Contributors

Ernesto R. Acevedo-Muñoz is Associate Professor of Film Studies, Comparative Literature and Humanities at the University of Colorado at Boulder. He is the author of the books *Pedro Almodóvar* (2007) and *Buñuel and Mexico: The Crisis of National Cinema* (2003). His essays have appeared in *Quarterly Review of Film and Video*, *Film and History*, *LIT*, and in the anthologies *After Hitchcock*, *Healing Cultures*, *The Processes of Adaptation* and *Genre, Gender, Race and World Cinema*. He is currently writing a book on *West Side Story* and preparing a book on Latin American cinemas and questions of film theory.

Jay Beck is Assistant Professor of Media and Cinema Studies in the College of Communication at DePaul University. He has published articles in *Southern Review*, *iris*, *Torre De Papel*, *The Journal of Popular Film and Television*, *The Moving Image*, *Kino-Ikon*, *Scope* and *Illuminance*. His dissertation, 'A Quiet Revolution: Changes in American Film Sound Practices, 1967–1979', received the 2004 SCMS Dissertation Award, and he recently co-edited a collection on film sound entitled *Lowering the Boom: Critical Studies in Film Sound* (2008).

Vicente J. Benet teaches History of Spanish Film at the Universitat Jaume I in Castellón, Spain, and is managing editor of the journal *Archivos de la Filmoteca*. He has written several articles on Spanish film of the transition period to democracy and on Spanish filmmakers such as Luis García Berlanga or Enrique Urbizu. He is currently writing on the representation of historical events in Spanish fiction film.

Josetxo Cerdán Los Arcos is Professor at the Predepartamental Unity of Communication, Journalism and Advertisement of the Universidad Rovira i Virgili, Tarragona, Spain. He has co-edited the volume *Mirada, memoria y fascinación. Notas sobre el documental español* (2001) and, with Casimiro Torreiro, *Documental y vanguardia* (2005) and *Al otro lado de la ficción* (2007). He is also co-editor of *Suevia Films-Cesáreo González. Treinta años de cine español* (2005). He has also collaborated in collective projects such as *Antología crítica del cine Español* (1997). He is author, with Luis Fernández Colorado, of a recent book about the Spanish producer Ricardo Urgoiti: *Ricardo Urgoiti. Los trabajos y los días* (2007). Now he is working on the history of Spanish television.

David Scott Diffrient is Assistant Professor of Film and Media Studies at Colorado State University. He has published articles in *Cinema Journal*, *Film Quarterly* and *Film and History*, and his essays can be found in such anthologies as *Horror Film: Creating and Marketing Fear* (2004) and *New Korean Cinema* (2005). His recently completed manuscript exploring the cultural history of *M*A*S*H*, from novel to film to award-winning TV series, will be published in 2008.

Juan F. Egea is Associate Professor at the University of Wisconsin-Madison, where he teaches contemporary peninsular poetry and film. He is the author of *La poesía del nosotros: Jaime Gil de Biedma y la secuencia lírica moderna* (2004). He has published articles on Víctor Erice's *El espíritu de la colmena*, Luis García Berlanga's *El verdugo* and Marco Ferreri's *El cochecito*, among others. His current book-length project on Spanish dark film comedy is entitled *Dark Laughter*.

Pietsie Feenstra is a lecturer in Film Studies at Sorbonne University in Paris, where in 2001 she received her PhD. Her dissertation has been published as *Les Nouvelles Figures mythiques du cinéma espagnol (1975–1995) : à corps perdus* (2006) and she recently edited a book with Hub Hermans on contemporary Spanish cinema entitled *Miradas sobre pasado y presente en el cine español (1990–2005)* (2008). She is currently preparing a book entitled *La Mémoire du cinéma espagnol 1975–2007*, and she is a member of the French research team *Les Théâtres de la Mémoire*.

Contemporary Spanish cinema and genre

MANCHESTER
1824

Manchester University Press

Contemporary Spanish cinema and genre

Edited by
JAY BECK AND
VICENTE RODRÍGUEZ ORTEGA

Manchester
University Press

Manchester and New York

distributed in the United States exclusively by Palgrave Macmillan

Published by Manchester University Press
Oxford Road, Manchester M13 9NR, UK
and Room 400, 175 Fifth Avenue, New York, NY 10010, USA
www.manchesteruniversitypress.co.uk

Distributed in the United States exclusively by
Palgrave Macmillan, 175 Fifth Avenue,
New York, NY 10010, USA

Distributed in Canada exclusively by
UBC Press, University of British Columbia, 2029 West Mall,
Vancouver, BC, Canada V6T 1Z2

British Library Cataloguing-in-Publication Data is available

Library of Congress Cataloging-in-Publication Data is available

ISBN 978 0 7190 9010 3 paperback

First published by Manchester University Press in hardback 2008

This paperback edition first published 2013

The publisher has no responsibility for the persistence or accuracy of URLs for any external or third-party internet websites referred to in this book, and does not guarantee that any content on such websites is, or will remain, accurate or appropriate.

Printed by Lightning Source

Contents

Part III   Genre and authorship

Part IV   Multilingual imaginaries, borderless Spain

Acknowledgements

A collaborative project from its inception, *Contemporary Spanish Cinema and Genre* has benefited from the contributions and support of many colleagues, friends and mentors. We owe a large debt of gratitude to many people without whom this book would not have been possible. The origins of this project date back to our mutual interest in Spanish cinema and a frustration with the lack of critical writing on genre in Spain. While we have each addressed the question of genre in our own writings, we decided to provide a critical framework for analysing genre in Spanish cinema by organising a panel on 'Contemporary Spanish Comedy' for the 2006 Society for Cinema and Media Studies conference in Vancouver, Canada. After subsequent presentations at The Transnational in Iberian and Latin American Cinemas conference in London, and Memories of Modernity: An International Conference on Hispanic Cinemas in New York, we decided to launch the current collection and started to collect essays. We both wish to thank Steven Marsh, Chris Perriam, Isabel Santaolalla, Peter Evans, Kathleen Vernon, Marvin D'Lugo, Mark Allinson, and the members of the SCMS Latino Caucus for their support and help during this time.

Jay would like to thank his colleagues in the College of Communication at DePaul University and the DePaul University Research Council for their support in the preparation of this manuscript. In addition, individual thank yous are extended to Kathleen Newman, Anna Brigido-Corachan and especially Cecilia Cornejo.

Vicente would like to thank his students and colleagues at New York University for their immense enthusiasm about Spanish cinema and their encouragement about the idea of putting together a collection of essays on contemporary Spanish cinema and genre. He also thanks Miguel Fernández Labayen, Josetxo Cerdán, Sonia

García López and Anna Brigido-Corachan for facilitating his research by providing necessary materials for the full realisation of this project. An individual thank you is extended to Mila Voinikova.

A very special thank you goes to Matthew Frost and the staff of Manchester University Press for their ongoing commitment to some of the finest scholarship on Spanish cinema. In particular, thank you to our anonymous readers who helped us to sharpen and focus our introduction and the overall structure of the book. Most importantly, we wish to thank the authors in this collection for their enthusiasm, interest and commitment to the project from the very beginning.

Finally, please note that all titles in this collection reflect the original language in which a film was produced. English titles are supplied only for films that have had verifiable releases in English-speaking countries as either theatrical or home video releases.

Mariana Johnson is Assistant Professor of Film Studies at the University of North Carolina at Wilmington. Her research focuses on Latin American cinema and cultural theory. She has published articles on Latin American and French avant-garde cinema and co-authored, with Toby Miller, a chapter on film and political economy in the forthcoming *Oxford Handbook to Film and Media Studies*. She is currently working on a book about transnationalism in contemporary Cuban film and media.

Miguel Fernández Labayen is Assistant Professor at the Universidad Autónoma de Barcelona. He is the author of a critical study of Woody Allen's *Hannah and Her Sisters* (2005) and has also published articles on the tradition of the American avant-garde for collective books such as *Dentro y fuera de Hollywood. La tradición independiente en el cine americano* (2004) and *El sonido de la velocidad* (2005) and journals such as *Archivos de la Filmoteca*. He is currently coordinating a special issue of *Secuencias. Revista de Historia del Cine* devoted to contemporary film comedy and researching the evolution of Spanish television and film comedy.

Antonio Lázaro-Reboll is Lecturer in Hispanic Studies at the University of Kent, where he lectures on European cinema and Spanish cinema and literature. He is co-editor (with Andrew Willis) of *Spanish Popular Cinema* (2004) and (with Mark Jancovich, Julian Stringer and Andrew Willis) of *Defining Cultural Movies: The Cultural Politics of Oppositional Taste* (2003). He has contributed to the following collections: *The Cinema of Spain and Portugal* (2005) and *Latin American Exploitation Cinemas* (forthcoming). Currently, he is writing a critical history of the horror genre in Spain.

Carla Marcantonio has a PhD in Cinema Studies at New York University and is an Assistant Professor of English (Film and Media Studies) at George Mason University. She has published articles on a variety of topics in *Women and Performance*, *Cineaste* and *Senses of Cinema*.

William J. Nichols is Assistant Professor of Spanish at Georgia State University. He specialises in contemporary Spanish literature and culture, specifically detective fiction and film studies. His manuscript, titled *Transatlantic Mysteries: Culture, Capital, and Crime in the 'Noir' Novels of Paco Ignacio Taibo II and Manuel Vázquez Montalbán*, is currently under revision. Currently, he is editing a special issue of the *Revista Iberoamericana* titled 'Crimen, cadáveres, y cultura: Siguiendo las pistas de la novela negra', which focuses on noir fiction in Hispanic literature. He has also written on themes of memory, space and textual fragmentation in the novels of such Spanish authors as Manuel Rivas, Antonio Soler, Rafael Chirbes and Rafael Reig.

Vicente Rodríguez Ortega has a PhD in Cinema Studies from New York University. He is a Visiting Professor in the Department of Drama and Film at Vassar College, and is a staff member of Reverse Shot. His interests include contemporary transnational cinemas, genre theory, and film and digital technology.

Robert Sklar is a Professor of Cinema in the Department of Cinema Studies, Tisch School of the Arts, New York University. His books include *Film: An International History of the Medium* (also issued as *A World History of Film*, 1993, revised and updated 2002), *Movie-Made America: A Cultural History of American Movies* (1975, revised and updated 1994), and *City Boys: Cagney, Bogart, Garfield* (1992). He is a member of the National Film Preservation Board and the US National Society of Film Critics.

Maria Van Liew is Associate Professor of Spanish Cultural Studies at West Chester University in Pennsylvania. She teaches film, literature, women's studies and cultural history courses in Spanish and English. Most recently, she has presented and published articles on various aspects of feminism and immigration in contemporary Spanish cinema, including 'Importing Love: Transnational Subjectivity in Iciar Bollaín's *Flores de otro mundo* (1999)' in *Letras Femeninas* (summer 2007).

Belén Vidal is Lecturer in Film Studies at King's College, London. She is the author of *Textures of the Image: Rewriting the American Novel in the Contemporary Film Adaptation* (2002) and has contributed articles on gender theory and the aesthetics of the period film to the journals *Screen* and *Archivos de la Filmoteca*. She is currently working on a monograph on the heritage film and on a project on cinephilia and Spanish cinema.

Andrew Willis teaches film and media studies at the University of Salford, UK. He is the co-author, with Peter Buse and Núria Triana-Toribio, of *The Cinema of Álex de la Iglesia* (2007) and the co-editor, with Antonio Lázaro-Reboll, of *Spanish Popular Cinema* (2004). He is also the co-editor, with Núria Triana-Toribio, of Manchester University Press's *Spanish and Latin American Filmmakers* series.

Foreword

Robert Sklar

For film historians and theorists, being able to hold two opposing ideas in the mind isn't a possibility. It is a necessity. The first idea is that 'national cinema' and 'genre' are valid concepts that are instrumental in understanding how films are made, distributed and received by spectators. The second is that they are not. The editors and authors of *Contemporary Spanish Cinema and Genre* animate these conflicting propositions with lively and probing dialectical flair.

To simplify, the notion of national cinema is tied to the state, and that of genre to the market. Historically, governments have founded and financed film industries and institutions. They regulate, legislate, censor, permit or forbid films to be made or shown. It seems sensible to denote films under the sway of such aegis and power as constituting a nation's cinema. The elements of culture, ideology, customs, styles, language and landscape that adhere to the state and its inhabitants, as they appear in films, provide further evidence of the coherence and usefulness of the national cinema idea.

Similarly, genre as a marketing tool predated the advent of cinema, and was imported and elaborated in the new medium for its utility in classifying and diversifying films. Film industries have used and still use genre as a tool of publicity and sales, first to the exhibitor, then to the spectator. It functions like a brand, evoking in the consumer familiar associations and tastes. It takes away the guesswork of deciding what film to see. Joined together, national cinema and genre can produce potent signifiers. Italian spaghetti westerns. Bollywood melodramas. Spanish horror films.

Against this – the negation of these formulations – is the fundamental premise that all definitions and categories in cinema are porous. Borders and boundaries are continually passed over or through. Transnational cinema is not only a phenomenon of late capitalism and twenty-first-century globalisation, it came into existence simultaneously with the invention of the medium. Exactly the same is true for genre hybridity. Ideas, sources, styles, languages, technologies, personnel, financing, production companies – all have moved across national frontiers with varying ease or difficulty in the century and more of cinema. How does one specify what is national or specifically generic in any given film? Is Alejandro Amenábar's *Los otros/The Others* (2001) a Spanish horror film? What makes it so, other than the nationality of its director?

I am writing from the perspective of a North American filmgoer. Although I have seen Spanish films at festivals and retrospectives, and of course DVD makes possible new opportunities and rediscoveries, my experience of Spanish cinema inevitably has been filtered through decisions made by US film distributors and exhibitors. Perhaps something similar could be said for spectators in the UK and other English-language venues. If so, then perhaps our experience suggests the existence of art cinema as a genre of its own, founded on the principle of authorship. Spanish cinema in US art houses has been a cinema of auteurs: Luis Buñuel (and what national cinema should we assign him to?), Carlos Saura, Pedro Almodóvar; latterly, Alejandro Amenábar and perhaps Isabel Coixet; with the exceptional one-off, Víctor Erice's 1973 classic, *El espíritu de la colmena/The Spirit of the Beehive*.

One might interrogate the extent to which this kind of spectatorship – in another country, in an art house – challenges the values of national cinema and genre even more thoroughly than transnationalism or hybridity, or perhaps hand in hand with them. How useful is 'Spanish cinema' or 'Spanish genre film' or even 'Spain' in this particular context? We know more or less of Spanish history, the achievements and conflicts of contemporary Spain, the look and feel of the Spanish landscape. A further complication is that the Spanish language, and Spain's colonial heritage, are strongly present in the Americas. The English speaker's ear and eye may not know how, or care, to differentiate among accents and cultural styles. Moreover, Spain is itself a construct in Latin American cinema, as a place of return, of exile or refuge, as in Alfonso Aristarain's 1997 Argentine film, *Martín (Hache)*. And to which national cinema belongs Guillermo del Toro's *El laberinto del fauno/Pan's Labyrinth* (2006)?

Many of the authors in *Contemporary Spanish Cinema and Genre* are concerned with this question of 'Spanishness'. It takes several forms. One involves the ways that a film may communicate or register the distinctive qualities of a place or a culture; what intonations, gestures, sights, manners, social relations mark a way of living that speaks specifically of Spain. And underlying this theme is a larger anxiety, or ambivalence, that several authors raise: maybe 'Spanishness' is an attenuated phenomenon; maybe it's too subtle or complicated or fraught to be addressed in the contemporary transnational cinema context; maybe the marketplace is not interested in what makes Spain Spain.

The framework for these concerns is Spanish history. A generation ago, Spain was emerging from a nearly forty-year dictatorship. Tourism notwithstanding, the view of Spain from outside – in Europe and North America – was of reactionary, repressive, backward society, out of step with the rapidly growing prosperity, sophistication and internationalism of neighbouring Western European countries. Then, seemingly overnight, to those observing from afar, Spain transformed itself, with much less strife and recrimination than might have been expected, in the template of its European counterparts. In no time, Spain, too, became prosperous, sophisticated and international. An underlying concern in several chapters here is whether, in so successfully becoming an equal partner, indeed in some ways a leader, in modern European culture, Spain may have lost something of its 'Spanishness'.

A related issue raised in these chapters, perhaps more fundamentally, concerns the 'Spanish imaginary'. If the topic of 'Spanishness' addresses the signs and appearances of what Spain is and what it looks and sounds like to be Spanish, then the 'Spanish imaginary' denotes how the Spanish nation and its peoples construe themselves discursively, how they view themselves and construct a set of values and narratives out of their recent experience, and the links and gaps between their present and their past. If one were to argue that sometimes it is difficult to locate 'Spanishness' – leaving aside flamenco and bullfighting – in contemporary Spanish films, nevertheless it is possible to make the case that nearly every Spanish film participates in, may illuminate, and perhaps shape, the 'Spanish imaginary'.

To be sure, there is another important difference between 'Spanishness' and the 'Spanish imaginary'. As an inventory of signs, 'Spanishness' is concrete and specific; a sign exists whether the spectator picks up on it or not. The 'Spanish imaginary', however, is a site of contestation. Any attempt to articulate it is liable to evoke dispute on ideological or regional or gender or generational grounds, or from whatever other configurations of conflict in Spanish society. To take one easily observable example, the visitor to Barcelona immediately encounters a Catalan cultural, historical and linguistic environment. In bookstores, the literature shelves are divided between works in Catalan and works in Castilian – 'Spanish' may be read and spoken here, but not by the unitary and dominant name with which we are familiar. From this perspective, what we think of as the Spanish language appears to be regarded as merely one regional idiolect among several within the borders of the Spanish state. Is this a major rupture in the 'Spanish imaginary' or merely an element of the nation's diversity, tolerable and picturesque? How does it compare in disruptive potential to the ideological struggles between right-wing and left-wing viewpoints in Spanish politics?

How to understand the role and significance of Spanish cinema within this larger discourse and its discontents is one of the challenges for the English-language spectator, in the UK, Australia, North America or elsewhere, viewing films from a social, cultural and geographical distance. Amenábar's *Mar adentro/The Sea Inside* (2004), which won an Oscar from the Hollywood industry as Best Foreign Language Film, could be appreciated as a moving individual story of a paralysed man, wonderfully portrayed by Javier Bardem, seeking death by assisted suicide, without awareness that the work was based on the actual life and death of a man fighting for the right to die against Spanish law and the Catholic Church, whose situation was highly publicised throughout Europe. How much further one follows this film into the realms of the 'Spanish imaginary' – for example, how Catholicism functions in contemporary society, the autonomy of Spanish institutions in the framework of new Europe, Spanish concepts of death and dying – is a matter for spectators to choose.

Almodóvar's *Carne trémula/Live Flesh* (1997), however, makes a different kind of demand on spectators. The film opens with a black-and-white graphic in large block letters declaring the establishment of an 'estado de excepción' ('state of emergency') throughout the country. As the document continues, certain words are highlighted in red, demarking the suspension of laws affecting freedom of speech, residence and association, as well as the right of habeas corpus. Only then does a further graphic identify the place and date as Madrid, January 1970. Then the narrative begins (in colour), at a brothel called Pensión Centro, with a working girl (portrayed by Penélope Cruz) going into birth labour, while in the background a radio voice explains that 'minority actions . . . part of an international plot' obliged the government to act. She and the Madame go into the deserted streets and hail an empty bus, in which the baby is born. The sequence concludes with black-and-white mock-NO-DO (*Noticiario Documental*) newsreel footage showing the mother and newborn being honoured by the state and receiving free passes for the buses. The action then jumps forward twenty years and no further allusion to 1970 is made.

The 'state of emergency' operates in part as a pun for the condition of Cruz's character, but also presents a deadly serious statement about the Franco dictatorship. Historically, no state of emergency actually was declared in January 1970, but that date was bracketed by states of emergency promulgated in January 1969 and December 1970: the first in response to strikes by university students; the second by actions of Basque separatists, in which the rights marked in red on the screen were each time abrogated. Almodóvar does not need this opening in order to tell a story set in the 1990s, yet it is clear that he is pointing the spectator to think about the gap between Spain the dictatorship and Spain the democracy, and how a very different past may lie like an unseen stratum beneath who we are and how we act.

Drawing on this cinematic moment, one might say that the problems of 'Spanishness' and of the 'Spanish imaginary' identified by the authors in *Contemporary Spanish Cinema and Genre* come together and find their strongest foundation in the problem of historical memory. It may be that neither the state nor the market is positioned to foster works that confront this aspect of Spain's contemporary circumstances, but one looks to the creative and resourceful filmmakers, who are the subjects of this provocative and illuminating book, to find a way.

Introduction

Jay Beck and Vicente Rodríguez Ortega

This collection analyses the significant changes in the aesthetics, production and reception of Spanish cinema and genre from 1990 to the present. It brings together European and North American scholars to establish a critical dialogue on the topic of contemporary Spanish cinema and genre while providing multiple perspectives on the concepts of national cinemas and genre theory. We start from the premise that Spanish cinema is a product of local, regional, national and global forces operating in diverse contact zones inside and outside of geopolitical borders. In recent years film scholarship has attempted to negotiate the tension between the nationally specific and the internationally ubiquitous in discussing how the global era has contributed to change films and the surrounding cultural practices. These broader social concerns have prompted scholars to emphasise a redefinition of national cinemas beyond strict national boundaries and to pay attention to the transnational character of any national site of film production and reception. Thus, our purpose is to provide a thorough investigation of contemporary Spanish cinema within a transnational framework by positing cinematic genres as the meeting spaces between a variety of diverse forces that necessarily operate within but also across territorial spaces. Paying close attention to the specifics of the Spanish cinematic and social panorama, the chapters investigate the transnational economic, cultural and aesthetic forces at play in shaping Spanish film genres today.

Spanish cinema is arguably one of the most fertile sites of cinematic production in the world. Since the 1990s the study of Spanish cinema has flourished in university programmes both in Europe and the US and, as a consequence, several books on Spanish cinema have been published over the last ten years. Building upon foundational texts in the field by Peter Besas, Virginia Higginbotham, John Hopewell, Vicente Molina-Foix, Juan Manuel Company, Vicente Vergara, Juan de Mata Moncho, José Vanaclocha, Marsha Kinder, Carlos F. Heredero, Román Gubern, Peter Evans and Marvin D'Lugo, we find a new generation of Spanish cinema scholars revising the established histories and deploying a variety of new approaches. Over the last decade, groundbreaking books by Núria Triana-Toribio, Jenaro Talens, Santos Zunzunegui, Barry Jordan, Rikki Morgan-Tamosunas, Steven Marsh, Jo Labanyi, Kathleen M. Vernon, Barbara Morris, Paul Julian Smith, Esteve Riambau, Casimiro Torreiro, Isabel Santaolalla, Antonio Lázaro-Reboll, Andrew Willis, Antonio Santamarina, Rob Stone, Mark Allinson, Sally Faulkner, Peter Buse and others have helped to redefine Spanish cinema as an object of study. With a marked shift toward cultural studies approaches, many of these texts position cinema within a larger framework of culture production and consumption. While these approaches are extremely valuable in exploring the modes of representation at work in the circulation of Spanish culture, they often tend to overlook one of the most powerful and salient methods for constructing meaning in cinema: namely, genre. Specifically, none of the texts are devoted to the study of post-1990 Spanish cinema or to an in-depth approach to the genres that populate Spanish cinematic production and reception today.

The mobilisation and application of genre studies is absolutely central to understanding the aesthetic approaches used by filmmakers in contemporary Spanish cinema. Even though international critics and scholars have identified generic constructions in the works of the most successful historical representatives of Spain's cinematic output – Luis Buñuel, Juan Antonio Bardem, Luis García Berlanga, Carlos Saura, Pedro Almodóvar, Alejandro Amenábar, among others – there is also rich generic experimentation at the core of Spanish cinema that is little known outside Spain and just starting to break through into international markets. In part this is because Spanish cinema does not exist only within the geopolitical coordinates of a fixed territorial boundary. Many Spanish filmmakers borrow freely from other cinematic traditions and modes of representation, while others have had to follow a diasporic route to realise their cinematic endeavours; such is the case of Isabel Coixet, Juan Carlos Fresnadillo and María Ripoll. In addition, many Spanish actors have established their names in several foreign film industries – Antonio Banderas, Victoria Abril, Sergi López, Penélope Cruz, Paz Vega, Leonor Watling, Javier Bardem – and alternate between their commitment to making films in their native country and exploring other acting challenges. Several Spanish companies often invest in international co-productions, most notably in Latin America and within the European Union. In these films, the artistic talent and the financial backing is typically multinational, pointing to the interstitial status of Spanish national cinema within the transnational vectors that shape contemporary cinema. Spanish cinema exists both inside and outside Spain (understood as an established territorial boundary) and it acquires different conceptual and pragmatic meanings as different players in the film business – from producers to marketing executives, from journalists to scholars – construct diverse forms of significations to promote their differing agendas.

This collection takes as a point of departure the beginning of the 1990s as a central epochal shift in Spanish cinema. There are several reasons for this periodisation: Spain's full integration in the European Union, the Barcelona Olympics, the Sevilla World Expo '92, the spiral of corruption as the leftist Partido Socialista Obrero Español (PSOE, the Spanish Socialist Workers' Party) was entering in the middle of its fourth consecutive legislature in power, and the moment before the rise of the Partido Popular (PP, People's Party) and a political return to the right. However, the main reason to choose this period to anchor our study is that Spanish cinema underwent a sea change at the start of the 1990s that was reflected in shifts in generic patterns and genre formations. Barry Jordan and Rikki Morgan-Tamosunas acknowledge that 'since the early 1990s, there appears to have been a massive injection of new blood into the [Spanish film] industry from virtually all quarters: directors, actors, scriptwriters, producers as well as audiences' (1998: 6). It would be simpler to choose a more definitive date to begin this project – such as the turn toward political filmmaking after the restoration of democracy in 1977 or the wave of prestige films after creation of *la ley Miró* in 1983 – but we prefer to avoid reductive historiographies in favour of an approach that maps cinematic changes against a growing resistance to those well-established genres in the 1990s. Núria Triana-Toribio puts forth a similar argument when she states that 'the most prominent filmmakers of the early 1990s advocated an aesthetic and thematic break with the politically responsible cinema' (2003: 141). For our work it is important to note that popular audiences favoured such changes and new directors set forth to reinvigorate genres such as comedy, horror, melodrama and the musical for both national and international markets. Therefore, we champion an interactive model that pays close attention to the manners in which the social, the cultural and the filmic cross-fertilise. The chapters in the collection highlight how Spanish genre films are in continuous dialogue with other cinematic traditions, both in the larger arenas of European and global cinemas.

Genre studies and Spanish cinema

Genre theory – including publications such as Rick Altman's *Film/Genre* (1999), Steve Neale's *Genre and Hollywood* (2000) and Linda Williams's *Playing the Race Card* (2001) – displays a strong bias favouring Hollywood cinematic production when attempting to define the historical and aesthetic functions of film genres. One of our main goals in this collection is to approach genre from what has been a marginalised body of works in genre theory – national cinemas – and by doing so construct an alternative method for understanding Spanish film genres. We seek to challenge Hollywood-based generic paradigms by putting the national, the transnational and the generic in direct contact. We explore how Spanish cinema may help film scholarship rethink the established hierarchies of genre theory by bringing to the fore the textual, social and historical idiosyncrasies of contemporary Spanish cultural production.

In recent years film scholars have emphasised the insufficiencies of clear-cut differentiations between genres. Rick Altman's historical enquiries articulate the mixed origin of widely accepted genre categorisations, such as the western or the musical, and the a posteriori inclusion of films into a generic corpus once the formal and thematic characteristic have been stabilised, while Steve Neale's topology of genres emphasises generic hybridity such as the action-adventure film. In addition, Linda Williams has intriguingly identified the 'melodramatic mode' as a dominant substratum running through American film history in a transgeneric fashion. In 'Rethinking Genre', Christine Gledhill has called for an understanding of genre that is capable of 'exploring the wider contextual culture in relationship to, rather than as an originating source of, aesthetic mutations and textual complications' (2000: 221) Films must be thought of in constant dialogue and exchange with the social context of their production, since aesthetic and ideological systems of signification act upon one another and cannot be dissociated. Moreover, the purity of genres has not only been contested but also summarily debunked and left aside as a limiting paradigm for a critical understanding of cinema.

If we approach film genres discursively, within the context of a dialogic interaction between filmmakers and viewers, the text is perpetually open to the shifting character of its intrinsic intertextuality. Furthermore, the filmmakers' creative activity is impregnated with their very cultural historicity and the discursivity of genre provides contingent entry points for spectators inside a wide variety of cultural signifying systems. Authorship and genre thus co-exist within an endless circulation of competing utterances that become alternatively dominant in the negotiated encounter between text and reader.

However, in the case of Spanish film scholarship, the relationship between genre and auteurism in cinema has been historically tempestuous. To discuss the friction between the two it is useful to parse the difference between genre as a classificatory label and 'genre film' as a pejorative used to describe formulaic filmmaking. Within the critical work on American film genres, the majority of genre theorists take the first perspective of genre as a category – sometimes neutral and sometimes active – that contains a number of films bearing stylistic or narrative similarities. Yet, in Spanish cinema history, the view of genre has almost exclusively been constructed negatively, often as a reaction against the functional definitions of genres adopted from American and European cinemas.

This trend is visible across a number of texts examining the history of film genres in Spain. Central to these is the pioneering *Cine español: cine de subgéneros*, a foundational text in Spanish genre theory co-authored by the Equipo 'Cartelera Turia'[1] (Juan Manuel Company, Vicente Vergara, Juan de Mata Moncho and José Vanaclocha). Published in 1974 – a year before the end of the Franco regime – the book offers a series of clues about how Spanish film scholarship conceptualised the role of genre within the wider terrain of Spanish cinema. In particular, the book examines the existence of genre in Spanish cinema through the filter of *subgéneros*, or subgenres: a term used here to classify Spanish genre filmmaking as subpar to American and European genres, rather than as an internal division within a larger genre's structure.

In his foreword to the volume, Román Gubern places the academic trajectory of the book within a historical and sociological scope. He notes that Spanish cinema had developed its own authentic genres – the *histórico-imperial, misionero, folklórico* and *Cruzada* – as an imperative under the unifying force of state-run production and distributing company CIFESA (Compañía Industrial Film Español S.A.) under Franco. Yet, with the weakening of both the state and the Spanish film industry, those prior genres were replaced by the subgenres: 'mimetic and repetitive simulations of other previous models, themselves repetitive, but having their own genuine and archetypal cultural character' (1974: 12).[2] For Gubern the subgenres the volume discusses – horror, spaghetti westerns, musicals and *sexy celtibérica (cine erótico)* – are fundamentally bankrupt in both ideological and aesthetic terms. However, from a sociological point of view, the interest in these films among popular audience 'surpasses the one that the works of Carlos Saura or Berlanga may have' (1974: 11).[3] Because Spanish audiences fundamentally consumed these types of films, while they seldom ran to movie houses to see the auteur-oriented cinematic products typically discussed in histories as constitutive of the core of Spanish national cinema, the book aims to point out the importance of these subgeneric categories in order to account for their undeniable relationship to the ways cinemagoers consume Spanish cinema.

In their choice of a prefix, the 'sub' of *subgénero* is not accidental. It signals the fact that, even though the diverse generic corpuses examined may function as legitimate genres due to their thematic and stylistic characteristics, there is also at work in each of them an 'inferiority' at the level of craftsmanship that immediately places them in a lower stratum of cinematic quality. In his discussion of Spanish horror films, Company, for example, explains that a 'sub-horror film offers the attentive spectator a deficient formal structure whose constitutive elements are in a state of chaos, beyond the control in their ultimate connotations of the director' (1974: 21).[4]

Despite its negative view of Spanish horror, Company's statement contains a number of significant points. First, it places the relationship between text and spectator at the centre of the historical process of genrefication, or the actual creation of a genre, anticipating Rick Altman's syntactic/semantic/pragmatic dimensions of genre films by over twenty years. According to Altman, 'a semantic/syntactic/ pragmatic approach refuses determinacy to textual structures taken alone, but in addition it acknowledges the difficulty of extracting those textual structures from the institutions and social habits that frame them and lend them the appearance of making meaning on their own' (1999: 211). For genres do not consist only of films; they are also systems that provide spectators with entry points to recognise, understand and rework generic categories. Spectators approach genres from specific social spaces, and rearticulate their meanings according to cultural demands. Company rightly recognised that genres are not a set of strict formal and thematic structures but an open meeting ground between spectators and texts, where different individuals inscribe their own understanding of how genre categories construct meaning. However, for the Equipo 'Cartelera Turia' and Company, Spanish horror films at this point in history were considered deficient in as much as they did not hold together as either tightly woven structures or as coherent directorial statements. In other words, they aspired to be genre films but failed because of their chaotic and mimetic character. This ties with the second main issue at work in Company's chapter. These subgenre films are 'auteurless' because, as he explains later, they were produced rapidly for both national and international markets, and they lacked the imprint true auteurs would be able to infuse in the cinematic products they create.[5]

These Spanish horror films were fundamentally designed to appeal to international markets due to a crisis in the Spanish film production that prompted producers to seek profits in the established European distribution and exhibition networks (Company 1974: 49). Therefore, subgeneric horror films did not redefine the genre by any means; instead, they repeated and recycled for the sake of pure commercial gain. Moreover, being a copy of an American genre, this type of films did not rise from a well-established cultural and mythological basis, like, for example, the Universal horror film from the 1930s or the westerns of the 1940s and 1950s. Spanish subhorror and spaghetti westerns were derivative of already degraded forms. As gifted as some of these filmmakers may have been, they were trapped by a commercial imperative that prevented them from elevating their craft to the realm of art (1974: 50).

Cine español: cine de subgéneros was a groundbreaking effort in both analytical and thematic terms and opened a line of study about Spanish popular genres, and only recently writers such as Núria Triana-Toribio, Antonio Lázaro-Reboll and Andrew Willis have treated the issue of subgenres with sufficient scope and detail in

English-language Spanish film scholarship. Yet the authors of the subgéneros book seem to be trapped in a clear-cut dichotomy between what constitutes 'good' cinema – films coming from auteurs working under Francoism who were able to display a superior degree of cinematic craftsmanship by taking cues from the great European masters – and 'bad' cinema – imitative, low-budget, aesthetically bankrupt genre productions.

This bias against genre filmmaking or, better, a bias against borrowing generic structures from American or European cinemas, is a trend present in the vast majority of Spanish-language film scholarship, not only in terms of discussions of subgenres in the 1970s but extensively in relation to genre studies up to the present. Taking a look at Román Gubern's canonical compilation, *Historia del cine español*, one notices that for Gubern and his authors the role of genres within the history of Spanish Cinema seems to be a secondary concern.[6] Even though they initially note that '*La historia del cine español* takes as a point of departure the analysis of a series of trends (currents, schools, genres)', they continue to frame the analysis in exclusively auteurist terms by 'studying in depth the more or less important authors without forgetting, of course, those remarkable filmmakers that have created their works on the margins of the dominant trends' (1995: 16).[7] Once again, in the collection genre filmmaking tends to be treated as inferior to authorial efforts. In his brief discussion of Spanish cinema from 1930 to 1939 – where only six out of fifty-eight pages address issues of genre – Gubern is fast to conclude that genre filmmaking, trapped in a commercial arena, superseded any kind of authorial endeavour (1995: 238). Even though Gubern and his co-authors chronicle the changing paradigms of Spanish cinematic genres throughout the book, especially in relation to comedy, they directly link genre filmmaking with commercialism and the repressive ideological projects during Francoism. Casimiro Torreiro, for example, addresses the status of genre filmmaking and consumption during the *apertura* period from 1961 to 1969 in a section dedicated to commercial cinema. He states that the period gave rise to a series of 'successful subgenres, constructed with garbage materials of classical genres, a type of opportunistic form of filmmaking in which the scarcity of resources and low investment were prominent, at the forefront of which were comedies "a la Española"' (1995: 332).[8] For him, the thematic and ideological conservatism and the diminished formal qualities of these films are unequivocal. However, following the arguments of the authors of the *subgéneros* book, he states that it is undeniable that vast numbers of people saw these films and, hence, their inclusion in the volume.

Historia del cine español does devote an extended discussion to account for the move away from subgenres in the wake of the demise of Francoism and how new directors took American film genres as a privileged reference point. It notes how José Luis Garci and Fernando Colomo developed noir and thriller genres during the early 1980s, while others such as Fernando Trueba used comedy as an arena to offer 'a distanced look at the growing disillusionment with democracy' (1995: 396).[9] Equally, the volume scrutinises the rise of Pedro Almodóvar as a new kind of auteur who reshuffled marginal artistic forms such as comic books and soap operas to change the contours of Spanish cinema. Esteve Riambau chronicles the growth of comedy at the forefront of commercial cinema, emphasising its move away from marginal *destape* circuits, helped by the favouring of high production values and exportability under *la ley Miró*, while giving a detailed account of Almodóvar's rise as a central figure of Spanish cinema throughout the late 1980s to mid-1990s. However, the whole volume seems to be structured around an underlying assumption that genre films are almost invariably designed for mass consumption. As such, they are aesthetically, ideologically and often thematically lesser to the 'true' Spanish cinema: films from auteurs who manage to resist the vicissitudes of the market and make personal films that engage the shifting realities of the Spanish social fabric while complying with the models of visual and aural narration in the tradition of European art cinema. Given this dominant school of thought within Spanish scholarship, it is no surprise that José Luis Borau's *Diccionario del cine español* (1998) does not include an entry for 'género' or even though there is an entry devoted to 'horror films', it is shorter than the section devoted to 'cine y toros'. Once again, genre is seen as a marginalised, almost unwanted surplus of the history of Spanish cinema.

This school of thought largely permeates the contemporary scholarship on Spanish film. For example, in 'El cine como realidad y el mundo como representación: algunos síntomas de los noventa', Ángel Quintana affirms that:

The social does not determine the point of reference of the cinematic. Instead, genres – in some cases subgenres – and a type of cinema that thrives on spectacle performs this function. Filmmakers are devoted to creating a series of re-readings and gameplays within the realm of genres. They have adapted them to *el costumbrismo ibérico*, without, on many occasions, being conscious of the roots of such a tradition. These new authors have established a certain distanced critical look in relation to the references that have inspired them, often creating a type of film that is a total pastiche. (2001: 17)[10]

In other words, Quintana laments that contemporary Spanish cinema does not engage with reality and he blames the rise of genre as a primary form of filmmaking for such a fact. Following Fredric Jameson's limiting conception of pastiche as 'blank parody', this commentator seems to affirm that contemporary Spanish cinema is trapped in a vortex of generic interplay that is closed in itself.[11] In addition, even though some of these directors consciously mobilise what they consider to be authentic forms of Spanish genre, such as the *costumbrismo ibérico*, they do so only apparently, through a variety of surface-driven cinematic efforts that fail to interrogate, approach or respond to the idiosyncrasies of the present historical juncture in Spain. This trend of thought leads José Enrique Monterde, for example, to dismiss Almodóvar's complex and multi-layered transgeneric marathons of disparate references as essentially shallow and inferior to the great tradition of great European auteurs such as Godard or Bergman. For Monterde, it is precisely because of his superficiality that Almodóvar is the ultimate representative breed of contemporary Spanish cinema. His value resides 'a lot more in his capacity for osmosis in relation to the realities he approaches than in his capacity to create his own poetic world. In the same way, his cinematic style stems from the digestion of several types of influences. He lacks the skills to put together a unique exploration of the expressive and narrative possibilities of mise-en-scène (1993: 193).[12]

Both Quintana's and Monterde's critical paradigms, in our view, are working under two unfortunate assumptions. First, they equate the aesthetics of active appropriation and genre revision with superficiality, favouring instead a kind of filmmaking that anachronistically places the 'original auteur' at its centre as a unifying consciousness. Hence, Almodóvar's inferiority to true European auteurs such as Bergman. What both authors fail to recognise is how critical frameworks developed in the field of literary studies – Bakhtin's dialogism, Kristeva's intertextuality, and Genette's intertextuality, among others – have problematised the concept of the author by introducing necessary intertextual dimensions to any given cinematic text. In the Bakhtinian world, the text only exists in the 'in-betweenness' of other texts, in a relational context with other cultural products. As Robert Stam claims: 'Within a Bakhtinian approach, there is no unitary text, no unitary producer, and no unitary spectator; rather, there is a conflictual heteroglossia pervading producer, text, context, and reader/viewer. Each category is traversed by the centripetal and the centrifugal' (1989: 221). Cinema and, thus, genre filmmaking, have always been the result of a process of multivocal, multistylistic and often transcultural exchange. Filmmakers are not consequently an original driving force, as Monterde and Quintana seem to imply, but mostly 'orchestrators' of this diverse set of influences that seek to engage audiences at different levels depending on their varied competencies in narrative storytelling. Second, the authors endorse the idea that genres are not able to convey political meanings or engage critically with reality. As several genre theorists have sufficiently proven, genre is indeed a powerful form of political intervention and it directly relates to the wider social and cultural landscape that gives birth to it, being potentially a privileged form of ideological dissemination due to its broad approachability by a diverse set of audiences.

In recent Spanish scholarship, Hollywood is mobilised to equate genre filmmaking with commercialism in counterpoint to the greater European tradition of the auteur film. In his discussion of contemporary Spanish horror and fantasy films in the collection *Miradas para un nuevo milenio: fragmentos para una historia del cine español*, Jesús Palacios states that the majority of contemporary Spanish genre films consume Hollywood, both in terms of purely commercial trends as well as auteurist endeavours like those of David Lynch and David Cronenberg (2006: 154). For him, this stems from lacks within the field of Spanish cinema: lack of historical and literary routes, lack of continuous praxis, and lack of positive reception for these genres by both audiences and the intelligentsia. While Hollywood provides the formulas, clichés and archetypes, the black humour at work in the well-established tradition of *esperpento* 'Spanishises' the films. For Palacios, the outcome is necessarily negative because the majority of the films of this genre 'either participate in the humoristic and esperpentic "negrorealista" trend or cheaply cheat the spectator, like Amenábar's films, which sell films that are completely Hollywood, both formally and

intellectually, as if they were Spanish' (2006: 156).[13] Due to their
unproblematic use of the term 'genre' without exploring the multiple nuanced meanings and variations that it signals, these authors
seem to simplify Hollywood as a monolith that, in its presumed technical flawlessness, produces mindless products aimed solely at pleasing the masses. Consequently, any Spanish film that appropriates the
generic structures of Hollywood genres, such as Amenábar's, are
invariably attacked for the vacuity and illegitimacy of their aesthetic
and ideological endeavours.

Underlying Quintana's and Palacios's arguments there is not only
a simplification in regard to Hollywood cinema and a defence of
European cinema as superior,[14] but also an inflexible understanding
of the concept of national cinema and how genres operate within a
process of continuous transnational cross-fertilisation and evolution.
This auteurist bias, as Josep Lluis Fecé notes in 'La excepción y la
norma. Reflexiones sobre la españolidad de nuestro cine reciente',
constructs a particular national cinema through its 'otherness':
privileging personal projects – or *francotiradores* (snipers) as many
Spanish-speaking scholars label them – as the creative and ideological
pinnacles of its history. Furthermore, while we may argue that most
genre theorists are guilty of applying Hollywood generic categories
transnationally while ignoring the variants that these formats adopt
in combination with vernacular forms of popular entertainment,
Quintana and Palacios seem to be guilty of the same critical misstep.
That is, they invariable identify a set of artistic project such as *esperpento* or *costumbrismo* as authentically Spanish, and either resort to
the unquestioning use of these terms to account for the co-existence
of Hollywood genres and Spanish genre films, or readily dismiss
those genre films that do not partake in the canon of 'true' Spanish
cinematic traditions they themselves have helped to consolidate. In
this sense, we agree with Fecé in considering that scholars need to
examine a variety of sociological, political and cultural aspects
beyond the straitjacket of canonical auteur-based conceptualisations
of Spanish cinema (2005: 84–5). In order to break this impasse
between the privileging of an authorial view of Spanish film history
and the dismissal of genre as a tool for analysis, we turn to the field
of genre theory and the concept of hybridity.

Recent scholarly writing on genre has examined the concept of
generic hybridity to properly historicise the continuous interaction
between different generic corpuses and to rescue genre theory from

its self-isolating taxonomy of generic masterpieces. Furthermore, as Steve Neale remarks, films belonging to a certain corpus can relate to films of the same genre, and, simultaneously, to films of other genres in several ways (2000: 219). Genres thus challenge homogeneity and permanence since they are the 'by-product' of an ongoing process in which filmmakers, production companies, distributors, exhibitors and spectators are fully involved – inscribing their own agendas into the genre object, making it, consequently, a multi-semantic phenomenon that defies fixity (Altman, 1999: 54). Furthermore, production studios and distribution companies encourage the creation of films that engage multiple genres, because their main goal is to appeal to a wide audience and achieve the best possible economic results. In fact, a hybrid generic label – like romantic comedy or psychological thriller – favours the studio's interest since it appeals to several audience groups under differentiated promises of cinematic pleasure. It is not only that generic hybridisation exists at the core of aesthetic creation but also that it is championed and institutionalised from a production point of view for financial reasons. Most importantly, when films travel from one culture into another, the role of generic categories and the function of film genres in selling a body of films to spectators typically change, building upon the cultural and social dominants of a particular mediascape.

Consequently, it is critical to understand genre as a discursive category that mutates in different cultural and media spaces, acquiring diverse sets of meanings, instead of simply identifying a particular Spanish comedy film as 'Hollywood plus *esperpento*'. The question is not as much about what representational templates are mobilised but how this combinatory process alters its different components, making them signify in diverse geographical, social and cultural contexts. In their analysis of *Torrente: el brazo tonto de la ley* and *Torrente 2: misión en Marbella*, Esquirol and Fecé attribute the success of Santiago Segura's comedic franchise to his careful and relentless cultivation of a media persona that manages to construct a wide-range community of *amiguetes* (2001: 34). Esquirol and Fecé rightly argue that Segura managed to tap into an audience group – the youth under thirty, who did not feel represented by any kind of Spanish film – to successfully beat Hollywood cinema at the box office. Instead of relying on the typical style of American teen and gross-out comedies, the *Torrente* series achieved its success in the way the films recycle forgotten film stars (e.g. Tony Leblanc), *casposo* icons (e.g. José Luis Moreno or El Fary), and capitalise on the appeal of well-known television personas (e.g. El Gran Wyoming) to anchor them in a Spanish tradition. Therefore, it is important to see how comedy becomes just one tool in Segura's method for competing successfully with foreign films and building a series of cultural, social and aesthetic bridges with Spanish audiences through a variety of media platforms. In other words, considering how Segura's work fits into the established hierarchies of Spanish comedy is less important than seeing how he does *not* fit into an established history and, consequently, how we may understand his deployment of generic categories via a study of Spanish cinema that both looks inward (to the local, the regional and the national) and outward (to the industrial, aesthetic and marketing models at work in the global film markets).

Genre in contemporary Spanish cinema

Hollywood has been the main focus of contemporary genre theory for several reasons. First, classical Hollywood narratives share a certain set of conventions that are easily identifiable and, therefore, favour a consistent grouping. Second, the Hollywood industry has traditionally been the most powerful economic arena of cinematic production in the world, and consequently its films were distributed globally and exhibited more than any others whereby Hollywood genres made a decisive imprint on other national cinemas. Third, due to its huge production output, the constant circulation of talent and the competition to win a greater market share, Hollywood favours 'controlled' generic reshuffling and hybridisation that is marked by an ongoing process of cross-fertilisation. However, we feel it is of paramount importance to expand the analysis of genre theory into other national cinemas in order to understand transnational cinematic cross-fertilisation as an ongoing process among geopolitical spaces. In discussions of the present multicultural, global era, the insufficiency of the nation-state to define the current sociopolitical situation has been widely debated by a number of different scholars from several disciplines: Fredric Jameson, Arjun Appadurai, Andrew Higson, Susan Hayward, Ella Shohat and Robert Stam to mention a few.

This does not mean that any critical enquiry into genre within a particular national cinematic field should exclude a thorough scrutinising of its relationship with the Hollywood industry. However, as Susan Hayward remarks, framing the concept of national cinema against the dominance of Hollywood runs the risk of 'reducing the idea of a national cinema to economies of scale and therefore to one concept of *value*: namely, economic well-being' (1993: 91). It also ignores the rich cinematic exchange that is occurring today as counterflow to Hollywood's domination of the global film market. In fact, individuals who are privileged enough to be hooked into the transnational spectrum of global media flow can access a quasi-infinite variety of audiovisual products. The social practices and imaginations of these individuals are likely to be shaped in a multicultural fashion and their cinematic productions can potentially challenge the dominant templates at work in the global film markets and offer alternative aesthetic and ideological choices to film spectators across different territories. In other words, the global exchange of aesthetics is not only shaped in the dark of a cinema or the executive offices of studios, but also in the *transmedia* landscape of television, DVDs, videogames, the internet, etc. Global filmmakers often attempt to appropriate and alter the very generic and narrative configurations of successful film genres and modes in order to capture a share of their domestic market and, occasionally, a piece of the international pie.

The transnational understanding of cinematic production and circulation displayed in this collection scrutinises the ideological and aesthetic modes through which diverse cinematic traditions and modes of production interact with one another and acknowledges their implications. The chapters address several layers of cinematic transnationalism in mapping out the relationship between cinematic traditions and modes of representation in contemporary Spanish cinema, understanding the latter category as a flexible concept that functions not only within Spain but also across the multilingual global mediascape. Cinema acts as a space of representation in which the tensions between the local, regional, national, supranational and global take place. It also functions as a central site for a range of competing discourses to understanding how these complex networks of cinematic and social relationships intersect in a multiplicity of complementary or antagonistic directions. Within the information saturation of the global era, the study of national cinema requires 'an analysis of how the actual audience construct their cultural identity in relation to the various products of the national and international film and television industries, and the conditions under which this is achieved' (Higson, 1989: 45–6). The critical model we employ acknowledges that the national cinematic is a fluctuating category that continuously circulates in a variety of transterritorial cultural fields, subject to redefinition as conflicting social, ideological and economic forces reconfigure it following differing agendas.

Specifically, our interest in understanding Spanish cinema as a national *and* transnational cinema hinges on how generic discourses are utilised both to advance and to hide markers of national identity. In our work on Spanish cinema it becomes clear that genre and nation are intrinsically and complexly linked, and that genre's ability to construct and contain meaning for an audience is very similar to how national discourses interpellate a citizenry. Therefore we are not proposing a treatise on genre nor on national cinema, but we hope that this is the first in a series of studies that will continue to examine the nexus of genre and national identity.

Our collection does not highlight any single genre primarily because our understanding of cinematic genres does not comply with a clear-cut taxonomy of generic categories. Conversely, it emphasises the cross-fertilisation of different genres historically and the theorisation of alternative models such as melodrama as a mode. Therefore, we have purposefully stayed away from structuring the collection along a discussion of specific genres. Instead of reiterating existing generic categories, which place the chapters into familiar constructs, we prefer the idea of mapping out alternative pathways as a way to provide different reading formations for the texts and to acknowledge competing discourses in relation to genre studies. We feel that this is a highly productive way of linking and theorising issues of film genre and national cinema that will not only increase the potential readership but also develop pedagogic dialogue across the collection's established conceptual boundaries.

We have structured the collection in four main sections that are far from being separate entities. Although we have thematically established a series of links to group together the chapters in different sections, we hope to foster an interactive form of readership that weaves its own narrative with the material we offer, establishing a series of connecting vectors between the different sections and the chapters included in them. Part I – Industry, marketing and film culture – approaches the existence of generic categories in contemporary Spanish cinema through an analysis of a variety of industrial and cultural fields. The authors of these chapters are not necessarily concerned with the intratextual generic characteristics of a set of specific genres. Instead, they study the mobilisation and changing meanings of intertextual generic categories as they enter the film market – via movie trailers, film reviews, fanzines and websites – and how the Spanish film industry negotiates between international market tensions and the cultural markers that define a national cinema. Part II – Generic hybridity: negotiating the regional, the national and the transnational – approaches how genres occupy an interstitial role in establishing a variety of both aesthetic and cultural links between forces defining the cultural and social fabric of a nation and its relationship with other geopolitical and economic constructs. While exploring the significance of genre production and reception in relation to understanding how regional initiatives have succeeded internationally, these four chapters also examine national (or even local) rearticulations of global genres such as the horror film and the indigenisation of 'indie' and thriller films. Part III – Genre and authorship – offers case studies of four prominent filmmakers in contemporary Spanish cinema: Pedro Almodóvar, Ventura Pons, Alejandro Amenábar and Isabel Coixet. Far from unproblematically accepting a tautological definition of cinematic auteurism, the authors approach the respective bodies of works with acuity. Manoeuvring through the often multilingual and multicultural discourses at play in each director's films, the authors trace the overlap between two critical categories within film studies – genre and authorship – by establishing links between the distinctive expression of a director and the role of genres to anchor their works in both the culturally specific and global markets. Part IV – Multilingual imaginaries, borderless Spain – looks at Spanish cinema and genre from a distinctly international perspective. Studying the emergent category of the 'immigration film', the mediation between Cuban and Spanish social and cultural imaginaries and the cross-fertilisation between Hollywood and Spanish musical productions, the authors explore how genre mediates change in Spanish society as it enters its most radical cultural shift in recent history.

In the wake of eight years of PP rule under José María Aznar, there has been a marked shift in Spanish media production after the election of José Luis Rodríguez Zapatero in March 2004 and the return

to a PSOE government. Esteve Riambau notes that 'beyond the continued sway of politics, [the Spanish film industry] is not controlled
as much by market criteria as by state dependence – or the biased
privatization of State interests. This dependence in turn becomes paradoxically indispensable in guaranteeing the survival of an industry
facing American colonization' (2003: 61). In this nexus of interaction – among state-sponsored support, international co-productions
and global circulation of films – Spanish cinema is changing, finally
coming to terms with its methods of production and its modes of representation in order to compete successfully in the contemporary film
mediascape. Specifically, filmmakers are negotiating the need to speak
to national and transnational audiences, and genre has become the
preferred method of discourse. We hope that this collection will help
scholars to examine the complex relationships between genre, cinema
and cultural identity in Spain, and that it makes a call for other studies
to explore the interrelationships between national cinemas, transnational media flow and genre as discursive frameworks for constructing meaning.

Notes

1 *Cartelera Turia* is an entertainment guide originating in Valencia, which
  has been published since 1964. It contains a variety of articles raging
  from film reviews to political commentary and features on porn film
  stars. It has been at the forefront of Spanish politics through entertainment from the days of Francoism, constantly championing a very liberal
  and, at points, countercultural spectrum of viewpoints.
2 'Los subgéneros son, como su propio nombre indica, sucedáneos
  miméticos y repetitivos de otros modelos previos, también repetitivos,
  pero de carácter cultural genuino o arquetípico.'
3 'Como sociólogo de la comunicación debo responder que su interés
  rebasa al que pueda ofrecer la obra de Carlos Saura y de Berlanga.'
  Vicente Vergara goes even a step further in this same volume in his discussion of the spaghetti western by stating that this genre is aimed at
  'broad audiences who are culturally underdeveloped and who are not
  reached by the educational policies; half of film production is aimed at
  this kind of public' ('un amplio público culturalmente subdesarrollado
  al que no llegan las politicas educativas; pensando en el, no lo lovi-
  damos, se planifica más de la mitad producción cinematográfica')
  (1974: 81).
4 'Una película de subterror se plantea, ante el espectador atento, como
  una estructura formal deficiente cuyos elementos constitutivos se

encuentran en un estado de caos, incontrolado en sus últimas connotaciones por el director.'

5 In *Cine español: cine de subgéneros*, Juan de Mata Moncho states similarly that a true Spanish musical tradition has never existed. The Spanish musical, for him, is an authorless and 'lazy' endeavour that recycles rising stars of the likes of Joselito, Marisol and Manolo Escobar, in a capital-driven environment in which the only goal is to produce films as fast as possible (1974: 136).

6 J. M. Caparrós Lera's *Historia crítica del cine español (desde 1897 hasta hoy)* (1999) shows a similar bias against genre filmmaking. While there is a whole section on the work of the partnership between Elías Querejeta and Carlos Saura, comparatively little space is devoted to the study of genre films.

7 '*La Historia del Cine Español* partirá de un análisis de las tendencias (corrientes, escuelas, géneros), profundizando las investigaciones sobre los autores más o menos importantes y sin descuidar, por supuesto, a los cineastas dignos de interés que han creado sus obras al margen de las tendencias dominantes.'

8 'Filones subgenéricos, ficciones construidas con los materiales de desecho de los géneros clásicos, filones oportunistas en los cuales la precariedad de recursos y la baja inversión son las notas dominantes, al frente de las cuales se encuentran las comedias a la Española.'

9 'Una mirada distanciada a una realidad democrática que ya comenzaba a distar de las ilusiones que en ella se habían puesto.'

10 'El referente cinematográfico no ha aparecido determinado por el entorno social, sino por los géneros – en algunos casos los subgéneros – y las construcciones dramáticas propias de un modelo de cine que ha querido buscar la espectacularidad. Los cineastas se han dedicado a establecer juegos y relecturas de los géneros, los han acoplado al costumbrismo ibérico sin, muchas veces, ser conscientes del peso de las propias raíces. Los nuevos autores han configurado una cierta distancia crítica respecto a los referentes que les han inspirado, llegando muchas veces a convertir las obras en auténticos pastiches.'

11 Quintana uses *Días contados/Running Out of Time* (Imanol Uribe, 1994) to exemplify his points. He argues that 'Uribe puts on the table two strong thematic elements and then binds them together through a story of love and death. His main concern is not to project reality but to make the cinematic apparatus to work. For this purpose, he does not hesitate in showing off all his skills to build up a film in which the story effects become clearly visible' ('Uribe pone sobre la mesa de montaje dos temas fuertes y los engarza dentro de una historia de amor y muerte. Su principal preocupación no estriba en proyectar la realidad, sino en conseguir que el dispositivo cinematográfico funcione, por lo que no duda

en mostrar todo su andamiaje, en construir una película donde en cada escena son visibles los efectos del guión') (2001: 23).

12 'Mucho más en su capacidad de osmosis respecto a ciertos ámbitos de la realidad que no a su capacidad de crear un mundo poético propio, tal como sus formas cinematográficas proceden de la digestión de multiples ámbitos de influencia, mucho más allá de una auténtica capacidad de explotar las posibilidades expresivas y narratives de la puesta en escena.' Monterde is not alone in this belief. José Maria Caparrós Lera, in both *La pantalla popular: el cine español durante el Gobierno de la derecha (1996–2003)* (2005) and *Historia crítica del cine español (desde 1897 hasta hoy)* (1999), unproblematically endorses Monterde's position.

13 'O bien participan de la esencia humoristica y esperpéntica de la corriente negrorealista, o bien engañan de forma artera al espectador, como las películas de Amenábar, al ofrecer como españoles productos de factura netamente hollywoodiense, tanto formal como estética e intelectualmente.'

14 Palacios affirms that the best alternative in the fantasy and horror genres comes from Filmax, since it is closer to a European type of filmmaking which offers a deeper, auteurist and more pessimist version of the genre, and is therefore, superior.

References

Allinson, Mark (2001) *A Spanish Labyrinth: The Films of Pedro Almodóvar*, London: I. B. Tauris.

Altman, Rick (1999) *Film/Genre*, London: BFI.

Appadurai, Arjun (1996) *Modernity at Large: Cultural Dimensions of Globalization*, Minneapolis: University of Minnesota Press.

Besas, Peter (1985) *Behind The Spanish Lens: Spanish Cinema under Fascism and Democracy*, Denver: Arden Press.

Borau, José Luis, Carlos F. Heredero and María Pastor (1998) *Diccionario del cine español*, Alianza Editorial: Madrid.

Buse, Peter, Núria Triana-Toribio and Andrew Willis (2007) *The Cinema of Álex de la Iglesia*, Manchester: Manchester University Press.

Caparrós Lera, José Maria (1999) *Historia crítica del cine español (desde 1897 hasta hoy)*, Editorial Ariel: Barcelona.

—— (2005) *La pantalla popular: el cine español durante el Gobierno de la derecha (1996–2003)*, Barcelona: Akal Ediciones.

Company, Juan Manuel (1974) 'El rito y la sangre (aproximaciones al subterror hispano)', in Equipo 'Cartelera Turia', *Cine español: cine de subgéneros*, 17–76.

de Mata Moncho, Juan (1974) 'El absurdo camino del "Musical" español', in Equipo 'Cartelera Turia', *Cine español: cine de subgéneros*, 129–92.

D'Lugo, Marvin (1997) *Guide to the Cinema of Spain*, Westport, CT: Greenwood Press.

Dyer, Richard and Ginette Vincendeau (eds) (1992) *Popular European Cinema*, London: Routledge.

Eleftheriotis, Dimitris (2001) *Popular Cinemas of Europe: Studies of Texts, Contexts and Frameworks*, London: Continuum.

Equipo 'Cartelera Turia' [Juan Manuel Company, Vicente Vergara, Juan de Mata Moncho and José Vanaclocha] (1974) *Cine español: cine de sub-géneros*, Valencia: F. Torres.

Esquirol, Meritxell, and Josep Lluis Fecé (2001) 'Un freak en el parque de atracciones: *Torrente, el brazo tonto de la ley*', *Archivos de la Filmoteca*, 39, 27–39.

Evans, Peter William (ed.) (1999) *Spanish Cinema: The Auteurist Tradition*, Oxford: Oxford University Press.

Faulkner, Sally (2006) *A Cinema of Contradiction: Spanish Film in the 1960s*, Edinburgh: Edinburgh University Press.

Fecé, Josep Lluis (2005) 'La excepción y la norma. Reflexiones sobre la españolidad de nuestro cine reciente', *Archivos de la Filmoteca*, 49, 82–95.

Gledhill, Christine (2000) 'Rethinking Genre', in Christine Gledhill and Linda Williams (eds), *Reinventing Film Studies*, London and New York: Arnold and Oxford University Press, 221–43.

Graham, Helen and Jo Labanyi (eds) (1995) *Spanish Cultural Studies*, Oxford: Oxford University Press.

Grant, Barry Keith (ed.) (2003) *Film Genre Reader III*, Austin: University of Texas Press.

Gubern, Román (1974) 'Prólogo', in Equipo 'Cartelera Turia', *Cine español: cine de subgéneros*, 9–16.

——, et al. (1995) *Historia del cine español*, Madrid: Cátedra.

Hayward, Susan (1993) *French National Cinema*, London: Routledge.

Heredero, Carlos F. and Antonio Santamarina (2002) *Semillas de Futuro. Cine español 1990–2001*, Madrid: Sociedad Estatal España Nuevo Milenio.

Higginbotham, Virginia (1988) *Spanish Films Under Franco*, Austin: University of Texas Press.

Higson, Andrew (1989) 'The Concept of National Cinema', *Screen*, 30: 4, Autumn, 36–46.

—— (2000) 'The limiting imagination of national cinema', in Mette Hjort and Scott MacKenzie (eds), *Cinema and Nation*, London: Routledge, 63–74.

Hopewell, John (1986) *Out of the Past: Spanish Cinema After Franco*, London: BFI.

Hutchings, Peter (1995) 'Genre Theory and Criticism', in Joanne Hollows and Mark Jancovich (eds), *Approaches to Popular Film*, Manchester: Manchester University Press, 59–68.

Jäckel, Anne (2003) *European Film Industries*, London: BFI.

Jameson, Fredric (1991) *Postmodernism, or the Cultural Logic of Late Capitalism*, Durham, NC: Duke University Press.

Jordan, Barry and Rikki Morgan-Tamosunas (1998) *Contemporary Spanish Cinema*, Manchester: Manchester University Press.

—— (eds) (2000) *Contemporary Spanish Cultural Studies*, London: Arnold.

Kinder, Marsha (1993) *Blood Cinema: The Reconstruction of National Identity in Spain*, Berkeley: University of California Press.

—— (ed.) (1997) *Refiguring Spain: Cinema/Media/Representation*, Durham, NC: Duke University Press.

Labanyi, Jo (ed.) (2000) *Constructing Identity in Contemporary Spain: Theoretical Debates and Cultural Practice*, Oxford: Oxford University Press.

Lázaro-Reboll, Antonio and Andrew Willis (eds) (2004) *Spanish Popular Cinema*, Manchester: Manchester University Press.

Marsh, Steven (2006) *Popular Spanish Film Under Franco: Comedy and the Weakening of the State*, Basingstoke: Palgrave.

Molina-Foix, Vicente (1977) *New Cinema in Spain*, London: BFI.

Monterde, José Enrique (1993) *Veinte años de cine español (1973–1992): un cine bajo la paradoja*, Barcelona: Ediciones Paidós.

Neale, Steve (2000) *Genre and Hollywood*, London: Routledge.

Palacios, Jesús (2006) 'Los últimos días de la bestia: cine fantástico español ante el nuevo milenio', in Hilario J. Rodríguez (ed.), *Miradas para un nuevo milenio: fragmentos para una historia del cine español*, Alcalá de Henares: Festival de Cine de Alcalá de Henares, Ayuntamiento de Alcalá de Henares, Fundación Colegio del Rey; Madrid: Comunidad de Madrid, Institut Valencia de Cinematografia Ricardo Muñoz Suay, 151–7.

Quintana, Ángel (2001) 'El cine como realidad y el mundo como representación: algunos síntomas de los noventa', *Archivos de la Filmoteca*, 37, 8–25.

Riambau, Esteve (2003) 'Public Money and Private Business (or How to Survive Hollywood's Imperialism): Film Production in Spain (1984–2002)', *Cineaste*, 29: 1, Winter, 56–61.

Riambau, Esteve, and Casimiro Torreiro (1999) *La escuela de Barcelona: el cine de la 'gauche divine'*, Barcelona: Anagrama.

Santaolalla, Isabel (2005) *Los 'Otros': Etnicidad y 'raza' en el cine español conemporáneo*, Madrid: Ocho y medio, Zaragoza University Press.

Smith, Paul Julian (1996) *Vision Machines: Cinema, Literature and Sexuality in Spain and Cuba, 1983–1993*, London: Verso.

—— (2003) *Contemporary Spanish Culture: TV, Fashion, Art, and Film*, Cambridge: Polity Press.

Stam, Robert (1989) *Subversive Pleasures: Bakhtin, Cultural Criticism and Film*, Baltimore: Johns Hopkins University Press.

Stone, Rob (2002) *Spanish Cinema*, Harlow: Longman.

Talens, Jenaro and Santos Zunzunegui (eds) (1998) *Modes of Representation in Spanish Cinema*, Minneapolis: University of Minnesota Press.

Triana-Toribio, Núria (2003) *Spanish National Cinema*, London: Routledge.

Vanaclocha, José (1974) 'El cine sexy celtibérico', in Equipo 'Cartelera Turia', *Cine español: cine de subgéneros*, 193–284.

Vergara, Vicente (1974) '10.000 dólares por una masacre (un estudio sobre el spaghetti-western)', in Equipo 'Cartelera Turia', *Cine español: cine de subgéneros*, 77–128.

Vernon, Kathleen M. and Barbara Morris (eds) (1995) *Post-Franco, Postmodern*, Westport, CT: Greenwood Press.

Williams, Linda (1998) 'Melodrama Revised', in Nick Browne (ed.), *Refiguring American Film Genres: Theory and History*, Berkeley: University of California Press, 42–88.

—— (2001) *Playing the Race Card: Melodramas of Black and White from Uncle Tom to O. J. Simpson*, Princeton: Princeton University Press.

Part I
Industry, marketing and film culture

1

The Fantastic Factory: the horror genre and contemporary Spanish cinema

Andrew Willis

There has been a significant increase in the production of horror films in Spain since the turn of the twenty-first century. In some instances, for example *Los otros/The Others* (Alejandro Amenábar, 2001), this has found some favour critically by being situated in conventional studies of authorship or into wider examinations of what constitutes national cinema. However, little critical attention has been given to the industrial contexts of horror film production in Spain during this period, and how these impact upon the actual products that find their way on to screens both within and outside Spain. In this chapter I want to address this by considering a particular production unit, the Barcelona-based Fantastic Factory, which was established in 1999, as part of the increasingly important Filmax group of companies, with the explicit aim of making genre films that would have an appeal beyond the Spanish market. The last Fantastic Factory products, *The Nun* (Luis de la Madrid) and *Beneath Still Waters* (Brian Yuzna), were released in 2005, after which Yuzna, an American producer and director who had helped establish the label, left the organisation. Filmax continued its commitment to horror and genre filmmaking but they now appeared under the Filmax label rather than that of the Fantastic Factory. Alongside looking at the development of the label and considering the shifts of emphasis within the films of the Fantastic Factory, I will discuss the continued importance of the idea of genre within both critical writing about film and its place within ideas of what constitutes Spanish cinema, in particular, the problems of defining a 'Spanish' film when looking at a production company that shows a continued commitment to making their films in English.

The continued importance of genre in film studies

Genre, as an approach to cinema, has long been established as a key critical perspective within film studies. Its first major impact was as part of an intellectual move to displace author-based approaches in the 1960s, in favour of ones that more clearly acknowledged the wider social and cultural influences upon, as well as the industrial nature of, cinema. However, much of the early work that appeared was primarily concerned with identifying the boundaries of what constituted film genres and cycles within such categories. An exemplary work in this regard is, for example, Will Wright's analysis of the western, *Sixguns and Society: A Structural Study of the Western* (1975). Andrew Tudor has identified this drive as the search for the 'X-factor' that links films together under a generic label (1973: 132). In terms of the creation of a wide-ranging analysis this search can become somewhat reductive and ultimately limiting. For this reason I will not attempt to define the output of the Fantastic Factory in terms of genre but acknowledge that they exist broadly within the generic boundaries of the horror film.

However, this does not mean that a genre approach is no longer useful. As Barry Keith Grant has observed, 'genre criticism has been able to accommodate the interests of newer approaches to film' (2003: xvii) and maintain its position as an important starting point for much contemporary writing on cinema, including this collection. That has been the case whether that work has been focused on the films themselves, their context of production or their audiences and the reactions they have to films and cinemagoing. Genre can therefore be usefully linked to a wide variety of aspects connected to the life of a film, including vitally those such as industry and audiences that exist beyond the simple projection of images on a screen. Again, as Grant notes, genre approaches 'have been exceptionally significant as well in establishing the popular sense of cinema as a cultural and economic institution' (2003: xv).

Whilst much of the landmark work on genre and cinema has concentrated on Hollywood, there is an increasing acknowledgement that genre filmmaking exists outside of the Hollywood industry, produced within and across other national cinemas across the globe. Grant acknowledges this, arguing that 'as one might expect, genre criticism has concentrated on (mainstream) American cinema . . . But such questions as the relation of genre to ideology have ramifications beyond Hollywood. From Japanese Samurai films to Italian westerns to French gangster films to Hong Kong action movies, almost all national cinemas have been influenced to some degree by American genre movies' (2003: xx). His argument echoes that of Peter Hutchings' comment that

> genres exist not only in American cinema but also in other national cinemas and for non-American audiences. The more one considers this geographical dispersal, the more genres seem to become rather fragmented entities. For example, as far as the horror genre is concerned, it arguably makes more sense to interpret British/Italian/Spanish horror films in relation to those institutions that characterise the local cinematic regime rather than lump them all together into a unified whole. (1995: 74)

Taking note of what both writers argue, I want to address the films of the Fantastic Factory as a body of work that has a strong relationship with the products of the American film industry but which also displays traits that can only be fully understood by placing them into contexts that exist beyond Hollywood. Therefore, what follows will acknowledge the influence of American horror cinema on the Fantastic Factory but will also consider the films in their own production contexts, one of the most significant of which is their existence as an example of popular cinema produced in Spain.

National cinemas and popular genres

In the introduction to their 1992 collection *Popular European Cinema*, Richard Dyer and Ginette Vincendeau identify that, traditionally, popular cinema produced in Europe has been perceived as not 'arty' enough for those who champion art cinema and not slick enough for those who celebrate the products of Hollywood. Falling between these two poles, the study of popular European cinema has lagged behind the academic and critical work produced about both conventional art cinema and Hollywood-produced popular cinema. In the case of European cinema, much of the critical writing produced still continues to consider, explicitly or implicitly, a clear distinction between the art cinema traditionally associated with the cinema of the Continent and those produced in more aggressively commercial contexts. Here, I want to argue that this overly simplistic division needs to be broken down in order to realise that the commercial industries across Europe have produced works that are of great critical interest. In the case of the Fantastic Factory these are films that in terms of both their ambition and achievement and their production contexts should be considered as worthy of a sustained critical examination.

Whilst decades of interest in Hollywood has managed to success-fully elevate the films of that industry to the status of justified objects of study in academic departments and on cinema courses, the product of European commercial cinema remains somewhat mar-ginalised. Indeed, when courses have included popular European films they have often been part of wider discussions of, for example, auteur directors. In these cases the European films of directors such as Alfred Hitchcock and Douglas Sirk have been continually seen as minor works when compared to their Hollywood output. V. F. Perkins (1992) has argued that this is often the case due to the fact that European commercial cinema is usually considered a poor rela-tion to the slickness of Hollywood's output. If one is interested in popular cinema there often seems to be an unwritten assumption that, at the very least, one should look at work with higher produc-tion values and that is seen by large audiences. Invariably, that is the output of the Hollywood film industry. The global reach of that industry has meant that other national cinemas that produce com-mercial work often struggle in what might be described as a kind of critical splendid isolation, their products rarely reaching the inter-national festival circuit, where critics will see them and then possibly write about them. By concentrating on genre one is able to move away from the traditional approaches to non-US cinemas that have focused on key art cinema directors, often isolated from their indus-trial production contexts due to their perceived auteur status.

In the case of the critical examination of Spanish cinema the turn towards an intellectual investigation of popular cinema has been a very slow one. This can partly be explained by the mistrust of popular film shown by many Spanish critics and intellectuals throughout the 1960s and beyond as they championed an anti-Franco art cinema. As Sally Faulkner has noted, many of these writers dismissed popular cinema for 'its saccharine optimism, facile humour and low production values' (2006: 8). More recently writing on Spanish cinema has sought to redress this imbalance by focusing on the popular films that had been largely ignored. This realignment has included a number of works—for example, Triana-Toribio (2003) and Marsh (2006)—that have looked closely at the popular cycles of comedies produced in Spain since the late 1950s and 1960s onwards. Other writers, such as Jo Labanyi (1997) and Eva Woods (2004), have considered the musical as a suitable genre through which to take Spanish popular cinema seriously. Here, by considering the output of the Fantastic Factory, I wish to continue this process by focusing on commercially produced contemporary horror cinema.

'Filmax presenta . . .': the Fantastic Factory

Today, Filmax Entertainment is a Spanish company that gathers together arms that are devoted to the production, distribution and exhibition of film and television. In a sense, through different companies that are gathered under its overall Filmax umbrella, it represents an example of contemporary vertical integration within the film industry. In the context of a study of the Fantastic Factory, one of the most significant things that the company states is that one of its main aims is to make products for 'the international film and television markets' (www.filmaxentertainment.com, 2007a).

However, whilst Filmax has not always been a film producer it has always had a commitment to looking at cinematic trends outside Spanish borders. It began in 1953 as an independent Spanish distributor specialising in 'film hits from the North American film industry', going on to release such noteworthy Hollywood products such as John Huston's *Moulin Rouge* in 1953, King Vidor's *War and Peace* in 1956 and Howard Hawks' *Hatari* in 1961 (www.filmaxentertainment.com, 2007b). The company was acquired by the current head and president, Julio Fernández, in 1987, and his incorporation of it into his wider group of companies led to a consolidation of Filmax's distribution work which was followed by a marked increase in activity. The company continued to expand and began its involvement in film production in 1995 with *Pareja de tres* (Antoni Verdaguer, 1995) and *A tres bandas* (Enrico Coletti, 1997). In 1998 the company took over new headquarters in the business district of Barcelona and this was followed by perhaps the most important of these increased activities, the creation of Castelao Production in 1999. This is described by Filmax as its 'content producer', and the establishment of this company in turn led to the creation of the Fantastic Factory in an attempt to reach international markets with their films. Filmax's commitment to popular forms of cinema was also reflected by their creation of Bren

Entertainment, a high-tech animation studio, which they chose to base in Santiago de Compostela.

Distribution has remained a significant part of the Filmax operation since those early days and more recently they have handled the Spanish releases of such varied titles as *Le Pacte des loups/ Brotherhood of the Wolf* (Christophe Gans, 2001), *Resident Evil* (Paul W. S. Anderson, 2002) and *Million Dollar Baby* (Clint Eastwood, 2004). One of the things that marks the contemporary Filmax distribution roster is the fact that it attempts to blend popular, genre films such as Kevin Costner's *Open Range* (2003) with more independent works such as John Sayles' *Silver City* (2003). Indeed, it is possible to see the roots of their production slate in this distribution history. They have attempted to mix potentially popular films with more artistically ambitious ones, and when possible mix the two elements together. On occasion this duality has also appeared in the Fantastic Factory films; for example, *Rottweiler* (2004), which director Brian Yuzna has argued offered clear generic elements alongside a more political or social commentary. He has stated that 'I had to make sure that I didn't just revert to a straight genre piece with a bunch of people being terrorised by a monster dog, even though that might be what some of the fans are expecting to see . . . so in the film the hero . . . is caught by the authorities with a group of immigrants coming up from North Africa' (Mendik, 2005: 8). This clearly indicates that even a commercial enterprise such as the Fantastic Factory can, in certain instances such as this one, find a place for something more ambitious in their products.

Trends in the early Fantastic Factory films
Following its creation in 1999, certain early works of the Fantastic Factory, *Faust: Love of the Damned* (Brian Yunza, 2001), *Arachnid* (Jack Sholder, 2001) and *Beyond Re-Animator* (Brian Yunza, 2003), for example, attempted to produce what might be termed 'American'-style genre films that had no obvious indication that they might be 'foreign' to those watching them. These films clearly aimed to sit alongside other low- to mid-budget American horror films without drawing attention to their production roots, attracting cinemagoers, and more likely DVD renters, through their generic elements rather than their national origins. To this end Filmax and the Fantastic Factory employed established and reliable American directors to make some of these early works. These included experienced

genre practitioners such as Stuart Gordon and Jack Sholder, who were well versed in the production of low- to middle-budget genre films, as indeed was Fantastic Factory head Brian Yunza, who directed their first release, *Faust: Love of the Damned*. All three also brought a reputation for genre direction which would have assisted in the marketing of the films internationally. For example, if *Faust: Love of the Damned* could be marketed internationally as 'from the makers of *Bride of Re-Animator*', that would work to further mask the Spanish origins of the film. Furthermore, the stories within the early films tended towards non-specific locations and settings, and the casting of both English-speaking actors and recognisable genre performers, such as Jeffery Coombs, in significant roles also assisted in camouflaging the films' national origins. Of course, such strategies had been prevalent in European genre production since the 1950s, for example in the casting of actors such as Steve Reeves in Italian peplum films such as *Le fatiche de Ercole/Hercules* (Pietro Francisci, 1958), John Saxon in early *giallos* like *La ragazza che sapeva troppo/The Evil Eye* (Mario Bava, 1963) and Clint Eastwood and Lee Van Cleef in the western *Per qualche dollaro in più/For a Few Dollars More* (Sergio Leone, 1965). In approaching their films in this way the Fantastic Factory were treading a well-worn and financially proven path.

One of the most strikingly similar attempts to produce American-style genre films in Europe is the Italian or spaghetti western. Produced in large numbers from the 1960s to the 1970s, Dimitris Eleftheriotis has argued that

> It is useful to understand the spaghetti western (at least initially) as a phenomenon closely linked to the process of globalization. This not only follows accounts of Hollywood as global cinema but also highlights the accelerated mobility of cultural products around the world and their increasing detachment from national contexts. Such a model implies the weakening of national identities and perceives cultural production as operating not only on a national but on a transnational, even global level. The spaghetti western offers an example of this process both as a response to Hollywood's global reach and as an economically and culturally transnational product. (2001: 97–8)

Certainly, the early films of the Fantastic Factory – *Faust: Love of the Damned*, *Arachnid* and *Beyond Re-Animator* – would seem to adhere to this model. They seem to disguise their Spanish origin in the way in which spaghetti westerns would use European locations to stand in for US and Mexican ones. Indeed, when asked about the idea behind the establishment of Fantastic Factory, Brian Yuzna has also reflected this, stating that 'We intend to create a line of genre films for the international market produced in Spain, but using talent from all over the world. We are going to employ Spanish talents, but we are of course shooting the movies in English, because we want to compete internationally. We are not just interested in being a success in Spain. We want to be a success internationally' (Mendik, 2004: 182). In attempting to achieve this goal the Fantastic Factory and Filmax were of course not the first, as there had been a number of previous producers who had wanted the same thing: internationally successful films produced in Spain, in English, for an international market. The most well-known recent, and highly successful, attempt to achieve this is perhaps *The Others*, which was a co-production between the Spanish companies Las Producciones de Escorpión and SOGECINE and the Hollywood-based Cruise/Wagner productions. Utilising a global star in Nicole Kidman, the film, according to IMDb.com, was made for a budget of $17 million and returned a profit of $210 million. However, this did not result in an ongoing relationship between the production companies or a production slate from these outfits designed to replicate the success of *The Others*. It is this fact that makes their one-off approach to genre film production in Spain for international markets significantly different to the ongoing project of Filmax. Perhaps the best-known previous example of a production company who did attempt to establish a base in Spain to produce films for the international market was Samuel Bronston's large-scale efforts in the early 1960s.

Filmmaking in Spain for an international market
There have been a number of companies and producers who have attempted to make genre films for international audiences in Spain. Perhaps the best known and certainly the most expansive of these was Romania-born Hollywood producer Samuel Bronston, whose operation provides an interesting precursor to recent attempts such as those of Filmax. Bronston arrived in Spain as an independent producer who had decided to shoot the large-scale *John Paul Jones* (John Farrow, 1959) there. The producer found the conditions in Spain, both in terms of climate and finance, so conducive to production that he decided that he would return there to make the biblical epic *King of Kings* (Nicholas Ray, 1961). In order to do so he

created his own company, Samuel Bronston Productions Inc., with offices in the Spanish capital, Madrid. Initially he rented the Chamartín Studios in the city as he set about establishing his own independent organisation. He would later purchase the studio as part of this aim, renaming it The Bronston Studios. Due to the politics of the time it is unlikely that this could have happened without the support of key elements in the Franco regime. As Peter Besas has observed,

> The government was delighted to see the American building a minia-ture Hollywood in Madrid, providing employment for thousands of people, bringing money into the country, turning to Spanish themes in his films, and professing himself openly pro-Spanish at a time when many governments looked askance upon the Franco regime. (1985: 55)

Increasingly committed to film production in Spain, and in order to access Spanish investors and finance, Bronston set up a Spanish sister company, Samuel Bronston Española, and it was this company that was involved in producing one of the most famous international films on a Spanish subject, *El Cid* (Anthony Mann, 1961). Following on from this very successful project, Bronston produced *55 Days in Peking* (Nicholas Ray, 1963), *The Fall of the Roman Empire* (Anthony Mann, 1964) and *The Magnificent Showman/Circus World* (Henry Hathaway, 1966), the latter two being box-office flops. As well as the large-scale international productions Bronston also made a number of smaller films that displayed much more obvious Spanish subjects and themes, including: *Objectivo 67* (Jaime Prades, 1964), *Sinfonía española* (Jaime Prades, 1964) and *El valle de los caídos* (Andrew Marton, 1965), which Besas describes as 'a present that Bronston gave the government' (1985: 60).

The failure of *The Fall of the Roman Empire* and *The Magnificent Showman* at the box office sent Bronston's production company into sharp decline and ultimately into liquidation. However, the fact that The Bronston Studios were owned by the Spanish arm of the organ-isation meant that they were able to survive. This was greatly assisted by the fact that the company was able to rent out facilities to TVE, the Spanish national television station, as well as to a number of independent producers seeking to shoot their films in Europe, many of whom were attracted by the highly skilled techni-cians present in the Spanish capital due to the experience they had gained on Bronston's large-scale productions. Indeed, it was this experience of working on genre films, such as the historical epic, designed for international markets, that also attracted smaller producers to Spain seeking to utilise their 'ready-made' skills in making their low-budget western, war and (later) horror films. Many of these involved co-productions with other European countries such as Italy and West Germany. However, whilst the early Fantastic Factory films seemed to follow the model established by these various productions that shot in Spain for international markets, for the most part using the landscape to stand in for other places, their horror products soon began to use their Spanish settings as an integral part of their identity.

Fantastic Factory and a shift to a more identifiable Spanish horror

So, whilst the Fantastic Factory seemed committed to this approach in some of their early films, with the production of H. P. Lovecraft's *Dagon* (2001) their output began to change slightly, with a slow revelation of the Spanish origins of their productions. It would seem that being Spanish was no longer seen as something to hide. *Dagon* is the first of the Fantastic Factory productions to clearly display its national origins, utilising locations in Galicia and incorporating an acknowledged Spanish setting. Alongside this, as would become familiar for the Fantastic Factory films, non-Spanish characters mixed with locals as the story unfolded. Of course, it would be foolish to suggest that this shift was driven by purely artistic aims as it also usefully utilised Filmax's growing relationship with the Galician local government. The company had set up their animation arm, Bren Entertainment, in Santiago de Compostela in 2000. Following on from this the regional government, the Xunta de Galicia supported the production of *Dagon* on location in the region and as a result they were given a production credit. Further evidence of a regional involvement in the production is another production credit for Televisión de Galicia. In fact this, along with the company's Barcelona base and support from the Generalitat de Catalunya, reveals that Filmax clearly has an ongoing artistic and business commitment to regional production in Spain.

However, in the case of *Dagon* the Spanish setting also allows for a reading that a less specific location would prevent. Therefore, the increased use of Spain as a backdrop for the Fantastic Factory opens the films up to particular interpretations that draw on, and are heavily informed by, knowledge of that backdrop and its specific history. In this way, one of the striking things about *Dagon* is the way in which the film uses religion. The villagers are led away from God by a character whose costume seems to suggest that he is some kind of revolutionary: a black great coat, a black cap and a goatee beard. In a key scene he bursts into a Catholic mass that is devoted to praying for a return of the fish that provides the villagers' livelihood, and calls them to follow Dagon. Once they take his lead they find their nets bulging with their catch and gold in amongst the fish. In response to this seeming good fortune they return to the village church and smash the statues devoted to Christ and a number of saints. Such actions seem to echo those of the Republicans in their fight against the power and influence of Catholicism in the 1930s. A less specific setting may have meant that such a reading would itself have to be less historically informed. Not for the last time the politics of a Fantastic Factory film would seem to be quite reactionary in its critique of anti-Christian ideas.

Romasanta: The Werewolf Hunt *(2004)*

Romasanta: The Werewolf Hunt is, as Filmax head Julio Fernández has argued, something that was 'very much a house effort' (2005: n.p.). For example, as well as a number of Fantastic Factory regulars on the film's crew, scriptwriters Elena Serra and Alberto Marini had previously been credited as 'Development Executives' on *Arachnid* and director Paco Plaza had made his debut feature, *Second Name* (2002), for Filmax. In a sense, then, the production staff involved in the creation of *Romasanta: The Werewolf Hunt* reflect an increasingly 'production line' style of working as they become more familiar with what might be described as a Fantastic Factory 'in-house' way of working. The film was also an early collaboration with London-based Future Films, who would become an important partner in the Fantastic Factory's next projects as well as with Filmax more generally. Alongside established star of European and US films Julian Sands, the film's casting also reflects a commitment to actors who had worked for the studio before, such as Spaniard Elsa Pataky, who had appeared in *Beyond Re-Animator*, and American John Sharian, who was in *The Machinist* (Brad Anderson, 2004), a film produced by Filmax's production arm, Castelao. Whilst the casting also continued to show that Filmax was still committed to shooting in English for international distribution,

Romasanta: The Werewolf Hunt is also the Fantastic Factory film
that most obviously reveals its Spanish roots and for this reason it
shows another important shift in emphasis for the production unit.
Unlike the early Fantastic Factory films which attempted to disguise their origins, the story of *Romasanta: The Werewolf Hunt* is a
very Spanish one. It is based on a real person, Manuel Blanco
Romasanta, who lived in Galicia in the eighteenth century. Known
widely as 'The Wolfman of Allariz', he was put on trial in 1851 for
a series of murders and accused of being a wolfman. Scriptwriters
Serra and Marini claim it was 'the only case of a wolfman being put
on trial in Europe' (2005: n.p.). In putting this tale on to the screen,
the Fantastic Factory once again shot on location in Galicia, a fact
acknowledged by an on-screen title at the start of the film. For director Paco Plaza the setting of the film was of vital importance, 'the
story is very Galician, the exuberance of its landscape, those stories,
those woods, I think they're unique and a beautiful asset to the film'
(2005: n.p.). Far removed from the non-specific world of *Faust:
Love of the Damned*, *Romasanta: The Werewolf Hunt* creates a
backdrop that is clearly Spanish and in doing so reveals a clear
change of focus for Fantastic Factory. This shift in emphasis did not
impact too negatively on the sales of the film outside Spain, as it was
picked up for distribution in a number of key territories including,
for example, the USA, where Lions Gate Films released it on DVD;
Australia, where Imagine Entertainment put it out on the same
format; and Russia, where it was released theatrically by Pyramid.

The Nun *(2005)*
One of the later films produced by the Fantastic Factory, *The Nun*
was directed by Luis de la Madrid. His presence in the director's
chair once again reveals the way in which Filmax and the Fantastic
Factory are willing to give an opportunity to personnel they know
and who have worked for them before. De la Madrid had been the
editor of *Faust* and had also worked on non-Fantastic Factory
Filmax works such as *The Machinist*. Again, a close look at *The Nun*
reveals an attempt to produce a film that might be described as both
international and local. The film opens in a Catholic boarding school
for girls where a class of international students is being taught and
treated very strictly by an overbearing nun. It then shifts to a high-
school prom in contemporary New York before taking its teenage
protagonists back to Barcelona for the main body of the film.

However, rather than hide the fact that the film has shifted to Spain, the makers of *The Nun* seem to celebrate it. As the youngsters fly into the city we see panoramic shots from the plane window and the excited attitude of the teenagers works to create the image of an international city that any young person would be excited by and happy to visit. In five years the Fantastic Factory films had shifted from passing Barcelona off as somewhere (indeed, anywhere) else, to celebrating the location as an attractive, vibrant and international place. The local setting had by this point, it seems, become bankable internationally. Once again, it might be argued that the 'Spanishness' of this horror film might be found in its interaction with notions of Catholicism, not something new for the Fantastic Factory. Here, the obvious setting of Catholic boarding school provides a backdrop that highlights religion.

Fantastic Factory: a transnational cinema?

Recently the idea of a transnational cinema has gained a greater currency within film studies, influenced by theorists such as, for example, Arjun Appadurai (1996), who argues that the increased mobility of people and culture will lead to the demise of the notion of 'the nation', and by extension ideas such as 'national cinema', resulting in the establishment of what Charles R. Acland calls a 'post-national imaginary' (2003: 42). However, in the field of cinema it is possible to argue that these changes exist alongside the rapid development of a global cinema dominated by large-scale international conglomerates. For many this means the extension of the domination of Hollywood across the world. Such a view is informed by the fact that, as Charles R. Acland has noted, 1993 marked the first time that 'international rentals for Hollywood films exceeded domestic', and that 'major U.S. film corporations received more revenue from films they had in theatrical release abroad than they did from those in the United States' (2003: 26). This meant that Hollywood increasingly looked to produce products that could be sold internationally and in doing so more forcefully targeted the domestic markets of other countries. The logic of this version of a 'transnational cinema' would see an organisation such as the Fantastic Factory representing the homogenising of world cinema. Their films were indistinguishable from those produced in the USA or anywhere else making 'international' products. Indeed, the early

films of the company – *Faust*, *Arachnid* and *Beyond Re-Animator* –
drawing as they did on creative talent from across Europe and the
US, would seem to illustrate a kind of 'post-national imaginary', one
where horror films looked the same wherever they were from. They
could also be seen as films that actively rejected being identified as
'Spanish' in favour of being international or global. However,
almost contradictorily, that situation would be challenged and ultimately change as the Fantastic Factory name became more saleable
internationally.

As already noted, one of the key components of the Fantastic
Factory films that indicates that they are international in scope and
aim is the fact that they were shot in English. As Anne Jäckel out-
lines, this reflects a Europe-wide trend, one that creates an environment where

> the more commercially ambitious producers argue that the future lies
> in productions able to cross borders. As a result, investments in
> English-language productions have grown despite concern expressed
> by independent producers from non-English-language territories
> about loss of cultural specificity. (2003: 64)

However, as we have seen, some of the Fantastic Factory films reveal
that the fact that the work is shot in English does not automatically
mean that cultural specificity vanishes. Indeed, with a film like
Romasanta: The Werewolf Hunt the Fantastic Factory managed to
make a film that is at the same time international in appeal, a horror
movie with an international star, and based on a story that is
absolutely historically and geographically rooted in Galicia. With
such a film the transnational does not lose its localness, but celebrates it in a manner that may be consumed internationally rather
than just within Spain. Therefore, part of the potential appeal of
Romasanta: The Werewolf Hunt is the somewhat exotic and little-
seen Spanish locations, in fact its very localness.

The increase in English-language European films has led to a
situation where 'Every significant film-producing country where
English is not the first language is now making films in the English
language' (Jäckel, 2003: 64). Increasingly, then, English has become
an important pan-European language for film producers. Again, in
her study Jäckel has argued that 'European English-language films
are certainly easier to sell than foreign-language films', stating that
according to Christian Boudier foreign-language films often suffer

from 'negative a-priori assumption outside their home territory' (2003: 101). Logically, then, when it comes to box-office returns, which one might argue may also later translate to other formats such as DVD, 'as far as European titles are concerned, it is largely British and other European produced English-language films that do well across European territories' (2003: 143). So, whilst the decision to make the Fantastic Factory films in English may meet the disapproval of purists, it certainly seems to fit the twenty-first century European trend to make popular films in English. Taking the Fantastic Factory and their genre films seriously as examples of Spanish cinema may therefore tell us more about current shifts and changes in the Spanish film industry and its attempts to compete in global markets.

Final thoughts

Even though the name of the Fantastic Factory has been retired after the release of *Beneath Still Waters* and *The Nun*, Filmax have continued their commitment to horror in its broadest term. The relationship they had developed with Jaume Balagueró, who had made *Darkness* for the Fantastic Factory in 2002, continued with their backing of his *Fragile* (2005), again shot in English with international actors such as American Calista Flockhart and Australian Richard Roxborough. They have also been behind Nacho Cerdà's *The Abandoned* (2006), which was shot in Bulgaria, Daniel Monzón's *The Kovak Box* (2006) and the six-part television horror compilation *Películas para no dormir* (2006). This reveals that Filmax clearly feel that their name alone now has enough credibility in the international genre market to leave behind the Fantastic Factory label. By removing the name from their films they have also removed themselves from the association with American Brian Yuzna. This, too, may be calculated to allow them to distance themselves from his link with FX-laden works in the mind of many genre fans, and create associations of their own. Later Fantastic Factory films such as *Romasanta: The Werewolf Hunt* and *The Nun* reveal that more atmospheric and less FX-led films are something the company can do well and, by increasing their reputation for such works, in doing so distancing themselves from a perceived 'Yuzna style'. The post-Yuzna, Filmax horror movies perhaps show a new willingness to move into a number of different sub-genres from the less gore-strewn and more psychologically driven horrors of the television films *Películas para no dormir* to projects such as Koldo Serra's *Backwoods* (2006), which exists on the more mainstream, almost thriller fringe of the horror genre. Indeed, the willingness to blend elements of out-and-out horror with those that may be more akin to psychological thrillers suggests the company are continuing to seek and develop new audiences, a fact reflected in their involvement in the production of the recent Mexican horror film *Kilómetro 31* (Rigoberto Castañeda, 2006). Whatever they choose to do, one thing is for certain: it does not look like Filmax are going to abandon their commitment to genre filmmaking, and for this reason they continue to be one of the most interesting production companies working in Spain today.

References

Acland, Charles R. (2003) *Screen Traffic: Movies, Multiplexes, and Global Culture*, Durham, NC: Duke University Press.

Appadurai, Arjun (1996) *Modernity at Large: Cultural Dimensions of Globalization*, Minneapolis: University of Minnesota Press.

Besas, Peter (1985) *Behind The Spanish Lens: Spanish Cinema under Fascism and Democracy*, Denver: Arden Press.

Dyer, Richard and Ginette Vincendeau (eds) (1992) *Popular European Cinema*, London: Routledge.

Eleftheriotis, Dimitris (2001) *Popular Cinemas of Europe: Studies of Texts, Contexts and Frameworks*, London: Continuum.

Faulkner, Sally (2006) *A Cinema of Contradiction: Spanish Film in the 1960s*, Edinburgh: Edinburgh University Press.

Fernández, Julio (2005) Interviewed in 'The Making of *Romasanta: The Werewolf Hunt*', on *Romasanta: The Werewolf Hunt*', Mosaic Entertainment DVD.

Grant, Barry Keith (ed.) (2003) *Film Genre Reader III*, Austin: University of Texas Press.

Hutchings, Peter (1995) 'Genre Theory and Criticism', in Joanne Hollows and Mark Jancovich (eds), *Approaches to Popular Film*, Manchester: Manchester University Press, 59–68.

Jäckel, Anne (2003) *European Film Industries*, London: BFI.

Labanyi, Jo (1997) 'Race, Gender and Disavowal in Spanish Cinema of the Early Franco Period: The Missionary Film and the Folkloric Musical', *Screen*, 38: 3, Autumn, 215–31.

Marsh, Steven (2006) *Popular Spanish Film Under Franco: Comedy and the Weakening of the State*, Basingstoke: Palgrave Macmillan.

Mendik, Xavier (2004) 'Trans-European Excess: An Interview with Brian Yuzna', in Ernest Mathijs and Xavier Mendik (eds), *Alternative Europe: Eurotrash and Exploitation Cinema since 1945*, London: Wallflower Press, 181–90.

—— (2005) 'Resurrecting Horror: *Rottweiler* and the Fantastic Films of Brian Yuzna', *Film International*, 17, 6–9.

Perkins, V. F. (1992) 'The Atlantic Divide', in Richard Dyer and Ginette Vincendeau (eds), *Popular European Cinema*, London: Routledge, 194–205.

Serra, Elena and Alberto Marini (2005) Interviewed in 'The Making of *Romasanta: The Werewolf Hunt*', on *Romasanta: The Werewolf Hunt*, Mosaic Entertainment DVD.

Plaza, Paco (2005) Interviewed in 'The Making of *Romasanta: The Werewolf Hunt*', on *Romasanta: The Werewolf Hunt*, Mosaic Entertainment DVD.

Triana-Toribio, Núria (2003) *Spanish National Cinema*, London: Routledge.

Tudor, Andrew (1973) *Theories of Film*, London: Secker and Warburg.

Woods, Eva (2004) 'From Rags to Riches: The Ideology of Stardom in Folkloric Musical Comedy Films of the Late 1930s and 1940s', in Antonio Lázaro Reboll and Andrew Willis (eds), *Spanish Popular Cinema*, Manchester: Manchester University Press.

Wright, Will (1975) *Sixguns and Society: A Structural Study of the Western*, Berkeley: University of California Press.

www.filmaxentertainment.com (2007a) 'The Trademark', accessed 28 April 2008.

—— (2007b) 'The Distributor', accessed 28 April 2008.

2

Trailing the Spanish auteur: Almodóvar's, Amenábar's and de la Iglesia's generic routes in the US market

Vicente Rodríguez Ortega

Anticipating the release of Pedro Almodóvar's latest effort, *Volver*, Sony Pictures Classics launched the 'Viva Pedro!' series in 2006. The retrospective, which played in art cinemas and repertoire houses all over the US, included those films that Sony previously held the theatrical rights to and two other films, *Matador* (1986) and *La ley del deseo/Law of Desire* (1987), that had very limited theatrical runs in the United States.[1] Sony also acquired the rights to *Mujeres al borde de un ataque de nervios/Women on the Verge of a Nervous Breakdown* (1988) which was initially released by MGM in the cinemas and the now-defunct Orion pictures in the video market. Significant absences in this retrospective were *¡Átame!/Tie Me Up, Tie Me Down* (1990), owned by Miramax and Almodóvar's 'confirmation' in terms of prestige after the critical success and Academy Award nomination of *Mujeres al borde de un ataque de nervios*, and *Tacones lejanos/High Heels* (1991), one of the Spanish director's most critically valued films.[2]

Sony's strategic manoeuvre hinges on an unambiguous asset: the director's name sells it all. The marketing tactic seems to stem from Penélope Cruz's hysterical scream 'Pedro!!!' when she announced that the Spanish director had won the Academy Award for *Todo sobre mi madre/All About My Mother* (1999). Pedro Almodóvar has become an unmistakable brand of sophisticated art cinema around the world; therefore, 'Pedro' is enough. It is no longer necessary to sell his films as coming 'from acclaimed international director Pedro Almodóvar'. Mark Allinson states that 'Almodóvar's work defies clear generic definition, the term "un film de Almodóvar" denoting almost a genre in itself'. What's more, the 'resistance to generic definition in Almodóvar is born out of an acute awareness of genre, how different genres can be mixed into a hybrid product, and most importantly, how it can be enlisted as a vehicle for the distinctive expression of an accepted "auteur"' (2001: 122). The Almodóvar brand is, in my view, a fully recognisable instance of art cinema rather than a genre, offering an example of how this type of cinematic endeavour functions as it circulates through different distribution and exhibition circuits around the world. Consequently, to fully map out the workings of Almodóvar-as-brand and the role of diverse genres in his films, we need to acknowledge that genres do not work identically for different audiences, since spectators are equipped with diverse cultural and social codes to approach generic categories and their encounter with films is invariably dependent on them.

In short, Almodóvar's use of generic categories functions differently for Spanish and American audiences. Sony did not necessarily market Almodóvar's recent retrospective in terms of his status as the internationally renown 'poster boy' for Spanish cinema but as 'poster boy' for global art cinema, who, since *Todo sobre mi madre*, has become fully recognisable and, most importantly, *understandable* for American audiences. In this sense, US audiences, according to Sony's marketing strategies, typically decode the generic heterogeneity of Almodóvar's works – from film noir to melodrama to slapstick comedy – through their recognition of the functioning of those elements as markers of the auteurist imprint the Spanish director has diachronically built through his body of works. In the Almodovarian universe for US audiences, genres thus function as markers of both his distinctive cinematic oeuvre and the multiple layers of intertextuality through which he connects his work with a variety of artistic practices from around the globe. Almodóvar's prominent status in world cinema offers us an entry point for analysing the interweaving concepts of auteur and film genres and, more specifically, their role in defining the position of Spanish cinema in contemporary global markets.

This chapter takes the genrification of the Almodóvar brand in the US media and cinematic imaginary as a point of departure to tackle how the concepts of genre, authorship and Spanish cinema itself acquire different meanings when transposed into a foreign film market. By scrutinising the marketing strategies deployed by the successive US distributors of three of the most economically and critically successful Spanish directors of the last decade and a half – Pedro Almodóvar, Alejandro Amenábar, Álex de la Iglesia – this chapter analyses the relationship between genre and Spanish cinema within a foreign film market. It studies how the films of these three directors come to occupy distinct generic positions in the US market, depending on which cinematic attributes a distributor chooses to highlight or downplay in order to enhance their marketability. Therefore, this chapter examines the function of film within a variety of circuits of cultural, economic and ideological exchange. As Steve Neale has noted, genres are indeed 'specific systems of expectations and hypotheses which spectators bring with them to the cinema and which interact with films themselves during the course of the viewing process' (2000: 31). But they are also the very discourses different players of the film business – producers, distributors, filmmakers and critics – mobilise to offer entry points for spectators into the multi-semantic discourses that engender the textual characteristics of films and their functioning within the broader social field. At the same time, genres work within a shifting dynamic across cultures and social formations since their decoding highly depends on a process of spectatorial intervention. When discussing films working within transcultural fields and across geopolitical borders, they become the very spaces of a variety of negotiations between different cultures and modes of cinematic address.

Either through websites, TV commercials, billboards, theatrical teasers or trailers, generic categories invariably emerge along with the star personas of the talent involved, the recognisable trademark of a director's specific style and the familiar brand of filmmaking a producer epitomises (e.g. Jerry Bruckheimer) as the prominent signposts disseminated in the transnational mediascape to allure spectators into viewing a particular film. Ultimately genres allow the spectator to engage with models of representation they can recognise, understand, appreciate and reimagine according to their own cultural codes as they continuously negotiate the dynamic between repetition and novelty that is central to the processes through which genrification addresses them.

The reasons for the centrality of these three directors in regard to contemporary Spanish cinema and genre are multiple. First, they are reference points in contemporary Spanish cinema in the commercial, journalistic and scholarly fields. Second, they have absolute control over all the phases of the filmmaking process. Not only do they write, produce and direct their films but they are also deeply involved in the design of the marketing campaigns and websites that advertise their products inside the Spanish cultural and social fields. In contrast, their promotional materials have been reconstructed entirely by their US distributors, and this process brings to the fore different understandings of the interaction between authorial status, generic categories and the adherence to the label of 'Spanishness' in terms of the marketing of their cinematic outputs. Third, they offer different 'faces' of Spanish cinema in terms of its engagement with generic categories. Consequently, they occupy different terrains in the international markets – and more specifically the US – in how they exemplify diverse deployments of film genres, transnational appropriation of film aesthetics and sociocultural negotiation of the historical junctures of Spain in the last decade and a half. Lastly, they each have cultivated a carefully self-constructed identity in the media (especially on the Web), as a key strategy to promote their works that reveals different attitudes toward the relationship between the producers and consumers of culture.[3]

In particular, the use of the Web has become a powerful tool for both the maintenance and construction of a director's identity, and for communicating directly with audiences and fans. For example, Almodóvar's site is an open portal to the inner thoughts, achievements and global recognition of his films. It includes a personal reflection about each of his films and 'Objective Almodóvar', a travelogue about the places that have impacted the Spanish director and a self-interview. It is thus a venue for Almodóvar to list his personal feelings and his cinematic references that only works in one direction, since the fans who enter his internet temple have no room to interact with the Spanish director. Amenábar's official site is equally closed off to user feedback.[4] The site is a technologically driven audiovisual tour de force that welcomes the Web user with an unmistakable message by the filmmaker himself: 'My movies are not movies about answers but questions.'[5] In other words, the website aims to produce the same degree of absolute immersion his films engender, without acknowledging explicitly the many influences at work in his films, like the Almodóvar site does. While giving the typical links to trailers, cast, production notes and stills, soundtracks for purchase and selected interviews, the site offers several of

Amenábar's reflections about his films. Like Almodóvar, he mobilises genre as a communicative asset for such a purpose. For example, discussing his 1997 film, Amenábar noted that 'What could have been a nice screwball comedy turns out to be the worst possible nightmare. *Abre los ojos* is a thriller with many elements: of love, suspense, terror, science fiction.'[6] De la Iglesia, conversely, treats his fans as bar-stool buddies. He keeps a regular online diary that is written in a colloquial style, informing his fans about both his upcoming and ongoing projects but also about his recent trips, opinions about the latest concert he went to and similar issues. The site also offers a venue for direct interaction with the director: 'Do you want to praise him? Maybe you have some complaints, secrets or (dis)honest propositions you wish to share with him? Write directly to Álex de la Iglesia, without intermediaries' – an open forum for de la Iglesia's zealots.[7] Even though the site also offers a self-interview in a very Almodovarian fashion, in terms of design it is the polar opposite of Almodóvar's and Amenábar's. The website is a direct communication bridge with the director himself, forming a continuum with his carefully designed public persona as an accessible movie buff who is always in *buen rollo* mood.[8] All the sites are available in both Spanish and English, capitalising on the borderless character of the Web and the use of English as a lingua franca to communicate with fans all around the globe.[9] The directors recognise the necessarily global dimension of their potential fan base and the necessary interstitial existence of Spanish cinema in a multilayered and multi-technological landscape of cultural exchange across borders. Thus the goal of this chapter is to analyse Almodóvar's, Amenábar's and de la Iglesia's cases to explore the necessary process of transcultural translation film products undergo when entering a foreign market and to pin down the shifting relationship between genre, authorship and national cinema utilising film trailers as a field of investigation.

De la Iglesia, Amenábar and Almodóvar in the Spanish and US markets

Thomas Elsaesser has provocatively theorised that contemporary European cinema may be better understood as a subset of world cinema, rather than through a model that directly opposes it to the imperialistic populism of Hollywood's global reach. The world cinema auteur – Wong Kar-Wai, Edward Yang, Wim Wenders, Olivier Assayas, etc. – operates within the terrain of this transterritorial field 'rather than the old national cinemas, thereby signaling a cinema that, while perhaps not suited for the national market, does well in international export markets, reaches the secondary markets of television or even the mass marketing of DVD releases with their vast network of internet-based fan sites and DVD reviews' (2005: 498). What makes these world auteur films travel well outside their national boundaries and often flop in their native lands? How do they neutralise the untranslatable elements of their locally and nationally inflected discourses to triumph globally and fully engage the universal audiences that hail them? Perhaps, as Yueh-Yu Yeh has suggested in her discussion of the musical discourses of Wong Kar-Wai films, in many cases it is precisely the heterogeneous multiculturalism of their soundscapes that appeals to this cultured, global spectator. Along these lines, Almodóvar's films are characterised for their vastly eclectic musical landscapes. He has worked with the likes of Ennio Morricone and Ryuichi Sakamoto – two worldwide musical powerhouses – and internationally renowned Spanish composer Alberto Iglesias. He repeatedly uses classical music, pop extravaganzas, camp classics such as La Lupe, African music such as Ismael Lo's 'Tajabone' and international favourites of cultivated intellectuals such as Brazilian singer Caetano Veloso. The soundscapes in Almodóvar´s films are indeed as diverse as his set of visual influences; in addition, as Mark Allinson states, 'his use of genre (the often wholesale borrowing of generic codes from Hollywood) is what sets Almodóvar apart from many of his European "art-house" peers', and other global art-house favourites such as Hou Hsiao-Hsien, Abbas Kiarostami and Tsai Ming-Liang (2001: 123). If anything, Almodóvar is closer to Wong Kar-Wai in terms of their constant recycling of American and Latin American multicultural discourses to compose multilayered audiovisual tapestries; even though their films are culturally rooted in the idiosyncrasies of their respective national cultures, they also operate centrifugally within a selected roster of multilingual and multimedia discourses (mostly cinematic and musical) to resist a clear categorisation attached to a single national border. Though Almodóvar seems to fit Elsaesser's above-mentioned description in the early stages of his career, the commercial success in Spain of most of his later films (with the notorious exception of *La mala educación/Bad Education* (2004)) would seem to signal otherwise. In other words, films such as *Todo sobre mi madre*, *Hable con ella/Talk to Her* (2002) or *Volver* belong to the mainstream within the Spanish film market; therefore, they do not occupy the peripheral position that Elsaesser ascribes to the world auteur inside their native countries.

Alejandro Amenábar is equally problematic in terms of his fitting into this framework of world auteurism. Ever since his early efforts, *Tesis/Thesis* (1996) and *Abre los ojos/Open Your Eyes* (1997), Amenábar was critically championed and recognised as the most commercially viable Spanish filmmaker among the new emergent generation. His films managed to manoeuvre the dictates of both commerce and art to create an innovative kind of Spanish cinematic product: one that recognised the demands of the filmmaking as an economic enterprise and, at the same time, showed a high degree of cinematic craftsmanship (Buckley, 2002; Maule, 2000). Significantly, whereas *Tesis* was fully funded by a Spanish producer – Jose Luis Cuerda's 'Las Producciones del Escorpión' – *Abre los ojos* was a French–Italian–Spanish co-production.[10] His next film, *Los otros/The Others* (2001), brought Hollywood to Spain in the form of the hottest star couple around at the time of its production: namely Tom Cruise as executive producer and his then wife Nicole Kidman as the protagonist of the film. *Los otros* was a massive worldwide commercial and critical success, giving Amenábar the global exposure he had not fully achieved with two previous features.[11] In addition, Cruise/Wagner productions bought the rights for *Abre los ojos* in the United States, and after Amenábar rejected remaking his own film Cameron Crowe was chosen to direct it as *Vanilla Sky* (2001), starring Tom Cruise and Penélope Cruz in the same role she played in the original. Amenábar's latest feature, *Mar adentro/The Sea Inside* (2004) showcases marketable transnational Spanish star Javier Bardem and won the Academy Award for Best Foreign Picture.

In generic terms, Amenábar's works are rather heterogeneous. *Tesis* is a horror thriller that succeeds in utilising a series of narrative and audiovisual tropes of two well-established transnational genres and, at the same time, 'Spanishises' them by pointing to the violence-ridden Spanish mediascape of the mid-1990s (Rodríguez Ortega, 2005). *Abre los ojos* is another generic hybrid, a sci-fi thriller, and *Los otros* is what has been traditionally defined as a 'gothic horror' film.[12] Finally, *Mar adentro* is a biopic. What binds Amenábar's films together is the masterful combination of a very *economic*, action-driven, narrative structure that varies according to the generic formations to which it attaches itself – from thriller to horror to biopic/drama – and a transgeneric sentimental substratum anchored in the problematic of the heterosexual couple.[13] In other words, his works explore a fundamental preoccupation: a genre-triggered crisis that impedes the full realisation of a heterosexual match.

His commercial success is undoubtedly rooted in the fact that he managed to capitalise on the mainstream appeal of genre films in a country where this tradition was notoriously underexploited within the mainstream arena. Unlike Almodóvar, a master of self-reflexivity and auto-appropriation, Amenábar ultimately makes what Christian Metz labels 'plausible texts'. Metz argues that the 'plausible' – the reiteration of discourse – is neither entirely absent from a film nor fully present. However, filmmakers can approach the plausible in two fundamental ways. They can choose to assume the conventions of a genre, like Almodóvar, and create a film as a 'performance' of a given discourse, playing out a set of rules the spectator knows and attempting to locate the spectator's pleasure in the aesthetic 'enjoyment of complicity, or of competence, of micro techniques and of comparison with a closed field' (Metz, 1974: 248–9). Or, conversely, they can select to create a plausible text that 'tries to persuade itself and spectators that the conventions through which it is built are not discursive, but true, reality' (1974: 249). Generic conventions are only plausible as long as they are naturalised as truthful, justifying the use of every single one of them through a plot move and creating the illusion of reality by attempting to efface the marks of discourse. Metz then proclaims that the modern filmmakers who broaden the field of the filmic 'sayable' profess a remarkable appreciation for 'true genre films' – namely, those films that embrace their discursive nature, making the auteur's imprint traceable (1974: 252). Perhaps, partly because of his appreciation for true genre films, Amenábar's first feature (conspicuously titled 'Thesis') and *Abre los ojos* did expand the field of the filmic-sayable within the terrain of the Spanish cinematic tradition. However, once we analyse his whole body of works, we encounter an erasing drive that attempts, above all costs, to hide any traces of the cinematic apparatus and pretends to offer 'slices of the real', even if this reality is a dystopic future as in *Abre los ojos* or a psychological paranoia as in *Los otros*.

Unlike in Spain, where Amenábar's name carries an immediate mark of recognisability in the contemporary transnational mediascape, in the US his role is easily subordinated to the able craftsman that allows his actors to fully shine in all their performing grandeur. In other words, from god-like editor, soundtrack composer, screenwriter and director of all his films, he has become the audiovisual and narrative substratum that facilitates Kidman's, Cruz's or Bardem's stardom to reach a higher plateau. Amenábar is not yet an entirely recognisable brand like Almodóvar. Nor is he a nationally successful maverick turned into genre craftsman with too many traces of cinematic untranslatability like Álex de la Iglesia. Amenábar is perhaps the ultimate genre filmmaker – one who knows too well the conventions of generic categories to merely repeat them but who is perhaps too calculating to let his oeuvre supersede them and break the illusionist drive that runs across most of commercial cinema worldwide. At the same time, his films exemplify the fact that the idea of national cinema has increasingly become a decentred concept, working within a variety of transnational networks of production, distribution and exhibition in the entertainment field. As Josep Lluis Fecé states, Amenábar's films bank on 'a set of images and symbols . . . easily recognizable in diverse cultural contexts but that are not necessarily perceived as "authentic" in their origin' (2005: 91).[14] In other words, the Spanishness of his films is a marketing strategy to function productively in both the national and international markets. His use of different generic discourses acts as the ultimate facilitator to accomplish such a goal.

Like Amenábar, de la Iglesia is an immensely successful commercial director in Spain. However, his films have not substantially impacted any foreign market, neither theatrically nor in DVD rentals. Nor are his films the centrepiece of auteurist paradises such as the New York, Cannes, Toronto or Venice film festivals. Furthermore, they remain deeply entrenched in the cultural specificity of Spanish popular culture, making their appeal worldwide utterly problematic. In fact, *El día de la bestia/The Day of the Beast* (1995), his big commercial breakthrough in Spain, was released in the US market dubbed into English and dumped in video-store shelves in the horror section instead of the more specific 'Spanish cinema'.[15] De la Iglesia exemplifies a current in world cinema that Elsaesser's framework does not fully encompass. I am referring to those films that carefully negotiate between the global appeal of certain generic mechanisms and modes of address – such as the porous contours of action, comedy and horror at work in *El día de la bestia* – and the emphasis on extremely specific cultural markers. Their goal is to have a significant impact in their national markets while simultaneously gaining 'legs' outside their countries of origin even if only succeeding in limiting market niches. De la Iglesia may be labelled as a *popular generic auteur* – that is, a filmmaker who is committed to ground his films in the specific sociocultural milieu of Spain and mobilises genre as a tool for both sociopolitical commentary and economic success, reinscribing myriad cinematic and cultural traditions (both Spanish and from other origins) in the specificities of his country of origin. It is thus a type of cinematic effort that, while aesthetically and generically transnational, remains deeply rooted in a variety of national cultural markers that are not easily understandable for foreign audiences.[16] This is why dubbing *El día de la bestia* into English becomes particularly significant since it calls our attention to an attempt, on the US distributor's part, to neutralise those cultural Others (Spanish, but also *madrileño* and *vasco*) that are barely comprehensible for the American spectator and enhance the globally recognisable markers of the film – via its identification as a horror genre piece – while perhaps mobilising the curiosity of the cult video junkie, who is always eager to discover a new exploitation gem or an unknown European auteur in the dark corners of a crammed video store.

Although *El día de la bestia* made a big splash in the commercial domestic market, the critical reception of de la Iglesia's satanic black comedy was far more diverse. While many critics praised the film, a part of the Spanish critical intelligentsia dismissed the film as a shallow enquiry in the mid-1990s Spanish sociocultural milieu, since it offered a surface-driven populist assortment of miscellaneous cultural references devoid of any kind of ideological substance (Rodríguez Marchante, 1995: 82). Alternatively, the film is seen as a part of an epochal trend in contemporary Spanish literature and cinema that responds to a state of 'transnational postmodernity', which is characterised by the extensive deployment of video clip aesthetics and ultimately favours the depiction of 'simple action' while lacking content (Moreiras Menor, 2000: 139). For others, de la

Iglesia's films are a symptomatic rejection of cinema as a cultural enterprise for the sake of commercial filmmaking that 'came hand in hand with a rejection of the Europeanization of the national cinema, since "European" is usually shorthand for "art cinema"' (Triana-Toribio, 2003: 152). His films epitomise the turn to comedy as an attempt to overcome the crisis of Spanish cinema in a global context and under the crushing power of the growing domination of Hollywood in the world film markets.

De la Iglesia had already produced a moderately successful film prior to 1995, *Acción mutante/Mutant Action* (1993), not coincidentally produced by Agustín and Pedro Almodóvar, and held a cult status in Spain after his short *Mirindas asesinas* (1991) in alternative circuits. After the success of *El día de la bestia*, de la Iglesia sought to conquer the English-speaking market with the critically demolished and commercially catastrophic *Perdita Durango* (1997).[17] He soon returned to Spain and has since then cultivated a taste for the combination of high-octane action and grotesque comedic universes with his successive works: *Muertos de risa/Dying of Laughter* (1999), *La comunidad/Common Wealth* (2000), *800 balas/800 Bullets* (2002) and *Crimen ferpecto/Ferpect Crime* (2004). None of his films have been a hit in the United States. In fact, *Muertos de risa* and *La comunidad* only made it into the film festival circuit, and *Crimen ferpecto* was given a limited released with a gross take in the US market of slightly over $400,000.[18] In short, de la Iglesia remains a quasi-anonymous director in the US whose works are alternatively dismissed by US distributors, Americanised via dubbing or played for short period of times by distributors who hope for a surprisingly profitable run, or at least a small profit.

As a platform to fully analyse the diverse degrees of translatability of the works of these three directors in a foreign market and the shifting role of film genres in such a transmutation, the next step of this chapter is to analyse the domestic and US trailers of Almodóvar's, Amenábar's and de la Iglesia's films. How do their different engagements with genre translate in terms of the marketing and packaging of their respective works in the trailer format? How does the functioning of generic categories change as these three 'total auteurs' lose total or partial control of their trailers, now under the rule of the marketing gurus of their US distributors? In brief, how do genres, Spanishness and auteurism interact in the US trailers of their films?

Trailing the foreign auteur and genre

First, let's set the record straight: US film distributors fear linguistic difference like the plague. Consequently, in the US market, cultural and linguistic difference becomes invariably a victim of marketing campaigns. This is the rule of thumb that applies to all foreign films, regardless of their aesthetic, narrative or cultural fabric. In the trailer format, the value of a director's name as a marker of authorship and the generic characteristics of his films undergo various processes of transformation as they interact with specific industrial, marketing and aesthetic models at play in different historical junctures.

The Dimension US trailer of *Los otros* is paradigmatic in this sense. It relies heavily on Nicole Kidman's star persona to the point that the name of the Spanish director is not even mentioned. Moreover, Dimension is a well-established powerhouse in the contemporary American horror genre and, at that point in Amenábar's career, his films had barely made it into the US domestic market. In contrast, the Spanish trailer for the film is shorter and much more quickly paced in terms of editing; though it also banks on Kidman's presence, at the same time it concludes by announcing the unmistakable imprint of its director. Whereas the US trailer attempts to build a feeling of suspenseful horror, the Spanish one is a purely kinetic ride that follows Kidman's character up the stairs into an attic with quick fades to black followed by glimpses of disturbing imagery that are rhythmically bound by a musical crescendo. In short, while the US trailer plunges the spectator into the horror ride the Dimension brand promises, in this instance via Kidman's persona, the Spanish trailer launches the latest twist in the Amenabarian exploration of horrific imagery already at work in *Tesis* and *Abre los ojos*. In contrast, the Fineline Features trailer for *Mar adentro* explicitly foregrounds the Spanish director's name – 'From Alejandro Amenábar, acclaimed director of *The Others*' – trying to build on the proven success of Amenábar's previous film. More importantly, Fineline explicitly avoids addressing the generic dissimilarity between *Mar adentro* and *Los otros*.[19] Genre is thus conveniently effaced and strategically subordinated to Amenábar's status as auteur. Similar to this, in the US trailer of *Abre los ojos*, Lions Gate Films legitimates the film through its official selection in the Sundance and Toronto film festivals, and the fact it won the Grand Prix in Tokyo. Whereas the Spanish trailer relies heavily on

dialogue and the construction of a story arc based on Pelayo's
(Eduardo Noriega) psychological imbalance and inability to distinguish between the real and the imagined, the US one capitalises
on quick-paced editing, the foregrounding of the sexual triangle
between Penélope Cruz, Najwa Nimri and Noriega with titillating
images of sex and romance. The trailer also promises that the film
comes 'from acclaimed director Alejandro Amenábar'. Even though
audiences could possibly infer that the film is a psychological thriller,
however, the distributor banks more heavily on the recognisability
of Cruz's persona and the allure of romantic sex.[20]

In Almodóvar's longer history as a *trailed* filmmaker, an analogous process occurs. The trailer of his first US-released film, *Mujeres
al borde de un ataque de nervios*, is one-minute and thirty-three
seconds long and relies heavily on a voiceover narration that emphasises the inseparable contact zone between the comedic and the
melodramatic the film cultivates: 'It's a romance but it's not about
love. It's a comedy but not everyone is laughing. It's a place
where the one thing you can expect is the unexpected.' While
emphasising Almodóvar's international prestige over his identity as
a Spanish director ('From internationally acclaimed director Pedro
Almodóvar'), the trailer also highlights the heavily generic fabric of
the film, presenting it as 'a deliriously deranged comedy that follows
no rules, spares no victims and takes no prisoners'. Even though the
voiceover stands as the most prominent 'organiser' in the trailer – a
sort of guide for the US spectator that filters his deliriously aestheticised images – few lines of linguistic alterity are present.

Two years later, Miramax used the Spanish trailer of *¡Átame!* with
added subtitles in English to launch the film in the US market. In this
case, it was not only a matter of striking a deal with a new and potentially profitable European film auteur who had already established
himself in the US with *Mujeres al borde de un ataque de nervios* but
also a perfect match between the film's polemical representation of
sex and violence and Miramax's aggressive push to become a mini-
major in the US. In 1989 Miramax released Steven Soderbergh's *Sex,
Lies, and Videotape*, which ushered in the era of the 'indie blockbuster', a type of film that, on a smaller scale, attempted to 'replicate
the exploitation marketing and box-office performance of the major
studio high-concept event pictures'(Perren, 2001–2: 32). Miramax
became notorious for the use of exploitative marketing tactics to
promote their movies.[21] On the one hand, they attempted to release

films that could be viewed as quality pictures, those that typically get critical support based on their cinematic qualities, such as Lizzie Borden's *Working Girls* (1986) or Bille August's *Pelle erobreren/Pelle the Conqueror* (1987). On the other, the Weinstein brothers' company launched a series of films whose controversial subject matters and representational templates, especially in terms of explicit sex and violence, would be ideally suited to disseminate a series of commercial hook-ups through which they could bridge the gap from the art house and the multiplex. *¡Átame!* was a perfect fit for Miramax's aggressive marketing manoeuvres. Even though far from the more than $24 million that *Sex, Lies, and Videotape* gained in the box office, Almodóvar's film made over $8 million in the US, consolidating his marketability in art-house circuits.[22]

As we move forward in time, we easily detect how the next Almodóvar films released in the US market built upon the critical recognition the Spanish director had increasingly garnered in the US media via the inclusion of brief praising capsules from reputed critics. In addition, these trailers disseminate a series of signposts that remind spectators who were already familiar with Almodóvar films of the kind of enjoyment they have already experienced with the Spanish director's previous works. Such is the case with the trailers for both *La flor de mi secreto/The Flower of My Secret* (1995) and *Carne trémula/Live Flesh* (1997). Whereas the trailer for the former is the Spanish one with English subtitles, the latter capitalises on the use of a voiceover that, in an introductory fashion, reminds spectators of Almodóvar's achievements. In *La flor de mi secreto*, it is worth noting that the 'Almodóvar' brand of authorship is at work in one of the Spanish director's trailers for the first time. While emphasising the extreme explosions of affect that characterise Almodóvar's work and the foregrounding of desire, jealousy and obsession along with nudity and hints of violent imagery, these trailers epitomise the progressive genrification of the Almodóvar brand as a marketable asset that functions within the recognisibility/novelty dynamic that characterises the different stages of the encounter between film spectators and generic categories. Almodóvar's oeuvre had reached a point in which marketability produced itself. It was not a matter of *telling* anymore but simply *showing* that the latest Almodóvar achievement was in store. Everything else seems to be unnecessary redundancy. In other words, the brand 'Almodóvar' was already immediately and unmistakably recognisable.

This is precisely why Sony Pictures Classics marketed his next three films in a similar manner. The *Todo sobre mi madre* trailer is designed – through the use of the font and colour palette in the inter-titles – to organically precede the film and visually rhyme with it as if they were two parts of the same whole. After the series of interti-tles highlight the importance of motherhood and/as performance and the centrality of affect in the film, a succession of images accom-panied by a musical crescendo close the trailer in quick succession, offering no clues about the narrative arc of the film nor any instance of linguistic Spanishness except for Cruz uttering the name of her dog Sapic. Once again, the brand 'Almodóvar' is favoured in con-trast to the name 'Pedro Almodóvar'. The trailers of *Hable con ella* and *La mala educación* follow a similar format in as much as they provide no information about the narrative fabric of the films, are devoid of dialogue altogether and are legitimated by either critics' capsules or the acknowledgement of the presence of the film in reputed film festivals. In this respect, perhaps, the *La mala educación* trailer reaches a new pinnacle of 'lack of information' since it is only twenty-eight seconds long. There is nothing else to sell any more, except perhaps that a new hot Hispanic transnational star, Gael García Bernal, has been added to the Almodovarian universe. In this respect, the Spanish trailer of *La mala educación* is radically differ-ent in as much as it is significantly longer, it includes several bits of dialogue, it explicitly foregrounds the metacinematic dimension of the film and it emphasises the central themes of homosexuality and transvestism and their relationship with the repressive role of the Catholic Church during the Francoist period. Whereas the Spanish trailer is historically grounded in a series of cultural icons easily deci-pherable for those who are minimally aware of the recent history of Spain, Sony Pictures Classics did not seem to believe the typical US spectator would be able to recognise these foreign historical markers and, perhaps, the film distributor simply avoided an unnecessary danger by letting Almodóvar the brand sell itself. Why should they risk alienating audiences with an array of images that, although deeply Almodovarian, may not be immediately comprehensible?

Volver, Almodóvar's latest feature, is perhaps an oddity in terms of its marketing. The film prominently features bits of Spanish dia-logue and is significantly longer than the last three Sony Picture Classics trailers of Almodóvar's films. This break in the pattern is directly related to Sony's attempt to achieve an Academy Award nomination (which they accomplished) for the biggest Spanish star in Hollywood: Penélope Cruz. For, unlike at the time of *Todo sobre mi madre*, when Cruz was trying to break through in the US, due to her artistic merits and sentimental affairs Cruz is now a regular fixture in the US cinematic and social imaginary. Since Sony attempted to cross-market the film from the scores of Almodóvar's fans to Cruz's devotees, the trailer displays the meeting ground between the emphasis on the sellability of an immediately recognisable auteur-as-a-genre-in-itself and the astounding beauty and acting skills of a well-known reputed star.

While the trailers for Álex de la Iglesia's films also rely on star discourse and genre, they diverge sharply from the function of Almodóvar's auteurist brand identity. The Spanish trailer of *La comunidad* uses a similar strategy in relation to *Volver* – it exclusively capitalises on the recognisability of its roster of actors and its main star, Carmen Maura – however it is a level of recognisability that is legible only within the Spanish market. As the trailer unravels through the rhythms of a suspenseful score and a series of stills linked through dissolves present well-known veteran Spanish actors such as Terele Pávez, Emilio Gutiérrez Caba and Sancho Gracia, we come to realise they are the residents of an apartment building who harbour mysterious and likely murderous intentions. Eventually all the members of this community are brought together on screen and the camera zooms into them as the title of the film salutes the spectator. Immediately after, Maura, trapped in a balcony, pleads for her life while armed with a knife. The trailer concludes with a quick glimpse of comedy through a short dialogue exchange between Maura and two of the neighbours that points to the centrality of money as the seed for the threat Maura's character is about to experience. In other words, the trailer sells the idea of a grotesque thriller that capitalises on the recognisability of Carmen Maura and a roster of veteran actors for Spanish audiences via the idiosyncratic combination of excessive violence and humour that is unmistakably de la Iglesia's. If *La comunidad*'s trailer is inextricably linked to de la Iglesia's previously built auteurist stamp, which remains almost unknown in the United States, the *Muertos de risa* trailer banks on similar assets but builds upon the aesthetics of Spanish TV and *destape* films of the 1970s through a string of images of tacky eroticism and a populist Spanish soundtrack. In a music video format it introduces the two main characters of the film, Nino and Bruno, who are played by two icons of contemporary Spanish culture – namely, El Gran Wyoming (TV superstar of the groundbreaking show *Caiga quien Caiga*) and Santiago Segura (who, after coming into stardom with his role in *El día de la bestia*, went on to become a commercially successful actor/director with his record-breaking *Torrente: el brazo tonto de la ley* (1998)). It is thus a film that is generically marked by its association with a type of Spanish popular culture that has never broken through into international markets and therefore does not open many points of contact for foreign spectators. While the trailers of *800 balas* and de la Iglesia's only English-language film, *Perdita Durango*, arguably attempt to transcend their Spanishness via their association with the iconicity of the spaghetti western and the erotic 'border thriller' respectively, the de la Iglesia factor – the combination of explicit sexual imagery, excessive action and grotesque comedic imagery – invariably rises and anchors their ultimate appeal in the recognition of the idiosyncrasies of the Spanish director's style.[23] Unlike Almodóvar's and Amenábar's, de la Iglesia's films for the most part do not capitalise on globally operative generic grounds to cancel out or, at least, make palatable the cultural specificities from which they stem. Consequently, they mostly fail to gain legs outside Spain, having limited or no impact in foreign markets.[24]

Genre, auteurism and crosscultural translation

Pedro Almodóvar continues to succeed internationally as his films constantly negotiate a multi-semantic melange of a variety of cinematic genres. He keeps on reworking the distinctive markers of an auteurist imprint he has long consolidated in the global cinematic imaginary. Alejandro Amenábar, for his part, remains the wunderkind of Spanish cinema, meeting critical and economic triumph in the domestic market and elsewhere. Álex de la Iglesia, however, represents the best virtues of remaining a populist filmmaker, filling up blog pages on his website, continuously cultivating his *amiguete* persona and feeding off a variety of generic categories while still relying on a core substratum of violent and grotesque comedy deeply entrenched in the idiosyncrasies of Spanish culture. The first two directors seem to be indeed fully translatable, and a study of the different meanders of their careers and the marketing of their films in the US market reveals how the ultimate success of a director's work and the mobilisation or minimisation of the role of genre in their films for marketing purposes is highly dependent on a variety of factors that have to do not only with the intratextual characteristics of their films but also with different industrial and cultural factors that are in continuous transformation.[25] Even if we recognise that genres are perhaps the ultimate meeting spaces between spectators and films within the multilayered mediascape in which filmmaking functions, we also need to notice that there are many other pieces in the complex puzzle of the crosscultural encounter between a film stemming from a given geopolitical territory and the foreign spectator. The diverse trajectories of Almodóvar, Amenábar and de la Iglesia offer us a starting point to tackle the understanding of this complex set of processes.

Notes

1 Cinevista released these films theatrically in the United States shortly after they came out in Spain. I would like to thank Robert Sklar for giving me this piece of information.
2 *Tie Me Up, Tie Me Down!* made $8,264,530 in the US box office.
3 For a thorough discussion of the impact of digital technology in the increasingly blurring distinction between producers and consumers of culture see Henry Jenkins' *Convergence Culture* (2006) and Mark Poster's *Information Please* (2006).
4 In fact, if one double-clicks on the 'Forum' icon, it brings the user to a dead link.
5 See www.clubcultura.com/clubcine/clubcineastas/amenabar/index.htm.
6 Almodóvar, for example, explains *Mujeres al borde de un ataque de nervios* in terms of his own idea of 'high comedy'. He also argues against the identification of *La mala educación* as a comedy despite its comedic elements.
7 The welcome message in de la Iglesia's Forum reads as follows: 'Discuss anything concerning the divine, the human or the extraterrestrial in this exclusive Álex de la Iglesia forum. Talk with experts and prove your knowledge about the life and works of the filmmaker. Most of the users speak Spanish as their first language.'
8 *Buen rollo* is a Spanish slang term that roughly translates as 'it's all cool' or 'having a good time'. For information regarding de la Iglesia's official site, see www.clubcultura.com/clubcine/clubcineastas/delaiglesia/ing/home.htm.
9 Almodóvar's site is also in French. It is worth noting that the Spanish director has always had a large fan base in France and that many of his films have been partially financed by French companies.

10 *Abre los ojos* was produced by Las Producciones del Escorpión (Spain), Sociedad General de Cine S.A. (Spain), Les Films Alain Sarde (France) and Lucky Red (Italy).

11 According to Rotten Tomatoes, www.rottentomatoes.com/m/1109257-others/numbers.php, *The Others* made $96,080,075 in the US domestic box office and an additional $23,010,000 in video rentals. Overseas the film made a total of $113,424,350. *Open Your Eyes*, released in the US in 1999, only made $368,234 in its short theatrical run.

12 For a full discussion of *The Others* in terms of the horror genre, see Chapter 10 in this collection.

13 In this respect, I follow the works of Linda Williams in *Playing the Race Card* (2001) and Christine Gledhill in 'Rethinking Genre' (2000).

14 'Un conjunto de imágenes o de símbolos . . . fácilmente reconocibles en diversos contextos culturales, pero que no se perciben necesariamente como "auténticos" en el de origen.'

15 According to the Spanish Ministry of Culture's official website, *El día de la bestia* made €4.367.321,16 when it was released in Spain. In the United States, the film had only a week-long theatrical run. It only made $8,000. See www.imdb.com/title/tt0112922/business.

16 In their essay 'The Spanish "Popular Auteur": Álex de la Iglesia as Polemical Tool', Peter Buse, Núria Triana-Toribio and Andrew Willis (2004) claim that the concept of the auteur is at best anachronistic. However, they continue to discuss the work of the Spanish director along this line of critical thought in order to 'attack Spanish auteur studies from within rather than without', given the privileged status of this kind of study in the discipline of film studies. The authors then proceed to extract auteurism from the safe box of art cinema and 'test' the term against the work of de la Iglesia within the realm of popular cinema.

17 The film was released straight to video in the US under the title *Dance with the Devil*.

18 For box-office data, see http://boxofficemojo.com/movies/?id=elcrimen-perfecto.htm.

19 The US trailer of *Mar adentro* also capitalises on the recognisability of Javier Bardem after his Academy Award nomination for *Before Night Falls* (Julian Schnabel, 2000). It is also worth noting that, while the Spanish poster of the film features Bardem as Sampedro in his older self, the US one capitalises on the masculine beauty of the young Bardem, promising a kind of encounter with the Spanish actor that is not necessarily fulfilled in the film since the young Bardem only appears in a few dream sequences.

20 The Spanish trailer does not even emphasise Cruz's presence in the film. She is one more in the list of actors that close the trailer.

21 As Perren reports, Miramax championed *Eréndira* (Ruy Guerra, 1983) actress Claudia Ohana posing for *Playboy* and set up Daniel Day-Lewis, who played Christy Brown in *My Left Foot* (Jim Sheridan, 1989), to testify before Congress on behalf of the Americans with Disabilities Act.

22 In fact, Miramax and Almodóvar sued the MPAA when the movie was given an X rating even though a settlement was reached with an NC-17 rating.

23 The clearest example of this is perhaps the opening of the *800 balas* trailer. An intertitle states 'It looks like a Western . . .' and is followed by a typical church bell in a Western town. The new intertitle reads 'But it is not exactly . . .', followed by the image of a ten-year-old boy dressed in a Samurai outfit.

24 *Perdita Durango* tried to use Rosie Perez as its main box-office appeal. Although Javier Bardem is the lead male in the film, he was not then the international superstar he is now. The lead in *800 balas* is Sancho Gracia, who is a central icon of the 1980s Spanish TV through his role in the series *Curro Jiménez*.

25 *Amiguete* is a term of Spanish slang that can be roughly translated as 'best buddy'.

References

Allinson, Mark (2001) *A Spanish Labyrinth: The Films of Pedro Almodóvar*, London: I. B. Taurus.

Buckley, Christine (2002) 'Alejandro Amenábar's *Tesis*: Art, Commerce and Renewal in Spanish Cinema', *Post Script: Essays in Film and the Humanities*, 21: 2, Winter–Spring, 12–25.

Buse, Peter, Núria Triana-Toribio and Andrew Willis (2004) 'The Spanish "Popular Auteur": Álex de la Iglesia as Polemical Tool', *New Cinemas*, 2: 3, December, 139–48.

Elsaesser, Thomas (2005) *European Cinema: Face to Face with Hollywood*, Amsterdam: Amsterdam University Press.

Fecé, Josep Lluis (2005) 'La excepción y la norma. Reflexiones sobre la españolidad de nuestro cine reciente', *Archivos de la Filmoteca*, 49, 82–95.

Gledhill, Christine (2000) 'Rethinking Genre', in Christine Gledhill and Linda Williams (eds), *Reinventing Film Studies*, London and New York: Arnold and Oxford University Press, 221–43.

Jenkins, Henry (2006) *Convergence Culture: Where Old and New Media Collide*, New York: New York University Press.

Maule, Rosanna (2000) 'Death and Reflexivity in Alejandro Amenábar's *Tesis*', *Torre de Papel*, 10: 1, Spring, 65–76.

Metz, Christian (1974) *Film Language: A Semiotics of the Cinema*, Oxford: Oxford University Press.

Moreiras Menor, Cristina (2000) 'Spectacle, Trauma and Violence in Contemporary Spain', in Barry Jordan and Rikki Morgan-Tamosunas (eds), *Contemporary Spanish Cultural Studies*, Arnold: London, 134–42.

Neale, Stephen (2000) *Genre and Hollywood*, London: Routledge.

Perren, Alisa (2001–2) 'Sex, Lies and Marketing: Miramax and the Development of the Quality Indie Blockbuster', *Film Quarterly*, 55: 2, Winter, 30–9.

Poster, Mark (2006) *Information Please: Culture and Politics in the Age of Digital Machines*, Durham, NC: Duke University Press.

Rodríguez Marchante, Oti (1995) '*El día de la Bestia*: de Madrid al Infierno', *ABC*, 21 November.

Rodríguez Ortega, Vicente (2005) 'Snuffing Hollywood: Transmedia Horror in *Tesis*', *Senses of Cinema*, 36, July–September, www.sensesofcinema.com/contents/05/36/tesis.html.

Triana-Toribio, Núria (2003) *Spanish National Cinema*, London: Routledge.

Williams, Linda (2001) *Playing the Race Card: Melodramas of Black and White from Uncle Tom to O. J. Simpson*, Princeton: Princeton University Press.

Yueh-Yu Yeh (2000) 'A Life of Its Own: Musical Discourses in Wong Kar-Wai's Films', *Post Script: Essays in Film and the Humanities*, 19, 120–36.

3

'Now playing everywhere': Spanish horror film in the marketplace

Antonio Lázaro-Reboll

Under the title 'Scare Tactics', *Screen International* provided a dossier on horror genre production in Europe's major territories (MacNab, 2006). Jennifer Green's brief profile on Spain offers us some preliminary points of entry to discuss Spanish horror production at the turn of the twenty-first century. First, horror film production in mainstream contemporary Spanish cinema rose in a boom that reached 'a peak in 2004 when seven of the top 25 local grossers were horrors'; second, international projection of Spanish horror cinema was favoured since it 'often travels better than other Spanish production'; third, 'a distinction [should be made] between the bulk of generally low-budget Spanish-language horrors from the likes of de la Iglesia, Barcelona-based genre specialists Filmax or upstart Valencia Pictures'; and finally, Filmax president Julio Fernández reminds us of the commercial realities of horror film production, observing that 'making genre films is about entertainment' and 'knowing our target: the public and international distributors' (Green, 2006: 12). This chapter looks at the 'scare tactics' deployed by three recent Spanish horror films – *El arte de morir/Art of Dying* (Álvaro Fernández Armero, 2000), *Darkness* (Jaume Balagueró, 2002) and *El laberinto del fauno/Pan's Labyrinth* (Guillermo del Toro, 2006) – focusing on their marketing practices, mechanics of distribution and exhibition, and critical reception abroad and in Spain.

Each of these three films is representative of a certain type of horror movie made in Spain, showing the variety and versatility of Spanish horror production. Whereas *El arte de morir* is a product calculated for the national market, and *Darkness* is conceived for the international market as part of Filmax's goal to produce competitive English-language films, *El laberinto del fauno* is designed with both the global and transnational markets in mind. Producers and directors have positioned their films in relation to international horror, mobilising specific commercial discourses and generic formations in order to reach beyond core horror audiences. Whilst del Toro has repeatedly proven his commercial expertise and knowledge of popular tastes and Balagueró has used to his advantage the service of leading professionals from Filmax, *El arte de morir* represents Fernández Armero's only incursion into the genre.

El arte de morir

Scream (1996) – the globally popular slasher directed by Wes Craven and written by Kevin Williamson – and its offshoots loom large in the production, marketing and reception of *El arte de morir.* Producer Francisco Ramos, screenwriters Juan Vicente Pozuelo and Francisco Javier Royo and director Álvaro Fernández Armero deliberately modelled *El arte de morir* on the teen horror films of the late 1990s, a hugely successful and popular Hollywood production trend. *El arte de morir* was a calculated commercial project designed to yield maximum financial returns. Its spectacular opening weekend (31 March 2000) made it an instant local hit and a much-needed injection of capital into the ailing coffers of national production; as *Screen International* dramatically described it, 'Spanish film stays alive with *Art of Dying*' (Green, 2000a). The film grossed $1.3 million in the two weeks following its nationwide release in 179 screens and a box-office domestic total of $3,328,702. That same year it was only outperformed in the box office by *Año Mariano* (Karra Elejalde and Fernando Guillén Cuervo), *La comunidad/Common Wealth* (Álex de la Iglesia) and *You're the one (una historia de entonces)* (José Luis Garcí). As for its life beyond Spain, *Variety*'s reviewer gives a realistic prediction of the possibilities of the film in the highly competitive horror market: 'pic is down-the-line mainstream . . . Offshore buyers and auds may feel material is too standard issue to perk much interest' (Holland, 2000); a fair assessment given the fact that *El arte de morir* grossed a meagre $36,207 and only lasted a few weeks (11 September–30 November 2001) in US cinemas.[1] My analysis of *El arte de morir* considers first the production and marketing strategies deployed by the producers and then moves on to discuss how the commercial aesthetic of being 'like *Scream*' fared among critics and reviewers.

Taking his cue from Andrew Tudor's (2002) label 'postmodern horror', Peter Hutchings asks whether the term 'postmodern slasher' is a useful critical category to describe the cycle of American teen horror films of the late 1990s and early 2000s.[2] For Hutchings it is because 'postmodern horror . . . has absolutely nothing to do with postmodern theory; it means . . . a film like *Scream* (1996)' (2004: 211). Films 'like *Scream*' were, among others, the two sequels of the franchise (Wes Craven, 1997 and 2000), *I Know What You Did Last Summer* (Jim Gillespie, 1997), *Urban Legend* (Jamie Blanks, 1998), and *Final Destination* (James Wong, 2000). How is *El arte de morir*, then, a film 'like *Scream*'?

Developed as an in-house project by Aurum Producciones, the Spanish distributor for New Line Cinema (which, in turn, is associated with several slasher hits), producer Ramos commissioned the script by Pozuelo and Royo and subsequently offered the project to Fernández Armero who took it as a genre assignment. The filmmaker had established his name as a comedy director with *Todo es mentira* (1994), *Brujas* (1996) and *Nada en la nevera* (1998), a series of films focusing on the lives of urban, middle-class adolescent and young people which had given him the credentials among this demographic to depict their lives realistically. His first and only foray into the horror genre had a considerable budget for a Spanish genre production, 300 million pesetas (approximately $2.5 million), plus the collaboration of TVE and the participation of Canal+.[3] The production and marketing strategy capitalized on the *Scream* series on a number of levels: script and production decisions, publicity and media commentary, and generic markers. Pozuelo and Royo explain the premise behind the project in the press book, namely to produce a Spanish version of contemporary American teen horror films: 'throughout the long process of its gestation we found that some elements of the latest American horror cinema were translatable into Spanish tastes' (*El arte de morir*, 2000). In what would become a common rhetorical operation throughout the promotional campaign, the acknowledgement of the source of inspiration is immediately followed by a disclaimer: 'but we also realized that Spanish audiences demanded something more, some narrative complexity which American teen horror films lacked' (*El arte de morir*, 2000). Their distancing from the 'unsophisticated', 'juvenile' American horror genre is replicated by the director in interviews: 'I am aware that my audience and that of *Scream 3* are the same' but 'we have added another turn of the screw to the narrative to give the story an European touch', or 'I believe [my film] is much more intelligent' (Fernández Armero in Belinchón, 2000). These promotional tactics reveal a two-pronged manoeuvre aimed at targeting particular audience segments, while, at the same time, presenting *El arte de morir*, through its thematic and stylistic association with 'European' art film, as a sophisticated alternative to the popular genres produced by Hollywood. The producers and creators are at pains in differentiating *El arte de morir* from the likes of *Scream*, asserting its qualitative difference and positioning it in a cinematic tradition that will elevate it to the higher end of the market and please middlebrow tastes. Let us examine the elements that shaped these tactics.

El arte de morir's poster bears an uncanny resemblance to those of *Scream 2* and *Scream 3*. A group portrait presents the defiant faces of the six young characters and in the background the menacing presence of Nacho (Gustavo Salmerón) hanging above them. The *Scream*-like scenario is counterpoised to the arty font of a title with marked artistic and intellectual pretensions far removed from the bodily and emotional reactions elicited by low body genres. '*El arte de morir* is the literal translation of *ars moriendi*' (*El arte de morir*, 2000), a Western medieval literary tradition, which provided guidance to those dying, write Pozuelo and Royo in the pressbook notes, in an attempt to lend the film an air of seriousness and respectability and to clothe the story in a philosophical and metaphysical subtext. Nacho, an up-and-coming avant-garde artist, who is obsessed with representations of death, is the character through whom this theme is articulated in the narrative. In spite of their studious framing devices, the *ars moriendi* motif is largely ignored by the media, though the philosophical and metaphysical subtext is picked up by some reviewers, who argue that the real protagonist in the film is conscience or the fact that the storyline involves the spectators in confronting their own ghosts (Villar, 2000; Piña, 2000).

Undoubtedly, death is the structuring element in *El arte de morir*. But so is that of any other slasher film where the protagonists are murdered one by one by the killer(s). Films like *Scream* present a 'whodunnit' structure populated by predominantly young characters who have to probe into 'the past – either their own past or the past of the community – in order to make sense of the present and then be able to act decisively on the basis of the knowledge thus acquired' (Hutchings, 2004: 215). What this probing into the past puts to the test is the group's interpersonal relationships, asking the individual characters to confront their past actions. *El arte de morir* is formulaic in this respect. The tagline for *El arte de morir* establishes squarely the presence of the past in the present: 'si tienes que desenterrar tu pasado, no excaves demasiado profundo' ('if you have to dig up your past, don't dig too deep'). Only Iván, ridden with a guilty conscience, is prepared to dig deep. A practical joke gone wrong ends with Nacho drowning in a swimming pool. The group subsequently denies that Nacho had been with them in the weekend trip and any involvement with his disappearance, but four years later when the case is reopened they have to confront their past. Panic emerges and friction sets in when the group decides to dispose of the body, buried in an abandoned country house. Their plan goes wrong when a fire breaks out and they have to escape. After this incident, one by one they begin to die.

Like its American counterparts, part of the cast of *El arte de morir* came from the world of television. Sergio Peris-Mencheta, Lucía Jiménez and Elsa Pataky had appeared in the popular Telecinco series *Al salir de clase* (1997–2002) which attracted audiences of three million in the afternoon slot (an audience share of 22 per cent). This TV series appealed to both male and female audiences in the 13-to-24 age group, a segment of viewers which would make up the main target audience for the film's producers. By exploiting the popularity of certain members of the cast, the producers succeeded in attracting a mixed-gender teen and youth mainstream audience. Casting decisions were also made to promote the film as a showcase for a new generation of actors whose looks, attitude and 'coolness' were highly marketable in the media; mainstream film magazines *Cinemanía* (Escamilla, 2000) and *Fotogramas* (2000) featured glossy reports on the cast and their roles in the film. But *El arte de morir* enticed not only TV audiences dying to see their TV crushes and the genre's core teen audience ready for the Spanish *Scream*, but also Spanish horror fans thanks to the casting of Fele Martínez as lead role Iván. This opened up cross-cinematic connections with Martínez' appearances in Alejandro Amenábar's *Tesis/Thesis* (1996) and *Abre los ojos/Open Your Eyes* (1997), and added (desperately) sought-after credibility to Fernández Armero – 'I'm a big horror fan and I've always wanted to make a horror film' (quoted in Belinchón, 2000) – and the scriptwriters, who describe their work as 'a pure exercise in genre filmmaking' (*El arte de morir*, 2000). Yet despite their claims for authenticity and their declared engagement with generic conventions – whether the American teen horror film or the psychological thrillers of Amenábar – it was a risky tactic that would be put to the test by reviewers.

Scream acts as a critical yardstick to measure the film's performance in almost every review: 'Gritos a la española' (Guillot, 2001); 'Terror juvenil a la española' (Calleja, 2000); the plot 'smells like *Scream* or *I Know What You Did Last Summer*', writes Belinchón in *El País* (2000). But Belinchón qualifies his statement: *El arte de morir* 'stays away from the usual commonplaces typical of the genre' (*El arte de morir*, 2000). This reviewer, like those in *Cinemanía*, *Fotogramas* and *Imágenes* (Boquerini, 2000), merely reproduce the call for distinction mobilised by producers and screenwriters in the pressbook and in the media, that is to say, to differentiate *El arte de morir* from the formulaic slasher films coming from Hollywood, and, at the same time, to differentiate Spanish audiences – discerning, sophisticated – from the average (American) teen consumer.

The genre-knowingness (or lack of it) displayed by *El arte de morir* is its major critical downfall. Genre commentators at home and abroad lambasted the horror competencies of Fernández Armero, Pozuelo and Royo. For British horror specialist magazine *Shivers*, the film is guilty of 'drawing heavily from several sources and doing justice to none of them' (Botting, 2000: 47). In *Cine para leer* journalist Borja Cobeaga Eguillor makes a clear distinction between the commercial aesthetics of the film and its attempt to engage generically with *Scream*. On the one hand, Cobeaga Eguillor applauds Aurum Producciones' ambitions to produce commercial cinema 'designed for immediate consumption' and 'to reach audiences' (2000: 50) by combining a charismatic cast, an efficient promotion machinery and an entertaining thrill ride that is profitable at the box office (2000: 49–50); on the other hand, *El arte de morir*'s pretensions to be 'like *Scream*' are cancelled out by the creators for they show a 'total ignorance of the horror genre (it looks as if neither the scriptwriters nor the director have ever seen a horror film in their lives) and their lack of humour (the main feature in the series created by Wes Craven and Kevin Williamson)' (2000: 51). Thus, as a purely commercial exercise, *El arte de morir* cunningly exploited the formula of a scary brand name and horror cycle, and delivered an 'energetic piece of entertainment' (Holland, 2000) for Spanish audiences. However, thematically it offered no meditation on 'the art of dying' nor on the *Scream* blueprint, failing to produce a local rebranding of contemporary American horror conventions. The commercial life of *El arte de morir* died after the summer of 2000[4] – may it rest in peace.

Darkness

The Spanish studio Filmax under its genre division Fantastic Factory produced Jaume Balagueró's second feature film *Darkness* in the wake of his critically acclaimed and award-winning debut *Los sin nombre/The Nameless* (1999) in international horror circuits. With a teaser trailer, the promise of an international cast and an English-language product to attract investors and pre-sales,[5] this project proved to be 'one of Spain's hottest sellers of the year' (Green, 2000b: 15). At the Cannes Film Festival in 2000, producer Julio Fernández struck a significant deal with one of the major American independent studios. He partnered with Miramax as co-producers of the film through its genre arm Dimension Films and sold them the distribution rights in the US and other English-speaking territories for $4 million. This commercial operation, plus other major pre-sales to European, Latin American and East Asian territories, helped boost the budget to $11 million. The film's financial success during the production process was confirmed in its world première in Sitges at the 35th International Film Festival of Catalonia, a key moment in the international horror film calendar, where it showcased for potential distributors and die-hard genre fans, and built enough momentum to release for the general public on almost 300 screens in Spain. Its opening weekend performance ($1.14 million) beat those of *Hable con ella/Talk to Her* (Pedro Almodóvar) and *El otro lado de la cama/The Other Side of the Bed* (Emilio Martínez Lázaro), the two top-grossing releases of 2002.[6] *Darkness* did not descend on American cinemas (1,700 screens) until Christmas Day 2004, yielding a total of $22,163,442 in the space of three months.[7] The delay was a matter of speculation in trade journals and special-ist horror film magazines; Dimension Films considered that the underlying theme of violence toward children could make it a tough sale, hence the trimming of the originally R-rated movie (toning down the dialogue and editing out some gore scenes like the tra-cheotomy operation scene) in order to obtain a PG-13 MPPA rating, broadening the audience reach. As these figures show, Balagueró's

film has been extremely lucrative for Filmax and a valuable investment for Dimension Films. To these profits one needs to add the
value of *Darkness* in the TV, home video and DVD markets for
which it was mainly conceived. In the Hispanic world, video and
DVD have been commercialised by Filmax Home Video, who have
marketed the film individually and as part of a DVD pack entitled
'El cine de terror de Jaume Balagueró', exploiting the horror fans'
and collectors' market. In the US Buena Vista released simultaneously the unedited and unrated version in what was just for many
DVD reviewers 'a marketing gimmick'.

Unlike *El arte de morir*, whose status as a horror film had to be
earned, the branding of *Darkness* as horror and, by extension, its
positioning in relation to generic traditions was relatively straightforward. Likewise, Balagueró's background poses no questions
about his horror credentials, in contrast to Fernández Armero's
phoney horror fandom. Editor and author of *Zineshock*, a
1990s fanzine devoted to trash and gore cinema, and author of two
experimental shorts, treading avant-garde and exploitation territory (*Alicia* (1994) and *Días sin luz* (1995)), Balagueró was a 'horror
auteur' in the making. The branding of *Darkness* relied on
two names: Filmax International (which at that time was establishing itself as a producer of commercial genre films)[8] and Jaume
Balagueró. Filmax International built awareness and expectancy
about these two brand names with a robust marketing campaign in
the industry journals, the press, mainstream film magazines and specialist horror magazines at home and abroad. Fans' appetites were
whetted in the film's official homepage, by daring potential browsers
to enter a house of horrors ('A House. A Past. A Secret. Will You
Dare Enter?') and emphasising the film's horrific elements. *Fangoria*
and *Shivers* kept an eye open for *Darkness* after Balagueró had being
hailed as one of the '13 rising horror talents' to keep audiences terrified for 'the next 200 issues and beyond' (Gingold, 2000: 80).
Screen International, Variety, as well as the Spanish *Cineinforme*,
had been following with particular interest the aspirational plans of
Filmax International and its genre arm Fantastic Factory, namely to
place their products in the international horror market,[9] and their
respective October issues are evidence of the publicity machinery
supporting the 2002 Filmax International flagship. Full-page
advertisements clearly conveyed the producers' and distributors'
marketing tactics: the traditional promises and 'frights' of horror

promotion ('You will fear it again . . . ') and the cultivation of an auteurist sensibility ('A film by Jaume Balagueró'). It is to this latter aspect that I now turn.

The air of expectation surrounding Balagueró's film enabled the producers to tap into discourses mobilised by cultural commentators in mainstream, specialised and subcultural publications. Here Timothy Corrigan's 'The Commerce of Auterism' and Catherine Grant's 'www.auteur.com?' provide productive ways to understand the value of the horror auteur as a commercial and critical practice. In his chapter, Corrigan argues that auteurism within the film industry functions not only as a critical concept tied to distribution and marketing practices but also 'as a commercial strategy for organizing audience reception'; moreover, 'in addressing cult fans and critical viewers' in the media, he 'can engage and disperse his or her own organizing agency as an auteur' (1991: 109). According to Grant, the end of the millennium saw 'an increasing commodification of authorship' (2000: 108) circulating via producers, auteurs themselves, audiences, critics and academics. A survey of Balagueró's profile in feature articles, his interventions in promotional interviews and the critical reception of *Darkness* will shed light on Balagueró's status as 'horror auteur'.

If auteur status is achieved over a group of films which present certain recurring characteristics formally and stylistically, Balagueró's short filmography is written about in auteurist terms. For many critics, Balagueró's work had already imprinted on it a personal stamp to be reckoned with. Such is the treatment reserved for him in the highbrow film magazine *Dirigido por . . .* which counts him in among the key directors of contemporary horror cinema (Navarro, 2006). In 'Jaume Balagueró ¿Quién puede torturar a un niño?', Tonio L. Alarcón maps out some of the director's recurrent concerns, his visual signature and his relation to international horror traditions. Among his obsessions, Alarcón credits Balagueró with physical and psychological torture, in particular that of children, an investigation of pure evil and the horrors of the past, and a 'dark vision of human existence', all conveyed through recurrent visual imagery (old photographs, medical paraphernalia, the presence of bodily fluids and water), cinematography and editing style (2006: 57). Reviews and interviews in *Dirigido por . . .* have consistently framed the reception of both *Darkness* and *Frágiles/Fragile* (2005) in auteurist terms. Thus Antonio José Navarro in his coverage of

Frágiles contributes further to the construction of Balagueró as an auteur by affirming that 'an oeuvre à la Balagueró is beginning to take shape' through the 'consolidation of a personal visual style of telling stories' (2005: 26). However, whilst there is a critical consensus on a Balagueró's visual signature, many critics have identified certain frailty in the construction of the narrative action. For Navarro, '*Darkness* confirms his remarkable talent to construct disturbing visual textures, while, at the same time, it evinces substantial lacks in narrating the story in a coherent manner' (2002b: 30); equally, the international industry press draws attention to the technical class present in *Darkness*, concluding that it 'is ultimately just an efficient exercise in style' and 'a series of powerful sequences that fail to cohere' (Holland, 2004). What these reviews seem to suggest is that Balagueró's name already performs a classificatory function in the fields of horror production and reception but that Balagueró, as a true 'horror auteur', is still 'in the making'.

Balagueró's and *Darkness*'s relationship to horror traditions, literary and cinematic, is uncontested. References to Lovecraftian themes and atmospherics abound: for Fernández in *Fotogramas*, 'the darkness of Balagueró's film could well be called Yog-Sothoth' and its conception could be out of *The Lurker at the Threshold* (H. P. Lovecraft and August Derleth) (2002: 20). Critics invariably rooted *Darkness* in the haunted house subgeneric tradition (Fernández, 2002; Navarro, 2002a; Zambrana, 2002), in particular classic contemporary films such as *The Amityville Horror* (Stuart Rosenberg, 1979) and *The Shining* (Stanley Kubrick, 1980), for in both films the house is linked to the father's process of derangement. The director himself acknowledges his debt to these films in interviews as a way of negotiating his horror heritage, engaging with generic conventions and creating a sense of belonging to a larger international horror tradition (Navarro, 2002a, 2006; Calleja, 2002; Lardín, 1999).

In interviews Balagueró praises the commercial work of the Fantastic Factory, with whom he shares their commercial vision ('the key thing is to make films for the audiences'), though he refuses to see all their products stamped with the same trademark and asserts the individuality of his work within the label (Balagueró in Navarro, 2002a: 33). Aligning himself with cult auteurs such as David Cronenberg and Dario Argento, among others, when listing his cinematic influences, serve also to 'disperse his own organizing agency as an auteur' and place his work primarily in a cult context. The reputation of Balagueró as a cult connoisseur and a horror auteur has been circulating in Spanish fanzine publications for some time now: 'He is one of us', writes Rubén Lardín in *ojalatemueras* (1999: 60), reassuring his readers that Balagueró is a *real* fan. It is worth noting that these references to Balagueró have seeped through to mainstream journalism with the arrival of fanzine writers into mainstream media. Thus, Pedro Calleja, frequent contributor to *2000 maniacos*, and these days also writing for the cultural supplements of major national dailies such as *La Luna* (*El Mundo*), described him as a 'true freak' who 'has an exquisite bad taste', crowning him as 'El Príncipe de las Tinieblas' ('The Prince of Darkness') (Calleja, 2002).

Generic formations and histories, authorship and authenticity, mainstream and underground circuits intersect in the production, distribution and reception of *Darkness*, shaping its marketability and international distribution. In true exploitation style, the marketing wheels had been set in motion before the shooting of *Darkness* began. The teaser promised 'a new brand of evil', a filmic experience 'beyond the limits of terror', and the Fantastic Factory product delivered what it said in the package. Made to engage horror audiences across the world, Balagueró and the Fantastic Factory produced a competitive product for the commercial horror film circuit.

El laberinto del fauno

El laberinto del fauno has already generated tons of material in trade journals, specialist film magazines, the press and online writing. As part of a trilogy of films on the Spanish Civil War, *El laberinto del fauno* (2006) will be no doubt revisited in the light of the first instalment *El espinazo del diablo/The Devil's Backbone* (2001) and the forthcoming *3993*, and will set in motion a revision of the texts. The last section of my chapter is a further contribution to the discourses surrounding del Toro's film, in particular an examination of the marketing strategies employed in Spain and the US, and a brief overview of the variety of ways in which critics, reviewers and fans talk about *El laberinto del fauno*.

With six films under his belt to date – *Cronos* (1993), *Mimic* (1997), *El espinazo del diablo*, *Blade 2* (2002), *Hellboy* (2004) and

El laberinto del fauno – del Toro is a bankable transnational figure whose name is highly regarded in the global film business, in the world of Spanish-language filmmaking and in the national film industries of Spain and Mexico. According to a recent survey in *The Hollywood Reporter*, del Toro is among the major players in the Latino film and TV industry, together with Alfonso Cuarón and Alejandro González Iñárritu (Galloway, 2007b). Such international status and commercial muscle have enabled them, for example, to intervene 'publicly in favour of the implementation of combined state and private measures to back the local film industry' (Grivas, 2006) during the Ariel awards ceremony organised by the Academia Mexicana de Artes y Ciencias Cinematográficas. Del Toro's international standing also means that smaller film industries like Spain benefit when he is helming co-productions and commercial ventures for his name is a guarantee to access international markets and to put Spanish cinema on the global filmic map. *El laberinto del fauno* has reaped nominations and awards all over the world: from the industry (three Oscars in Hollywood, three BAFTAs in the UK, six Goyas in Spain, nine Ariels in Mexico), the critical establishment (Film of the Year for the National Society of Film Critics in the US, the UK Regional Critics Film Awards, and included in hundreds of critics' ten best films of 2006) and the horror festival circuit (Zone Horror Fright Fest, Fantasporto). To date, its box-office takings have been phenomenal and have broken some industry and personal records in the American, Spanish and Mexican markets. In the US, *Pan's Labyrinth* has become the top-grossing Spanish-language film of all time, surpassing *Como agua para chocolate/Like Water for Chocolate* (Alfonso Arau, 1992 – $21,665,468) and *Y tu mamá también* (Alfonso Cuarón, 2001 – $13,839,658) and is currently ranking fourth in the list of top foreign language films behind *Wo hu cang long/Crouching Tiger, Hidden Dragon* (Ang Lee, 2000 – Taiwan), *La vita è bella/Life is Beautiful* (Roberto Benigni, 1997 – Italy) and *Ying xiong/Hero* (Zhang Yimou, 2002 – China). And 'after its second weekend on release . . . *Pan's Labyrinth* had already surpassed the final Spanish grosses of *The Devil's Backbone* and *Hellboy* having taken $4.9 m' (Mitchell, 2006). With a worldwide gross of $82,048,724, del Toro's film appealed, and continues to appeal, to broad and diverse audiences across the globe.

A Spanish/Mexican co-production, *El laberinto del fauno* brought together five producers – Bertha Navarro (Mexican Tequila Gang),

Alfonso Cuarón, Guillermo del Toro, and Frida Torreblanco (Spanish OMM) and Álvaro Augustín (Spanish Estudios Picasso, the production arm of Spanish TV channel Telecinco) – and a budget of $19 million. Executive producer Augustín stressed the potential of a project which will 'enable the Spanish film industry to access international talent' and will 'consolidate in Spain an industry fully capable of competing internationally' by profiting from del Toro's familiarity with Hollywood commercial strategies and genre production.[10] His predictions were confirmed when Warner Bros Pictures International acquired the multi-territory distribution rights for the film in Spain and Latin America, while Wild Bunch bought the rights for international sales and Picturehouse picked up all North American rights. At a national level what the participation of Telecinco highlighted is the productive synergy between cinema and television, in particular the key role of private TV channels in the successful placing of products in the marketplace through an aggressive advertising and promotional campaign across the whole media spectrum from traditional media to the internet in order to reach the widest possible audience.

While *El arte de morir* exploited the 'look' of *Scream* and *Darkness* brought to the foreground the generic markers of horror, the marketing strategies used to present *El laberinto del fauno* to audiences relied on a number of elements to drive its box-office success. First and foremost, the gregarious public persona of del Toro; second, an approach to filmmaking that goes beyond generic borders and is amenable to cross-genre marketing; and, third, the story the director is telling – a fairy tale for grown-ups. The spot advertising campaign on television was vigorous, with TV spots and trailers shown repeatedly on Telecinco, promoting the specific sellable elements in *El laberinto del fauno*: the director, the art direction and the use of special effects. Horror and fantasy are the main generic markers in the promotional posters, where the gothic imagery and the monstrous creatures – the faun, the toad, the Pale Man – suggest the fear invoked in horror films, while the fairy-tale atmosphere and the magical creatures – the fairy, the mandrake – transport us to a land of fantasy and draws us into a young girl's universe. The central position of an innocent little girl, Ofelia (Ivana Baquero), immersed in a fantastic world and surrounded by menacing creatures, conveys the childlike sense of wonder that links the story to the tradition of fairy tales. This connects the film to a long-standing Spanish cinematic tradition in which the main protagonist is a child dealing with traumatic experiences, and it evokes del Toro's own *El espinazo del diablo*[11] along with Víctor Erice's *El espíritu de la colmena/The Spirit of the Beehive* (1973) and Carlos Saura's *Cría cuervos/Cria!* (1976). The international success of the film in art-house and genre film festivals in Cannes, New York, Toronto and Sitges, as well as the prestige attached to being selected as the Mexican entry to the Academy Awards, enters the picture; the critical endorsements in the advertisements come in the form of quotes from the nation's main newspapers: Carlos Boyero (2006) from *El Mundo* calls the film ('imaginative and disturbing' and Jordi Costa (2006) from *El País* says it is 'the best work of Guillermo del Toro'.

Like *Darkness*, *El laberinto del fauno* premiered in the Sitges Festival (6 October 2006) and it acted as the launching platform for the film in the Spanish media. Press attention escalated in the cultural sections and weekend supplements of the two main national newspapers – *El País* and *El Mundo* – which published interviews with del Toro and focused on the creative process of the Mexican director, as well as in popular and specialist film publications. The film was released on 10 October in Madrid and the following day nationwide on 300 screens. Meanwhile del Toro himself was the main spokesperson for the film with a grassroots campaign targeting mass, niche and micro media and different segments of the audience: general public in the mainstream press and Spanish television, cinemagoers and critics in popular and specialist film magazines, and fans in festivals, online Q&A sessions and discussions. The film's official homepage – hosted by ClubCultura.com, the cultural magazine published by FNAC España – invited the prospective viewer to enter the 'labyrinth' and the potential consumer to purchase the DVD.

Describing the American marketing strategy behind *El laberinto del fauno* in the *Hollywood Reporter*, Bob Berney, president of Picturehouse, confessed that 'the challenges of marketing a Spanish-language film were daunting' and that the risk was that specific segments of the audience could have shied away from the film since 'the traditional art audience, the older audience, might be put off by the extreme violence and that the younger audience might not understand the period and the politics of the film' (quoted in Galloway, 2007a). In order to retain these two demographics, Picturehouse decided 'to promote Guillermo as the star', thereby capitalising on del Toro as 'writer-director' who would attract genre fans and art-house audiences. By using this promotion tactic, the distributors also wanted to target Spanish-speaking audiences. A forceful and sustained promotional campaign was devised to reach other audiences from mid-2006 onwards, from the critic establishment to the comic fan. Thus, through their French distributor Wild Bunch, the film entered Cannes nominated for the Palme d'Or, and by extension the 'high-end critic aspect'. At the same time, it featured in comic book conventions such as the Comic-Con at San Diego and genre festivals such as the Austin Fantastic Festival, which, according to Berney, 'kept the fantasy genre crowd happy by screening the trailer and setting up a Q&A session with del Toro'. In the words of Berney, 'Guillermo is a master filmmaker and the ultimate film fan as well', a true star 'who is equally comfortable talking eloquently about the movie in Cannes as he is discussing it in front of the fans' (quoted in Galloway, 2007a). Del Toro's himself actively supports these promotional activities by showing his ability to pitch at very different audiences and tastes and to exploit his many personas: star, fan, cinephile, popular auteur. He continuously positions himself as fan and acknowledges the fundamental role of fandom for genre cinema; speaking at the Comic-Con in San Diego: 'I'm first a fan and then a filmmaker . . . I find that amongst the people . . . genre conventions or comic conventions you find some of the most articulate, passionate, loyal, fierce and well-cultured and well-read people that you will ever meet' (podcast at www.panslabyrinth.com). Del Toro considers these conventions as platforms as important as any festival. It was the role of Picturehouse to secure the film's presence in the latter; Toronto (September) and New York (October) acted as launching platforms for the film in North America. A second phase of the marketing strategy was the actual release and the weeks leading to the Oscars, with a limited release on 29 December 2006 in major cities (seventeen cinemas in New York, Chicago, Los Angeles and San Francisco) followed by a wider stateside release on 19 January 2007 (609 cinemas), cranking up for the Oscars campaign. The six Academy Award nominations and its consideration for the Best Foreign Language Film exposed *El laberinto del fauno* to audiences across the globe. By early February the film reached maximum industrial exposure by featuring on the front cover of *Variety* (12–18 February 2007).

With his latest film del Toro demonstrated once again that he is not only a talented cinematic craftsman but also an accomplished storyteller when it comes to explaining the genesis of his individual works, promoting his films, talking about cinema in general, or commenting on the making of the film for DVD viewers. There is no space here to analyse the kind of stories that del Toro has told us about his film in interviews, podcasts or infotainment extras (autobiographical elements, fan confessions, political remarks, to name but a few), but they certainly provide productive ways of exploring *El laberinto del fauno*. Likewise, critical commentary on the film has been multifarious and a variety of aspects of the filmmaking process is being scrutinised. Professional industry publications such as *American Cinematographer* (Calhoun, 2007) and *Cinefex* (Fordham, 2007) have published extensive articles on the visual style and on the technologies employed in the film, respectively; leading international film magazines have offered in-depth analyses of the themes, aesthetics and influences in *El laberinto del fauno* (Kermode, 2006; Atkinson, 2007); horror film publications *Fangoria* (Turek, 2007) and *Shivers* (Jones, 2006; Nazzaro, 2007) have read and evaluated the film in terms of its generic status and del Toro's status as a 'horror auteur', and informed horror fans of the work behind the scenes (Nazzaro, 2006); and weblogs have been updating the blogging community, enabling online discussions with del Toro and generating debate on a range of topics.[12] In contrast to the modest critical reception of *El arte de morir* and *Darkness*, which were mainly considered through the lens of genre, *El laberinto del fauno* has reached a broader spectrum of audiences and critics who are more than willing to dare enter del Toro's creation.

Conclusion

Del Toro, Balagueró and Fernández Armero knowingly trade in the horror genre by exploiting mainstream commercial film culture and engaging with international examples of horror. But their films owe their commercial success to the role played by their respective production and distribution companies, whose marketing and publicity 'scare tactics' drove audiences to the cinemas and mediated the reception of the film. Mainstream critical response in Spain is coming to terms with what is perceived mostly as a purely commercialising film culture; however, genre critics and fans consume and write about these films in a different way by engaging with generic conventions, diverse horror traditions, or the cross-fertilisation between films and comics, cinema and television – in other words, participating in the construction of a Spanish horror film culture. As a culture (and industry), 'it's alive' and well, and finding a place in the international horror market.

Notes

1 Box office and rental grosses have been obtained in www.variety.com and www.mec.es.
2 See Hutchings' analysis of the slasher and post-slasher horror subgenre in his *The Horror Film* (2004: 192–217).
3 Television channels were complying with current film legislation whereby TV operators had to invest 5 per cent of their annual revenues in local cinema.
4 The film's afterlife is limited to its distribution abroad for US Hispanic video and DVD market via Venevision International, and to screenings on Spanish TVE-2 (11 October 2002 in TVE-2 *Versión española* featuring a discussion with director Fernández Armero, scriptwriter Royo and actress María Esteve, and 25 August 2006 in *Cine con Ñ* as part of a late-night horror double bill with *Mucha sangre* (Pepe de las Heras, 2003)).
5 Anna Paquin, Lena Olin, Iain Glen, Giancarlo Giannini and Stephan Enquist made up the international cast, supplemented with the Spanish Fele Martínez and Fermí Reixach. The producers used the same modus operandi for Balagueró's latest film *Frágiles* (2006), where the lead role is played by Calista Flockhart.
6 At the end of 2002, *Darkness* was the fifth top-grossing film in Spain with a total box-office gross of €3,987,669.68 and 885,361 spectators.
7 Worldwide the film has grossed $34,409,206.
8 Other Filmax products were out by the time *Darkness* was released: *Faust: Love of the Damned* (Brian Yuzna, 2001), *Arachnid* (Jack Sholder, 2001), *Dagon* (Stuart Gordon, 2001). See Chapter 1 in this collection.
9 See Green (2000a, 2000b, 2001, 2003).
10 Augustín in Kay (2006b: 36).
11 Del Toro refers to *El laberinto del fauno* as a 'sister' film to the more masculine look of *El espinazo del diablo*.
12 See, for example, www.blogdecine.com, www.otrocine.com or www.periodistadigital.com/cinedigital and follow the tag for *El laberinto del fauno*.

References

Alarcón, Tonio L. (2006) 'Jaume Balagueró. ¿Quién puede torturar a un niño?', *Dirigido por* . . . , 358, July/August, 56–8.

El arte de morir (2000) Pressbook, Madrid: Aurumn Producciones.

'El arte de morir' (2000) *Fotogramas*, 1878, April, 170–1.

Atkinson, Michael (2007) 'Moral Horrors in Guillermo del Toro's *Pan's Labyrinth*', *Film Comment*, 43: 1, 50–3.

Belinchón, Gregorio (2000) 'El terror también da dinero al cine español', *El País*, 23 April.

Boquerini (2000) 'El arte de morir', *Imágenes*, 191, April, 102.

Botting, Jo (2000) 'El arte de morir', *Shivers*, 79, 47.

Boyero, Carlos (2006) 'La imaginativa e inquietante "El laberinto del fauno" despide con brilliantez la grisácea sección oficial', *El Mundo*, 28 May.

Calhoun, John (2007) 'Fear and Fantasy', *American Cinematographer*, 88: 1, January, 34–45.

Calleja, Pedro (2000) 'Terror juvenil a la española', *Metrópoli*, 31 March.

—— (2002) 'El Príncipe de las Tinieblas', www.el-mundo.es. Accessed 3 August 2007.

Cobeaga Eguillor, Borja (2000) 'El arte de morir', *Cine para leer*, January/June, 49–52.

Corrigan, Timothy (1991) 'The Commerce of Auteurism: Coppola, Kluge, Ruiz', in *A Cinema Without Walls: Movies and Culture after Vietnam*, New Brunswick, NJ: Rutgers University Press, 101–36.

Costa, Jordi (2006) 'Un laberinto para perder el sentido', *El País*, 7 October.

Escamilla, Bárbara (2000) 'Terror español taquillero', *Cinemanía*, 56, May, 108.

Fernández, Fausto (2002) 'Darkness', *Fotogramas*, 1908, October, 20.

Fordham, Joe (2007) 'Into the Labyrinth', *Cinefex*, 109, 32–45.

Galloway, Stephen (2007a) 'Marketing Movies with VW Vans and Lots of Blood', www.hollywoodreporter.com. Accessed 27 July 2007.

—— (2007b) 'THR's Latino Power 50', www.hollywoodreporter.com. Accessed 27 July 2007.

Gingold, Michael (2000) 'The Future of Fear', *Fangoria*, 200, 80.

Grant, Catherine (2000) 'www.auteur.com?', *Screen*, 41: 1, 101–8.

Green, Jennifer (2000a) 'Filmax Develops English-Language Trio', www.screendaily.com. Accessed 24 July 2007.

—— (2000b) 'Filmax Partners with Miramax on *Darkness*', www.screendaily.com. Accessed 24 July 2007.

—— (2000c) 'Spanish Film Stays Alive with *Art of Dying*', www.screendaily.com. Accessed 23 July 2007.

—— (2001) 'Filmax Closes More Cannes Slate Deals', www.screendaily.com. Accessed 24 July 2007.

—— (2003) 'Filmax Funds Boosted by Spanish Investors', www. screendaily.com. Accessed 24 July 2007.

—— (2006) 'Spain', in 'Scare Tactics', *Screen International*, 29 September, 12.

Grivas, Alexis (2007) 'Del Toro's "Tres Amigos" Question Mexican Production Incentives', www.screendaily.com. Accessed 24 July 2007.

Guillot, Eduardo (2000) 'Gritos a la española', *El Levante*, 31 March.

Holland, Jonathan (2000) 'The Art of Dying', www.variety.com. Accessed 14 August 2007.

—— (2004) '*Darkness*', www.variety.com. Accessed 14 August 2007.

Hutchings, Peter (2004) *The Horror Film*, London: Pearson Longman.

Jones, Alan (2006) 'Pan's People', *Shivers*, 130, 14–18.

Kay, Jeremy (2006) 'Faun-language market', *Screen International*, 15 December, 36.

Kermode, Mark (2006) 'Girl Interrupted', *Sight & Sound*, December, 20–4.

Lardín, Rubén (1999) 'Jaume Balagueró', *ojalatemueras*, 1, 60–5.

MacNab, Geoffrey (2006) 'Scare Tactics', *Screen International*, 29 September, 12–13.

Mitchell, Robert (2006) 'Spain/Mexico. Pan-Demic', *Screen International*, 3 November, 39.

Navarro, Antonio José (2002a) 'En el corazón de las tinieblas', *Dirigido por . . .*, October, 316, 30–1.

—— (2002b) 'Jaume Balagueró', *Dirigido por . . .*, October, 316, 32–3.

—— (2005) 'Jaume Balagueró', *Dirigido por . . .*, September, 348, 26–8.

—— (2006) 'Dossier nuevo cine de terror. Diez directores fundamentales del género, *Dirigido por . . .*, July/August, 358, 36–55.

Nazzaro, Joe (2006) 'Creature Features Great and Small', *Fangoria*, 253, 60–5.

—— (2007) 'Monsters in the Labyrinth', *Shivers*, 132, 15–17.

Piña, Begoña (2000) 'Fernández Armero explora el género del terror en su nuevo filme *El arte de morir*', *La Vanguardia*, 30 March.

Tudor, Andrew (2002) 'From Paranoia to Postmodernism? The Horror Movie in Late Modern Society', in Steve Neale (ed.), *Genre and Contemporary Hollywood*, London: BFI.

Turek, Ryan (2007) '*Pan's Labyrinth*. A Maze Thing', *Fangoria*, 259, 42–7.

Villar, Carmen (2000) 'Terror de diseño', *El Faro de Vigo*, 21 April.

Zambrana, Manuel (2002) 'Darkness', *Cinemanía*, 85, October, 24–5.

Part II

Generic hybridity: negotiating the regional, the national and the transnational

4

From Sevilla to the world: the transnational and transgeneric initiative of La Zanfoña Producciones

Josetxo Cerdán and Miguel Fernández Labayen

Relocating the concept of 'nation'

If we are to study contemporary Spanish audiovisual production, it can be fruitful to start from its geographical and cultural margins and move towards the centre, destabilising the usual approach towards Spanish cinema and decentring the power of Madrid's industry. Therefore, one can observe the changes that arise from the interaction of two different but interdependent fields since the 1980s: film and television. Moreover, this framework can help us draw a temporal periodisation and define two concrete moments. The first period, whose origin can be traced back to the late 1970s and up until the early 1990s, is defined by a mode of film production tied to the renaissance of the so-called historic nationalities and the arrival of regional televisions. A second period begins after the celebration of 1992 and reaches until the present. This second stage is characterised by a growing abandonment of nationalist preoccupations in film production and a definitive hybridisation between film and television, equally in aesthetic (genres and formats) and industrial terms (i.e. production companies that converge in both fields thanks to the digitisation process).

The course of decentralisation that starts with the arrival of democracy in Spain allows the emergence of a small peripheral audiovisual industry. The new powers of the *Comunidades Autónomas* design a cultural map with two strong points – first of all, the consolidation of a televisual offering for the territory, creating regional communication groups with public funds that deal with local issues, so as to construct an identity for the inhabitants of each community. The regional communication groups, starting with the creation of Basque (Euskal Irrati Telebista (EITB), 1982) and Catalan (Corporació Catalana de Ràdio i Televisió (CCRTV), 1983), appear all around the country during the 1980s and are fundamental to the implantation of the regions' nationalistic imaginaries. Through the revision of the past and the re-elaboration of their own local history, as well as the use of the territorial languages, television plays one of the central economic, social and cultural roles in building the new map of post-Franco Spain.

Parallel to the exploration of nationalism by the Basque and Catalan regional governments' TV and radio stations, there are the politics of promoting a patriotic national cinema especially in films produced in those areas. Several movies intend to rewrite local history and myths, going back to a practice close to the patriotic panegyrics of the early years of Francoism, now to serve an apparently opposite ideology: *Crónicas de las guerras carlistas* (José María Tuduri, 1988) or Antoni Ribas's *¡Victoria!* series (1983–84) are but two examples. This approach can also be found in biopics of relevant historical figures, such as *Companys, procés a Catalunya* (José María Forn, 1979) and in literary adaptations of the 'classics' of each community, with titles like *Solitud* (Romà Guardiet, 1991) adapted from a novel by Víctor Català. At the same time, urban comedies from *L'orgia* (Francesc Belmunt, 1978) to *Què t'hi jugues Mari Pili?* (Ventura Pons, 1991) work with the same goal in mind; that is, to give enough signs for local communities to recognise themselves in a democratic multinational context. In order to achieve this, production companies arise in the *Comunidades Autónomas*, getting funds from the regional and central governments as well as from the participation of the different television networks in the financing of the movies.

A quick look at the increasing regional production of this era reveals a nationalistic concern with local languages and an institutionalised programme to establish a basic nationalistic imaginary. Moreover, a growing investment in cinema by both local and national communication groups and especially funds by political institutions link the production of feature films with the nationalistic agenda, transforming the cinematic medium aesthetically and economically. Television becomes both a platform for new ideas and creators as well as an ideal vehicle to promote audiovisual goods.

Along with these new television stations and the deregulation of the television market, the country faces the modernisation of the whole audiovisual industry in the early 1990s. It is the time of the arrival of the private TV networks (1989–90), the expansion of a new university degree in Media Studies (*Comunicación Audiovisual*), the opening of cinema schools in Madrid (ECAM) and Barcelona (ESCAC) and the rise of other schools and postgraduate programmes over the country. Thus, over the last twenty years, Spain has faced the formation of a new filmic and media imaginary, one that tries to suit and feeds on the sociocultural reality of Spanish political landscape. New professionals with a different cultural background and new channels to promote and give birth to other audiovisual offers help to include Spain in the communication era.

A second phase begins with the internationalisation of Spain and a conscious play between the local and the global, exemplified by the uprising of new production companies helped by international programs such as European Union Media I (1991–95) and Media II (1996–2000) programmes. The Spanish involvement in the European Union impulse implies a progressive decentralisation in the modes of production and, more important to our argument, a reconfiguration of the politics of production of the *Comunidades Autónomas*, which implies a new way of thinking about identity and genre now in the context of the EU and the world.

In this new framework, genre comes up in Spanish cinema in a completely different way. During the 1980s, genre as a discourse was erased from a film industry based in auteur politics and the cultural mirror of French cinema. In their quest for a European modernist quality in films, legislative and economic measures accounted for the disappearance of a whole part of the industry based on the exploitation of cheap subgenres (basically sexy comedy but also horror movies and soft porn). The forge of a democratic cultural imaginary was oriented towards the rescue of Spanish cultural legacy (especially through literature and theatre) and its recuperation for the big screen through big budgets and an intention to achieve highbrow cultural products (in other words, to locate Spanish cinema in the realm of Art). That approach obviously did imply the renunciation and marginalisation of whatever was considered lowbrow and representative for cultural and political authorities of the worst of Spanish culture; namely, gross comedies identified by critics and politicians with the expression of a primitive long-repressed society and an embarrassing uneducated popular culture. Paradoxically enough, all those films produced in the 1980s after *la ley Miró* that were supposed to rescue Spanish cinema in the name of Art and Culture not only did not obtain their international goals (recognition for a new-born democratic society) but their stylistic similarities lost the interest of national audiences. It is symptomatic that in those years 'Spanish films' found a specific place in local video stores, artificially transformed into another genre classification next to comedy, drama or action.

However, in the new transnational media configuration of the 1990s, Spanish cinema finds in genre an ideal way to renew audience interests and gain some attention back from both local and foreign spectators. In the early 1990s, we find a group of films that work with generic elements as a way to express and relate to narrative: *Todo por la pasta* (Enrique Urbizu, 1990), *Acción Mutante/Mutant Action* (Álex de la Iglesia, 1993), *La madre muerta/The Dead Mother* (Juanma Bajo Ulloa, 1993), *Todo es mentira* (Álvaro Fernández Armero, 1994), *El día de la bestia/The Day of the Beast* (Álex de la Iglesia, 1995), *Tesis/Thesis* (Alejandro Amenábar, 1996). In the ongoing debate about what is Spanish cinema and how it should look, some critics and part of the public despise this generic approach since they find it intrusive and culturally alienating.[1] However, if the debate about national cultural specificity is indeed an idealistic field of opinions and misconceptions about the role of popular culture, the crosscultural terrain of the late twentieth century is an ideal milieu to explore the presence and mixture of regional/national legacy with different cultural traditions from around the globe. If we take into consideration Rick Altman's three-way definition of genre through a semantic, syntactic and pragmatic approach (1999: 207–15), it becomes necessary to revisit Spanish film history in terms of generic play, understood as an arena where discussions about cultural legacy, political direction and social commitment find a new meaning and give birth to a more open-minded understanding of Spanish cinema, based on popular culture practices and far away from auteur determinism or the limitations of semiotics.

This audiovisual outburst of the 1990s permits the existence, along with an institutional and official line, of new and smaller production companies, which, far from dealing only with their surroundings' problems, develop imaginative works with formats and genres, blending local issues with transnational approaches. These new films play with elements of TV narration and TV formats (i.e. ironic subversion of news programmes and reality shows in *Acción Mutante* and *Todo por la pasta*) and also with homemade and digital technology, such as in the visual conception of Amenábar's debut film, *Tesis*. All this hybridity of formats is, at the same time, unified under generic conditions. Genre becomes the basic element to understand the renovation of not only the Spanish film industry but also world cinematography from 1992 until today. Movies by Quentin Tarantino, Guy Ritchie or Matthieu Kassovitz are obvious examples of a transgeneric trend that is also present in some of Latin America's recent cinema (for example, Guillermo del Toro's or Fabián Bielinsky's films) and in Western interest in Asian subgenres (yakuza films, manga or Asian horror). This movement consists of a number of audiovisual entrepreneurs who experiment with media, adopting an international aesthetics mixed with identity policies, local flavour and the mobility of cultural and monetary capital.

If we go back to the Spanish case, it is remarkable that most of them come from the *Comunidades Autónomas* TV experience and not from cinematic production. Given that in most of these territories there has never been a film tradition of their own, these producers find it easier to forge their own production lines, including an approach to genre and film production liberated from an orthodox and more professionalised way of dealing with the cinematic institution of places such as Madrid or Barcelona. Then again, if the agenda of most of Catalan, Basque and Galician companies dealt with the incorporation and naturalisation of bilingual contexts, other places fought to reverse the Francoist imaginary and set their own referents, playing with regional accents, local sceneries and other iconographic referents. Two different examples here could be the Andalusian *Solas* (Benito Zambrano, 1999) or the Galician *Lena* (Gonzalo Tapia, 2001). The first draws a Sevilla far away from flamenco, sevillanas and Feria de Abril iconography, but with the characters deeply rooted in their context (strong Andalusian accent), and both face the urban and rural realities of the south. *Lena* is a road movie in a country that lacks the cinematic road-trip referent and that is going to be adopted to refresh the image of the Spanish landscape (one only needs to think of other 1990s road movies such as *Fugitivas/Fugitives* (Miguel Hermoso, 2000) or *Airbag* (Juanma Bajo Ulloa, 1997)).

Such is the same case in Andalusia, which has been trying to overcome a folklorist approach and, at the same time, capitalise on its cultural background mainly associated with exoticism and flamenco. With the appearance of Radio Televisión de Andalucía (RTVA, integrated by Canal Sur Radio in 1988 and Canal Sur Televisión in 1989), all these small companies find economic and communicative backing for part of their projects.

Therefore, the redefinition of the audiovisual arena, the recuperation of the interest in/from the audience and the decentralisation of the production activities promote a return to generic imagination, as well as a hybridisation of formats (most of them from TV aesthetics), and a historic and aesthetic revision of the Spanish landscape through the identification with a local generic and subgeneric tradition and the assumption of cultural diversification of the multicultural reality of the twenty-first century. Thus, genre becomes the perfect discursive engine to provide popular variations easily recognisable, economically fruitful and yet critically significant for Spanish cinema of the 1990s and 2000s. This flexibility calls for permeability in recent concepts of trans- and intracultural inscriptions and, in the Spanish case, liberates both spectators and the industry in terms of cinematic creation, distribution and consumption. Although more rigid schemata still disregard popular culture and argue in terms of Spanish auteur cinema, generic hybridisation seems a proper way to question and dismantle these assumptions about cultural transitions in postmodern Spain.

Concept of a production company: La Zanfoña before La Zanfoña, or what happens when the amateurs meet the institution

Over the last thirty years, Andalusia has moved from a central position in its identification with Spanish culture to a peripheral one, following the vast post-Franco crisis of Spanish identity and an ambiguous way of dealing and addressing two of Andalusia's best-known images: flamenco and bullfighting. Traditionally related to Franco's national project or with a romantic idealisation of cultural essence and folk, Andalusia has tried to reinvent itself and design new ways to picture its diversity. If the official operation of an image renewal of the Andalusian landscape can be said to climax with Sevilla's World Expo '92, it must be taken into account the extensive cultural activity overshadowed by such an acclaimed event.

Therefore, while the administration powers tried to actualise and hail Andalusia's modernisation, there were other artistic endeavours more interested in alternative and subcultural manifestations. The economic and cultural failure of the Expo was counterpointed by an increasing subcultural field, one that defied a homogenising definition and freely moved across different styles and patterns. It is the case of popular music, which presents different manifestations of crosscultural and transnational fertilisation, such as the so-called 'indie' rock of the early 1990s (with bands such as Los Planetas or Sr Chinarro); the rewriting of flamenco through its mixture with blues (Pata Negra), pop (No me pises que llevo chanclas), rock (Los Delinqüentes) and socially concerned world music (Mártires del Compás) as well as the consolidation of Andalusian hip-hop in the mid-2000s (with Tote King or Mala Rodríguez).

The clean, intellectualised, high-art flamenco films of Carlos Saura[2] find their counterpart in the guerrilla, low-budget amateurism of *Carlos contra el mundo* (Chiqui Carabante, 2002) and, as we are about to see, the Cinexín project or *El factor Pilgrim* (Santiago Amodeo, Alberto Rodríguez, 2001). Other recent revisits of Andalusia's romantic imaginary – Vicente Aranda's *Carmen* (2003), *Muerte en Granada/The Disappearance of Garcia Lorca* (Marcos Zurinaga, 1997) with Andy Garcia as Federico García Lorca, or internationally exotic approaches to gypsiness in *Gitano* (Manuel Palacios, 2000) and *Vengo* (Tony Gatliff, 2000), as well as recent titles by Miguel Hermoso, *La luz prodigiosa* (2002) and *Lola, la película* (2007) – fit into more evident tactics of an industrial transnational-oriented cinema, appropriating Andalusia's internationally known myths for their circulation in mass markets. However, there are other films that escape this immediate identification, situating their references in a different sphere of subcultural roots and pop culture consumerism. In cinematic terms, the work of La Zanfoña bridge together localism and the new global arena of the twenty-first century, escaping the clichés of official culture and considering other alternatives of relating to the codes of late capitalism by an unprejudiced mode of fusing diverse cultural practices. This implicates a deep renovation of generic elements in a new negotiation with the teen publics that empathised with these new cultural configurations.

La Zanfoña Producciones S.L. is a production company created in Sevilla in 2001 and chaired by Gervasio Iglesias, Mercedes Cantero,

Alvaro Garrido and Florencio Ortiz, and with the later incorporation of Alex Catalán and Jorge Casanova. La Zanfoña has developed an ever-increasing manufacture of a wide variety of products, being involved in advertisement, music videos, post-production facilities, animation, experimental video and short films.[3] So far it has produced six feature films,[4] over ten short films, seven documentaries for institutions and television and a few art videos. It is then a melting pot of media currency, an initiative that includes all sort of audiovisual experiences and practices. In this scenario, the mixture of different media also implies generic hybridisation, where feature films and documentaries are thought in terms of their aesthetic and narrative crossover and transgeneric resolution, mixing different genres to offer a postmodern conception of film. This inventiveness and the company profile make it an interesting example of what we have called the second stage in the production development of Spanish media landscape since the arrival of democracy. In addition, La Zanfoña has built its reputation in the cinematic field by the appropriation of part of Sevilla's subcultural world, one that goes all the way back to the late 1960s and that La Zanfoña has actualised and relocated in a transnational and transgeneric framework.

Last, but not least, La Zanfoña commercialises its products in the productive array of media venues in the global world: following the well-established film festivals tournée, opening in cinemas all over Spain and negotiating broadcasts with the different TV channels. Its situation within the tropes of cultural cosmopolitism that the actual expansion of cinematic consumption makes available turns it into an attractive case study to analyse the politics and cultural dissemination of so-called Spanish twenty-first century-cinema. The way La Zanfoña's films work with a postmodern and transgeneric conception is important so that audiences all around the world can identify elements of contemporary cinema in their work.

The genesis of La Zanfoña can be traced back to the early 1990s. Halfway in between the official audiovisual institutions and the subcultural milieu of the 1990s, some of the founders of the company, former workers of Televisión Española, found themselves collaborating on a series of underground projects made by friends, relatives or college mates. One of these is the collective venture known as *Cinexín* (1997).[5]

The origins of the project go back to a 16mm camera that director Alberto Rodríguez got as a present from his father. A group of friends decided to buy footage and each shoot a three-minute reel, adding up to a total of fourteen Cinexins. What is most shocking of the Cinexín experience is the way the different films use the camera and its technical possibilities. Some of them, like *La vaca lechera* (Julio Sánchez and Mariano Agudo) or *El Caminante* (Álex Catalán), explore the potentiality of film photography, playing with the stock-grain in a documentary style or using solarisations. Others, like *Deuce* (Daniel de Zayas) or *PiPiPiPiPiPi o el Teorema de la Felicidad* (Inma R. Cunill and Juanjo Domínguez), work closer to the narrative concept of Spanish comedy short films of those years, including a humorous twist at the end of the dramatic structure. Finally, most of them fall closer to video art compositions than to narrative cinema. This third and final strand is somehow anomalous to the Spanish film industry. Mixing a punk, 'do-it-yourself' philosophy with the neat fashionable composition of video art, *Cinexín* is an interesting struggle to overcome the rigid patterns of narrative applied to what could be called the short-film comedy. The success of the collective film led to a second part.

Following this same spirit of experimentation and amateur play, the next project of some of the people present in *Cinexín* was a feature film entirely shot in 16mm in London during twenty days in summer. *El factor Pilgrim* (Santiago Amodeo and Alberto Rodríguez) tells the audacious vicissitudes of an international group of roommates who find a tape by Pilgrim, the 'real' writer and composer of The Beatles' songs. With a total crew of ten people and a very small budget, *El factor Pilgrim* reflects a co-operative spirit, where everyone feels committed to their various task in the shooting of the movie (the post-production took more than two years to be finished and everyone earned the same amount of money based on the days each one had worked). It received a special mention at the San Sebastián Film Festival and was finished thanks to investment from Tesela Producciones Cinematográficas producer José Antonio Félez, starting a productive collaboration between Tesela, directors Alberto Rodríguez and Santiago Amodeo and, finally, La Zanfoña.

In addition, it must be taken into account that *Pilgrim*'s delirious plot is built upon the demystification of pop bands. Its partisan amateurism gives birth to a narrative of artisan passers-by who live on the fringes of the system, a system as lunatic and capricious as the four lost souls of the movie (only the former represents the official powers and social, political and economical institutions). Transnational in its narrative conceit, an Italian, a Swedish, a Spanish and an English roommate, all in their thirties, try to make their way through London selling old relics or just plain garbage at flea markets. The movie is a melting pot of accents and types, far away from the middle-class Erasmus dream[6] depicted in *L'auberge espagnole/The Spanish Apartment* (Cédric Klapisch, 2002). Outside of the industry, Amodeo, Rodríguez and their team build a narrative based on their own experience of being far and away, geographically, economically and culturally speaking. All these practices come together through the deconstruction of the music industry and the remaking of pop history. The opposition to transnational homogenisation is depicted through the parody of one of the most acclaimed bands in history and, at the same time, through a resistance to the appeal of the commoditisation markets. It is not a coincidence that it has become a cult movie in Spain, through its cheap alternative mode of production and its uninhibited pop and musical revisionism.

Thus, the features and characteristics of La Zanfoña can already be seen in some of the works done by its main perpetrators, as well as the oeuvre of two of its most representative filmmakers, Alberto Rodríguez and Santiago Amodeo. *Cinexín* and *El factor Pilgrim* are examples of the Sevillian scene of the 1990s, one determined by a subcultural and marginal drive. If 'subcultures are groups of people that are in some way represented as non-normative and/or marginal through their particular interests and practices, through what they are, what they do and where they do it' (Gelder, 2005: 1) and are characterised by their heterogeneity and normlessness, then *Cinexín* and *Pilgrim* represent audiovisual experiences that are basic to understand the development of a wide range of meanings, actors and institutions, in which generic hybridisation becomes a logical means of expression. The range of proposals and styles is overwhelming and the convergence of an amateur mode of production with the diffusion via a wide variety of outlets brings together two of La Zanfoña's greatest accomplishments: that of manufacturing hybrid products with aesthetic aspirations, and selling the marginal and subcultural both through subcultural and official media channels.[7] The role of generic hybridisation in this option is remarkable and far away from cinematic genre formation. *Cinexín* and *El factor Pilgrim* not only mix up concepts of cinematic genres but, in the search of new patterns, also bring into the field elements of other formats to reinforce the relationship with subcultural and popular spectatorship. These elements are even more important in films made such as *Cabeza de perro/Doghead* (Santi Amodeo, 2006), in which Amodeo uses the parody of a situation comedy (sitcom) to represent a flashback to the previous life of the female's lead character. Following Gelder's explanation of subcultural organisation, we are reminded that subcultures imply the existence of both a collection of *people* and *institutions*. As a result, La Zanfoña was born as a logical extension of these activities, through which the community gathered around *Cinexín* and *El factor Pilgrim* could express and organise themselves.

Undergrounding Sevilla

It is then not a coincidence that La Zanfoña looks back to Sevilla's underground of the early 1970s for one of its first projects. A co-production with Canal Sur, TV3 and financial support from La Junta de Andalucía, *El underground: la ciudad del arco iris* (2003) becomes a perfect way to legitimate La Zanfoña's world by linking it to the countercultural tradition of Sevilla's flamenco-rock and theatre scene. Directed by Gervasio Iglesias himself, the documentary traces the emergence of a cultural Sevillian scene of its own, far from the institutionalisation of Andalusian symbols.

By juxtaposing original footage from NO-DO newsreels with dramatizations, interviews and graphic work by Miguel Brieva,[8] *El underground* visually echoes the psychedelic sounds of Smash and other bands influenced by the arrival of US pop and rock music to the military bases located in southern Spain during the late 1960s. Iglesias and screenwriter Santiago Amodeo emphasise Smash's path from being a non-professional band to recording with the popular singer Manuel Molina (from the duet Lole y Manuel) and being commercialised by Catalonia's intelligentsia. *El underground* not only exemplifies the always-difficult relations between subculture and power, but also delineates the hybridisation of the Sevillian cultural scene in the 1970s. The physical and geographical itinerary is the same as the journey depicted by another La Zanfoña movie, *¿Por qué se frotan las patitas?* (Álvaro Begines, 2006), which implies moving from Andalusia to the northern riches of Catalonia. Both movies subvert a popular collective narrative. If traditionally southern emigration to Catalonia has been depicted as an economic need to improve material conditions, *El underground* and *¿Por qué se* *frotan las patitas?* develop stories in which southern artistry goes north just to be exploited by Catalan mercantilist powers.

If Andalusian hybridisation has commonly been associated with gypsy and Arabic influences, this time it comes from the assimilation of US popular culture, from comic books to rock 'n' roll, from performance art to psychedelic trance. The reification of the hippie counterculture under the dictatorship fell short of finding a great echo in Spanish youth culture. However, it did make its way and was mirrored by a small community in Sevilla which was introduced to the sex-drugs-rock 'n' roll credo without having any other means than having a good time against some of the conservative local prejudices.

El underground plays with the structure of a television documentary introducing avant-garde aesthetics. Not only does it mix the classic 'talking-heads' interview format with found footage and other appropriation techniques, but the deconstruction of the archival material by Miguel Brieva brings the result closer to underground fanzines than to orthodox representations of the past. Finally, the recreation of this same past by a contemporary group of hippies (who actually take the leading voice in the documentary) invites us to reflect on those old experiences, not from a nostalgic point of view, but more from an actual and contemporary re-vision and repetition of some of those cultural schemes. It is then not a historical reconstruction, but a cultural claim in favour of cultural hybridisation as well as visual and musical generic crossovers. All these elements move this film away from what can be considered a classic documentary work – for *El underground* does not follow traditional patterns of documentary representation, and instead mixes different genres and borrows elements from fiction (the narrative) and avant-garde filmmaking (parody reconstruction or found footage as a way to resignifying images).

We could then trace a direct line from late 1960s Sevillian underground (with all its mythological US implications) to La Zanfoña's productions and other current Andalusian subcultural practices that still hold on to an amateur philosophy. Furthermore, recent efforts from La Zanfoña such as *Fosforito: la voz, el genio, la leyenda* (José Francisco Ortuño, 2005) and *La Giralda perdida de Nueva York* (Pedro Barbadillo and Diego Carrasco, 2005) prove the amalgam of cultural hybridisation with marginal positions and the rewriting of cultural history that successfully recognises some of those 'other stories' and locates them in their probably more suitable context: the transnational arena. The narrative of *La Giralda perdida de Nueva York* provides a perfect example of this. This documentary works *in the voice of* (as the opening credits says) Antonio Dechent, one of the most popular Andalusian actors of the last decade, who tells the story of the reconstruction of the Sevillian Giralda Tower in the centre of Manhattan in the early twentieth century. The appropriation of resignification of this monument in that moment is a perfect illustration of the way La Zanfoña's films use generic elements of transnational filmmaking to deal with local concerns.

Presenting the past: rewriting traditional narratives in a global context

La Zanfoña not only deals with this appeal towards global (especially US) culture and its assimilation through the recycling of mass culture. This new global and multicultural scenario affects the actualisation and discovery of new contexts for storylines based in old Spanish narrative tradition. A similar way of working was used by Álex de la Iglesia and the inclusion of the *esperpento* tradition in his films from the early 1990s.[9] What is most important here is not the update of a long-established tradition, but how this renovation is done through popular genres. Such is the case of *El traje* (Alberto Rodríguez, 2002), produced by Tesela with support from La Zanfoña in the post-production stage, a movie that re-enacts the story of two *picaros* trying to survive in a miserable milieu, in a way very much similar to *Fulano y Mengano* (Joaquín Romero Marchent, 1956). The mise-en-scène of postwar Madrid is substituted by a post-1992 Sevilla filled with crumbling luxury hotels and homeless shelters. Whereas Eudosio and Carlos in *Fulano y Mengano*[10] were kicked out of the system by Franco's *Nueva España*, Patricio (a black sub-Saharan teenager) and Pan con Queso (a low-down trickster) are marginalised by late capitalist society, with its globalisation process that has located these losers outside the limits of the system, in a continuous no-place. Patricio tries to fit in by using an elegant suit that a black basketball player has given to him. However, that same suit will be the beginning of the end for him, in a down-spiral of misunderstandings based on false appearances and prejudices. His friendship with Pan con Queso relies on the terms of the common interest already present in *Lazarillo de*

Tormes and basic to understand the picaresque tradition. However, Alberto Rodríguez's film does not intend to just play with that reference, but it is the base to develop a plot with tragicomic elements in transgeneric terms. The actualisation of traditions is self-conscious and referential, creating a tension between comedy and melodrama on the frontier of two of the traditional Spanish genres. This generic mixture can be found in most of La Zanfoña's productions, where the principal characters are losers taken from the melodrama schemata, but the point of view is closer to comedy, with a treatment that swings freely across comedy and other generic codifications, such as suburban teen films or even romantic comedy.

On the one hand, this rewriting process in *El traje* is a postmodern exercise of appropriation of the past. On the other, this is a habitual practice in Spanish cinema from the 1920s to the 1960s, when some stories are brought back time and time again depending on the specific historical period in which they are reborn. Thus, we find four versions (one of them Mexican) of *La casa de la Troya* between 1925 and 1959; three adaptations of *La verbena de la paloma* between 1921 and 1963; and three revisions of *Malvaloca* between 1926 and 1954. Recently, *Solas* (Benito Zambrano, 1999) actualises the now-aged three lead roles of *Malvaloca*; and *El laberinto del fauno/Pan's Labyrinth* (Guillermo del Toro, 2006) rewrites in a cruel fashion Víctor Erice's *El espíritu de la colmena/The Spirit of the Beehive* (1973).

If we consider *¿Por qué se frotan las patitas?*, a musical with covers of greatest hits from the Spanish-speaking repertoire of the last thirty years (with songs adapted from Raphael, Camilo Sesto, Andrés Calamaro and Jeanette), we find an unlikely marriage between *copla* and pop. The movie defies standard musical categories and the soundtrack – composed by Raúl Ruiz, Manuel Ruiz 'Queco' (writer of hit songs for Las Ketchup and Niña Pastori) and director Álvaro Begines (former lead singer of the unorthodox pop band No me pises que llevo chanclas) – is a tour-de-force presentation of popular culture with squatters singing a hip-hop version of Las Ketchup's 'Aserejé' or the inclusion of a character named Niña María (with similarities to Lola Flores' biography and echoes – the name, the flamenco pop style of the performances – of Niña Pastori's cultural significance) covering Raphael. This musical admixture is another case of how La Zanfoña's fiction films play with elements from different genres, not only to create a transgeneric product, but also to cater to a larger transnational market. In *El traje* and *¿Por qué se frotan las patitas?*, the presence and survival of cultural interests comes to life through the engagement with pop aesthetics while making their way through political and social urges. Pop becomes a dialectical and referential process that allows the repetition of fragments of everyday life by relocating their meaning in new configurations that cross generic and sociocultural borders. Pop appropriation of melodramatic and comedic elements becomes a key concept to understand how all these films talk to their audience.

Stranger in a strange land: pop-modern replacement and musical re-contextualisation

It is then this new configuration of cultural dialogue that calls for the rereading of geographical and historical forms. If Spain's process of modernisation has been, to say the least, anomalous, the space of the city and the place of subcultures in social history enable La Zanfoña's movies to explore other connections through the investigation of popular culture and its endless recycling. Far from movies like Mateo Gil's *Nadie conoce a nadie/Nobody Knows Anybody* (1999), films such as *Astronautas* (Santi Amodeo, 2004) and *7 vírgenes* (Alberto Rodríguez, 2005) explore the lost zones of postmodern architecture and the black holes of Spain's economical upheaval. Whereas Gil's *opera prima* opts for spectacular aerial views of Sevilla and an integration of the myths and common sites of the southern city (the celebration of *Semana Santa*, the killing at the bullfighting arena) just to modernise them through obvious transnational intertextuality (the Internet, role-playing games), Amodeo and Rodríguez offer an almost unidentifiable Sevilla, with suburban blocks under construction, public swimming pools and dirty old cafés in out-of-the-way places. While both options deal directly with the process of globalisation and transgeneric influences (those of the new Hollywood, but also European postmodern cinematic reconfigurations of the 1980s and the 1990s), it is shocking to see how the more obvious approach falls into mockery and superficiality, with Jordi Mollà playing an Andalusian and Eduardo Noriega a would-be journalist/writer frustrated by the limitations of his work as a crossword inventor and day-dreaming of writing a literary masterpiece.

In contrast, *Astronautas* tells the story of Daniel, a junkie who is trying to quit his habit by following a Decalogue that can take him back to 'normal' life and social acceptance, and *7 vírgenes* follows a messed-up teenager on a weekend leave from a juvenile correction facility. Both movies insist on the importance of alternative lifestyle choices and what is usually considered marginal. Despite their main characters' failures, one cannot help but feel shaken by the honesty of their choices. *Astronautas* and *7 vírgenes* reveal a cinema concerned both with local issues (immigration, drug addiction, juvenile delinquency) and new trends in global cinema (the defiance of narrative conventions, pop appeal and visual invention).

If *Astronautas* presents an aesthetic closer to *El underground* and even *El factor Pilgrim* (with Miguel Brieva's animations and a musical score played by the director's band, Lavadora, that refers to the parallel non-canonical history of pop music), *7 vírgenes* deals with teenage subcultures and hobbies deeply rooted in contemporary Spanish culture but basically forgotten by the media: customising cars, wandering around shopping centres and hip-hop singing as expressive tools. Through the mixing and crossing of boundaries, these films present an 'unmanageable textuality that refuses to play by the old rules' (Collins, 1993: 250), and thus break limits within generic intermixing and collapse the differences between new and old media, modern and postmodern approaches to the Spanish landscape.

Two images are sufficient to support what we are saying. First of all, Daniel's shopping trip to a record shop in *Astronautas*. After numbly strolling through the shopping centre (carefully recorded through the security cameras of the different stores), Daniel and his teenage companion Laura return to his favourite musical shop. We see how Daniel frantically goes through all the LPs in a crazy *batida* (raid) while complaining about other costumers that stand in his way. The song that marks the rhythm of the scene underlines Daniel's preference for cool, alternative bands. A power-pop song by Amodeo's band Lavadora recounts a litany of pop cultural icons – Soviet basketball player Kurtinaitis, Freddy Krueger, the Pink Panther, Richard Burton – while Daniel flips through an equal array of popular music artists. The generational blink of an eye operates as a pop condensation of sentimental value, with a fetishistic recognition of the wide cultural spectrum that shapes the main character's (as well as the viewer's and the director's) identity. The visit to the music shop is then not only a musical journey but a passage through which most music and other pop cultural fans (from comic books to video stores) recognise themselves. It operates as a signifying practice common to viewers and listeners all over the world, not only present in other recent movies (for instance, Stephen Frears's *High Fidelity* (2000)), but extending to the cultural formation of a generation of 1990s audiovisual creators and consumers (Quentin Tarantino, Kevin Smith, Danny Boyle).

This importance of the acoustic hybridity of the soundscape can also be found in *7 vírgenes*. The marriage of Tano's brother or the assault and fight between Tano's friends and some bullies at the street brings together different musical and iconic textures, from the repetitive choreography of the wedding and its celebration to the eruption of violence that some critics have related to Carlos Saura's *Deprisa, deprisa* (1980) and José Antonio de la Loma's films of the 1980s (Monterde, 2005: 17). *7 vírgenes* calls, then, to a revision of juvenile delinquency depicted on the screen, reflecting on the identity problems of youth and claiming for alternatives to official and politically correct outtakes on adolescence. The choice of teen idol Juan José Ballesta as Tano is symptomatic of the cultural and economic tactics of the movie. Having starred in other Tesela productions – *El bola/Pellet* (Achero Mañas, 2000) and *Mi casa es tu casa* (Miguel Álvarez, 2002) – Ballesta has built a character recognisable for his closeness to lower-class hoods and especially his origins in Parla, Madrid. It is remarkable that Ballesta's Castilian accent is very much foregrounded in *7 vírgenes*, in a context where everyone else speaks with a strong Sevillian accent (director Alberto Rodríguez even commented on the possibility of subtitling the movie for other regions in Spain, since its dialect is difficult to follow for non-Andalusian speakers). The vernacular speech is a highly distinctive characteristic of the film and operates as a generic mark of subcultural gangster cinema. In a way this slang option connects *7 vírgenes* with other gangster films that use slang and strong accents to identify different communities as well as racial and ethnic origin in US and global cinema (with examples ranging from Martin Scorsese's movies of the 1970s to Guy Ritchie's films of the early 2000s). It is important to argue that in Spanish cinema accents were almost forbidden during Francoism: all Spanish cinema was spoken in a neutral Castilian accent, while Andalusian or Galician accents were used only for comic purposes. From the 1990s to the present, characters with accents and talking in other languages like Catalan or Galician have become more frequent. From the Basque priest of *El día de la bestia* to the Catalan anti-Francoist in *El calentito* (Chus

Gutiérrez, 2005), not to mention the language mixture of *Salvador* (Manuel Huerga, 2006), recent Spanish cinema is filled with examples that depict these plurinational and linguistic realities.

Having been shown at international festivals and forging a deep connection with young audiences as well as with cult circuits, these films show a very different side of Spanish contemporary culture. Teenage spectators are finally being considered in Spanish cinema and the movies are highly designed to meet their expectations. The rereading of genre is relocated in a postmodern world, where the consumption of the movies and their themes (drugs, sex and music) is experienced by the audience as a countercultural pose.

Based in such a rooted and stigmatised culture as southern Spain, these films defy classical mythological views of the south and offer a different look at the post-industrial, post-1992 World Expo Sevilla. Not only have *Variety*'s critics hailed *Astronautas* as one of Europe's top ten movies of 2004, but in general most of La Zanfoña's works have achieved greater recognition and subcultural value. If film festivals are, as Thomas Elsaesser has optimistically defined, 'the symbolic agoras of a new democracy' (2005: 103), La Zanfoña's movies constitute themselves as works that bring different cultures and practices together, finding a balance between regional codes, transnational heritage and international appeal. Obviously genre reconfiguration is essential to understand how La Zanfoña's films achieve this status. Generic referents let these films mix tradition with innovation, local subcultural expressions with transnational cinema.

It is mandatory that we situate these different alternatives to the official culture to analyse the postmodern impulse in contemporary Spain. Whether in music, theatre, performing arts or cinema, the channels of democracy and the new status of consumerism and global culture allow the exploitation of several cultural movements throughout the national territories. If media convergence calls for a melting pot of filmmakers-authors-gamers-creators that can easily move from one spot to the other, covering different angles, then the initiative of La Zanfoña functions as a dialogue between historical international change and local practices, moving between the stabilisation of local continuities and its constant disruption. The importance of institutional infrastructures is fundamental to the invention of this tradition, one that moves through temporal and spatial references to build a local offer of transnational meaning through the legacy of popular culture and counterculture. Furthermore, genre becomes the space where this renovation of Spanish cinema takes place since the 1990s, and La Zanfoña is one of the clearest examples of this new reconfiguration, one in which films are built from popular genres in order to break through national culture and international markets.

Notes

The authors would like to thank the extreme generosity of Gervasio Iglesias and Sonia García from La Zanfoña and José Antonio Félez and Ana Ferri from Tesela Producciones Cinematográficas. Without their help this work would not have been possible.

1 See Losilla (1997, 2005).

2 We cannot forget that Saura's films are one of the main cultural products that help bring to the surface the new cosmopolitan face of flamenco. Nonetheless, his film *Sevillanas* (1992) is produced by Expo '92 and movies such as *Flamenco* (1995) promote the values of a new generation of flamenco artists, closer to design and fashion than other generations, such as internationally acclaimed Joaquín Cortés. Furthermore, Saura has been working on this reconfiguration of the flamenco imaginary since the early 1980s, when he started rewriting flamenco traditions by adapting the plays of Federico García Lorca.

3 In fact, La Zanfoña is divided in three areas: La Zanfoña Producciones, a television and cinema production company; LZ Producciones, a post-production and digital editing branch that invests in new multimedia contents and develops websites; Zanfoña Móvil, a musical production company with several bands under contract (www.lzproducciones.com, visited June 2006).

4 The movies produced and already released by La Zanfoña are: *Astronautas* (Santi Amodeo, 2004), *7 vírgenes* (Alberto Rodríguez, 2005), *La furia de Mackenzie* (José Luis Reinoso, Félix Caña y Paco Campano, 2005, yet not released in the cinema), *Cabeza de perro* (Santi Amodeo, 2006), *¡Qué tan lejos!* (Tania Hermida, 2006, released in Ecuador) and *¿Por qué se frotan las patitas?* (Álvaro Begines, 2006). The company also collaborated on *El traje* (Alberto Rodríguez, 2002).

5 During the 1970s and the 1980s the Cinexín was a very popular toy for kids. The Cinexín is a kind of Super 8 projector that permits watching short films, specially commercialised in this format, and play it forward and backward in an endless loop. Since the Cinexín functioned manually, children could also accelerate, slow down or stop the images. The malleability was very important in the game, for it let kids play with the narrative of the films, always silent and most of them slapstick comedies or cartoons.

6 The Erasmus is a EU-funded exchange programme in which students from all the countries of the Union get to spend a term or a year studying at a foreign university from one of the other countries of the EU. Despite its feeble economic help to students, it has become an easy way to travel abroad and immerse oneself in a cultural experience that goes beyond its academic reach.

7 In the case of *Cinexín*, it was shown both in alternative screens (local bars, alternative film festivals) as well as in national TV stations like Canal+. In a way, *Cinexín* recall contemporary experiences such as the Microcinema movement in the US.

8 Miguel Brieva is a social activist whose graphic work has appeared in magazines, comic books, fanzines and three of La Zanfoña's films: *El underground, Astronautas* and *Cabeza de perro*. One of his more famous series is called *Dinero*, a critical look at consumerism and capitalism.

9 About Álex de la Iglesia, *esperpento* and postmodern hybridisation, see Cerdán (2004) and Buse *et al.* (2007).

10 *Fulano* and *mengano* are Spanish expressions to call someone a 'nobody' or a John Doe.

References

Altman, Rick (1999) *Film/Genre*, London: BFI.
Buse, Peter, Núria Triana-Toribio and Andrew Willis (2007) *The Cinema of Álex de la Iglesia*, Manchester: Manchester University Press.
Cerdán, Josetxo (2004) 'España fin de milenio. Sobre *El día de la bestia* (1995)', in Rafael Ruzafa Ortega (ed.), *La historia a través del cine: transición y consolidación democrática en España*, Bilbao: UPV/EHU, 235–55.
Collins, Jim (1993) 'Genericity in the nineties: eclectic irony and the new sincerity', in Jim Collins, Hilary Radner and Ava Preacher Collins (eds), *Film Theory Goes to the Movies*, London: Routledge, 242–64.
Elsaesser, Thomas (2005) *European Cinema: Face to Face with Hollywood*, Amsterdam: Amsterdam University Press.
Gelder, Ken (2005) 'Introduction: The Field of Subcultural Studies', in Ken Gelder (ed.), *The Subcultures Reader*, London: Routledge, 1–15.
Losilla, Carlos (1997) 'Adónde va el cine español. Los jóvenes realizadores y la búsqueda de una nueva estética', *Dirigido por . . .*, 257, May, 34–42.
—— (2005) 'Contra ese cine español. Panorama general al inicio de un nuevo siglo', *Archivos de la Filmoteca*, 49, February, 124–45.
Monterde, José Enrique (2005) '*7 vírgenes*. Nada nuevo bajo el sol', *Dirigido por . . .*, 349, October, 17.

5

Justino, un asesino de la tercera edad: Spanishness, dark comedy and horror

Juan F. Egea

When asked to classify the Spanish movie *Justino, un asesino de la tercera edad* (La cuadrilla, 1994), its directors, Luis Guridi and Santiago Aguilar, invent a curious, almost untranslatable film category. The black-and-white film about a retired *puntillero* (assistant bullfighter) turned serial killer is, according to them, a *chascarrillo negro*, a dark little joke. Even if in jest, the creation of such a generic label reveals, first of all, a willingness to anchor one's work in a national, even local specificity; and, second, a playful problematisation of the concept of film genre. A *chascarrillo*, in fact, is not really a joke – a *chiste* – in Spanish. The *Real Academy Dictionary* defines the term as a 'light and racy anecdote' ('anécdota ligera y picante') and as a 'witty short story or phrase with equivocal and funny meaning' ('cuentecillo agudo o frase de sentido equívoco y gracioso'). Neither an 'anecdote' nor a 'short story' or 'phrase', *Justino* cannot be described with this hard-to-translate term. The term, rather than describing the movie, brands it, makes it 'local' or, at least, points towards some problems of translation. Whether these problems are cultural as well as linguistic is precisely one of the questions to be addressed in these pages.

A cross between an indigenous dark comedy and an indie horror movie, *Justino* provokes generic considerations that are necessarily linked to questions – and questionings – of national cinema, which, in turn, raise issues of genre formation, cultural specificity and viewer expectations. These will be the first areas developed as I am guided by the following questions: How is the concept of national cinema strengthened or debunked by the use of 'indigenous' and 'foreign' film genres? What does 'Spanishness' mean as a notion reflected or performed in this story about life after bullfighting and serial killing? And what image (or images) of Spain does this movie add to the constellation of 'national images' being produced during the first half of a decade in which the adjective 'transnational' would be so frequently invoked? For if *Justino* displays a 'family resemblance' – to use Wittgenstein's expression – with some Spanish dark comedies from the early 1960s, the Spain in which the movie is produced and exhibited is not the Spain of Francoist *desarrollismo*. *Justino*'s Spain is the Spain of the tumultuous fourth consecutive term of the PSOE's government: a Spain only two years removed from the complex fair of regionalism and Europeanness that were the Barcelona Olympics, Madrid's term as European cultural capital and the Sevilla's Expo '92. The country was indeed at a cultural crossroads: looking simultaneously backward and forward, projecting triumphant images of modernity and yet unable to forgo a very distinct and problematic model of national history that has 1492 as its ultimate referent. Caught between micro- and macro-levels of imaginable communities, the country was visibly searching for images to represent its alleged essence and ambitions both to an international and intranational audience. The nation's film production of this period echoes the same cultural and representational anxieties, as does the film analysed in this chapter.

Armed with the very Spanish *puntilla* – the special dagger used in a bullfight to ultimately kill the bull – *Justino* enters this early 1990s cultural landscape as a low-budget, genre-blending production to become one of the first cinematic serial killers in the country. The second part of this chapter will read closely the character and crimes of this assistant bullfighter to elucidate how his displaced usage of the *puntilla* adds blood, irony and darkness to the representational anxieties of Spain on the eve of the twenty-first century.

Questions of genre

Justino is a Spanish dark comedy. This filmic genre does not need to be understood as one in which its members share common aesthetic properties; nor does it need to be seen as one in which there is any particular ideological factor that grants membership. *Justino* belongs to the film genre of Spanish dark comedies because of the 'family resemblances' it displays with movies such as *El pisito* (Marco Ferreri, 1959), *Plácido* (Luis García Berlanga, 1961),

Viridiana (Luis Buñuel, 1961), *El verdugo* (Luis García Berlanga, 1963), *El extraño viaje* (Fernando Fernán Gómez, 1964) and, especially, *El cochecito* (Marco Ferreri, 1960). 'Family resemblances,' as Wittgenstein envisioned them in his famous philosophical remarks on games, do not necessarily entail the existence of common factors among all members of a presupposed category. Family resemblances have more to do with an 'act of seeing' that results in the appreciation of 'a complicated network of similarities overlapping and criss-crossing: sometimes overall, sometimes in detail' (1958: 32). As qualified by Stanley Cavell in his *Pursuits of Happiness*, this concept acquires more relevance in the study of film genres where the conditions of recognisability depend less on common aesthetic features among the members of a given genre than on each and every member's capability for mutual illumination. Cavell's 'comedies of remarriage' constitute a genre 'not merely [because] they look like one another or [because] one gets similar impressions from them'; they do so because 'they *are what they are* in view of one another' (1981: 29, emphasis in the original). Even if we have a ready-made category such as the 'dark' or 'black comedy', the series of movies enumerated above constitutes a particular kind of dark comedies when viewed in light of one another. To call them Spanish dark comedies is, of course, to factor in considerations of nationality into the discussion of film genre. Yet to determine what makes them Spanish is, or could be interpreted as, a more complex issue than acknowledging their geopolitical origin. The question, then, is if there is such a thing as a *Spanish* dark comedy whose Spanishness does not solely depend on the obvious fact that the movie in question has been produced, filmed and exhibited in Spain. At this stage of this discussion, the critic is brought to the thorny issue of national specificity with regards to subject matter, filmic narrative form, aesthetics and, in this case, sense of humour. I will address some of these questions during my analysis of *Justino*.

I am embarking, therefore, in a context-specific analysis of a film seen through the lens of the different film genres this particular movie invokes, and where the connection between object and context is a two-way street. The film genres in question are the Spanish dark comedy and the horror movie. All in all, there is a double critical move that involves looking back to the past (to the corpus of Spanish dark comedies of the early 1960s) and planting one's analytical feet in the present, in this movie's present (the Spain of the early 1990s). However, it is all still a question of familiarity, of cultural familiarity with a filmic past and with a sociopolitical present. It is a question of resemblances – of family resemblances, that is. It is a question of how this cinematic text is read in light of other films and, furthermore, in light of other cultural phenomena. And yet, it is also a question of variation, of *un*familiarity, since this is also a serial killer movie, a cinematic genre with very few members in the Spanish film tradition.

Justino's family resemblances and cultural interventions

According to Wes Gehring, dark comedy is a genre of 'comic irreverence which flippantly attacks what are normally society's most sacredly serious subjects – especially death' (1996: xiv). Implicit in Gehring's subsequent elucidations on the genre is the premise that such an attack on society ought to be historicised. Even when the final indictment of the work in question may appear to be something as all-embracing as the absurdity of life, that indictment has been triggered by very specific sociocultural circumstances.

Spanish dark comedies had their heyday in the early 1960s transition from Franco's autarchy to the greater cultural permissiveness under the *apertura desarrollista*. This period provides the political and cultural context to undertake a generic study of the landmark movies in the history of Spanish cinema enumerated above. Death figures pre-eminently in each of aforementioned Spanish dark comedies; as does old age and laughter. Or, more precisely, we are dealing with cinematic narratives that mixed death, old age and laughter. Death, old age and laughter play a significant part in the making of *Justino* as a film story told through images. The differences between those movies and *Justino* can be easily discerned, of course. Yet the familiarity, the 'resemblances', are equally noticeable in images that conjure up *El cochecito*, for instance, and in situations where characters are forced to prove their consent with, or flaunt their defiance towards, the moral order surrounding them. Simultaneously compliant and rebellious, I have argued elsewhere that the characters featured in these filmed stories are morally ambiguous; that their key actions, in their excess, change the field of choice in which they are taken; and that their needs, the object of their desires, redefine the very idea of necessity within a given socioeconomic environment (Egea, 2003; 2006–7). *Justino*'s killings could be placed in this interpretative framework. However, what it is worth emphasising in the case of this particular dark comedy is that, by recuperating the spirit of those dark comedies of the 1960s, *Justino* explores the possibility of going as local or as indigenous as possible in order to intervene in the Spanish cinematic and cultural scene of the 1990s.

Indeed, *Justino* intervenes in the Spanish cultural scene of the 1990s in the sense that it interferes with the creation of a trans- or post-nationalist imaginary, throwing into the field of cultural production a very archaic and autochthonous set of figures and references. The Spanish cinema of the 1990s is a national cinema at a crossroads, both as a representational practice and as cultural industry. As a representational practice films produced in Spain during this period were not typically engaged with Francoism. The late 1970s and the 1980s experienced the furore of cinematic revisionism; those years also witnessed Pedro Almodóvar's break with both the recent past and the obsession to deal with it. Spanish cinema needed to look for a new image, or rather images, which do not necessarily invoke, contest, undermine or simply make reference to the trauma of the Spanish Civil War and its traumatic aftermath.[1]

As a cultural industry, Spanish cinema of the 1990s sees its audience shrinking due to the ever more aggressive post-Franco presence of Hollywood films in Spain that, year in and year out, take the lion's share of distribution revenues in the country. As Marvin D'Lugo has argued, Spanish cinema during that decade started to show clearly a 'liminal position' of sorts (2002: 79). At the same time asserting itself as a European cinema and reaching across the Atlantic towards its cultural and linguistic area of affinity in South America, Spanish cinema is simultaneously searching for a 'visual identity' and for a viewing market. Subsidies from the different European cultural agencies and co-productions are part of the equation.[2] Regional, national and global audiences are all factors that influence the national image the movies rehearse, question or simply mock, and as such need to be taken into consideration in an analysis. It is at this junction that the *Justino* indie quality is worth emphasising.

The movie was first filmed in 16mm and transferred later to a 35mm format. The grainy look of the images and the barely audible dialogue between two non-professional actors earmark these images from the beginning: this is a low-budget, independent film. The rough look of some movies has been taken as an act of cultural, national or even hemispheric affirmation and defiance rather than as the logical consequence of a modest budget.[3] *Justino's* 'rough look' (in the majority of the acting, its overall aesthetics, the improvised feeling of some of the shooting locations) may display a humble oppositional look, but an oppositional one nonetheless; after all, *Justino* is to be seen in stark contrast with the lavish commercial productions that surround it contemporaneously – productions such as *La pasión turca* (Vicente Aranda, 1994) and *Todos los hombres sois iguales* (Manuel Gómez Pereira, 1994). These Spanish blockbusters from the same year as *Justino*, however different they may be in subject matter and tone, epitomise the attempts of the Spanish industry to be commercially successful mainly through a production of technical quality, conventional narratives and the star-power of a very recognisable cast: the exact opposite of La cuadrilla's film.

Justino also intervenes in the Spanish cultural scene of the 1990s in the sense that it confronts the country's official representations of itself as a smooth-running organism that has finally managed to become a successful fusion of tradition and innovation, of local and national specificities with European and global inclinations. Among the institutional events that took place in 1992, Sevilla's universal exhibition was the one that produced the most spectacular images of such a nature. Since Expo '92 was compulsively promoted not as a trade fair but as a cultural one, not only Spain but the vast majority of the 109 participating countries had to confront the problem of creating and projecting a national image; a problem that ultimately had to do more with questions of representivity than with that of representation. As Penelope Harvey (1996) has shown compellingly, the tension between nation and state haunted many of the exhibitors' pavilions. Likewise, the invitation that was made to the different countries to reflect on the last 500 years of national history forced many of them to impossible essence-staging acts and complex identity-politics statements. Quite frequently, national stereotypes were simultaneously fought and invoked.

Spain portrayed itself as a community unproblematically anchored in 1492: a country of discoveries and also one being 'discovered' as a harmonious blend of autonomous regions and brand-new Europeanness. With so many representational dues to be paid – with so many overlapping communities to be imagined – the national entity projected at the Expo was one of a Spain at the same time idealised and highly self-reflexive, where cultural and socioeconomic optimism carried the day. Against the background of this idealised state-sanctioned spectacle, *Justino*'s grainy images of *pun-tilleros*, *almohadilleros*, *puyeros* and retirees' residential homes function as a strategic, low-budget return to an underworld of archaic cultural forms. *Justino* is in fact the first member of a trilogy that its directors labelled 'Spain through the back door' ('España por la puerta de atrás').[4] The name was inspired precisely by a scene in *Justino* in which the main character exits the bullring through the back door, in clear contrast with what a triumphant matador does ('salir por la puerta grande'), and in contrast with the triumphant institutional images of the nation-state promoted in Sevilla two years earlier. Bearing in mind the representational strategies deployed by both the national film industry and the nation's official images of itself in the early 1990s, we can embark on a close reading of *Justino* as an ironic staging of Spanishness, and a deliberate 'going local' and 'looking rough' in the midst of all the refined global and transnational image-projection. Yet, in this case, the close reading requires beginning with an analysis of how this visual text *sounds* and not with how it *looks*.

A serial killer *made in Spain*

The first scene of *Justino*, inserted in the middle of the movie's opening credits, sets the tone, literally, for the rest of the moving images that are to follow. In this first scene, the music score alternates between a threatening tune and a festive, semi-folkloric melody. The former is a clear reference to horror films; the latter, reminiscent of the soundtrack that scored *El cochecito*, *Plácido* or *El verdugo*. The soundtrack in a dark comedy may become one of the most significant resources to widen the breach between narrative's subject matter and its tone. In the classical Spanish dark comedies mentioned previously, the audience has to wait until more sombre aspects of the plot appear in the film to truly perceive the mismatch between images and sound. In *Justino* this mismatch can be heard from the very beginning. Furthermore, the horror soundtrack is heard over the opening credits and the carnivalesque, vaguely folkloric music starts the instant an axe begins chopping the horns of a recently defeated bull. When Justino launches his criminal career, the image/sound clash will also be underlined in a very particular way. Indeed, each use of the *puntilla* to kill actual people and not bulls is punctuated by an ironic sound effect, a musical underlining that makes the killings less horrific and turns each murder into less of a slaying. Later in the movie, a *pasodoble* will add more local flavour to the soundtrack. On the other hand, a whole sequence in which Justino struggles to dispose of his neigh-bour's body will be scored by a jazzy, Henry Mancini-like theme that pulls the musical references of this film towards a more cosmopol-itan sound and even to a different era. There are also two festive tunes. One is 'a Finnish party music' ('una música de fiesta finlan-desa'), as the directors call it; the other animates the celebration of Sansoncito's retirement. Regarding the latter, the directors speak of their intention to make it sound like 'the kind of music in one of those tapes you have in your car'.[5] These are melodies that, because of the musics' transnational qualities, decontextualise the story as much as the *pasodoble* anchored it as national folklore. This movie wants to be heard in a very particular way; it sounds either very local or it has the sound of a caricatured elsewhere. The killings it shows, in turn, are 'softened' by a sound effect that belies their horror.

So the tone – or rather the dissonance – has been set. From the opening scene onwards we will not only hear but also witness the making of a Spanish serial killer. And Spanish it is. The cultural speci-ficity of this serial killer is of course determined by his profession or, to be precise, by the continuation of a profession from which he had been forced to retire prematurely. This killer kills as if he were per-forming the last *suerte* of the so-called *fiesta nacional*. At this point, what a *puntillero* does in the bullfight is in fact a merciful killing. The bull is dying but not yet dead, and this assistant bullfighter, without any glamour or drama, puts the bull out of its misery. Justino does a mini-lecture on how to perform such a *suerte*. It is not an art, he reminds his group of friends, and, when done properly, there is not even that much blood. The ironic Spanishness of this serial killer is then established through references not to the world of bullfighting, but to the lower ranks of that world in particular. Other movies have borrowed from the bloody *fiesta nacional* to interrogate the role of stereotypical images and cliché icons in both local and foreign per-ceptions of a Spanish national cultural identity. Pedro Almodóvar's *Matador* (1986) and Bigas Luna's *Jamón, jamón* (1992) are, of course, the first ones that come to mind. Regarding the former, since it features two serial killers and hence a possible resemblance to what this movie concerns itself with, it bears repeating that Justino is not that high in the hierarchy of bullfighting. In fact, a *puntillero* these days – and certainly the one the movie depicts – does not belong to any team at the service of a bullfighter, as they once did. A *puntillero* works for and in a particular bullring; he is that extremely specialised worker tied to a very concrete facility that cleans up the mess left by the most prestigious *matador* precisely when he cannot be true to his name. Class considerations are present in *Justino* right from the outset and they have to be taken into account when the killing starts and when motives are to be elucidated.

Why people kill, kill themselves or wish somebody to be dead are integral components of the darkness, the moral ambiguity and the 'politics of death' differently invoked in *El verdugo*, *El cochecito*, *Viridiana*, *El extraño viaje* or *El pisito*. Why this early-retired *puntillero* kills, and kills repeatedly, brings about something new to this family of cinematic Spanish killers and death-wishers. It brings about, first and foremost, a degree of excess that results in a figure that has to be read in light of those who populate this subgenre of horror that the serial killer movie is; a subgenre, as previously indicated, with virtually no tradition in Spanish cinema.[6]

A serial killer film is not just a matter of the number of killings; it is also a matter of motives. The combination of numbers and motives make serial killer movies horror stories where the monsters may walk among us and look like us, yet be involved in the production of some sort of deadly mathematical sublime. A serial killer movie is, then, as much about monstrosity as about normalcy; even identification – in the concrete way the term is used within the medium of the moving image – may play a part in how this type of movie influences the spectator. Or in other words, cinematic serial killers have been provoking more than just repulsion or horror in their audiences.[7]

Justino presents us with another ambiguous killer, with a likeable one at least, a fact that complicates passing judgement on his murderous acts. What I have called elsewhere – in connection with José Isbert's characters in *El cochecito* and *El verdugo* – an investigation on the 'ethics of empathy' is very much present in the way this movie introduces its Spanish serial killer. In leading the spectator to disapprove at one level (intellectually and morally) and condone at another (emotionally and symbolically) the character's actions, the potential viewers of these movies are themselves confronted with their own moral dilemmas. In consonance, precisely, with what a dark comedy is supposed to do (to problematise the moment of and occasion for laughter), these Spanish dark comedies make it problematic to manage efficiently any kind of moral compass. This is done in a variety of ways.

First, we could speak of a 'structural' redemption of the serial killer: a way of putting scenes together so the spectator is forced to identify and even empathise with characters that, from all we know, do not deserve our sympathies. When Justino struggles to hide Doña Pura's body from his friends, the possibility of the criminal being caught activates the audience's empathy. In those scenes, this possibility feels more like a moment of danger than that of an occasion for justice. In Justino's first killings, the redeeming qualities of the killer appear also in images of macabre tenderness, in moments of absurd post-crime warmth towards his victims. Justino covers his son's slain body as if he were putting him to sleep one last time, and places a pillow below his daughter-in-law's head to make her eternal rest more comfortable. These are more than humorous oddities; and they are not the only ones that complicate the visual description of our serial killer. Very early in *Justino* the main character helps a handicapped person in a vehicle whose primitiveness refers back to the less affluent members of Don Anselmo's physically challenged friends in *El cochecito*. What Justino does with the invalid by pushing him in the wrong direction despite the man's repeated complaints amounts to another one of those visual descriptions of this character's moral fibre: his actions, his motives, his now-kind-now-murderous intentions are equally unclear. The number of times in which we see his face partially shadowed could point to nothing more symbolic than the final visual clue to this man's ambiguous moral grounds and to his problematic likeability.

Ultimately, the likeability of this killer is inversely proportional to how unlikeable the characters around him are. The directors surround the murderer with unpleasant, when not despicable, individuals that range from an abusive boss to neglecting family members. 'Social rage' explains, if not condones, the crimes, if only at a symbolic level. Yet as the film progresses Justino's victims do not seem to deserve, not even symbolically, their deaths. What drives Justino to kill is not as clear to discern as it may appear.

Our serial *puntillero* kills his son and his daughter-in-law first. Then he murders a woman on a Metro platform right in the middle of her being mugged by teenagers. Doña Pura, his annoying neighbour, becomes Justino's fourth victim. The list continues with a one-armed drunk who insults him and his friend Sansoncito, two policemen who laugh at his confession and all the residents of a nursing home. Justino kills family members for living space and possibly to extract revenge from the way he has been treated. He kills an unknown woman for money, a neighbour so that a party he is throwing can continue and a handicapped person plus two police officers out of either pride or spite. The final mass killing is also for money, but this time behind the financial need there is a very humble dream to fulfil: the possibility of retiring to Benidorm with his friend, which is in fact the possibility of making Sansoncito's dreams, rather than his own, come true. Justino starts killing to have a room of his own and ends up annihilating a group of old people to make a friend happy.

Early retirement under very unfavourable conditions seems to be the first recognisable cause of emotional distress for Justino in the film. It is one of the measures aimed at lessening the effects of one of the worst recessions in the European Union during the 1990s. By 1993, Spain's honeymoon with Europe was over. The other transition, the economic one that allowed the Spanish economy to enter the European Common Market in 1986 and remain competitive, had officially ended. The country was exposed to the full force of EU competition. Reduced investment, falling output and public deficit ensued. By the beginning of the 1990s, Spain was becoming the oldest EU country, while its unemployment rate remained one of the highest in the continent. However, finances and morals are two sides of the same coin in this national picture, just as in *Justino*. The 1990s witnessed the infamous Torras-KIO and Banesto bankruptcies (1993 and 1994, respectively), and the downfall of 'star' bankers such as Mario Conde and 'maverick' financiers such as Javier de la Rosa. The so-called *cultura del pelotazo* (a culture of political corruption and abuse of power for financial gain) was in full swing.

Taken as a whole, this economic, demographic and moral context reframes Justino's killing. The outcome of financial hard times and a get-rich-quick boom, Justino's actions express not only rebellion against but also communion with the spirit of his times. If in the first two murders the murderer seems to have lost his mind, and in the next four he appears either impulsive or desperate, the mass killing in the nursing home is done with premeditation and for a rather calculated financial gain. In fact, the final mass killing partakes of certain modest proposal logic, however unaware the killer is of his Swiftian ways. What is there to do with so many elderly people living under such sad retiree's life conditions? Justino just kills them all, takes their savings, and consolidates them towards a truly satisfying retirement plan for himself and Sansoncito. The absence of remorse and the businesslike attitude of the killer match the moral climate of a period in Spain where a banker nicknamed 'the shark' (Mario Conde) seemed to be a model of social success. The dark comedies of the 1960s had to contend with or respond to not only Francoism but also the new Opus Dei-affiliated technocrats taking the country to modern capitalism. They had an economic reform that forced them to emigrate along with the beginning of an 'economic' miracle that involved the boom of the national tourist industry. These movies took account of an economic openness that did not match the climate of cultural and political repression suffocating the country. These movies had individuals struggling in a social order in which the repressing forces were getting blurrier, and the acts of true rebellion more problematic.

Justino, in turn, depicts a Spain of bust economy following the boom of the 1980s determined to make a splash in the world's concert of nations. The film has an established and stable democracy, yet still somewhat dark and threatening, where the sources of social evil are harder to pinpoint and their perverse ideology misrecognised as finances. *Justino*'s Spain is struggling economically because of its new *apertura*, its opening: first, to a European and world economy for which it is not entirely ready; and, second, to an international audience whose perception of the country's past and present has to be at once contested and confirmed. In the early 1960s, whatever image the Spain of Manuel Fraga Iribarne wanted to sell to the international community *El verdugo* was sure to discredit by bringing its reluctant and clumsy executioner to the touristy island of Mallorca to apply a brutal death penalty. In the early 1990s, whatever triumphant images of transnationalism the Spanish film industry and the Spanish national institutions were bent on producing *Justino* takes care of questioning them through its underworld of taurine figures and its scavenger-produced look. How to look Spanish, for whom or for what, matching whose preconceptions and revealing which hidden anxieties in the process remain questions at the core of what this series of movies has to offer as either serious or ironic screenings of Spanishness. In that respect, *Justino* belongs to the cinematic family of the Spanish dark comedies of the early 1960s, and its close cousins are Bigas Luna's 'Ruedo

Ibérico' series – *Jamón, jamón* (1992), *Huevos de oro* (1993) and *La teta i la lluna* (1994) – and Alex de la Iglesia's *Acción mutante/Mutant Action* (1993) and *El día de la bestia/The Day of the Beast* (1995). Like in these other excessive, nationally fixated dark comedies, in *Justino* there is a deliberate performance of Spanishness that mixes the transnationality of generic conventions (the horror film, the serial killer movie) with a heavy dose of local references, local humour and national clichés for global consumption. *Justino* carries this throughout, all the way to its final scene.

The final shot of the movie shows a bus on its way to Benidorm with the famous Osborne bull in the horizon. More than the retiree's paradise Sansoncito champions, Benidorm represents the epitome of urban planning atrocities and cheap tourism wonderland, where fish and chips and happy hours have altered for ever the coastline and its culture. The Osborne bull silhouette is visual shorthand for a national stereotype fully embraced. Still standing by popular demand after the passing of the law that banned this kind of commercial advertisement boards on Spanish motorways, they display the image others may expect to see associated with Spain. A real bull was quartered in the opening images of the film, which is, of course, the unseen fate of the animal after being so visibly fought and killed. The stereotypical, two-dimensional bull points one last time to a mocking Spanish imaginary that is there for others to see, that is produced for the passing onlooker, and that offers an ironic display of Spanishness after a gruesome one has been acknowledged. Whether the joke is on us or on them, it is hard to tell; just as difficult as telling the difference between what really represents 'us' and who constitutes the 'them' we are representing for. *Justino*, as an independent Spanish dark comedy about a retiree serial killer that comes from the lowly provinces of bullfighting, plants itself firmly in that representational interregnum to keep us wondering, simply, who are we kidding.

Notes

1 Post-Franco Spanish cinema have been divided and 'mapped' in different ways, but the most frequent periodisation dates its true beginning to 1982, seven years after the dictator's death. This is the year of the PSOE victory in the general elections. One year later a new law for the national cinema industry, the so-called Miró law (named after the recently

appointed *Directora General de Cinematografía*) was passed. A left-wing party whose leaders had a history of opposition to the old dictatorial regime, the PSOE remained in power until 1996, when a combination of economic and political scandals propitiated its defeat in favour of the right-wing Partido Popular (PP). One of the most interesting studies that focuses on that period is the collection of essays *Refiguring Spain* (or *Refiguring Socialist Spain*, as the title of the introduction reads), edited by Marsha Kinder (1997). This 'socialist Spain' could be subject to further subdivisions. In fact, other approaches to the Spanish film production of that period speaks of the 'socialist decade' (Riambau, 1995), focusing on the years 1982–92 and disregarding that ill-fated socialist fourth term during which *Justino* is produced.

2　See Peter Besas's article in Kinder (1997) and Riambau (1995).

3　Glauber Rocha's 'aesthetics of hunger', Solanas and Getino's 'third cinema' and García Espinosa's 'imperfect cinema' are exemplary on this score.

4　The other two movies in this trilogy by La cuadrilla (a taurine name itself that makes reference to a matador's team of assistant bullfighters) are *Matías, juez de línea* (1996) and *Atilano, presidente* (1998). They were both received very unfavourably by the critics. Before *Justino*, between 1980 and 1990, the tandem Luis Guridi and Santiago Aguilar 'perpetrated' (as they put it) thirty shorts in Super 8 and six in a 35mm format.

5　All quotes from the directors are from their commentary in the DVD edition of the movie.

6　The aforementioned *Matador* is the story of two serial killers. *El bosque del lobo* (Pedro Olea, 1971) could be the only other forerunner for *Justino*. The serial killer movie, in its 'modern' tradition, has in fact been recognised as an 'American genre' (i.e. from the US). Films as different as *Henry: Portrait of a Serial Killer* (John McNaughton, 1986) and *Silence of the Lambs* (Jonathan Demme, 1991) constitute part of this 'national' corpus of serial killers.

7　'Serial killer' is a term coined in the 1970s, although the 'modern age of the serial killer' may be dated to 1888, when the Jack the Ripper murders took place in Victorian London (Cettl, 2003: 5). The serial killer film has been periodised differently and has been made to reflect a variety of philosophical and social points or concerns. For a good introduction on the topic, although restricted to serial killers driven by sexual impulses, see Cettl (2003). For a more comprehensive study of the serial killer figure focused on the US cultural production, see Simpson (2000).

References

Cavell, Stanley (1981) *Pursuits of Happiness: The Hollywood Comedy of Remarriage*, Cambridge, MA: Harvard University Press.

Cettl, Robert (2003) *Serial Killer Cinema: An Analytical Filmography*, Jefferson, NC: McFarland & Company.

D'Lugo, Marvin (2002) 'The Geopolitical Aesthetics in Recent Spanish Films', *Post Script: Essays in Film and the Humanities*, 21: 2, 78–89.

Egea, Juan (2003) 'Paralítico o no: comedia irónica, disidencia e identidad en *El cochecito*', *Anales de Literatura Española Contemporánea*, 28: 1, 77–93.

—— (2006–7) 'Para una anatomía de la complicidad: *El verdugo* de Berlanga', *Letras peninsulares*, 19: 2/19: 3, 211–26.

Gehring, Wes D. (1996) *American Dark Comedy: Beyond Satire*, Westport, CT: Greenwood Press.

Harvey, Penelope (1996) *Hybrids of Modernity: Anthropology, The Nation State and the Universal Exhibition*, London: Routledge.

Justino, un asesino de la tercera edad (2002) Dir. La cuadrilla. Perf. Saturnino García and Carlos Lucas. José María Lara P.C., 1994. DVD. Suevia Films.

Kinder, Marsha (ed.) (1997) *Refiguring Spain: Cinema/Media/Representation*, Durham, NC: Duke University Press.

Riambau, Esteve (1995) 'La "década socialista" (1982–1992)', in Román Gubern *et al.* (eds), *Historia del cine español*, Madrid: Cátedra, 399–447.

Simpson, Philip L. (2000) *Psycho Paths: Tracking the Serial Killer through Contemporary American Film and Fiction*, Carbondale: Southern Illinois University Press.

Wittgenstein, Ludwig (1958) *Philosophical Investigations*, G. E. M. Asncombe (trans.), 2nd edition, New York: Macmillan.

6

Tracing the past, dealing with the present: notes on the political thriller in contemporary Spanish cinema

Vicente J. Benet

Spanish cinema has often made use of the generic conventions of political thriller films not only to chronicle present events, but also to critically analyse the past. This chapter presents several points for understanding how the political thriller has played an important role in the collective processing, both social and political, which occurred after the traumatic years of the Franco dictatorship. The political thriller is especially pertinent for comprehending how the past is worked through in the public sphere, in the sense laid out by Theodor Adorno as *Aufarbeitung* (working through/coming to terms with the past). The term was coined by Freud and taken up by Adorno, who applied it to the public realm, arguing that there was a point of juncture between individual processing of traumatic experiences and the posterior collective reformulation that processes them at the social level (1986: 116). Mainstream films that rely on standard genre formulas offer us the unique possibility of tracing symptoms of those past traumas in order to understand how they are worked through at the social level.

The political thriller comes into its own in Spanish film in the mid-1970s in the upheaval of the transition period from the Franco dictatorship to democracy. The appearance of this genre came about from the interrelationship of three key factors. First was the international trend for political themes and narratives of the 1960s and 1970s. Second was the iconography in film noir and other related genres (such as gangster films, prison dramas, etc.), which was developed in films *d'auteur*. And lastly were the film reconstructions of recent historic and political events.

The political thriller thus took hold in Spain, saturated with the emblematic productions of European film typical of the times. Imbued with the political environment at the end of the 1960s, several film-makers oriented the genre conventions in terms of an ideological agenda geared to unveiling corruption or critiquing capitalist society and its political structures. Films such as *Stavisky* (Alain Resnais, 1974), *Z* (Costa Gavras, 1969), *Il caso Mattei/The Mattei Affair* (Francesco Rosi, 1972), *Il conformista/The Conformist* or *Strategia del ragno/The Spider's Stratagem* (both Bernardo Bertolucci, 1970) are examples of just how far these didactic, critical films aimed to go, usurping stereotypical genre formulas directed at the widest audience possible.

The didactic force of these films was not merely a function of the archetypical characterisations within clear ideological and moral parameters. It was also a function of the narrative, often presented in a non-linear, fragmented structure, which corresponded to the formal characteristics typical of the auteur film. With a marked style that self-consciously established differences with the conventions of Hollywood cinema, European filmmakers utilised known generic conventions within a sophisticated dynamic of renewal. Despite this, they attempted to maintain a balance with the spectator's expecta-tions to find a communicative ground of exchange. Fragmented nar-rative structure and hermeneutic plots were very effective in keeping the audience interested. Something scandalous or criminal happens to get the ball rolling for an investigation that ultimately leads to the political sphere. The search is closely guided either by a narrative voice (through titles, voiceover, etc.), or through a character who becomes the narrator. The spectator tags along with the character and participates, to a greater or lesser degree, in the deductive process as the events unfold. This participation is essential because the way that who knows what (i.e. narrative focalisation) is established – for the investigating character, the narrator and the spectator – and it determines the complexity of perspectives. And it is from these perspectives that the spectator is enabled to process the events and judge the outcome. This was the typical strategy used in the political thriller to present complex social processes and ideas in a way that was easy to understand. If the film dealt with past events, its allegorical reference to the present was made fairly obvious.

In the mid-1970s, at the beginning of the transition period, Spanish political thrillers took a didactic turn, reinforcing structures

of social control and political power through several different strategies. Most notable were adaptations of fiction novels. These novels
integrated political issues into the detective novel formula. We have
a striking example with Manuel Vázquez Montalbán and his detective Pepe Carvalho. Pepe Carvalho's novels were adapted for film by
Bigas Luna (*Tatuaje*, 1977) and a few years later were made into
what would be the first of several TV series called *Las aventuras de
Pepe Carvalho*. Vázquez Montalbán, a militant communist and
popular media personality, characterised his detective in the conventional stance of being morally superior to the world surrounding
him. Carvalho was rather cynical, yet was as consistent in his moral
standards as he was in his taste for fine cuisine. His journeys through
Spanish society of the 1970s and early 1980s often brought to light
the complex process of transition from the old entrenched institutions of the Franco regime to the new forms of democracy. This
transformation was occurring not only in the main core of political
and economic power but also in leftist groups which, in turn, had
to adapt to the new circumstances and were likewise not free of
corruption.

Another important example of literary adaptation to film is
Eduard Mendoza's *La verdad sobre el caso Savolta* (1975), directed
by Antonio Drove in 1980. The novel was a bestseller during the
transition years and was closely tied to the film conventions of the
political thriller where a historical event is used to make allegorical
reference to circumstances easily recognised by the 1980s spectator.
Mendoza wrote two other novels: *El misterio de la cripta embrujada*
(1978) and *El laberinto de las aceitunas* (1982). In these, he used the
perspective of an anonymous detective, just out of a mental institution, to create a paradoxical vision of Spanish society during the
transition period. These two films were adapted to the big screen,
respectively, as *La cripta* (Cayetano del Real, 1981) and *Soldados de
plomo* (José Sacristán, 1984), but were not very successful given that
they lacked the grotesque tone of the original novels.

Apart from literary adaptations, there was an evolution of narrative style from the conventions of film noir toward plots that dealt
directly with the political transition. This comes out very clearly in
El arreglo (J. L. Zorrilla, 1983), a daring film for the time by por-
traying police corruption in the fight against terrorism. This film fits
our second model, where a story is constructed about the present,
using a criminal case that brings politics into play. This happens, for

instance, in *Matar al Nani* (Roberto Bodegas, 1987), *El Lute I* and *II* (Vicente Aranda, 1987 and 1988) or *El caso Almería* (Pedro Costa Musté, 1983). These films were meant as an immediate reflection of *faits divers* one could read about in the newspapers – criminal cases that could be used to reveal how Franco regime repression was still in place, or perhaps the failings of the recently implanted democracy.

Yet, without a doubt the most important films of the first phase of the political thriller are *Operación Ogro* (Gillo Pontecorvo, 1979) and *La fuga de Segovia* (Imanol Uribe, 1981). Both films focus on two key events that took place during the transition years. First is ETA's assassination of the Prime Minister, Admiral Luis Carrero Blanco, in 1973. Second is the escape of several terrorists imprisoned since 1976, the year after Franco's death and shortly before all political prisoners would be set free. As we can tell from the short time span between when the events happened and when the films were made, they were taking part in the debate on an extremely serious and sensitive issue. Yet both films relied on conventional genre formats that allowed the debate to be guided along lines that were quite touchy for the turbulent and conflictive times, such as focalising the narrative through the perspective of the terrorists.

Operación Ogro and *La fuga de Segovia* give the impression of being objective through a journalistic-style account of events. This formula proved extremely effective, especially for two complementary questions: on the one hand it brought to the public sphere a rendition of recent events that was diametrically opposed to official versions, often in an explicitly confrontational stance; on the other hand, conventional genre formulas were used to codify those events, converting them into film dramatisations that were easily internalised by the vast public.[1]

In the years following the transition period, the political thriller underwent new revisions. The beginning of the 1990s was a particularly significant time. These were crucial years for Spanish culture. The grand celebrations in 1992 marked the symbolic end of a repressive dictatorship and the beginning of a democracy that would bring Spain into the European context. In this light, the Olympic Games in Barcelona and the World Expo '92 in Sevilla represent Spain as having surpassed its totalitarian past, bolstered by the political strength of the Socialist Party headed by Felipe González. Some scholars of the Transition period, however, view this catharsis as purely superficial.[2] In any case, from a film genre perspective, it is

clearly revealed as symptomatic of these processes in which there is
a radical departure regarding both the social implications of the
political thriller and in the narrative and stylistic formulas they use.
These transformations need to be considered in context. The first
phase of the transition period was geared mainly toward a didactic
reflection on the changes society was undergoing. Yet there were also
signs that something else was there, something which would continue to develop as time passed: a growing feeling of malcontent. In
certain sectors of society there was a strong feeling of frustration
with the process of how the Franco regime had been disassembled.
To put it briefly, people began to question the way in which the
regime had been dissolved, especially since it had been based on
political pacts that made it possible to keep things rather peaceful,
at the cost of not bringing past actions to justice or demanding political accountability of those who had supported the regime. The
result, according to several scholars, was a feeling of *desencanto*
(disenchantment) or, in a sense, mourning for the loss of an object
(the dictatorship), since an entire generation had built their identity
on the fight against the Franco regime. Characterising the transition
period in this way, however, renders a fairly uniform and restricted
sense to political and cultural processes that were actually quite
complex and contradictory. As Paul Julian Smith points out, this
interpretation overlooks the complexity and richness of many cultural productions of the 1970s and 1980s – free, uninhibited and
effective elaborations of the past that far surpassed the level of pacts
among the political elite (2007: 51–2).

The symptoms of discontent crystallised as well in a few unique
genre films. These complex, allegorical films were quite baroque in
the mise-en-scène and in the plotlines. The dense imagery and
metaphorical elaborations were, however, based on the conventional
plot of a detective story well exemplified by *Beltenebros/Prince of
Shadows* (Pilar Miró, 1991), *Madregilda* (Francisco Regueiro, 1993)
or *El detective y la muerte* (Gonzalo Suárez, 1994). In these films, the
narrative construction leaves behind the didactic function that we see
in the first phase of transition films, and is directed toward a more
poetic level, by which I mean to say that these narratives present a
dense, metaphoric discourse on the issue of totalitarianism itself. The
Franco regime was put into a parallel relationship with what was
happening at the time in Europe. Communism was falling in Eastern
Europe, and there was a fairly clear comparison drawn between what

was going on in the countries newly freed from Soviet control and the process undergone in Spain two decades earlier. So in these films we find a gloomy, dense, pictorial style to accentuate the allegorical notion that the totalitarian past still lives on. After all, the idea was to project the feeling of discontent in the present that had developed out of the public sphere of the past, and this use of *Aufarbeitung* was meant to serve as an example for other countries.

Both the didactic model of the early 1980s and the allegorical model of the 1990s have continued to evolve. Auteur film style is left behind, while film noir and action thriller conventions with a political twist are again taken up. Yet we are currently at a very complex moment for film, given the fact that a critical reading of how past events have typically been reconstructed (*Aufarbeitung*) is in vogue and has become part of the policies of the Spanish Government and the mass media. The history of the Civil War and the Franco regime has become, without a doubt, the most intense debate in the cultural and mass media scene of our time. As soon as we take an interest in this topic, we are inundated with books, television dramas and documentaries, movies, open debates, and web pages in all shapes and sizes. Some of these are directly related to specific circumstances. For example, the Socialist Party president, José Luis Rodríguez Zapatero, implemented a series of projects, in particular one called *La ley de memoria histórica* (The Law of Historic Memory). This law incited biting debates within the standard media and brought out disputes among new media producers as well. The arguments were invariably tainted by the political leanings of the media producers. The so-called 'obituary wars' among the major Spanish newspapers during 2006 is an example of a new genre that reflected a generalised feeling of malcontent. In this media war, the descendants or relatives of the victims of the Civil War would publish an obituary claiming criminal responsibility for his or her death. Whereas during the last decade the memory of the Spanish Civil War was clearly marked by the disinterment of those who had been executed and communally buried by the Franco regime, the newly posted obituaries served to bring the dead back into the collective imaginary, and to reopen the debate that had yet to be resolved.

The present reconstruction of the transition years is no longer projected into a poetic, baroque rendition as we find in the second phase of the political thriller. Instead new parameters must be established. On the one hand, we find films that return to a didactic stance, to a simplified account of historic events such as the Civil War, the Franco regime or the transition period. These films use standard, highly predictable film genre conventions. The melodrama, as well, has once again become an essential point of reference for memory, constructing films that simplify the bitter events of the past through historical figures who represent resistance and dignity as opposed to (the) absolute evil (of the regime). We can see this in recent rereadings of the Franco era in films by José Luis Garci, and in films that render a fictionalised account of the 'recovering the past' such as *El lápiz del carpintero* (Antón Reixa, 2003), *Silencio roto/Broken Silence* (Montxo Armendáriz, 2001) or even in *Salvador* (*Puig Antich*) (Manuel Huerga, 2006).[3]

In addition to the political rhetoric behind the didactic films, there is an important consequence related to the new structure of the Spanish film industry, specifically in terms of the recent consolidation of media conglomerates. In the mid-1990s several major sectors converge: the television industry, the film industry, telecommunications and the leisure industry. These media conglomerates directly influence what stories reach the public and even the way they are told, since distribution no long privileges public consumption for exclusively moviegoers, but now includes distribution through television, DVDs, etc. (Benet, 2001). The well-recognised relationship between film and television industries increasingly affects key factors in production and distribution. In fact, it has become practically impossible for a film to ultimately reach the audience without the financial backing of a television channel (Álvarez Monzoncillo, 2002: 118).

Yet there is an even more important issue. Of course, media conglomeration is occurring not only in Spain but also in Italy, the US and other developed countries. And in the process there is an inevitable fusion of groups that share similar political agendas. The process of conglomeration of the 1990s in Spain has affected both major political parties, the PSOE (Partido Socialista Obrero Español) and the more conservative PP (Partido Popular), headed by ex-president José María Aznar. Two important factors help explain the strong ties between the communication sector and these two political parties. On the one hand, the massive state-owned communications industry *Telefónica* was privatised and began to invest in the new TV and radio stations. In conjunction with this were the accompanying policies for granting radio and television licences, which highly determined how the Spanish mass media scene would pan out. These issues go beyond the scope of this chapter, but suffice it to say that they ultimately affect several questions regarding our discussion of the political thriller.

Perhaps the most representative example of media conglomeration is the PRISA group. PRISA (Promotora de Informaciones, S.A.) is a consolidation of the major national newspaper *El País*, the national radio station SER, the pay television channel Canal+ TV along with its respective theme-based channels and the recently added free-access television channel Cuatro. In the mid-1990s the group acquired the Santillana publishing group (which subsumes several other publishers such as Alfaguara, Aguilar, Taurus, etc.), thus further reinforcing their potential to make an impact on cultural productions. The PRISA group's film branch, called Sogecable, is comprised of three sectors: a production company (Sogecine); a distribution agency (Soge-Warner Sogefilms); and an exhibition company (Warner Lusomundo Sogecable).

PRISA's dominant role in the production of cultural contents goes hand in hand with its political agenda, which it consolidates through the media, especially in the editorial line of its newspaper *El País* and the radio station SER. Its overall identification with the political agenda of the PSOE has, in turn, incited new alliances among groups that support the conservative party. Many of these new alliances were formed when the PP was in power, both at the national level and in the autonomous communities, which allowed them into the bidding process for licences of private radio and television stations, as well as for television and film production companies.

We have a very clear example of this with the newspaper *El Mundo* and its television and film production company, Mundo Ficción. Mundo Ficción, run by the journalist Melchor Miralles, has produced various television programmes and, most importantly, two full-feature fiction films which echo back to the didactic rhetoric of the political thriller: *El Lobo* (2004) and *GAL: en el punto de mira* (2006), both directed by Miguel Courtois, a highly experienced director of action series for French television. In this sense, these films are most remarkably characterised by their reliance on the most typical conventions of the genre, precisely those that have been thoroughly utilised within the TV arena.

Both films return to the issue of ETA terrorism during the last years of the Franco regime through the transition period. Here, we find absolutely no trace of auteur film techniques that we likely would have seen in films of the early 1980s. On the contrary, the action film format completely dominates the genre formula and the narrative composition so much that both the storyline and the mise-en-scène become extremely predictable. Any historical implication is typically resolved by a series of titles at the beginning and end of the film, which contextualise the events. But, as one of the producers of *El Lobo* admitted in a press conference, the most important thing was the action, above and beyond any supposed political message.[4]

With due justice having been paid to the conventional patterns of the action film, Mundo Ficción presents the two films in a carefully studied, international marketing plan, using famous performers coming out of the Spanish star system like Eduardo Noriega in the lead role, and secondary roles given to well-established actors such as José Coronado, Santiago Ramos or Jorge Sanz. The film narrates the real story of how a young man infiltrated the terrorist group, finally reaching the upper ranks. It uses the typically strategy of a made-for-TV action series. The political facet to the story is in no way emphasised. What is emphasised are the customs and fanaticism of the terrorists, as well as the wide range of political corruption and the police force's vested interest in keeping terrorism alive in order to justify itself as a necessary branch of power within the state structure. This was Mundo Ficción's first major production, and was supported by television channels such as Canal+ and Telecinco. The film was a box-office hit, bringing in nearly €8 million, and thus led the way for another, much more ambition production, *GAL: en el punto de mira*.[5] This time around, the film was supported by television stations of all the autonomous communities governed by the PP (Valencia, Baleares, Madrid), and even by the autonomous Basque television station, naturally very sensitive to the topic.

Melchor Miralles, the head of production of Mundo Ficción, was in fact one of the journalists implicated in the investigation in the GAL case. José García, a well-known French actor, plays the part of Miralles. The film again uses the star system, including Jordi Mollà and Natalia Verbeke. The political dimension of the film is loosely brought out through clues that the spectator can easily recognise. Even though names have been changed, as well as any physical resemblance to the characters has been erased, it is not difficult to identify the real people behind the characters such as ex-president

Felipe González, Judge Baltasar Garzón or Minister of Interior José Luis Corcuera. Nevertheless, in spite of having full access to first-hand documentation, the film remains within simplistic formulas. The movie never really goes beyond mere clichés for the characters and the plot. Consequently, *GAL: en el punto de mira* was a box-office disaster and brought in barely over 300,000 spectators.

The productions by Mundo Ficción offer a reading of historic events through the conventions of the political thriller, but what they actually give us is a view of the state of contemporary mass media. In contrast to transition period films, these are not a look back at the past or a search for clues from the past to teach us something about the present, i.e. they do not offer a didactic or critical reconstruction of the past. Nor do they use a dense, baroque style for the plot or the malcontent that emerges as symptomatic of the 1990s. Lacking in political reflection, uninterested in stylistic elaboration, the way that current cinema is reconstructing historical events is far from rekindling the debate in the public sphere in the sense of *Aufarbeitung*. Is this a sign that the past has been sufficiently and adequately processed by Spanish society? Absolutely not. The pain and resentment that still come out in debates on the Civil War, the dictatorship, and even the transition period, lie just under the surface, and will remain there for a long time to come. The last vestiges of totalitarianism continue to be felt as witnessed by the survival of the Basque terrorist group ETA. Yet, in contrast to the situation thirty years ago, perhaps cinema is no longer the best medium for analysing the present or for reconstructing the past in the public sphere.

Notes

1 ETA terrorism has also been dealt with in genres other than the political thriller. This is the case with the melodramatic film *La muerte de Mikel*, also directed by Imanol Uribe in 1983.
2 See, for example, Subirats (1993), or Vilarós (1998).
3 For a detailed account of this process, see Sánchez-Biosca (2006).
4 The comment was later softened in the same press conference by Melchor Miralles, who defends the film's political and social relevance, rather than it being merely an action film. The press conference is available in the DVD edition of *El Lobo*, Filmax, 2005.
5 'GAL' stands for 'Grupo Antiterrorista de Liberación', an illegal anti-terrorist organisation that operated within the Spanish government from 1983 to 1987.

References

Adorno, Theodor W. (1959) 'What Does Coming to Terms with the Past Mean?', in Geoffrey Hartman (ed.), *Bitburg in Moral and Political Perspective*, Bloomington: Indiana University Press, 1986, 114–29.

Álvarez Monzoncillo, José María (2002) 'La industria cinematográfica: enfermedades crónicas e incertidumbres ante el mercado digital', in Enrique Bustamante (ed.), *Comunicación y cultura en la era digital. Industrias, mercados y diversidad en España*, Barcelona: Gedisa.

Benet, Vicente José (2001) 'El malestar del entretenimiento', *Archivos de la Filmoteca*, 39, October, 40–53.

Sánchez-Biosca, Vicente (2006) *Cine y Guerra Civil Española. Del mito a la memoria*, Madrid: Alianza.

Smith, Paul Julian (2007) *Spanish Visual Culture: Cinema, Television, Internet*, Manchester: Manchester University Press.

Subirats, Eduardo (1993) *Después de la lluvia. Sobre la ambigua modernidad española*, Madrid: Temas de Hoy.

Vilarós, Teresa M. (1998) *El mono del desencanto: una crítica cultural de la transición española (1973–1993)*, Madrid: Siglo XXI.

7

Selling out Spain: screening capital and culture in *Airbag* and *Smoking Room*

William J. Nichols

'Genre', Christine Gledhill declares, 'is first and foremost a bound-ary phenomenon', and genre critics act as 'cartographers' concerned with exploring and defining the 'fictional territories' that distinguish certain kinds of films, like westerns, from others, such as gangster films (2000: 221). Within the discourse of film genre studies, such use of spatial metaphors is not uncommon. Critics often talk about genre referring to their 'borders' or 'territories', or attempt to 'map' the 'terrain' or 'location' of genre, or hope to explore the 'imaginary landscape' and plot the 'cognitive mapping' of one genre or another. Such vocabulary conveys the idea that genres occupy an overtly delineated space and 'have clear, stable identities and borders' (Altman, 1999: 16), a general assumption about film studies that Rick Altman critiques, such that a romantic comedy would not infringe into the realm of musical, or horror into that of thriller, etc. This perceived stability is important, asserts Altman, for much more than reasons of aesthetic purity, but constructs a 'structure and conduit through which material flows from producers to directors and from the industry to distributors, exhibitors, audiences and their friends' (1999: 15). Genre, in other words, can be understood as the key cog in the industrial machinery that defines the production and consumption of film, a kind of contract for the 'mode of exchange' between those who pay to make films and those who pay to see them. In *Film Genre: Hollywood and Beyond* (2005), Barry Langford's answer to the question 'Who needs genre?' seems to bolster Altman's critique of genre as a market tool. The film indus-try, not critics, defines genre hierarchically through institutional practices (marketing, publicity, studio policies, etc.) that organise production to 'reduce commercial risk' and ensure the 'promise of attracting and retaining audience'. Spectators, on the other end, not only use genre, then, to differentiate one product from another, but also derive pleasure from the familiarity genres offer and which assure 'some guarantee that the price of admission will purchase another shot of an experience already enjoyed before' (Langford, 2005: 1). If genre can be understood in spatial terms, then it would seem a ludic space designed to ensure the spectator's pleasure with the aesthetic familiarity of a recognisable narrative structure. The illusion of the narrative diverts the attention of the spectator away from the market strategies that frame genre construction as a mode of exchange and, instead, mask the machinations of capital by legitimating genre as a 'cultural norm'. This 'generic pleasure' would ultimately legitimise, or at least normalise, the narrative in question by creating a unified 'constellated community' of spectators who have accepted the rules as a way of communicating and sharing knowledge about the world (Altman, 1999: 157, 161).

Such a consideration of the exchange between those who produce film and those who consume it, however, would seem to view the spectator as an unwitting, passive receptacle whose gaze is constant and uniform. More accurately, the spectator may interact, and even intervene, in the construction of genre, making it a space of contention where power is negotiated through the spectator's gaze. Cinema is not, then, a mimetic device that would attempt to offer concrete truths through the stability of the spectator's gaze supposedly conferring upon him knowledge relating to verifiable, discernible facts about an objective, outside world in a visual manner. Rather, cinema threatens to 'deterritorialise' the spectator and destabilise his gaze by subsuming him into a fetishised cinematic space and commodifying the visual in order to negate the spectator's intervention and undermine his ability to intervene and determine objective truth. Film, in other words, as a cultural product consumed visually within the context of market demands, ultimately communicates much more than an aesthetic awareness of narrative structures. Ironically, the illusion of reality communicated by the cinematic narrative masks the 'invisible hand of the market', described by Adam Smith, thus ensuring the perpetuation of the logic of capital.[1] In his article, 'Film Theory and the Revolt Against Master Narratives', Bill Nichols notes a fetishisation of the visual as a primary characteristic of modernity in which he includes video, digital graphics, art, performance pieces, and virtual realities as well as film as components of the 'symbolic economies of knowledge production' (2000: 42) that mould social identity. Labour, Nichols asserts, imbues such objects with an exchange value. The fact that these objects come to be desired, then, establishes the 'basis for commodity fetishism as a symptomatic expression of the symbolic economy of capital' (2000: 44).

Genre understood as a discursive mode allows for the global circulation of capital and, more importantly, allows for the active interaction on the part of the spectator whose gaze may legitimise the reality represented in cinema or subvert it. The purpose of this chapter, then, is to analyse the interpenetration of culture and capital in two recent Spanish films: *Airbag* (Juanma Bajo Ulloa, 1997) and *Smoking Room* (Roger Gual and Julio Wallovits, 2002). These two films, I argue, offer a curious aesthetic juxtaposition and present a unique insight into the influence of capital on cultural production in Spain. On a superficial level, these two films seemingly have nothing in common and would be at opposite ends of the genre spectrum. Dismissed by critics as a *película gamberra*, *Airbag* set box-office records in Spain with scenes of gratuitous violence, explicit sex and blatant drug use that seemingly invoke the Hollywood formula for big-budget blockbusters. *Smoking Room*, on the other hand, offers a minimalist aesthetic typically associated with an 'indie' film tradition that seemingly adheres to the tenets of such Dogma 95 directors as Lars von Trier. Inspired by such Cassavetes films as *Faces* (1968) and *Husbands* (1970), Gual and Wallovits achieve a cinéma-vérité quality through the use of digital cameras while suppressing special effects and soundtrack in favour of dramatic action motivated by dialogue and personal conflict. Whereas *Airbag* seems to 'buy in' to such (stereo)typical Hollywood genres as melodrama, film noir, gangster films, road movies, coming-of-age films, buddy flicks and the comedy of manners, *Smoking Room* is notoriously devoid of any perceived genre framework suggesting an intentional distance from the aesthetics associated with Hollywood.[2] What these two films have in common, however, is an exploration of capital and its influence on both physical and narrative space, culture and identity. Through a self-aware aesthetic that acknowledges both the spectator's consumerist gaze and their own commodified status, both *Airbag* and *Smoking Room* expose the machinations of capital that mould the construction of the films themselves while at the same time they depict the destabilising effects brought about by the flow of capital across regional, national and transnational borders.

Airbag 'goes Hollywood'

I would like to begin the discussion of *Airbag* with a quote that frames the polemic surrounding the film's use of techniques typically associated with Hollywood blockbuster films. In *El Criticón*, Antonio Méndez Casanova writes,

> A change of pace for the overrated director and screenwriter Juanma Bajo Ulloa, who on this occasion opts for a story that attempts to mix esperpentic black comedy, social satire, road movie and over-the-top adventure with touches of the absurd, only to achieve a tasteless con-coction of enormous commercial success . . . The cause of the com-mercial triumph is clear. Disguise the vulgarity of the film through the manufacture of a Hispanic product that integrates the aesthetic model of American cinematic style. (2002)[3]

This review, like many others, dismisses the aesthetic quality of the film by the young Basque director by obeying an artistic hierarchy erected upon a dialectic that is not only false but also archaic and classist as well. The review suggests that what it considers to be aes-thetic quality and commercial success mutually exclude each other. This position accepts only one of two possibilities: if the film (or any type of artistic creation for that matter) witnesses any sort of com-mercial success, this presupposes a low aesthetic quality; while, on the other hand, a film of high aesthetic quality is doomed to suffer a lack of commercial success. Moreover, in the case of *Airbag*, vitriol aimed at its offensive vulgarity equates bad taste with commercial success by the fact that the film in question appropriates a specific-ally American (read Hollywood) style of filmmaking that supposedly appeals to the lowest common denominator for the sole purpose of increasing earnings.[4]

This binary opposition projects a myopic vision that not only underestimates a film because of a commercial success, but, more-over, disdains a Spanish film because it imitates the generic conven-tions and aesthetic style perceived as American. I suggest that *Airbag* polemicises this tendency to adhere to easy dichotomies that oppose what is supposedly a Spanish, national (non-commercial) cinema from specifically American Hollywood movies that market block-busters not on stories, character and dialogue but with mind-numbing special effects and explosions, scintillating scenes of heterosexual sex and gratuitous violence, and formulaic plots and stock characters of little psychological depth. *Airbag* represents a contradiction in Bajo Ulloa's cinematic style developed in his first two feature films, *Alas de mariposa/Butterfly Wings* (1991) and *La madre muerta/The Dead Mother* (1993). Both films exhibit a narra-tive and stylistic sophistication, touch on themes of feminine trauma and masculine violence, offer a dark treatment of family psychology, and incorporate innovative visual techniques. Especially when we consider the previous cinematic endeavours, the manic energy, overly aestheticised violence and wanton sexuality would seem to support the notion that Bajo Ulloa 'sold out' his artistic integrity to go 'Hollywood'. Yet, a deeper reading of this film reveals a more subtle self-aware interrogation of the influence of Hollywood films and genres on Spanish cinema in the era of globalisation.

Airbag at several moments demonstrates a keen consciousness about its own visual construction as it evokes stylistic references to American cinema of such directors as Quentin Tarantino, John Woo and Oliver Stone. Bajo Ulloa's film blends styles and confuses tropes from genres considered typical American cinematic staples like melodrama, thrillers, noir, road movies, coming-of-age, screwballs, romantic comedy and comedy of errors. Likewise, he populates scene after scene with visual cues that reference such icons of American film and television as *Star Wars* (George Lucas, 1977), Indiana Jones, *Starsky and Hutch*, and even *Little House on the Prairie*. What is more, such overt references to American pop culture find themselves juxtaposed alongside other forms of cultural production more typi-cally associated with Iberian and Hispanic culture ranging from the traditional – *tortilla de patatas* (Spanish omelette), Golden Age comedies, *pelota vasca* and folkloric Basque clothing – to the realm of mass media – South American telenovelas, soccer and the star power of actors like Javier Bardem – and even including the exotic allure of contraband – Brazilian prostitutes, Portuguese drug runners and a mysterious, beautiful Portuguese assassin who practises black magic. Add to this uncanny moments of ironic awareness where char-acters on screen become acutely conscious of the spectator's presence and, more importantly, his gaze, and *Airbag* can be understood to offer a self-aware critique of the ways in which capital subsumes diverse modes of cultural production to offer them as fetishised commodities for the spectator's consumption. Boundaries – generic, geographic, social and cultural – are blurred, to borrow from the title of Bill Nichols's book on documentary film, as people, goods and cultural production move across borders propelled by the demands of and desires for capital.

Airbag follows Juantxo (Karra Elejalde), a young man from a well-off family in the Basque upper class, who loses his wedding ring, valued at 30 million pesetas, in the 'dark corners' of a *mulata* prostitute during his bachelor party. Setting out to recover the lost ring takes Juantxo and his two friends, Konradín and Pako, from bordello to bordello across the Basque Country and unleashes a series of implausible events that involve them with Spanish Mafiosi, Portuguese drug traffickers, paedophiliac politicians, philosophical *Guardia Civiles* and exotic assassins. With its scenes of chaotic shootouts, wild car chases, exaggerated explosions, scatological humour, drug abuse and lustful sex, *Airbag* most definitely offers an artistic detour in the cinematic production of Bajo Ulloa that frustrates any attempt to categorise the Basque director. Rob Stone, for example, in his book *Spanish Cinema*, connects Bajo Ulloa with Álex de la Iglesia as two Basque directors that do not follow the social, militant line of other directors from that region like Imanol Uribe, Montxo Armendáriz, Ana Díez, Víctor Erice or, in some films, Julio Medem, which consequently, argues the author, poises them dangerously close to the brink of anonymity. Stone declares, 'In the nominally Basque cinema of the new millennium De La Iglesia and Bajo Ulloa are typical of a generation that makes films for pleasure instead of political commitment or militancy. Both are talented filmmakers with unusual visual flair; yet, in disregarding their roots in Basque cinema, they might be risking anonymity' (2002: 154–5).

Such a commentary would seem to pigeonhole both the directors Stone mentions as well as Basque film in general. I share the opinion of Mark Allinson in his article 'Not Matadors, Not Natural Born Killers: Violence in Three Films by Young Spanish Directors' (1997) where he examines the duality of films like *El día de la bestia/The Day of the Beast* (Álex de la Iglesia, 1995), *Nadie hablará de nosotros cuando hayamos muerto* (Agustín Díaz Yanes, 1995) and *Tesis/Thesis* (Alejandro Amenábar, 1996). According to Allinson, the violence in the films mentioned reveals the influence of Hollywood in Spanish cinema, which, ironically, liberates a new generation of directors from the 'introspective, politically engaged or otherwise commercially unpopular manifestations of violence'. These films represent, then, a rupture with the personal vision of 'auteurs' like Carlos Saura, Pedro Almodóvar, Julio Medem and others who explore the Spanish condition (in national and cinematic terms), investigate issues of memory and trauma, and 'obsess' over Spanish idiosyncrasies. Nevertheless, Allinson affirms that the new films and the new directors employ violence in their films in a way that reconciles the perceived discrepancy between art (and/or message) and commercial attraction. Incorporating violence allows them also to question its excess, offer self-referential commentaries about its use, and propose investigations about its cultural relevance.

As the article was published the same year in which *Airbag* appeared in theatres, Allinson does not mention the film, but it does not require much effort to extend his argument to include Bajo Ulloa's film, since it embodies the 'duality' signalled by Allinson in the films mentioned above. The juxtaposition or, more accurately, the interpenetration, of generic conventions and stylistic characteristics typically associated with Hollywood blockbusters with thematic elements and narrative structures associated with Spanish culture endow *Airbag* with a self-referential hybridity.[5] The scene that opens *Airbag* prepares the reader for a film with an aesthetically blurred identity when the viewer observes a game of *pelota vasca* while the players and spectators come in and out of focus as the voices of the commentators in Spanish and Basque blend into each other and become indecipherable. Many other scenes offer a similar juxtaposition. For example, after the match, Juantxo's father, Don Serafín (the famous Basque chef Karlos Arguiñano), participates in a contest of *tortilla rusa* in which several people must each consume an omelette, only one of which is not poisoned, and the survivor wins sixty million pesetas. The light in this scene enters at distorted angles, the atmosphere is darkened by cigarette and cigar smoke, and figures are barely visible in the shadows, all of which creates a visual composition very similar to that typically associated with American film noir of the 1930s and 1940s. Nevertheless, rather than a gun, the weapon of choice is an omelette with poisoned mushrooms prepared by a French chef. When one of the participants excuses himself from the competition and the others die, Don Serafín, as a (stereo)typical Spaniard, considers it poor taste to eat without bread or wine and refuses to consume the tortilla until he can enjoy it '*en condiciones*'.

Together with the treatment of the gastronomic elements and the social institutions mentioned above, the narrative structure of *Airbag* culminates with a convention normally associated with Golden Age comedies: the wedding. Many times the wedding at the conclusion of a comedy functioned as a kind of deus ex machina to restore the social order and re-establish aesthetic harmony, but in *Airbag* it provokes destabilisation when the *mulata* prostitute with whom Juantxo had fallen in love interrupts the ceremony, rescues Juantxo from an arranged but certainly loveless marriage, and flees with him in a supposedly happy ending. The juxtaposition of a religious ceremony with Basque dancers dressed in folkloric attire and members of the upper bourgeoisie in attendance alongside prostitutes of diverse ethnic identities dancing aerobics incites an absurd musical scene where the traditional Basque rhythms fuse with a pop song performed by Albert Pla (who also plays a priest in the film).[6]

Similarly, the film often offers the viewer such traditional elements of Spanish and Basque culture as the regional clothing of the Basque Country, other forms of regional music as well as Spanish *coplas*, and scenes of peasants walking along the side of the road or working in the fields alongside a highway. Such a 'pre-modern' identity contrasts with the infiltration of a consumer culture exemplified by the overabundance of mobile phones and brand names like Volvo, Marlboro, Mizuno, Cadillac and Goodyear. Far from lamenting the loss of the former or celebrating the presence of the latter, *Airbag* problematises the possibility of maintaining a traditional cultural identity in the era of global capitalism, and reveals a hybridity that exposes the interpenetration of traditional and modern elements that have been assimilated into the 'logic' of late capitalism.

Understanding *Airbag* then, within the framework of global capitalism and consumer culture, becomes indispensable. This fusion between the national and the foreign, the sacred and the profane, the highbrow and the lowbrow, the traditional and the (post)modern needs to be understood as a self-reflection about the place of the film itself within a culture of consumption and mass media. As Juantxo's fiancée, Araceli (Raquel Meroño), in her wedding dress, prepares for the ceremony her gaze acquires ideological repercussions while she and her family watch a Latin American telenovela, ironically titled *Amor obsoleto* (*Obsolete Love*), in which the protagonist of the television programme undertakes a mythical search for his father. In a large, austere room with stone floors, incense swings above the characters as the women discuss Juantxo's disappearance while the men play cards. Organ music emanating from a television that projects the image of a saint confers a sacred aura to the box as it rests atop a pedestal in the centre of the expansive room. Araceli contemplates herself in the wedding dress between two mirrors, but runs to the television and changes the channel when she realises *Amor obsoleto* is about to begin. Ironically, the television substitutes for the mirrors when Araceli sees herself in Miranda, the female character of the telenovela, who struggles to understand why José Alberto (Javier Bardem) must leave her only days before their wedding. Visually, the identification between Araceli and the female character is compounded with a graphic match. After José Alberto tells her he plans to return once he finds his biological father, the camera slowly zooms in on Miranda's tearful eyes. A quick cut to a slow zoom on Araceli's tearful eyes underscores her cathartic identification with Miranda's plight. The camera cuts back and forth between Miranda and Araceli several times, slowly closing in on their eyes, suggesting the television as a mirror image in which Araceli sees her own situation reflected. Nevertheless, Araceli's gaze is ultimately reflected by the television, and her consumption transforms into a catharsis that normalises and legitimises the 'illusion' of the telenovela's narrative and, more importantly, the ideology behind it. Yet, Araceli's gaze, as our own, becomes demystified if we consider it part of a mise-en-abyme, as it is suggested at the outset of the scene by the two mirrors facing each other. Her gaze, that is, reflects our own and elicits our own consumption of *Airbag* as we voyeuristically watch her as she watches the telenovela.

The telenovela, moreover, anachronic and of an aesthetic quality beyond camp, breaks the 'illusion' of the narrative as microphones appear over the heads of the actors, portions of the set collapse, and production assistants scurry as the camera pans toward them. Such scenes where the viewer becomes keenly aware of the construction of the narrative he or she is viewing are complemented by inverse scenes in *Airbag* when the characters demonstrate an ironic awareness of their position as objects observed by the camera and consumed by a spectator. For example, as Juantxo drives, the movie suddenly and unexpectedly transforms into an advertisement when a hand appears through the sunroof of the car with an energy drink named 'Reanimator'. Overtly mocking the product placement associated with Hollywood blockbusters, Juantxo gulps down the fictitious drink with exaggerated emphasis and comments on its refreshing effects, giving the 'thumbs up' while openly conscious of the consumer's gaze. These examples of 'meta-observation' stress more than an ironic self-awareness on the part of *Airbag* about its own generic or narrative construction, but, more importantly reveal an understanding of its own commercial production and consumption with a capitalist system proposing genre, then, as a contentious space where power and ideology are negotiated with the spectator.

In general, the path of a 'road movie' acquires a metaphoric value where the journey through physical spaces represents an evolution in the character toward some sort of self-understanding or anagnorisis. For *Airbag*, such a genre trope acquires a double meaning. As Mafiosi and assassins chase after the three protagonists while a truckload of South American prostitutes race toward them from Portugal, such a movement across borders evokes the transnational and transregional migrations of people, capital and cultural production evoked in the film. *Airbag*, likewise, journeys inward to explore its own cultural and commercial identity through a fusion of aesthetic conventions that expose the film with a space in which genre discourses travel beyond national boundaries to intersect and interact. The aesthetic chaos and confusion provoked by this interaction makes us acutely aware of the spectator's gaze and, in turn, the power behind the representation of reality constructed through genre.

A cinema of resistance, a resistance of cinema: *Smoking Room's* anti-Hollywood aesthetic

Smoking Room depicts the reactions of several employees in a Spanish subsidiary of an American multinational company that imposes its own corporate culture by forcing its workers to smoke outside. Seen as a significant cultural marker associated with Spanish national identity, one especially combative worker begins to circulate a petition and accumulate signatures requesting an abandoned storage room be transformed into a *sala de fumar*. Fear, paranoia, selfishness, cowardice and envy sabotage the attempts at solidarity and thwart any possibility for reserving and protecting any semblance of a contestatory space in which to protect them, even one seemingly as silly and superficial as a room for smoking, from the demands of and desires for capital. Much like *Airbag*, physical spaces in *Smoking Room* act as more than mere backdrops for the film's dialogue or action, but acquire a metaphorical significance related to the commodification of culture and its effects on individual, national and cinematic identity. Yet, whereas the characters in *Airbag* transgress boundaries travelling fluidly across geographic and generic borders, the vast majority of *Smoking Room* is set inside the austere interior of the building with its cold atmosphere of the isolated offices, closed doors and clouded glass windows. Visually, then, the film offers no recognisable markers with which to locate the characters but, rather, emphasises the alienation and dehumanisation of the individual characters. Even the few outside scenes destabilise the viewer with extreme close-up shots at street level that impede any attempt to discern spatial markers and identify the Spanish city, and with medium shots on rooftops that provoke vertigo in the viewer by setting characters against an open sky. Filmed on digital video, the movie's texture endows the film with a realistic drive and immediacy which, along with the noticeable lack of any type of soundtrack or sound effects, creates an unsettling, ironic minimalist aesthetic style. Extremely tight close-up shots, shaky camera movement, staggered reframed cuts and quick edits within extended scenes frustrate continuity and destabilise the viewer to further deepen the sense of dislocation, disconnection and displacement. The often improvised dialogue, quick and choppy, likewise provokes a sense of imbalance and anguish in the viewer where the futility of their actions is exacerbated by the furious rhythm and superficial pseudo-intellectual themes of their discussions.

The focus on character-driven dialogue, the lack of sound and special effects, the absence of music, the attention to action motivated by character conflict (rather than plot devices), the lack of props and the use of hand-held cameras not only situate *Smoking Room* at the opposite end of the aesthetic spectrum from *Airbag*, but also suggest an intentional decision on the part of the directors to avoid those techniques specifically associated with Hollywood filmmaking. Yet, while *Smoking Room* overtly avoids the tropes of American filmmaking and the preoccupation of the characters revolves around the preservation of cultural idiosyncrasies associated with some kind of Spanish national identity, Wallovits' and Gual's film exudes nothing in terms of genre that might connect it with films considered to be 'Spanish' or exemplary of Spain's national cinema. Ironically, *Smoking Room*, with its blatant absence of identifiable generic markers, shares this sense of displacement, dislocation and deterritorialisation with *Airbag*, considered un-Spanish precisely because of its integration of genres specifically considered 'Hollywood'. Interestingly, the characteristics of *Smoking Room*, especially the lack of generic devices, coincides almost exactly with the those proposed in the 'Vow of Chastity' that is part of the Manifesto for Dogma 95 proposed by Lars von Trier and Thomas Vinterberg as a way to create an alternative, international cinema that might oppose the dominance of Hollywood films. Moreover, these techniques suggest a desire to jar the viewer out of his complacent consumption of the film's narrative, thus demystifying the film's own construction and what von Trier and Vinterberg call 'an illusion of pathos and an illusion of love' (1995) perpetuated by Hollywood. Yet, in her article 'Dogma 95: A Small Nation's Response to Globalisation', Mette Hjort attests that the aesthetic rules outlined in the 'Vow of Chastity' have less to do with innovating an avant-garde form of cinematic expression and more overtly reveal 'the inequalities of globalising processes . . . as a defence of the margins of cinematic production [to which] small nations and minor cinemas inevitably are' (2003: 31). At its heart, then, Dogma 95 is supremely concerned with the homogenising effects of capital and offers itself as a means to contest the hegemony of Hollywood film in both aesthetic and economic terms.

In *Todo por un largo: diario de* Smoking Room, Roger Gual curiously distances himself from any intentional emulation of the Dogma 95 aesthetic, fearing they would be seen as a 'copia española y barata' ('cheap Spanish knock-offs') of Lars von Trier: 'I would be upset if they called us the Spanish dogma, or the Cassavetes of 2001' (2003: 62).[7] The use of digital video cameras to produce *Smoking Room*, for example, has less to do, it turns out, with evoking a kind of cinéma-vérité and more with the prohibitive cost of film. But Gual does suggest a revolutionary resistance to the film aesthetic and marketing techniques typically associated with Hollywood film production, referring to his project as 'la guerrilla del cine' ('guerrilla filmmaking').[8] Once their requests for funding from Canal+ and TVE had been rejected, Gual, contemplating the possibility of soliciting money from the Spanish government, offers the following distinction about so-called independent film, 'This is what I call independent film, independent film with public money doesn't do much for me. Now, if they were to tell us they were giving us the money and we could do the movie we'd be much more at ease, long live the "dependent" film' (2003: 40).[9] Ironically, despite Gual's desire to distance himself from the aesthetic of Dogma 95, his inability to access capital not only mirrors the issues of dominance and subjection at the thematic heart of *Smoking Room*, but exemplifies the economic dangers that threaten the production of truly independent films at the margins of mainstream commercial cinema as Hjort outlined above. Despite the increased globalisation of film production, the international dominance of the Hollywood industry in international markets problematises a 'national cinema's' ability to thrive, suggests Ana M. López in 'Facing up to Hollywood'. The historical access to distribution outlets, the easy ability to market themselves, and the technological sophistication establish the hegemonic occupation of Hollywood films in foreign markets and force 'national cinemas' into a 'dialogue with Hollywood' (2000: 423–4).

On a narrative level, the employees find themselves in a similar predicament in which they face an 'occupation' by a hegemonic American presence. Yet, while the Spanish employees, led by the confrontational Ramírez, attempt to resist the loss of hegemonic space by collecting signatures to present to 'los americanos', the viewer never sees any human representative of the American company.[10] Rather, the American presence and the infiltration of capital are reified in an imposing, glowing Coca-Cola machine that drones monotonously, keeping guard outside the storage room in question. Space, physical and cinematic, is not overtaken by individuals but infiltrated by the symbols of capital that impose themselves and establish spatial hegemony, thus impeding self-representation. Physical spaces in *Smoking Room*, like the cinematic space of the film itself, become a symbolic battleground in which individual identity is protected or relinquished as capital begins to impose its hegemony in both spatial and psychological terms.

Ramírez's understanding of this unused space and our understanding of *Smoking Room*'s cinematic space coincides with Edward Soja's notion of 'Thirdspace' in which physical, built environments exist simultaneously as imagined, conceived symbolic spaces and interact with individual and collective awareness becoming 'lived' social spaces. Mysterious, subliminal and secretive, these social spaces become 'sites of struggle' and 'spaces of representation'

(1996: 68) where the physical, symbolic and ideological planes interact simultaneously to construct consciousness. The construction of
space acquires an 'illusion of transparency', a phrase Soja borrows
from Lefebvre (1991), that denies the underlying interplay of power
and dominates individual and collective awareness by endowing the
material world with a seemingly invisible innocent, and even ludic,
nature. 'These spaces', declares Soja, 'are also vitally filled with
politics and ideology, with the real and imagined intertwined, and
with capitalism, racism, patriarchy, and other material spatial practices that concretise the social relations of production, reproduction,
exploitation, domination, and subjection' (1996: 68). If understood
in spatial terms, genre, and film in a larger sense, may similarly be
seen as a 'space of representation' in which individuals, as spectators, contend with the 'illusion of transparency' that masks the negotiations of power, identity and ideology with narrative.

When Ramírez approaches Rubio to sign the petition, he literally proposes the *sala de fumar* as a 'space of representation'
within which one might express cultural difference and resist
assimilation into the 'logic of capital'. While Ramírez views the
petition, perhaps naively, as an inherent right for a worker to
demand respect, Rubio, perhaps more astutely than Ramírez, sees
the personal political repercussions that could threaten his ascent
within the company's hierarchy and his incorporation into a space
of hegemony. Whereas Ramírez seeks solidarity among the
workers to demand a space for self-representation, Rubio focuses
on his individual survival and desire to occupy a space of power
within the corporate infrastructure. The conversation is presented
in standard shot/reverse shot close-ups to communicate the dialogue exchange, but with a slight alteration. The camera, positioned behind the listener above his shoulder, captures the back of
Ramirez's head and right shoulder as Rubio talks and part of
Rubio's head and left shoulder as Ramirez speaks. Each, then,
becomes an obstacle to the other impeding the co-existence of both
a contestatory and hegemonic space.

Ramírez's own desire for resistance transforms into anarchic revolution after he is confronted and beaten by his fellow co-workers
when he refuses to take their names off the list. He returns late at
night, douses the room with gasoline and ignites it with a lit cigarette, destroying the physical space in an attempt to purge it of its
symbolic value as a site of dominance and subjection. As the flames

engulf the room, the screen fades to white and cuts to black. Then, as two characters, Fernández and Martínez, begin a dialogue off screen, the scene fades in to still shots of empty lit rooms in the building, each a setting for a previous dialogue, conflict or argument. Without the presence of human beings, the spaces themselves become protagonists, ironically underscoring their ideological significance and influence over the employees that work there. In their dialogue, the two men establish urban space as a site of conflict and tension that moulds and frames human awareness, infusing it with fear and alienation. Fernández explains, 'The city makes you feel alone. Helpless and vulnerable. The city makes us all feel a little crazy.'[11]

The men ironically expose what David Harvey refers to as the 'urbanisation of consciousness' where the symbolic order of the material environment imposes 'ways of thinking and doing which reinforce existing patterns of social life' (1989: 250). When Martínez declares that the violence and fear infused in individuals by the city is 'lo normal', Fernández counters, stating, 'It depends. It remains to be seen. It remains to be seen what is normal, right? Is it normal what we think is normal? We are living in a world of crazy people. What is normal isn't normal.'[12] By questioning *lo normal* they dismantle the 'illusion of transparency' and reveal the patterns of capital that permeate the spaces of the building and instil individuals with narcissistic fetishes within an atmosphere of alienation and impossible self-realisation.

Similarly, such an interrogation of *lo normal* extends to the film itself in which *Smoking Room*'s awareness of its own construction implicitly suggests an awareness of the spectator's gaze and, thereby, offers the film as a 'site of struggle'. The sense of deterritorialisation expressed by the two men quickly, ironically, dissipates, and the last scene of *Smoking Room* seems to contradict the apparent impossibility of self-realisation with a suggestion of solidarity, cohesion and camaraderie among the various characters. The final scene ironically integrates an 'illusion of transparency' by filming on 16mm film rather than digital video, which endows the composition with a smooth appearance and projects steadiness and continuity, avoiding the abrupt edits seen throughout the film. This abrupt alteration in the texture of the visual image at the end of *Smoking Room* demonstrates both an awareness of the spectator's gaze and an understanding of the film itself as a 'space of representation' that has the capacity either to shock its audience with quick edits and shaky camera movements or lull its viewers with a ludic 'illusion'. Over the course of *Smoking Room*, as Ramírez futilely attempts to motivate support for 'cultural' resistance, another character gathers signatures for a different kind of cultural phenomenon: a soccer game. The physical space of the soccer field offers not the opportunity for resistance and revolution but proposes an avenue of escape where solidarity is achieved only in the most frivolous of circumstances. Visually, the texture of the scene is smoother, the choppiness and movement are substituted with longer takes that follow individual characters as they play. Seemingly liberated from the confines of the office and their own pettiness, the characters seem to have achieved the solidarity they were unable to attain earlier.[13] As the characters play, cigarettes hanging from their mouths, Joan Manuel Serrat's 'Hoy puede ser un gran día' from his 1981 album *En tránsito* plays in the background. The only music of any kind in the film, the upbeat tempo of the song parodies the light-hearted sounds of mass media pop music while it mirrors the contentment of the characters as they defeat the opposing team of mechanics from the garage across the street. With the upbeat music, the more 'transparent' film techniques, and ludic atmosphere of the soccer game, the final scene in *Smoking Room* not only abandons its 'avant-garde' techniques but feels more like a commercial attempting to sell the viewer the bliss of a happy ending.[14] Yet, the lyrics' call for individual responsibility and moral resistance to mediocrity underscores the characters' hypocrisy and moral vacuity. Culture, then, is presented in the last scene with two opposing possibilities. While Serrat's song suggests culture as a space for resistance and urges self-realisation, the soccer game offers a place of pleasure and acts as a utopian escape that masks and, thus, perpetuates the dominance behind the 'illusion of transparency'.

A happy ending?

If genre may be understood in spatial terms as a terrain occupied by discourse, then what both *Airbag* and *Smoking Room* expose is the fluidity, not the fixity, of the boundaries that define and delimit it. While the former assimilates a wide range of genres, tropes, styles and conventions associated with Hollywood blockbusters, the latter distances itself from any aesthetic characteristic that might suggest an adherence to a discernible Hollywood style or genre. Yet, what both *Airbag* and *Smoking Room* reveal, by their appropriation of Hollywood aesthetics or their rejection of it, is a poignant commentary on capital's ability to infiltrate the space of genre and transgress national, regional, cultural and aesthetic borders in the era of globalisation. By fracturing the symmetry of the narrative's illusion these films ironically recognise the spectator's gaze and, in so doing, reveal their own status as fetishised, commodified objects. Film, and cultural production in general, can be understood, then, as a 'space of representation' that becomes battleground, a space of contention and negotiation. The awareness of *Airbag* and *Smoking Room* toward the spectator demonstrates a keen understanding of the power of the viewer's gaze that may legitimise the narrative's ludic illusion or pierce through its transparency.

Notes

1 Smith refers to the 'invisible hand' to address the factors that motivate individual decisions and which seemingly subvert free will, 'As every individual, therefore, endeavours as much as he can both to employ his capital in the support of domestic industry, and so to direct that industry that its produce may be of the greatest value; every individual necessarily labours to render the annual revenue of the society as great as he can. He generally, indeed, neither intends to promote the public interest, nor knows how much he is promoting it. By preferring the support of domestic to that of foreign industry, he intends only his own security; and by directing that industry in such a manner as its produce may be of the greatest value, he intends only his own gain, and he is in this, as in may other cases, led by an invisible hand to promote an end which was no part of his intention' (2003: 572).

2 It may be argued that *Smoking Room* might be seen as a kind of 'corporate drama' in the vein of such films as *Wall Street* (Oliver Stone, 1987), *Glengarry Glen Ross* (James Foley, 1992), *The Big Kahuna* (John Swanbeck, 1999) and *The Boiler Room* (Ben Younger, 2000), among others. Interestingly, another recent Spanish film, *El método/The Method* (Marcelo Piñeyro, 2005), adapted from the play *El método Gronhölm*, strikes the same minimalist chord as *Smoking Room* and offers a strong critique of corporate culture. One may even propose a genealogy of Spanish films with a focus on corporate culture that stretch back to the early 1970s with such films as *Los nuevos españoles* (Roberto Bodegas, 1974), *Reina Zanahoria* (Gonzalo Suárez, 1977) and *Las verdes praderas* (José Luis Garci, 1979).

3 'Cambio de registro del sobrevalorado director y guionista Juanma Bajo Ulloa, que en esta ocasión opta por una historia que pretende mixturar comedia esperpéntica, sátira social, road movie y aventura enloquecida con toques absurdos, logrando únicamente un desaborido potingue de enorme éxito comercial . . . La causa del triunfo comercial es clara. Coartar la vulgaridad del film en la facturación de un producto hispano con una maquetación al estilo americano.'

4 In 1997, *Airbag* was the highest grossing Spanish film, earning €7,205,891.99. At the time, it was the Spanish film that had earned the most money at the box office. However, it was later surpassed a year later by *Torrente: el brazo tonto de la* ley (Santiago Segura, 1998) with €10,902,631.95. *Torrente* was later surpassed by *Torrente 2: Misión en Marbella* (Santiago Segura, 2001) with €22,142,173.13. *Torrente 3, el protector* (Santiago Segura, 2005), however, did not take the record from *Torrente 2*, earning a 'meagre' €18,168,171.58. All statistics on box-office earnings in Spain come from the database at the web page for Spain's Ministerio de Cultura at www.mcu.es/bbddpeliculas/cargarFiltro.do?layout=bbddpeliculas&cache=init&language=es.

5 Such hybridity, 'duality' for Allinson or 'double-coding' according to the definition of postmodernism proposed by Charles Jencks (1986), suggests what Marsha Kinder calls 'transcultural reinscription' in her landmark study on Spanish film, *Blood Cinema*. Her term, moreover, seems more appropriate as it refers to the appropriation of hegemonic cinematic traditions by the culturally colonised to build a syncretic film language. For Kinder, like Allinson, this transgression of artistic borders and the apparent conflict between cinematic conventions appropriated from cultures outside Spain ultimately test the boundaries of what might be considered a 'national cinema' and possibly 'carv[e] out a new aesthetic language' (1993: 11).

6 Curiously, this final scene is strikingly similar to the last scene in Pedro Lazaga's *El turismo es un gran invento* (1968), in which a small Aragonese town rejoices in song and dance a traditional jota at the prospect of building a parador which would attract tourism. Whether or not Bajo Ulloa intentionally attempts to imitate this scene is unclear, but both films do offer a critical reading of the effects of capital on cultural identity and cultural production.

7 'Me indignaría que nos llamaran el dogma español, o el Cassavetes del 2001.'

8 Throughout the diary, Gual sets himself (and those involved in the filming of *Smoking Room*) apart from mainstream film, epitomised in Spain by Alejandro Amenábar, who Gual sarcastically refers to as the 'niño prodigio' (2003: 44). He also jokingly suggests that a way to raise capital for the film would be to imitate Hollywood by including

'product placement' (2003: 41) and convert the film into a kind of cinematic billboard. (This idea is followed closely by the possibility of robbing a bank.) When Planeta 2010 expresses interest in the film, but asks Gual to show what they have to a 'target group', he vehemently refuses on the basis that submitting film process to market strategies would compromise his artistic integrity. The representatives at Planeta 2010 chastise the directors, claiming that they would have no future in Hollywood where all films are 'tested' first. This prompts Gual to ponder, '¿Quién quiere ir a Hollywood de todos modos? Estos tíos no tienen ni puta idea de con quiénes hablan' (Who wants to go to Hollywood anyway? These guys don't have a fucking idea who they're talking to) (2003: 74). Ironically, before the suggestion to test the film, Gual and others involved in the film had jokingly toyed with the idea of a possible Hollywood remake of their independent, guerrilla film, 'El tema del remake con Robert De Niro, Kevin Spacey, Al Pacino y Ed Harris lo dejamos para otro proyecto, pensamos que no era el momento' (We left the talk of a remake with Robert De Niro, Kevin Spacey, Al Pacino and Ed Harris for another project, we didn't think it was the time or place) (2003: 73).

9 'Esto es lo que yo llamo cine independiente, no me va el cine independiente con dinero público. Ahora si nos dijeran que nos dan la pasta y podemos hacer la peli mucho más tranquilos, bienvenido el cine "dependiente".'

10 In this regard, *Smoking Room* is strikingly similar to Luis García Berlanga's 1953 film *Bienvenido Mister Marshall*. Though the 'Americans' never appear physically, the social and psychological effects of their supposed visit and, especially, the promise of capital and modernisation are patently and painfully clear.

11 'La ciudad te hace sentir sólo. Como desamparado, vulnerable. La ciudad nos hace sentir a todos uno poco locos.'

12 'Depende. Está por ver. Está por ver qué es normal, ¿no? ¿Es normal lo que es normal para nosotros? Estamos viviendo en un mundo de locos. Lo normal no es lo normal.'

13 The script explicitly notes that this final scene is the first, and only, in an exterior setting away from the offices and building: 'Partimos de un cielo azul refulgente. Finalmente, estamos al aire libre. Se ven árboles, se escuchan pájaros. Detrás de ellos comienzan a escucharse voces que grieten y ríen. Es un campo de fútbol improvisado, sobre un hermoso césped de color verde, todos los empleados de la oficina – excepto Ramírez, Sotomayor y Armero – corren de un lado para otro. Patean con entusiasmo la pelota, y parecen funcionar muy efectivamente como un equipo conjuntado' ('Open with a bright, blue sky. Finally, we are outside. You can see trees, and you can hear birds. Behind them you

start to hear voices that yell and laugh. It is an improvised soccer field, upon a beautiful field of green grass, all the employees of the office – except Ramírez, Sotomayor and Armero – run from one end to the other. They kick the ball with enthusiasm, and seem to function very effectively as a team') (2003: 140).
14 Interestingly, Roger Gual worked freelance in advertising for a time in New York City while he studied film.

References

Allinson, Mark (1997) 'Not Matadors, Not Natural Born Killers: Violence in Three Films by Young Spanish Directors', *Bulletin of Hispanic Studies* (Liverpool), 74, 315–30.

Altman, Rick (1999) *Film/Genre*, London: BFI.

Gledhill, Christine (2000) 'Rethinking Genre', in Christine Gledhill and Linda Williams (eds), *Reinventing Film Studies*, London and New York: Arnold and Oxford University Press, 221–43.

Gual, Roger (2003) *Todo por un largo: diario de* Smoking Room, Madrid: Ocho y medio, Libros de cine.

Harvey, David (1989) *The Urban Experience*, Baltimore: Johns Hopkins University Press.

Hjort, Mette (2003) 'Dogma 95: A Small Nation's Response to Globalisation', in Mette Hjort and Scott Mackenzie (eds), *Purity and Provocation: Dogma 95*, London: BFI, 31–47.

Jencks, Charles (1986) *What is Postmodernism?*, New York: St Martin's Press.

Kinder, Marsha (1993) *Blood Cinema: The Reconstruction of National Identity in Spain*, Berkeley: University of California Press.

Langford, Barry (2005) *Film Genre: Hollywood and Beyond*, Edinburgh: Edinburgh University Press.

Lefebvre, Henri (1991) *The Production of Space*. Donald Nicholson-Smith (trans.), Malden, MA: Blackwell Publishers.

López, Ana M. (2000) 'Facing up to Hollywood', in Christine Gledhill and Linda Williams (eds), *Reinventing Film Studies*, London and New York Arnold and Oxford University Press, 419–37.

Méndez Casanova, Antonio (2002) 'Airbag [Review]', www.alohacriticon. com/elcriticon/modules.php?name=News&file=print&sid=386.

Nichols, Bill (1994) *Blurred Boundaries: Questions of Meaning in Contemporary Culture*, Bloomington: Indiana University Press.

—— (2000) 'Film Theory and the Revolt against Master Narratives', in Christine Gledhill and Linda Williams (eds), *Reinventing Film Studies*, London and New York: Arnold and Oxford University Press, 34–52.

Smith, Adam (2003) *The Wealth of Nations*, New York: Bantam Classics.

Soja, Edward (1996) *Thirdspace: Journeys to Los Angeles and Other Real-and-Imagined Places*, Cambridge and Oxford: Blackwell Publishers.

Stone, Rob (2002) *Spanish Cinema*, Harlow: Longman Pearson Education.

von Trier, Lars and Thomas Vinterberg (1995) 'Dogma 95 Manifesto', www.dogme95.dk/menu/menuset.htm.

Wallovits, J. D. and Roger Gual (2003) *Smoking Room: guión cinematográfico*, Madrid: Colección Espiral.

Part III
Genre and authorship

8

The transvestite figure and film noir: Pedro Almodóvar's transnational imaginary

Carla Marcantonio

Melodrama has been a narrative and representational form tied to the imagining of the nation. In the wake of the global era, melodramatic parameters have necessarily mutated in order to account for a new imaginative experience, one where national boundaries are permeated by global trajectories, replacing the imagined, homogenous and bounded landscape of the nation with the hybrid and unbounded grid of transnational interconnection. I claim that one of the ways in which the melodramatic imaginary has been reconfigured in order to produce a transnational imagination has been by mixing with elements of film noir, an expressionistic genre that arose as a response to the anxiety of a post war era that had lost faith in the very institutions that upheld the national imagination. Central to this reimagination of the global landscape is the reconfiguration of the body in relation to narrative and genre.

In his films, Pedro Almodóvar has always made connections to the world beyond Spain's border. *Laberinto de pasiones/Labyrinth of Passions* (1982), for example, begins with the arrival of the son of the Emperor of Tiran in Madrid and ends with his departure from Madrid's airport, along with his female companion, to Panama's Contadora Island. The Tiranian kidnapping team of this film is later replaced by the Shiite terrorist with whom Candela (María Barranco) has an affair in *Mujeres al borde de un ataque de nervios/Women on the Verge of a Nervous Breakdown* (1988); this film also resolves in Madrid's airport. One of the nuns in *Entre tinieblas/Dark Habits* (1983) has disappeared in Africa, the same place where in *Hable con ella/Talk to Her* (2002) Marco, a travel-guide writer, had once travelled with a long-lost love. Sister Rosa

(Penélope Cruz) in *Todo sobre mi madre/All About My Mother*
(1999) is scheduled to depart for Guatemala to replace slain fellow
sisters. Becky del Páramo (Marisa Paredes), the mother in *Tacones
lejanos/High Heels* (1991), achieves stardom while in self-imposed
exile in Mexico, whereas the mother at the centre of *Todo sobre mi
madre* is an Argentine transplant to Madrid. Tina (Carmen Maura)
in *La ley del deseo/Law of Desire* (1987) reveals that she went
through her sex change in Morocco. The husband in *¿Qué he hecho
yo para merecer esto?/What Have I Done to Deserve This?* (1984)
travels to Germany to meet a lover with whom he is forging Hitler's
love letters. In *Kika* (1993), Nicholas (Peter Coyote) is an American
author who takes his inspirations from his travels, specifically in
Latin America.

The insistent presence of these international connections, despite
their cursory or tangential inscription, is at least partially a response
to the decades of isolationism Spain suffered under Franco's rule. At
the same time, interconnectivity in the director's work is undoubtedly
also a response to an increasingly globalised landscape. This interconnectivity is tracked all the way down to the level of the body,
which is, in fact, a more explicitly dominant axis in his work. *Todo
sobre mi madre*, in particular, picks up the motif of organ transplants
that was introduced in *La flor de mi secreto/The Flower of My Secret*
(1995) and melodramatically expands it into a story of a mother
whose dead son's heart is implanted into the body of a man in La
Coruña (the most important city in Galicia), where it arrives from
Madrid. The heart transplant provides the film with its thematic
centre, as it also dramatises the idea that community, however imagined, presupposes our interconnectedness. The narrative thus brings
together a haphazard community of women through mothering that
they perform for each other – a riff on the theme of transplantation –
given that they become substitute caregivers for each other. Huma
(Marisa Paredes) says to Manuela (Cecilia Roth), at a moment when
Manuela offers to help her find Nina (Candela Peña), 'I've always
depended on the kindness of strangers.'[1] The film thus builds an
entire emotive universe on this cue taken from the Tennessee
Williams play, and Elia Kazan's film adaptation,[2] *A Streetcar Named
Desire*. Huma plays Blanche in the play within the film, whereas
Manuela, in a past outside the diegesis of the film, had once played
Stella. As the director's penchant for citation and appropriation in
this brief example reveals, the notion of the transplant has proven to

be a core and multilayered motif in his cinema, whether it be the
litany of transplants and surgical interventions that Agrado (Antonia
San Juan) lists as having endured during her monologue in the same
film – breasts, cheeks, lips, etc. – or the way intertextual references
are interweaved throughout his work. Transplantation and interconnectivity are also conditions that characterise globalisation. The
body is central to this process, as it is both trapped by national narratives and ensnared by transnational articulations.

Crucial to this play of intertext as transplantation is the director's
hybrid use of genre. Almodóvar, for example, consistently works
within the parameters of melodrama, yet its conventions are always
interrupted and subsequently reorganised by elements of comedy,
the musical, the thriller and film noir. In this chapter I will focus on
the latter: the director's use of noir alongside melodrama. *Tacones
lejanos* and *La mala educación/Bad Education* (2004) are his most
explicitly noir narratives, and for this reason my analysis will rely on
these two films. Film noir has from the outset been interested in the
in-between, its characters move along the edges of society: they are
drifters, private eyes and femme fatales, identities constructed
outside the bounds of the nuclear family – the family at the centre of
the discursive strategies of the nation and the affective nexus dramatised by the melodramatic mode. Furthermore, the transvestite characters in each of these films provide a figure of embodiment for these
transnational articulations informed, in part, by their iconographic
status as femme fatales.

Given that the director is one of the dominant creative voices
associated with the democratic transition in Spain and that he has
continued to work, prolifically, throughout the country's rapid
transformation, it should hardly seem surprising that the dominant
generic container for his work is melodrama. Melodrama has been
an expressive form that arose in conjunction with transitional social
moments: '[it] becomes the form both to register change and to
process change, in particular mediating relations between a lost but
problematic past and the present' (Bratton, *et al.*, 1994: 3).[3] Crucial
to its articulating the social landscape is the pressure it applies on the
body's representational capabilities. The body is the place where
melodramatic meaning both stakes its battles and from which it
emanates: what Peter Brooks has called the form's 'aesthetics of
embodiment' (1994). In Almodóvar's case, melodrama is employed
to deconstruct the sanctioned/sacrosanct family structures that

defined Spain under Franco and that were heavily dictated by the regime's inextricable relationship to the Catholic Church. The director's films propose a new model of the family, reconfiguring the mode of imagining nationality in the process. This aspect of his work has been amply analysed.[4] Following Alejandro Yarza, Ernesto Acevedo-Muñoz describes the moment of Spain's transition as a moment of cultural anxiety and argues that this anxiety derives from the period's national identity crisis.[5] He argues that transsexual and transvestite characters represent this anxiety; he thus reads the transsexuals in later Almodóvar films (specifically Agrado in *Todo sobre mi madre*) as finally resolving this anxiety, performing reconciliation with the nation's past. Because I am interested in transnational articulations, I read the transvestite figure as embodying a claim to a new, hybrid identity, rather than expressing an anxiety about identity. But, whether reading the transsexual figure from a national or transnational frame, we both agree that it reveals Almodóvar's sense that 'the human body [is] one of the locales of negotiation, tension, and trauma, suggesting the body itself as a sign of the social contradictions of a country involved in a process of profound cultural transition' (Acevedo-Muñoz, 2004: 25). This contrast in our readings of the trans-figure underscores the fact that bodies signify differently depending on context.

Film noir marks a break with melodramatic representations tied exclusively to national narratives and thus updates the stakes of the melodramatic project. It is a narrative and representational form that, like melodrama, arises during a moment of transition – extending Thomas Elsaesser's observation about melodrama, one could argue that noir's popularity also coincides with periods of social and ideological crises (1987: 45). Film noir arises during the post-World War II era: one that sees the rise of the United States as an international power, a period when the seeds of our present-day globalisation are planted. Moreover, this also coincides with a time period when film culture becomes a truly global enterprise – the very talent behind film noir is largely made up of transatlantic émigrés to the United States. Aesthetically, film noir's emphasis on the ambivalent status of knowledge, truth and visibility is central to updating the melodramatic imagination for a postmodern, global era.

As with the work of Douglas Sirk, Almodóvar's melodramatic output is known for its deconstruction of the genre and the sociocultural parameters it upholds. Yet, his emphasis on mixing genres adds a further dimension. Never fully inscribing his narratives within the conventions of a single genre, Almodóvar's films' power resides in their capacity to negotiate the in-between. The director is linked historically to an important transitional period in Spain, particularly to the counterculture movement that thrived during the democratic transition, known as *la movida*. In *La mala educación*, during a scene that takes place in 1977, Zahara gives voice to Almodóvar's condemnation of the old order as she says to the Priest who abused the young Ignacio, 'this society values my liberty over your hypocrisy'. The pursuit of liberty, if not of happiness, has consistently been a driving force in his films as well as his investment in representing and producing a new Spain. Yet the mood of his films, beginning perhaps with *La flor de mi secreto* and cemented by *Carne trémula/Live Flesh* (1997), has by all accounts acquired an air of gravitas that was absent from his early output. One must thus conjecture that as Spain's role mutated from that of promising democratic debutant in the early 1980s to present-day global player,[6] so has the tone of his films. Released in 1991, *Tacones lejanos* benefits from the felt exuberance of a newly achieved democratic freedom and Spain's increasing visibility on the global landscape. The mood in *La mala educación*, which was released in 2004, is radically different and reflects the director's uncharacteristic turn toward reckoning with the past. At the same time, for as much as it is set in the past, *La mala educación* is Almodóvar's thinly veiled outcry against a present-day government he sees as usurping the very freedom that the end of Francoism heralded and that his early films both paraded and gleefully proclaimed.

The differences between *La mala educación* and *Tacones lejanos* have to be understood within this context. In 1991, Spain was still swept up in the upsurge of post-Franco freedom and was fighting for global economic relevance. After forty years of existing in the cultural and economic backwater of Europe, Spain saw an unparalleled surge in its cultural, social and economic modernisation. It democratised its political system, modernised its economy, and restored social and personal liberties. By 1986, only a decade after Franco's death, Spain gained access to the European Economic Community (later to become the European Union), becoming the twelfth country to do so. The government, eager to confirm the emergence of a new Spain both to its citizens and to the world, placed 1992 as a deadline for its progress. 1992, the year of the Barcelona Olympics and the World Expo in Sevilla, also coincided with the five-hundred-year anniversary of Columbus's voyage to America. (Given this context, it is perhaps not a coincidence that *Tacones lejanos* begins with a flashback to Isla Margarita in the Caribbean, an island that was discovered by Columbus in 1498.) This deadline shortly preceded the 1 January 1993 date set for Spain's (and Western Europe's) entry into the borderless world of the EU. Spain's infrastructure had been given a boost by government investment in highways, airports and communications to support the Olympics and the Expo, a process that also transformed the country's image. After the defeat of the PSOE in 1996, the PP began an even more aggressive push toward achieving global economic relevance, pressing for the privatisation of domestic industries and the rapid acquisition of foreign industries, particularly in Latin America (Spanish companies own a large share of the telephone and banking industries in the region).[7]

During this time Almodóvar himself went from underground singing and filmmaking sensation, to internationally acclaimed director, to nationally recognised, cultural figurehead (in October 2006, he received the prestigious Prince of Asturias award for the arts). Thus, what becomes clear is that his trajectory, for as much as it may be grounded in the moment of *la movida*, has actually straddled more than one important national transition. In fact, tracing the transnational articulations in Almodóvar's films is complicated by the fact that his filmmaking encompasses this rapidly changing historical period. At the same time, because Almodóvar spends many years developing his scripts, it becomes impossible to claim that there is a direct correlation between current events and his narratives. The change in tone and mood that is evidenced in his films is clearly a mark of his maturing status as an individual and a filmmaker. But what remains equally true is that, from the beginning of his career, his films have been very close to Madrid's, if not also Spain's, heartbeat. And thus, these shifts are undoubtedly also a reflection of the changing tides in the social and economic landscape of the country.

In order to elucidate the distinctions between *Tacones lejanos* and *La mala educación*, I propose to focus on the figure of the femme fatale, specifically the respective films' transvestite figure as femme fatale. In a gesture that serves both as decoy and homage, Miguel Bosé's character in *Tacones lejanos* is named Femme Letal. Garcia Bernal's character, Zahara, in *La mala educación* is a clear echo of

Bosé's character in the earlier film. The transvestite (or transsexual, transgendered) figure has been the recipient of much attention in analyses of the director's work. It is particularly responsible, though by no means solely, for the perception that Almodóvar's films respond to queer concerns over the performative nature of identity. Yet, little has been said about how transgendered characters function within the generic parameters that the director employs in his narratives.

The femme fatale's duplicity and ambivalent relationship to the visual field is literalised in the cross-dressing performances of the characters played by Bosé and Bernal.[8] Bosé's Letal turns out to be an impersonator concocted by clever Judge Domínguez (who is in turn concocted by a man named Eduardo, all played by Bosé). Yet, the duplicitous aspect of the femme fatale is, in this case, used more as a commentary on the Law embodied by the cross-dressing character than on the character himself, who ultimately harbours good intentions. Bernal's Zahara, conversely, is a true femme fatale: plotting, deceptive and manipulative. As with the case of Bosé, Bernal also embodies multiple characters in the film. The radical difference in the noir/melodrama narrative of *Tacones lejanos* versus that of *La mala educación* is that the former positions Spain within the context of the global, whereas the latter marks an explicit turn to the past, and the irreconcilable divisions that mark Spanish nationality and its push toward global relevance. In *La mala educación*, in particular, Almodóvar employs the narrative structure of noir to investigate the problem of history as memory, or memory as history. Thus, despite its specific national character, this latter emphasis in the film links it to transnational concerns over identity, exile and the human rights abuses perpetrated by military regimes – a way of imagining a different kind of community. The transsexual and abject body of Ignacio, absent from the narrative and present only as a trace (and disembodied voice), stands as a figure of irreparable loss.

One of the conventions of the classical-era femme fatale is that she seems to materialise out of nowhere: Phyllis Dietrichson (Barbara Stanwyck) in a bath towel at the top of the stairs as Walter Neff (Fred McMurray) walks into her home in *Double Indemnity* (Billy Wilder, 1944); in *Out of the Past* (Jacques Tourneur, 1947), Kathie Moffet (Jane Greer) appears twice to an expectant Jeff Bailey (Robert Mitchum), out of the moonlight and out of the sunlight; Alice (Joan Bennett) appears as a reflection in a window to Professor

Wanley (Edward G. Robinson), the man who was already ogling her portrait on the other side of that window in *The Woman in the Window* (Fritz Lang, 1944); a descendant of the noir femme fatales, Kim Novak's Madeleine theatrically materialises out of the red background at Ernie's as James Stuart's Scotty fatefully awaits at the bar in *Vertigo* (Alfred Hitchcock, 1958). These are just a few iconic examples. An ancestor of noir's femmes fatales is undoubtedly Marlene Dietrich (as Phyllis Dietrichson's last name might indicate), an actress with transgender performativity and a dangerously ambivalent sexuality. Introduced on stage in each of their respective films, Femme Letal and Zahara respond to this long tradition; the exception is that men play both of these characters. On the one hand, this gender inversion recognises the fact that the classic femme fatale is already largely a projection of masculine fantasy. On the other hand, it updates the figure of the femme fatale for a contemporary context, where her sexual ambiguity is best rendered through the very motif of gender as performance.

No character in the noir imaginary, nor perhaps in the entire history of film, has come to embody duplicity and falsehood more than the femme fatale, a woman of suspect intentions with a shady, or nonexistent, past who never is what she seems to be. Traditionally, her presence undermines the central male lead's identity, essentially emasculating him, and often leaving him dead. A figure of castration either way one cuts it, she portends loss. Loss is perhaps the central organising trope around the narrative construction of film noir, especially when speaking of noir films that function in the mode of retrospective narration: flashbacks accompanied by voiceovers. In this world, the femme fatale is a mirage, pure narrative catalyst (Doane, 1991). When she is present in a film's narrative (noir narratives do not always require her presence), she is there to definitively mark the before and the after. It does not matter whether she first appears from behind a set of curtains or out of the moonlight; the problem for the narrative, and for the main protagonist, is the very fact of her apparition. A modern version of Eve, she enables the narration of a fall from innocence as our hero, or anti-hero, often laments not having known then what he knows now.[9] The temporal trick of noir, at least of those films functioning in the mode of flashback narration, is not merely that their narratives present us with images from the past, but precisely that present knowledge is overlaid onto those images. In doing so, noir transforms the past into a narrative of and for the present, ensuring a discontinuity rather than a continuity of time.

In the noir framework, truth, like the femme fatale, remains elusive, perhaps all the more reason that words and more words incessantly stumble upon each other. What the femme fatale reveals, with her propensity for demarcating the before and after, is that identity is always a narrative. It should then come as no surprise that in the world of noir, where narrative is itself a subject, identity is less a given than a problem. Film noir, after all, might be the first moment in the history of film when narratives came into full, self-reflexive consciousness of themselves as such. Identity in these films, like truth, proves to be a mercurial quality.[10] This characteristic of noir, more so than is the case with melodrama, lends it to express the contested status of identity as it is detached from its national context. In *La mala educación*, in particular, Almodóvar employs the structure of noir, and its constitutive ambivalence to approach history.

If noir protagonists are not trying to make sense of the past, they are, like Sam Spade in *The Maltese Falcon* (John Huston, 1941), too busy parsing through layers and layers of present-time stories and lies. This is clearly the case in *Tacones lejanos*, where the Judge must tangle with a mother–daughter pair who have an inclination for lying, telling stories and leaving dead men in their path. In the process he impersonates different characters that serve as his informants (in other words, he is his own informant – a figure of the Law as hyperbolically self-referential, or even schizophrenic). Letal first meets Rebeca at a transvestite club, where Letal is impersonating Becky. As it turns out, Rebeca's murderous impulses are closely tied to her unresolved Oedipal issues with her mother – this is the narrative line that drives the melodrama in the film. Letal falls in love with Rebeca, and thus, when the Judge is assigned to the case of her murdered husband (who also happens to be her mother's lover), he does more to try to save Rebeca than to solve the case. In the end, once it is revealed that Rebeca is pregnant (likely by Letal), Eduardo reveals himself as the man also impersonating the Judge and asks Rebeca to marry him. In the end, a dying Becky confesses and takes the fall for Rebeca, fooling even the Judge in the process and finally repaying a debt to her daughter, setting her, literally and metaphorically, free. In this respect, *Tacones lejanos* follows in the footsteps of a film like *Gilda* (Charles Vidor, 1946), where melodrama ultimately derails the noir narrative. More specifically, we are also in *Mildred Pierce* (Michael Curtiz, 1945) territory, where a maternal melodrama is really at the heart of the film's narrative.

Nowhere in Almodóvar's oeuvre is the confluence of a global and national culture more explicitly grafted onto the body of a trans-character than in *Tacones lejanos*. Shortly after Becky's arrival at Madrid's airport, we learn that there is a drag performer that imper-sonates her 'pop-phase' (an important distinction because, as Becky puts it, she has now become a *grande dame* of song). The transgen-dered character is employed both as the mark of new identity possi-bilities as well as a nostalgic body. In *La mala educación*, the character of Sandra, who is an actual drag performer called Eden, impersonates a young Sara Montiel in her thirties, even if Eden herself is in her fifties.[11] Rebeca has befriended Letal because she reminds her of her mother. Echoing many of Marlene Dietrich's on-stage entrances in her Von Sternberg collaborations, Letal emerges on to a stage, and into the diegesis of the film, from behind a set of curtains. The backdrop of the stage is decorated with paintings depicting an *españolada*, a stereotypically Spanish scene, of folklor-ically dressed flamenco dancers, mostly women. Letal performs in the foreground of this tableau, in the process complicating, under-mining and critiquing, through mere visual juxtaposition, tradi-tional standards of femininity, while it replaces the image with an updated and non-nationally specific pop style.

As Marsha Kinder notes of this scene, the painted backdrop fur-thermore serves to underline the stereotypical aspects of Spain 'pro-moted for foreign consumption, which Almodóvar's postmodernist transsexuals have come to replace in the post-Franco era' (1995: 151). The choice of Miguel Bosé stands in contrast to actors whom Almodóvar is largely responsible for launching onto the interna-tional plane, such as the case with Antonio Banderas and Penélope Cruz. Bosé, already a star, is best known as a pop icon who cata-pulted into superstardom and sex-symbol status in the early 1980s and who owes much of his early, and continued, success to the Latin American music market (this closely matches the fictional Becky's professional trajectory). The emphasis on pop culture also replaces an exportability based on the exoticism of regional specificity (the flamenco dancers) for one based on the hybrid identity of global culture. The function of the transvestite character thus goes beyond deconstructing gender distinctions; it also underscores the complex process of appropriation and reinscription that characterises global/local cultural exchanges.

This process of exchange is dramatised through the hyperbolic chain of impersonations that take place in the narrative of this film. Kinder describes the moment when Letal appears on screen thus:

> The chain of simulations is dazzling, for the impersonator is really a male pop-star (Miguel Bosé) doing an impersonation of an ordinary man (Eduardo) doing an impersonation of a detective ('the Judge') doing an impersonation of a female impersonator (Letal) doing an impersonation of a female pop singer (Becky), who is there in the audience with her daughter, Rebeca, who has been impersonating her mother all her life. (1995: 151)

The culture of exchange is further emphasised during the sequence that follows Letal's performance, where Becky and Letal swap mementoes: Becky gives Letal an earring, Letal gives Becky one of her fake breasts (1995: 152). Given that Kinder reads the film through the lens of the mother–daughter Oedipal scenario, she notes about this scene: 'This exchange of fetishes reveals that their referents come from the mother's body, which is the point of origin of all fetishes – a revelation that contradicts the co-optive phallocentric theories of Freud and Lacan' (1995: 151). Linda Williams echoes this reading of the scene of exchange, of fetishes and illicit desires, at El Villarosa: 'these illicit desires are mediated by these aural and visual fetishes once connected to, but now detached from, the body of the mother' (2004: 276). This emphasis on the all-pervasiveness of the mother as referent and the possibility that Femme Letal opens, through the chain of impersonations, for a simulation of that mother (he tells Rebeca during their sex scene, 'I would like to be more than just a mother to you'), dislodges the maternal body not only from the patriarchal Oedipal scenario but also from the exclusively national scenario, where her body represents and fulfils the duties of nationally sanctioned, heteronormative reproduction. The mother's body thus radically becomes a metaphor for the imagining of an unbounded community that exchanges gifts with each other and is bonded, instead, through the experience of loss and substitution. *Todo sobre mi madre* will precisely emphasise this through the motif of adoption and organ donation.

Tacones lejanos and *Todo sobre mi madre* are narratives set in motion by a mother's return to reckon with her past – the quest before Enrique in *La mala educación* as well. *Tacones lejanos* opens at Madrid's airport, with Rebeca waiting for her mother's return – she has been waiting for fifteen years. Becky does not share with anyone that she has returned to Madrid to die: she has an ailing heart and knows her time is limited. As discussed, the resolution of the film falls squarely within the parameters of the maternal melodrama, with Becky taking the blame for a murder her daughter committed; before her death, Becky places her fingerprints on the murder weapon. In this respect, Becky vindicates Mildred, from that earlier melo-noir narrative, whose bluff is called by the Law as she tries to take the blame for Veda. Not so in *Tacones lejanos*, where the Law is fooled by its own need for proof – its reliance on the visual field for truth, its search for evidence, becomes its own downfall. As Williams has also argued, 'Almodóvar's film is a melancholic revision of *Mildred Pierce* that acts out the queer incestuous romance that the heteronormative Hollywood classic violently represses at its end' (2004: 277). *Tacones lejanos* is, nonetheless, a film about justice, but just not institutional justice. Becky and Rebeca fix their own debts to each other.[12] The chain of substitutions and impersonations that function to dislodge the Oedipal narrative from its patriarchal narrative function, as discussed by both Kinder (1995) and Williams (2004), lays the foundation for a different type of narrative, one that echoes in its own displacements those of culture in the global era – and, through it, the mechanisms for identification. For example, Williams notes that the tragedy of the mother–daughter passion in *Tacones lejanos* ultimately has to do with the fact that Rebeca and Becky are 'perpetually out of phase; they cannot bring voice and body together in the same, present, space of desire' (2004: 279). *Tacones lejanos* proves to be a maternal melodrama deeply infused with a sense of deterritorialisation. Almodóvar thus provides a global landscape increasingly determined by deterritorialisation with its own Oedipal narrative.

Thirteen years later, Letal's remarkable screen entrance would be echoed in the star-entrance of another multiple impersonator played by Gael García Bernal in *La mala educación*. Zahara, like Letal, also first emerges on to a stage, this time one depicting the fake landscape of a tropical island (also echoing the opening flashback scene of *Tacones lejanos* in Isla Margarita). Zahara dons a similar blonde, French-twist wig as Letal's. But, underscoring the only skin-deep femininity of this character, Zahara is introduced wearing a Jean-Paul Gaultier gown, spectacularly sequined to look like a nude female body. García Bernal is a Mexican actor who rose to international stardom and sex-symbol status almost overnight after his feature film debut in 2000's *Amores perros* (directed by Alejandro González Iñárritu). As with Bosé's Letal, Almodóvar once again employs a ready-made international star in the role of impersonator/transvestite. But the similarities between Letal and Zahara stop there. Gone from *La mala educación* and the figure played by García Bernal is the hope that surrounds the new masculinity emblematised by Bosé and his character's matriarchal lineage.[13] The benign role of Letal/Judge Domínguez/Eduardo is replaced by the much darker and devious persona of Ángel/ Ignacio/Zahara/Juan. The character played by Bosé has self-serving but noble intentions; his motivation is to save Rebeca and conquer her love. García Bernal, on the other hand, is one of the darkest characters to have thus far been given life in an Almodóvar narrative. Selfish, ambitious, and conniving, he is a true 'femme' fatale who will manipulate and stop at nothing to achieve his goals. García Bernal's character is a figure that breeds death and destruction – despite his internationally marketable sex-symbol status and pretty face. The lure of the global market, exemplified by Bosé's Letal, seems to have lost its liberatory appeal. This will ultimately be made explicit through the figure of the transsexual Ignacio in *La mala educación*, whose abject status stands in contrast to Juan/ Zahara's glamorous impersonation.

In the case of *La mala educación*, the noir-style flashback narration entraps the narrative, almost claustrophobically, in a past that cannot escape itself. The melodrama in this film revolves around a lost and corrupted childhood that comes to haunt the present – this is rendered quite literally, since the absent presence in the film is that of Ignacio, who, in the fashion of films like *Sunset Boulevard* (Billy Wilder, 1950) or *Letter from an Unknown Woman* (Max Ophüls, 1948), is already dead at the start of the film's narrative. The reference to *Letter from an Unknown Woman* is particularly relevant because the past is not only narrated in voiceover, but also through letters and a written text. As in *Letter from an Unknown Woman*, the written text will be the vehicle through which the narrative jumps from present to past and vice-versa. The text, an autobiographical story titled 'La Visita' ('The Visit'), functions as a ghostly apparition, which haunts the present in search of reckoning.[14]

La mala educación poses a challenge in that it is unlike any other Almodóvar film, not only because its narrative is completely encased in the past (a first), but because its subject is so stubbornly national in character. It is entrenched in the excavation of a personal past closely linked to the repressive (and repressed) past of the nation. The motif of division that drives the narrative and representational universe of *La mala educación* answers to this sense of a Spain divided between its global ambition and its repressed past. Division, and its varied implications, is a guiding motif in *La mala educación*, where division speaks to the problem of identity, split between a past that haunts it and a present invested in the denial of that past. If the imbrication of identity with narrative is perhaps implicit in noir films, *La mala educación* makes this link explicit.

In *La mala educación*, Almodóvar thus employs film noir's flash-back convention in order to investigate the problem of history as narrative. As J. P. Telotte has noted, beyond its amply noted stylistic parameters, film noir is fundamentally a form that investigates our cultural discursive formations. In Telotte's view, 'the form manages to articulate a rising awareness of the limitations and paradoxes that shape our culture, our lives, and the stories we tell of them both' (1989: 12). *La mala educación*'s historical representation mimics the noir narration's 'struggle between different voices for control over the telling of the story' (Christine Gledhill cited in Telotte, 1989: 15). The purpose of the narrative and flashback device in noir, as Telotte has described it, is that it points 'not only to truth's elusiveness but also to the very contentiousness of what often passes for truth' (1989: 12). This is a theme at the heart of *La mala educación*.

Yet, despite its juggling of different time frames – 1964, 1977, 1982 – only one narrative strand in the film is explicitly a flashback; the rest have been segments of the film within the film that tells the story of Ignacio as a young boy and his unjust death as Zahara at the hands of the same priests responsible for his abuse. The film uses the extreme close-up of the text of 'La Visita' to jump from time frame to time frame, but at a point about two-thirds through the film a sequence begins from an extreme close-up of the inside of a film camera. The accoutrements of the film are at this point themselves laid bare. We briefly cut to the close-up of a man we have never seen, who emerges as if from the darkness of the frame (it will turn out to be the real-life Father Manolo, now going by the name of

Sr Berenguer). Our suspension of disbelief is finally broken by the image that follows, which is of a clapboard in front of Zahara signalling the start of the final shot of the film within the film. This is the first time we are made aware that what we are watching is a fictional representation of past events and not a flashback; storytelling, but from a different temporal position.[15] As the shoot wraps up, and the film production setting is revealed, we have yet another splitting of the frame into two (once again reminding us of the visual and narrative motif of division in the film): the left side corresponds to the fictional setting, whereas the right side of the frame contains all the equipment and crew filming (fictionally) the film within the film. This entire sequence emphasises a dressing down, not only of the set, which begins to be dismantled, but also of Ángel as Zahara, who is divested of his feminine clothing by one of the female assistants on set. The tearing down of the set, like the undressing of Ángel, prepares the way for the entrance of the real-life Ignacio into the narrative of the film.

The real Ignacio is still dead. But, as Berenguer pays a visit to Enrique in his office, he reveals the truth of how Ignacio died. The unveiling of the truth is presented in flashback, no longer contained within the world of the film within the film. As the flashback segment begins, we observe Berenguer, who arrives to meet Ignacio. We are here presented with an unexpected image: the man/woman who opens the door to meet Berenguer, compared to the glamorised Zahara, or even Sandra (the female impersonator Ángel models Zahara after), is an abject figure. With a deep voice, big tits, long hair, polished nails, bad teeth and a masculine face, the transsexual figure that meets Berenguer at the door passes neither as a man nor as woman and lacks all the glamour of Bernal's Zahara. As Berenguer walks in, a point-of-view shot of the surroundings also reveals the scattered paraphernalia of a heroin addict. In voiceover, Berenguer describes Ignacio to Enrique quite simply as 'that wasn't the Ignacio you and I loved'.

Truth is not a pretty thing. And neither is Ignacio, who announces the subject for his blackmail: 'looking pretty costs a lot of money'. He is referring, of course, to his intent to pursue further surgery, prior to entering rehab and 'cleaning up' completely. He is blackmailing Berenguer, threatening to expose the truth of their past together, in order to achieve this. The charm and light-hearted wit we have come to associate with Almodóvar's transvestites and transsexuals is missing from Ignacio's announcement and from the very persona of Ignacio. Ignacio's comment, for example, should remind us of the clever and heartwarming monologue performed by Agrado in *Todo sobre mi madre* that revolves precisely around the theme of how much it costs to be authentic. Standing on a stage, Agrado shares with the audience assembled at a theatre (both that within the film and outside of it) the history of how much she has spent in her pursuit to become authentic, or, as she puts it, 'one is most authentic the more she resembles what she's dreamed of being'.[16] Her monologue is introduced by a close-up tracking shot of the theatre curtain, Agrado stands at the very threshold between the stage and the theatre audience. The stage as a representation of reality, and reality as a stage for the everyday, is a subject that Almodóvar's films never cease to explore. The image of Agrado on stage, thus, is one that speaks to the very epistemology of the Almodovarian trans-subject, straddling the theatrical and the real, male and female, she places on display the constructed character of all identity or, more explicitly, the individual's freedom to claim her own. Agrado's credo is not far from Almodóvar's surrealism-inspired project of approaching the mundane aspects of daily existence through the artifice of a boldly coloured world. This has been true, in different hues, of characters like Tina (Carmen Maura) and Ana (Bibí Andersen) in *La ley del deseo*, or of Femme Letal and La Cimarrona (Bibí Andersen) in *Tacones lejanos*.[17] But in *La mala educación*, Ignacio presents us with a different paradigm, as if Almodóvar's camera was for the first time acknowledging that embodied identity is not unproblematically pliable (or one might say that through the figure of Ignacio he explores the limits of his own future-tensed project – the past is not so easily shed nor forgotten). Only *Todo sobre mi madre*'s Lola (Toni Cantó) displays some of the darker elements evidenced here in the adult Ignacio. Despite her brief appearance in the film, Lola, with her big tits and macho attitude (as the main character, Manuela, puts it), is a figure that breeds misery, death and destruction in the world of the narrative. Yet, if Lola is an agent of tragedy in that film, here Ignacio is the film's true tragic figure.

The juncture between consumerism and identity, the subject of Agrado's monologue and Ignacio's blackmail, is not treated as kindly in *La mala educación*'s depiction of souls crushed and dreams gone awry. In voiceover, Berenguer narrates the film's only formal flashback sequence. He notes that his sexual interest was peaked by the young Juan, who lived with Ignacio. He decides to capitalise on Ignacio's blackmail, turning it into an investment. In order to keep seeing Juan, he stalls Ignacio's request for money, and we witness him engage in a series of perfectly ordinary and mundane encounters with the two brothers at their home. One scene is particularly telling despite its thirty-second duration. Berenguer and Ignacio are alone and Ignacio is reminiscing about his time at the school. He asks Berenguer, 'do you remember Don Narciso, the Nazi? He loved my illustrations. Look at this one, "Children of Spain"'. The camera cuts to an extreme close-up of one of the drawings decorating a school notebook, it is a drawing of the Spanish flag. As the camera holds on this image, Father Manolo places some bills over the flag. Ignacio closes the notebook. The camera then cuts to another extreme close-up image, this time of a needle full of heroin that Ignacio is injecting into his arm. The implication is that the small sums of money that Berenguer provides go directly toward perpetuating Ignacio's drug habit. Yet, the image of the flag being eclipsed by the money carries inevitable symbolic implications. The notebook and drawing in question are actual mementoes from Almodóvar's childhood. The director recounts that during the nationalist fervor of the Franco years, children were rewarded and encouraged to decorate their notebooks with such themes.[18] Clearly, Almodóvar has an allegorical association in mind: he seems to suggest that the 'Children of Spain' did not only receive abuse and a 'bad education' during the Franco years, but that they have also been sold off to private interests in the post-Franco years. Abuse and commerce, mixed with national fervour, have, in this view, eclipsed the Spanish nation.[19] Ignacio, Enrique finally learns, died from the pure version of heroin Juan procures and Berenguer delivers – what else is purity to do in a world that has done nothing but snuff it out?

The division in question is not only about before and after Franco, Nationalists and Republicans, Right and Left, the PP and the PSOE, nor the move from economic backwardness to globalised prosperity. Starting around 2000, the denunciation of Spain's wilful forgetfulness of its past was beginning to be voiced more forcefully than it ever had.[20] The practice of pretending as if Franco had never existed was, after all, not purely an Almodóvar phenomenon. *Desmemoria* is a term that refers to a collective pact of forgetting, sometimes translated as 'pact of oblivion' or 'willful forgetting' (Richards and Ealham, 2005: 9). Almodóvar's initial stance toward history was thus not as unique as it appears to his international audience. His filmmaking has changed from one that refused to look toward the past into one that is willing to reckon with it. What has not changed is his ability to respond to, or anticipate, larger historical tendencies. The look toward the past in *La mala educación* is no exception. This new turn toward a politics of remembering is undoubtedly a social undercurrent informing, if not necessarily inspiring, *La mala educación*.

In *Carne trémula* and *Todo sobre mi madre*, Almodóvar melodramatically inscribes the birth of a baby with the symbolic weight of the birth of a new Spain, or of a new possibility for the creation of community. The third Esteban in *Todo sobre mi madre*, born to Sister Rosa and adopted by Manuela, is born on the same day, as Manuela tells Rosa, that Videla is incarcerated in Argentina. This repeats a motif that was first introduced in *Carne trémula*, given that the main protagonist, symbolically named Victor, is born (also to a mother played by Penélope Cruz), on the day Franco dies in 1975. General Jorge Videla was responsible for the 1976 coup d'état and presided over the dark period in Argentine history known as the Dirty War. Many who were potential targets of the Military Junta's persecution fled into exile; a large number of these fled to Spain (just as decades earlier, persecuted Spaniards had gone into exile in Argentina). The family of actress Cecilia Roth who plays Manuela was one of them – she moved to Spain with her family at the age of 17. The presence of Roth, furthermore, is a throwback inscription to Almodóvar's early films (she plays the lead character, Sexi, in *Laberinto de pasiones*, but also has an uncredited appearance in the director's first feature, *Pepi, Luci, Bom y otras chicas del montón* (1980)). Almodóvar thus suggests the existence of a transnational community joined by the memory and experience of exile and of the human rights violations perpetrated by military regimes such as Franco's and Videla's. Thus, even if *La mala educación* is rooted in the excavation of a personal past tied to a traumatic period in Spain's history, its project of unearthing truth, especially because it revolves around Ignacio's absent body, links it to this larger project.

Film noir, we must recall, is a genre that, as much as it is considered to have had its origins in Hollywood, is rooted in the experience of exile – European émigrés comprised an important part of the talent behind much of film noir. It was rooted as much in the tradition of American hard-boiled detective fiction as it was in the visual style of German expressionism, and even though the films were American productions the concept of film noir as a distinctive cinematic style was born in postwar France. Transplantation and interconnectivity, along with its obsession with memory, and its consequent organizing trope of loss, are thus built into the fabric of the genre. Whereas in *Tacones lejanos* Almodóvar employs noir in a more jocular tone, used to undermine patriarchal narratives of truth and knowledge and present us with an ambivalent figure of the Law, in *La mala educación* the structure of noir is used in order to complicate the question of identity, especially of the narratives essential in constructing it. Ultimately, both of these films resolve melodramatically. Ultimately, they inscribe noir, a genre prototypically sceptical about truth and justice, against the grain. In Almodóvar's films, justice is to be found outside the channels of the State and in allegiances forged despite them and beyond it.

Notes

I would like to thank Elena Gorfinkel and Paula Massood for their feedback on drafts of this chapter.

1 *All About My Mother* was, in turn, performed as a play in London's Old Vic Theatre during the autumn of 2007. It was written by Samuel Adamson and directed by Tom Cairns.

2 Kazan also directed the first theatrical production of the play in 1947.

3 Thomas Elsaesser has also echoed this observation: '[melodrama's] height of popularity seems to coincide . . . with periods of intense social and ideological crises' (1987: 45).

4 See Vernon (1995), Kinder (1995), Allinson (2001), D'Lugo (2006). These are just a few examples.

5 Acevedo-Muñoz cites Yarza (1999).

6 In 2005, the World Bank ranked Spain as the eighth largest economy in the world.

7 As the title of a *Business Week* article put it, Latin America was not the only goal: 'Its companies are already a power in Latin America. Now, Spanish execs are prowling the globe for deals.' See 'Spain's Surge', *Business Week (international edition online)*.

8 On the relationship of the femme fatale to the visual field, see Doane (1991).

9 In *La mala educación*, this knowledge is expressed by Enrique in reference to the woman who willingly let herself be eaten by crocodiles (sort of the very predicament of the noir subject in the hands of the femme

fatale): 'I wanted to see how far you were capable of going, and how much I was capable of withstanding.' Enrique, having uncovered the truth, says this triumphantly, sending off Ángel with his bags and shutting the door on his duplicitous ways.

10 J. P. Telotte finds that noir narrators, for example, 'set about providing us privileged access to a world, only to find that the path they staked out is full of obstacles and pitfalls, in fact that like truth itself, it seems virtually to disappear before us' (1989: 8–9).

11 In the DVD commentary Almodóvar recounts the following anecdote about the transvestite impersonator he finds to play Sandra, the performer who Ángel models Zahara after: 'I found Eden, the performer who plays Sandra in the film, who is, let's say, the official impersonator of Sara Montiel [a legend and icon of Spanish cinema]. The one who best imitates her. Sandra is now over 50 and she impersonates a Sara who is unrealistic and impossible because she imitates Sara when she was 20 or 30. When Sara was 50 she was nothing like Sandra, she was much heavier.'

12 This theme of justice exacted between individuals through private rather than public channels also guides the relationships between the women in *Volver* (2006), where moral debts are paid outside of legal, religious, or media-driven venues.

13 In *Tacones lejanos*, Eduardo and Rebeca are set to have a baby by the film's end; they will thus form one of Almodóvar's non-heteronormative families and give birth to a baby boy. This element of *Tacones lejanos*, which it inherits from *La ley del deseo*, will be echoed in *Carne trémula* – another noir-inspired film that problematises traditional notions of masculinity – where Victor (Liberto Rabal), who has had to learn how to please women sexually, also embodies this new masculinity and is rewarded by the film's end both with his long-sought-after object of desire, Elena (Francesca Neri) and a baby boy.

14 Paul Julian Smith begins the introduction to his book on Almodóvar, published well before the release of *La mala educación*, with a paragraph referring to an unpublished story that had been deposited by a 26-year-old Almodóvar on the day of his birthday at Madrid's Biblioteca Nacional in 1975, the same year Franco died, for purposes of obtaining copyright. The title of the typewritten manuscript is also 'La Visita' and from Smith's description it echoes the narrative of *La mala educación* quite closely, especially the key scene where Zahara visits Father Manolo. It even includes the double ending alluded to in the finished film. Smith also notes the similarities of the manuscript scene with the scene in *La ley del deseo* where transsexual Tina confronts her 'spiritual director'. See Smith (2000: 1).

15 This is a self-reflexive gesture in the film, which underscores the fact that everything we see in the film, the film within the film or otherwise, is a fictional representation.

16 Agrado's breakdown of costs: 'Look at this body! All made to measure. Almond-shaped eyes, 80,000; Nose, 200,000, a waste of money, since another beating the following year left it like this, I know it gives me a lot of character, but if I'd known, I wouldn't have touched it; Tits, two, because I am no monster, 70,000 each, but I've earned that back; Silicone in the lips, forehead, cheeks, hips, and ass, a litre costs about 100,000 so you work it out, I've lost count; Jaw reduction, 75,000; Complete laser depilation, because women, like men, also come from apes, 60,000 a session depending on how hairy you are, usually two to four sessions.'

17 Bibí Andersen (now known as Bibiana Fernández) is a real-life transsexual woman, and a popular television personality in Spain, who is always summoned to play a biological woman in Almodóvar's films, but whose high-profile presence provides a contrast to the fictional transsexuals in his early films (she also has a brief appearance in *Matador*, as a fortune-telling gypsy, and in *Kika*, as an eventual murder victim of the film's serial killer).

18 DVD commentary, *La mala educación*.

19 The visual motif of the 'eclipse' runs throughout the film: Father Manolo's body eclipses the image of a young Ignacio before a rape in the sacristy, a point at which the young Ignacio's voiceover tells us, once the screen has faded to black, 'I sold myself for the first time in that sacristy.' The body of Father Manolo is often the subject of said 'eclipses'; it is also his body that eclipses that of a soon-to-be-dead Ignacio for the camera. When he returns as Berenguer at the end of the film shoot, and claims he will no longer allow Juan to escape him, his body eclipses that of Juan's as he walks to the door that frames his figure. Yet, it is Enrique who provides the final eclipsed image of the film, as he slowly shuts a sliding door from right to left on a close-up of Juan's face.

20 In December 2000, the Association for the Recovery of Historical Memory (ARMH) was founded with the purpose to collect testimonies about the victims of Franco's rule (from rapidly dying survivors) and to excavate and identify bodies in mass graves, and in some cases the mass graves themselves (again, as a generation of people who could help do this was disappearing, the need for this type of work became imminent). This work has culminated in the recent, and controversial, historic-memory law passed before parliament in 2006 (seventy years since Franco came to power). Some accuse the Prime Minister of unnecessarily opening divisive and painful wounds; others accuse him of not going far enough (the law proposes to name victims but not those responsible).

References

Acevedo-Muñoz, Ernesto R. (2004) 'The Body and Spain: Pedro Almodóvar's *All About My Mother*', *Quarterly Review of Film and Video*, 21: 1, 25–38.

Allinson, Mark (2001) *A Spanish Labyrinth: The Films of Pedro Almodóvar*, London: I. B. Tauris.

Bratton, Jacky, Jim Cook and Christine Gledhill (eds) (1994) *Melodrama: Stage, Picture, Screen*, London: BFI.

Brooks, Peter (1994) 'Melodrama, Body, Revolution', in Jacky Bratton, Jim Cook and Christine Gledhill (eds), *Melodrama: Stage, Picture, Screen*, London: BFI, 11–24.

D'Lugo, Marvin (2006) *Pedro Almodóvar*, Urbana: University of Illinois Press.

Doane, Mary Ann (1991) *Femmes Fatales*, London: Routledge.

Elsaesser, Thomas (1987) 'Tales of Sound and Fury: Observations on the Family Melodrama', in Christine Gledhill (ed.) *Home Is Where the Heart Is*, London: BFI, 43–69.

Kinder, Marsha (1995) 'From Matricide to Mother Love in Almodóvar's *High Heels*', in Kathleen M. Vernon and Barbara Morris (eds), *Post-Franco, Postmodern*, Westport, CT: Greenwood Press, 145–54.

Richards, Michael and Chris Ealham (2005) 'History, Memory, and the Spanish Civil War: Recent Perspectives', in Chris Ealham and Michael Richards (eds), *The Splintering of Spain: Cultural History and the Spanish Civil War, 1936–1939*, Cambridge: Cambridge University Press, 1–22.

Smith, Paul Julian (2000) *Desire Unlimited: The Cinema of Pedro Almodóvar*, 2nd edition, London: Verso.

'Spain's Surge', *Business Week (international edition online)* http://www.businessweek.com/2000/00_20/b3681125.htm (accessed 23 March 2007).

Telotte, J. P. (1989) *Voices in the Dark: The Narrative Patterns of Film Noir*, Urbana: University of Illinois Press.

Vernon, Kathleen (1995) 'Melodrama Against Itself: Pedro Almodóvar's *What Have I Done to Deserve This?*', in Kathleen M. Vernon and Barbara Morris (eds), *Post-Franco, Postmodern*, Westport, CT: Greenwood Press, 59–72.

Williams, Linda (2004) 'Melancholy and Melodrama: Almodovarian Grief and Lost Homosexual Attachments', *Journal of Spanish Cultural Studies*, 5: 3, October, 275–88.

Yarza, Alejandro (1999) *Un canibal en Madrid: la sensibilidad* camp *y el reciclaje de la historia en el cine de Pedro Almodóvar*, Madrid: Ediciónes Libertarias.

9

Caressing the text: episodic erotics and generic structures in Ventura Pons's 'Minimalist Trilogy'

David Scott Diffrient

Spanish cinema exhibits a range of tendencies as disparate and divergent as the country's varied geography and contentious sub-national identities. (Dapena, 2001: 53)

Thanks to their generic hybridity and stylistic audacity, not to mention their array of talented transnational stars, several recent motion pictures by internationally renowned auteurs, including Pedro Almodóvar, Iciar Bollaín, Álex de la Iglesia and Alejandro Amenábar, have helped Spain to emerge from the long shadows cast by its European neighbours and gain a venerated place in the pantheon of national cinemas. Spanish film is today recognised as one of the world's most dynamic sites of cultural intermixing and convergence, not to mention a testing ground for narrative experimentation. With so much attention now being focused on Spanish cinema, the time is right to begin cultivating an awareness of the country's diverse cultural traditions and reassessing the distinctiveness of Catalan-language films.

In the years since the November 1975 death of Franco, Catalonia – a geographically defined *place* as well as a symbolic subnational *space* of resistance – has witnessed a partial restoration of its cultural and political autonomy (D'Lugo, 2002: 167). It has also seen some of its brightest talents – novelists such as Quim Monzó, playwrights such as Sergi Belbel, painters such as Alicia Grau Pérez-Agustín, installation artists such as Eulàlia Valldosera, animators such as Luis Eduardo Aute, and filmmakers such as Manuel Huerga, Pere Portabella, José Luis Guerín, Bigas Luna and Marc Recha – expand the textual horizons and aesthetic boundaries of their respective fields while rising to the challenge of representing heretofore repressed elements in contemporary society. Of this latter group, one filmmaker in particular, the prolific writer-director Ventura Pons, stands out due to his persistence in reclaiming long-suppressed subject positions (specifically, gay, diasporic and subcultural identities) and his insistence that ideologically dominant values (linked to such perennial stock genres as melodrama, *folklórico* and the *thriller policíaco*) be dismantled through acts of aesthetic provocation and parody.

The Barcelona-born theatre director first burst on to the film scene in 1978, when his debut feature, the intimate documentary *Ocaña, retrat intermitent*, was released to critical acclaim. This unconventional portrait of José Ángel Pérez Ocaña, a transvestite Andalusian painter who spent much of his adult life in Catalonia, was a milestone in the history of Spanish cinema, heralding a new era in post-Francoist cultural production when more open and honest expressions of sexuality were being permitted by a liberalising government.[1] Produced and released a mere three years after Franco's death, amidst free elections and party reconfigurations, *Ocaña* entered into the public's ongoing conversation about Catalonia's relationship to the Spanish state at a pivotal moment, when the old guard was giving way to youthful idealism and a constitutional regime. This was also a time when a heightened awareness of the 'triple subordination' – political, commercial and symbolic (Fernàndez, 2004: 69) – faced by heretofore 'invisible' members of the Iberian peninsula's population encouraged government officials to implement new programs, reforms, and incentives designed to stimulate independent filmmaking in Barcelona (Fernàndez, 2004: 69). In the lead-up to that moment, after the transitional period of *apertura* (1963–69) paved the way for economic growth, trade liberalisation and decentralisation in the early 1970s, Pons took time out from staging and directing theatrical plays (by Shakespeare and Zorrilla, among others) to participate in the counterculture revolution sweeping throughout the autonomous geopolitical community. In that context, *Ocaña* – an independently produced, low-budget 16mm film shot in a single week – was a defiant gesture as well as a kind of 'coming out' for the artist, a Catalonian corrective designed to undermine reductive assumptions about national unity and subvert heterosexist discourses by way of an experimental cinematic framework in which performative camp, generic hybridity and narrative anti-illusionism all operate.

Utilising a novelistic structure steeped in theatrical techniques, with the extravagantly dressed title character performing 'fragments of popular plays' on a tiny stage (Smith, 2003: 127), *Ocaña* is both remarkable and representative, signalling a radical break from earlier depictions of drag queen culture and gay subjectivity while setting the template for subsequent attempts to denaturalise heteronormative precepts related to masculinity, femininity, friendship and family. Beneath *Ocaña*'s supposedly 'transparent' style are subtle attempts by Pons to parlay episodicity – the segmentation of the subject's life into discrete vignettes – into a '(micro)political form of cultural resistance', a potentially subversive dismantling that rejects those monolithic 'categories of classification created by the state', which has historically treated both homosexuals and Catalans as 'indigenous foreigners' whose very existence threatens to contaminate or taint the imagined purity of the nation (Fernàndez, 2004: 71–2).

Pons's deployment of disruptive narrative devices in this and other films undermines traditional forms of storytelling as well as essentialising conceptions of national consciousness and belonging. His eventual decision to embrace the critically maligned and industrially marginalised genre – or, as I'll explain later, *meta*-genre – of the episode film can therefore be seen as his way of responding to Catalonia's own marginalised status as well as the region's ability to fissure the nation's historical narrative. Such strategies allow him to represent the fragmentary aspects of everyday life while commenting on the various means of constructing an 'imagined community', one brought together and sustained not only by print capitalism, popular culture, and other shared traditions outlined by Benedict Anderson (1991), but also through linguistic assimilation and compulsory heterosexuality.

The kinds of *procesiones* (religious-themed parades during Holy Week) in which drag artist Ocaña is seen partaking throughout the film are worth mentioning here, for the camp sensibility that infused them can also be detected in the three anthology films comprising Pons's self-defined 'Minimalist Trilogy', the Catalan-language motion pictures *El perquè de tot plegat/What's It All About* (1994), *Carícies/Caresses* (1997) and *Morir (o no)/To Die (Or Not)* (2000). Despite their seemingly streamlined appearance and membership in a transnational art-house movement partially founded on the principles of formal austerity and aesthetic rigour, these three films (which Pons produced through his own company, Els Films de la Rambla, founded in 1985) can be codified as 'camp objects' – exuberant if sometimes depressing, bold if frequently meditative narrative ensembles or carnivalesque 'parades' consisting of discrete units following one after the other and moving to the percussive pulse of the postmodern city. Together they illustrate Pons's adeptness in pioneering alternative approaches to storytelling as well as his commitment to socially marginalised communities. The filmmaker thus deserves consideration for having cast light on the Catalonian experience and reinvigorating narrative form in the years leading up to the new millennium.

The episode film: an 'odd-duck' genre?

The following pages examine the thematic profundities of these intricately plotted, episodic features. Although *El perquè de tot plegat, Carícies* and *Morir (o no)* have all travelled the international festival circuit and earned critical accolades as well as industry awards, as episode films they appear to be exceptions to the rule. Indeed, few types of cinematic praxis have been more universally reviled, or have received less attention in critical genre studies, than the 'episode film', a term I have opted to use in describing a feature-length motion picture made up of several stories, sketches, vignettes or variations on a theme. Also known as 'anthology film', 'omnibus film', 'portmanteau film' and 'sketch film', the episode film is a multi-part feature, segmented into two or more tales, with or without explicit linking devices or wraparound narratives. Each constituent episode in such a work is thus placed into a chain, either by a single filmmaker or, in the case of multi-director films, by a producer responsible for the entire piece. Perhaps owing to their inherent heterogeneity, to their discursive movement between ostensibly 'small' stories lacking the magnitude and narrative depth of a traditional feature, such motion pictures frequently frustrate viewers who have grown accustomed to linear plots organised around a single protagonist or a core group of characters.

Distinctions can (and should) be made between the various junior categories comprising episodic cinema. Both single- and multi-director anthology and omnibus films may be organised around a central theme, genre, object or setting. In the case of those metrophilic films like *Paris vu par . . .* (1965), *Paris vu par . . . vingt ans après* (1984) and *Paris, je t'aime* (2006), wherein each episode is not only contributed by a different director but also set in a different neighbourhood of the City of Lights, the structural organisation of the entire piece promotes a 'flaneurial' spectatorial engagement, one that invites the audience to metaphorically 'move' with the text from one group of characters to the next. This is distinct from quasi-episodic picaresque films, such as Alfred Hitchcock's *The Thirty-Nine Steps* (1935), Alain Tanner's *Messidor* (1979) and Agnès Varda's *Vagabond* (1985), whose overriding narrative trajectory is shaped by a *single* protagonist's pitstop-peppered land journey. Spatial linkages can be even more explicit, if also less ambulatory, in those multi-character works with episodes that are all largely confined to a single building (as in *Si Versailles m'était conté/Royal Affairs in Versailles* (Sacha Guitry, 1955) and *Four Rooms* (1995)) or a single room (as in *Plaza Suite* (Arthur Hiller, 1971) and *Motel Seoninjang/Motel Cactus* (Ki-Yong Park, 1997)).

Narrative structure itself may be shaped or determined by a film's funding. Made in 1999 by screenwriting-directing team François Girard and Don McKellar, *Le Violon rouge/The Red Violin* (1999) was financed by American, Canadian, British, Italian and Japanese companies, and features English-, Italian-, German-, French- and Mandarin-language dialogue (with a dash of Latin sprinkled in for good measure). Even the credit sequence, in which the title of the film is scrawled in five superimposed languages at once, floating and overlapping, bears out the effects of this trend toward multinational co-productions. Indeed, the film's opening credits read like a parodic pedigree: 'A New Line International/Channel Four Films/Telefilm Canada presentation of a Rhombus Media/Mikado/Sidecar Films production'. Spanning three continents, four centuries and five languages, *Le Violon rouge* tracks the life of the titular instrument from its creation in seventeenth-century Cremona, Italy to its eventual resting place in modern-day Montreal, with in-between forays into Oxford, Vienna and Shanghai.

Writing about *Le Violon rouge*, Andy Klein says, 'Anthology films are an odd-duck genre: While there once was a time – long ago – when books of short stories were published with nearly the frequency of novels, their cinematic equivalent has never amounted to even 1 percent of the fictional films released' (1999: 45). True though this statement may be, one ought not mistake paucity for inferiority; nor should one neglect to account for the many 'classics' of international cinema whose uniqueness hinges upon episodicity, from single-director films like Dziga Vertov's *Tri pesni o Lenine/Three*

Songs about Lenin (1934), Jean-Luc Godard's (*Vivre sa vie/My Life to Live* (1962), and Andrei Tarkovsky's *Andrei Rublev* (1966) to multi-director works such as *Dead of Night* (1945), *Amore in città/Love in the City* (1953) and *Deutschland im Herbst/Germany in Autumn* (1978).

However, some anthologies are merely the result of enterprising producers; perhaps those who have bought the rights to pre-existing works and brought together, in a single package, the short films of internationally recognised directors (who may or may not have had designs on seeing their work positioned alongside that of other filmmakers). Others are conceived of as cohesive units with some degree of stylistic continuity, thematic reverberation and/or narrative parallelism. This is true of many single-director efforts, particularly those cinematic 'rondos', like Max Ophüls's *La Ronde* (1950), Luis Buñuel's *Le Fantôme de la liberté/The Phantom of Liberty* (1974) and Chantal Akerman's *Toute une nuit* (1982), which accentuate the adjacencies of multiple characters, settings and events by way of a 'baton-passing' plot device that links the episodes. Despite their many differences, though, all of these (and several other) subcategories have at least one thing in common: they are simultaneously singular and multiple, made up of two or more discretely demarcated segments that each have at least a modicum of spatiotemporal autonomy.

From this working definition, we can assume not only that the term 'episodic' (which comes from the Greek *epeisodion*, meaning 'parenthetic story') refers to any text composed of a series of separate, loosely connected (or unconnected) tales or vignettes following one after the other, but also that films featuring discretely demarcated narrative zones differ from chronologically scrambled, spatially fragmented, often non-linear ensemble films employing what might be called a 'braided' storytelling structure, in which multiple plotlines dovetail and diverge. D. W. Griffith's *Intolerance* (1916) is the earliest example of this latter type of film, with more recent, less historically expansive examples including Edward Yang's *Kongbu fenzi/The Terroriser* (1986), Robert Altman's *Short Cuts* (1993), Wong Kar-Wai's *Duoluo tianshi/Fallen Angels* (1995), Goran Paskaljevic's *Bure Baruta/Cabaret Balkan* (1998) and Barbara Albert's *Böse Zellen/Free Radicals* (2003). There is, in each of the films making up Ventura Pons's Minimalist Trilogy, some degree of narrative and/or character convergence, suggesting that his work is similar to these braided features. But all three films maintain the clear demarcations between stories unique to episodic cinema, even as his sober yet 'camp' sensibility collapses distinctions between aesthetic modes and undermines the hierarchical schemas pitting art-house cinema against popular fare.

As suggested above, Pons is not the only contemporary filmmaker to depart from classical narrative formulas and embrace the intertextual as well as *intra*textual complexities of episode films. Over the past fifteen years, several filmmakers throughout the world have made similar interventions in plot (de)construction and character development, from Rodrigo García to Jim Jarmusch to François Girard. These and other auteurs have created polyphonic works whose internal fragmentation provides a structural foundation for expressing psychological uncertainty, epistemological ambiguity, perspectival disjuncture and thematic reverberation while suggesting an affinity for various literary and artistic avant-gardes of the twentieth century. However, among these individuals Pons deserves special consideration for the way he mobilises the narratological genre of the episode film as a means of cultural recovery and political resistance.

Although each film in the trilogy derived from a literary or theatrical source (the stories of Quim Monzó and the plays of Sergi Belbel), Pons exerted authorial control over these texts by eliciting psychologically nuanced performances from his actors and by injecting his trademark stylistic virtuosity. More importantly, in foregrounding the underlying connections between disparate individuals who at first glance appear to be emotionally and/or physically estranged, he allows the spectator to ruminate on the erotic and polygamous disposition of episodicity – the literal and figurative entanglements of several characters as well as our own potentially fetishistic yet frustrated relationship to the texts – while forming hypotheses about the very nature of cinematic narration. This is what I explore in the ensuing parts of this chapter, which interrogates the classificatory status of episodic cinema before taking the above-mentioned motion pictures as intersecting case studies through which to examine Pons's distinctive reworking of popular genres (romance, melodrama, comedy, fantasy, etc.) and ability to generate complex philosophical questions within narrative miniatures that are rooted in the social problems and urban landscapes unique to post-Franco Spain.

Pons's Minimalist Trilogy can be situated within a narratological lineage that recognises the significance of earlier anthology, omnibus, portmanteau and sketch films produced in Spain. An adumbrated list of notable titles would include *El cerco del diablo/Besieging the Devil* (1951), *Las cuatro verdades/The Four Truths* (1962), *Los Desafíos/The Challenges* (1969), *Pastel de sangre/Blood Cake* (1971) and *Cuentos para una escapada/Stories of an Escapade* (1979), all part of Madrid's venerable film tradition and local industry. Suffice to say, though, that two particular genres – the horror film and the literary adaptation – have been especially predisposed toward the emplotment of multiple stories within a feature-length framework. Produced only a few months before Amicus's popular *Tales From the Crypt* (1972), the multi-director *Blood Cake* (featuring the contributions of Francesc Bellmunt, Jaime Chávarri, Emilio Martínez Lázaro and José María Vallés) is perhaps the most famous example of a Castilian-language omnibus film comprised of not one but several terrifying tales, each presented in a consecutive fashion yet given narrative autonomy as a stand-alone unit.

If Pons did not necessarily inherit earlier Spanish filmmakers' penchant for shock effects or their predilection for horror, he nevertheless drew upon a vast number of antecedent texts in preparing to adapt the written word of Quim Monzó and Sergi Belbel for the big screen. Besides his avowed interest in the multi-character films of Joseph L. Mankiewicz – director of the quasi-episodic tale of an extramarital affair, *A Letter to Three Wives* (1949), not to mention *All About Eve* (1950), a work that inspired the Catalan filmmaker to helm *Actrius/Actresses* (1997) – Pons followed a path cleared by such disparate international auteurs as Max Ophüls, Luis Buñuel and Chantal Akerman. However, due to their circularity (with the final episodes returning us to the themes, characters and/or iconography of the first episodes), such films as *La Ronde*, *The Phantom of Liberty* and *Toute une nuit* ultimately present the audience with 'the impossibility of escape', with the spectre of continued corruption, entrapment and repression. As we shall see, Pons utilises a similarly cyclical pattern in his three episode films, yet deftly manages to convey both containment and freedom by leaving those narrative circles partially open. Moreover, in creating episodic films largely, if not exclusively, about disparate individuals striving to connect with one another across ruptures and discontinuities, he foregrounds the associative hermeneutics and inherent hybridity at the heart of *all* multi-story, multi-character, multi-genre works, as well as the often strained linkages between cinematic adaptations and their literary or theatrical sources.

Genre, mode or meta-genre?

An important question arises: Is it correct to speak of the episode film as a genre? Given the fact that episode films appear to lack unifying iconographic elements and can mobilise any number of generic conventions in a combinatory – indeed, promiscuous – way, might this type of cinematic praxis be more accurately described as a narrative *mode*, a *method* of audiovisual representation and *presentation* not bound by particular taxonomies or producer–consumer pacts, but rather by the rhetorical devices employed by filmmakers to illicit certain responses? Or, conversely, might it be referred to as a *meta-genre*, one conducive to mise-en-abyme structures and self-reflexive gestures that call attention to the permeable and shifting boundaries between constituent narrative units as well as traditional genres (such as the musical, the western and romance)?

I wish to posit the latter possibility as a means of reconceiving the relationship between the syntagmatic and paradigmatic dimensions of textual signification, and suggest that questions of content and form are italicised in episodic cinema, which twists the 'spigot' of the semiotic axis so as to visually manifest structural components that in other types of film are concealed. This ninety-degree turn of the syntagmatic/paradigmatic axis thus renders visible otherwise invisible relations. By extension, it provides filmmakers with a wide yet limited repertoire of narrative possibilities for breaking texts into separate sections, and therefore facilitates our attempts to uncover resemblances between seemingly dissimilar episode films.

Division markers, such as title cards, thus become the iconographic features to look for, the visual *content* rather than a structural function or formal property of a larger narrative system of signification. Just as the syntagmatic becomes paradigmatic, so too does the paradigmatic become syntagmatic, with the motivic emphasis on couples in conversation superimposed atop the couplet structure of thematically linked episodes, which share a kind of 'dialogue' across the breach of space and time separating them. The staged encounters between two people in each of the eleven episodes comprising Ventura Pons's *Caricies* effectively illustrate the structural machinations involved in linking up one section of the film to another. For a serial chain of stories – especially one like *Carícies*, which circles in on itself – is made up of *coupled* links, a dyadic configuration multiplied over time and occasionally made dissonant through narrative 'disagreements'.

If the episode film is indeed a genre (or, as I am inclined to think, a meta-genre), then it is the most Bakhtinian of all genres, a dialogic and carnivalesque mishmashing of elements that has the latent capacity to level social fields, demolish aesthetic hierarchies, and provide alternative visions of life free from conventional rules and restrictions. Besides its hybridised status, as a text of limited if not infinite replenishment the episode film allows the spectator to laugh in the face of death; for the withering away of one story is followed by the blossoming of another (at least until the very end). The death of the old and birth of the new, so central to Mikhail Bakhtin's conception of carnival, is marked by extreme contingency as well as moral quandaries in the context of episodic cinema, wherein what is 'new' (here indicative of renewal and the future) quickly becomes 'old' (itself indicative of stasis and the past). In the case of Catalan cinema, the multiple apertures and closures that pepper a single episode film can effectively conjure the sociopolitical turmoil, the series of rapid transformations, that brought both welcome liberalisation and moral uncertainty to Spain from the 1960s onward.

Moreover, since many episode films are *about* the crossing of boundaries, this type of cinematic praxis seems especially prone to Bakhtinian metaphors – in particular the breaching of 'borders, thresholds, and territorial demarcations' that can emancipate people from their confined sociopolitical states so as to challenge the status quo. Such thresholds may be literal or figurative, spatial or corporeal, and indeed few types of film lend themselves so readily to 'body language' as the anthology. Not coincidentally, in his assessment of Ventura Pons's fifteen-episode *El perquè de tot plegat*, Gerard Dapena refers explicitly to 'the body of the film', which corporealises the quest for romantic love and/or sexual fulfilment (2001: 54). In our own 'caressing' of that text, our own fetishistic stroking of the spaces between its autonomous vignettes, a similar pursuit can be ascertained, one that betrays the spectatorial drive for narrative fulfilment in the face of closure's continuous deferment. Finally, because carnival offers its participants and onlookers the opportunity to 'taste the world' – to paraphrase Bakhtin (1984: 281)[2] – the banquet of elements on display in episode films – the sheer abundance of stories, sketches, characters and situations – suggests a remarkably democratic alternative to traditional storytelling, a spreading out (or spreading *thin*, some might argue) of narrative. This showcasing of abundance in miniature(s) is literalised in a scene from *El perquè de tot plegat*, when several tiny desserts on a buffet are served to a female patron at a restaurant – an image that reminds us that we are sampling a variety of dishes and delicacies in this rather 'promiscuous' film.

Having now served an 'appetiser' of sorts, one that details the classificatory status of episode films, I shall now move to the 'main course' of this chapter – the case studies that explain, through textual analysis, how the three above-mentioned films consolidate Pons's most frequently mobilised themes, 'homosexuality, literarity and urbanism' (Smith, 2003: 127), while painting a complex picture of contemporary life marked by marital infidelity, urban alienation and communication breakdown.

'Lumpen comedies' and 'limpid dramas': a minimalistic mix

As stated earlier, Pons's first entry in his Minimalist Trilogy – *El perquè de tot plegat* – consists of fifteen episodes, or rather thirteen vignettes framed by a prologue and an epilogue. These bookending boundaries of the film are themselves porous and prone to perpetuity. After a five-second opening shot of a middle-aged man standing against a photo-shop backdrop and uttering the word 'Prologue' while looking at the camera, the film begins with the same individual – now surrounded by mountainous terrain – trying to teach a stone to say 'Pa'. From the outset, and in a very primal way, *El perquè de tot plegat* self-reflexively foregrounds the enunciative act, the putting-into-words of personal desires.

Quickly, however, the man's frustrations begin to mount, as the rock (roughly the size of a newborn baby) remains obstinately silent. Between puffs on a cigarette, our befuddled protagonist carries on a one-sided conversation, the first of many throughout the film. Lacking answers to his spoken questions ('How should I communicate? How shall I go about establishing contact?'), he tries to reason with the stone (crouching down to its level) and even treats it to breakfast before hurling the object across an improbably vast space in anger. The prologue thus culminates with the disconsolate man sending the stone across the countryside, past golf courses and river gorges, into the heart of Barcelona, where it lands on a street outside a cathedral and finally yells 'Pa!' This humorous ending to the prologue marks the beginning of the film proper, and puts forth a metaphor of communication in which the desired response to the man's prodding of the rock comes *after the fact*, suggesting a kind of temporal delay or narrative deferment that takes on additional meaning throughout the rest of the film, which is filled with missed opportunities and similar moments of melodramatic pathos.

Besides initiating a fable-like tone for the ensuing episodes, which are primarily set in claustrophobic apartment buildings far removed from the mythological landscape of the opening minutes, the prologue of the film (subtitled '*Voluntat*', meaning 'Will') hinges upon the protagonist's rhetorical enquiries about communication and contact, which are significant insofar as they reflect Pons's own inquisitive search for ways to link up several self-contained episodes, each marked off from one another by introductory title cards yet filled with thematic echoes, audiovisual repetitions and characters striving to connect with one another. The prologue's flirtation with fantasy and magical realism is later echoed in the epilogue (entitled '*Dubte*', or 'Doubt'), when a forest gnome magically appears out of thin air to grant a similar-looking man a wish. When told to choose something tangible within the next five minutes (like gold or a palace rather than health or happiness), the surprised hiker considers a litany of possible answers – 'A mansion! A Range Rover! An airline! Claudia Schiffer! Julia Roberts! The throne of a Balkan country!' – before ultimately deciding, at the last second, to wish for another gnome, thus extending the duration of the event and inscribing the idea of infinity, something also connoted by the film's episodic yet serial narrative, which threatens to continue unfurling even after this final vignette.

Not coincidentally, each of the thirteen episodes contained between this film's prologue and epilogue average five minutes in duration, some of them ending almost immediately after they have begun. This has the effect of leaving audiences in a breathless state, still processing what has just transpired even as a new set of characters is being introduced. Each episode in the film bears a different title, covering such psychological qualities and emotional states as 'Jealousy', 'Spite', 'Desire' and 'Love'. These individual words are spoken directly to the camera by each episode's main characters, who are likewise introduced in the interstitial moments. Significantly, the first vignette to follow the prologue is entitled 'Wisdom' ('*Enteniment*', more accurately translated as 'Understanding'). It features a married couple debating what it takes to become 'intoxicated' by the opposite sex. For the wife, little more than a physical caress makes it difficult for her to resist a man's advances; an admission that troubles her husband, as does her comment that she has 'known' lots of men over the course of her adult life. She believes that the adage 'all men are equal' may be a cliché, but it nevertheless carries a measure of truth. In fact, this saying becomes our basis for adducing the similarities and differences among the film's assortment of male characters, many of whom fail to meet their partners halfway in relationships that are strained by anomie, distrust and disillusionment.

The titles of the second and third episodes, 'Honesty' ('*Honestedat*') and 'Sincerity' ('*Sinceritat*'), might seem to counteract such themes, suggesting an optimistic alternative to the treachery on display throughout the film. But in fact these segments express equally pessimistic takes on male–female relations. In the first of these two, a nurse looks forward to the end of her shift, for it means that she will soon be meeting the improbably named Ztt for dinner (the unseen man's moniker, like the names of the main characters in the ninth episode – Grmpf and Piti – recall the fairy-tale aspects of the prologue and epilogue). However, after a patient dies (an unfortunate nuisance insofar as 'death means a lot of paperwork'), she catches a glimpse of the insinuating smile of a doctor in the hospital and decides to postpone her date, one among many deferrals throughout the film.

Although the title of this episode, 'Honesty', conveys the nurse's candour (if not integrity), it could just as easily have been applied to the episode that immediately follows, which features a young woman and her fiancé pledging undying love over dinner, their romantic words punctuated by bursts of fireworks lighting up the night sky. Entitled 'Sincerity' (a word spoken only by the man in the interstitial), this brief vignette not only recapitulates a food motif that will become more apparent, but also finds the couple promising to be completely honest with one another (for, according to her, 'one single lie would destroy their love'). Then, in a matter of seconds, they begin bickering. Their argument is the result of his being *too honest* about her questionable taste in restaurants. Calling her fiancé

a 'chronic idiot', the woman throws down her engagement ring and
walks out of his life, bringing a sudden end to this discombobulat-
ing series of events. Her precipitous change of heart reminds us that
abrupt shifts in milieu, character, pacing and tone are what partially
define the episodic format, and that we should be prepared for anything and everything in submitting to these interruptive fictions.

The film's fourth episode, 'Submission' ('*Sumissió*'), concerns an
older woman in contrast to the younger couple, and it begins with a
tracking shot of a restaurant waiter putting four small pastries on
her plate. As suggested earlier, the array of dishes in this scene can
be taken to mean the enormous spread of stories made available to
viewers of episode films, which are narrative banquets offering
something for everyone. The film's appeal to its own audience is
made explicit in this segment, since this woman of wealth and experience (something denoted by her appearance and demeanour)
delivers a salty monologue to the camera in the manner of a direct-
address confessional. 'I want a man who doesn't listen to what I say',
the woman states, before musing, 'I want a man who bosses me.'
This masochistic character, who admits to being turned on 'when
they hit me', derives pleasure only by pleasing men, a polymor-
phously perverse state of being that is later echoed in the film's
eleventh episode, 'Jealousy' ('*Gelosia*'), which pivots on the image
of a woman performing endless fellatio on an increasingly anxious
man. In that case, though, the receiver of sexual gratification is the
one who expresses the episode's titular sense of envy; for the man
thinks that his partner is so obsessed with his penis that she has forgotten the person to which it is attached. 'I exist too', he tells the
unnamed woman, who simply falls asleep atop his groin.

Significantly, this tale of penis obsession and male depression
follows the tenth episode, entitled 'Desire' ('*Desig*'), which reiter-
ates, almost shot for shot, the restaurant scene from the fourth
episode, complete with pastries; only this time with a different older
woman speaking to the camera from her table. Featuring the only
flashback in the entire film, this segment delves into the emotional
pain of someone whose husband would rather masturbate than have
sexual intercourse. The speaker recalls a recent moment when the
two of them, staying at a posh hotel and sleeping in separate twin
beds, overheard the groans of a couple next door, their audible love-
making and post-coital conversation filtering through the wall and
casting in relief the distance separating husband and wife. She likens

the vast silence between the two, broken only by his muffled sobs into a pillow, to an emotional gulf filled 'with the cobwebs of years'.

Entitled 'Competition' ('*Competició*'), the fifth episode concerns three apartment dwellers: office worker Morell, his girlfriend Baba, and Veïna, an exotic beauty living in the high-rise dwelling opposite theirs. In a scene that might remind viewers of Hitchcock's *Rear Window* (1954), Morell becomes so obsessed with the mysterious woman across the courtyard that he begins peering at her through a recently purchased telescope. Veïna parades around her apartment in various states of undress and entertains different men each night of the week, something Morell becomes privy to in his growing obsession with this stranger. Once Veïna returns the look and begins peering through Morell's bedroom window, he too becomes an exhibitionist, performing for this woman whose prying eyes turn his personal space into a 'private theatre'. The title of this episode refers to an unspoken contest between the two voyeurs/performers, each trying to top the other in terms of sexual feats and partners. Not only does Veïna literally get the *first* word (she is the one who announces the title, 'Competition', in the brief interstitial), but also she figuratively gets the *final* word. To Morell's surprise, his girlfriend Baba becomes Veïna's latest sexual conquest; a twist ending that suggests that she has won this game of one-upmanship, an ending that is not unlike the humorous denouement of the next episode.

'Compenetration' ('*Compenetració*') is a comically inflected conversation between two people, this time a middle-class man and woman speaking on the telephone, each playing a prankish game on the other by masking their identities and inventing sexually explicit scenarios that suggest that their lives are filled with little more than lies. With both individuals speaking *past* one another as if existing in two separate worlds, this episode illustrates the self-created yet unnecessary impediments to human contact and communication. This theme returns in the next episode, 'Ego', in which a talkative man, taking a break from performing cunnilingus on his partner in a parked car, complains about his inability to listen to other people. Speaking nonstop about how he feels like a creep for being so self-involved, he ironically shuts down communication and transforms a two-person scene into a monologue, one that finally ends when the silent woman in the passenger seat returns his head to her lap.

'Spite', the ninth episode, is the most 'polygamous' section of the film, dipping into several romantic pairings, yet largely focusing on

Grmpf, a woman who cannot seem to settle down with the man of her dreams. 'Love', the twelfth episode, follows the tempestuous relationship between a zoological librarian and a rugged football player, the latter seeking tender caresses from the woman until she suggests that they live together; a comment that ironically drives the young man away. In the build-up to that twist ending, the librarian gives her boyfriend a bounty of gifts, from books to shirts to compact discs to jewellery. This array of goods is a mise-en-abyme assisting in the 'visualisation' of episodicity, putting it into a material context that helps us to 'see' this meta-genre's spectatorial appeals.

As stated earlier, *El perquè de tot plegat* ends on a quirky note, with a hiker in the forest being greeted by a diminutive gnome after kicking a toadstool and sending fairy dust into the air. His last-second wish for a second gnome, chosen so as to extend his decision-making another five minutes, resonates with the way in which short episodes are presented to us in anthology, omnibus, portmanteau and sketch films, which gesture toward infinity within a finite structure. This implied infinity is also detectable in *Carícies*, Ventura Pons's 1997 follow-up to *El perquè de tot plegat*. Adapted from a *La Ronde*-like play by Sergi Belbel, and broken into eleven interlocking episodes that form a circle or narrative chain, this low-budget independent production kicked off a fragmenting trend in Spanish filmmaking, one reflected in the forking-path narratives of Julio Medem's *Los amantes del Círculo Polar/The Lovers of the Arctic Circle* (1998) and María Ripoll's *Lluvia en los zapatos/If Only* (1998). Perhaps the most sophisticated example of subjunctive or forking-path cinema came two years later, when Pons's *Morir (o no)* was theatrically released in Spain before hitting the film festival circuit. Rather than conclude this chapter with a discussion of that film, which – given its complexity – deserves a lengthier analysis on its own,[3] I wish to briefly examine some of the aspects of *Carícies* that distinguish it from Pons's other entries in his Minimalist Trilogy.

Although less generically hybridised than *El perquè de tot plegat*, which schizophrenically shifts from fantasy sequence to marital drama to workplace comedy and other types of narrative, *Carícies* manages to convey a broader array of lifestyles and social contexts for its many disconsolate characters, who can be seen in apartment buildings, city parks, a retirement home, a railway station and a deserted alleyway at night. Whereas most of the protagonists in the former film are middle-class and straight, a number of the characters in *Carícies* appear to come from working-class origins and are homosexual. But they do not fit into convenient moulds, and indeed exist as liminal figures set adrift in a nocturnal landscape, a bleak vision of Barcelona filled with poverty, drugs and malaise. So there is greater diversity in *Carícies*, a film that ranges across different settings and communities. And yet, while the characters in *El perquè de tot plegat* have names, the men and women in this film do not, and are listed in the credits in the most rudimentary way: as 'Young Man', as 'Older Woman', as 'Kid', etc. Such anonymity is problematised, however, by the presence of recognisable stars and character actors, from Julieta Serrano to Rosa María Sardá and several other famous thespians from the big screen and small.

The first individuals to appear in the film, though, were relative newcomers at the time of the film's production: David Selvas and Laura Conejero. Here they play a young married couple whose tense relationship is a throwback to the final, pre-epilogue episode of *El perquè de tot plegat*. As if a continuation of that scene, the man and woman are shown in a claustrophobic domestic space, in close quarters yet separated by an emotional distance. As the man looks out of their apartment window on to an abandoned street corner, his wife flicks through a magazine on the sofa. An argument quickly ensues. She has grown tired of 'filling their idle time with empty words and insults', and in communicating this raises her voice each time that he interrupts her. He does this, the woman argues, every time she puts together a coherent argument. This connects to the idea that interruptions are what partially define the episodic film experience, wherein coherency is habitually broken for the sake of narrative diversity and thematic counterpoint.

In contrast to the caresses that one might expect to find in a loving relationship, the man's backhand slap of his wife brings this domestic argument to a climax. He hits her two more times before she asks him what he wants for dinner. The man's request that she make a salad 'with lots of different things' thrown in not only reminds us of the earlier film's fixation on food, but also reinscribes the idea that episode films feature 'lots of different things'. When told that they have 'lettuce, tomatoes, carrots, sweetcorn, olives, celery, onions', the husband tells her not to use onions, since they 'repeat' on him. This comment, while seemingly insignificant, assumes allegorical meaning toward the end of the film, when the opening scene is *repeated* in the penultimate episode from a different audiovisual perspective. A typically 'twisted' twist ending caps this first episode, with the wife turning the tables on her abusive husband. Kicking him in the testicles and slamming the salad bowl against his head, she tells him to go fetch the ingredients for their dinner.

Following this violent skirmish is the first of many interstitials in which the camera takes us racing through the streets of Barcelona at night, here accompanied by sped-up death-metal music. As a linking device between two episodes, this and the other in-between scenes, which pepper the entire film with shots of the Catalonian capital, suggest that the restless city is in fact the main character. In a sense, *Carícies* – while filled with faces and in many ways an anthropological exploration of human desire – is a *city film*, one that is similar to such multi-director omnibus features as *Paris vu par . . .*, *Sipurei Tel-Aviv/Tel-Aviv Stories* (Ayelet Menahemi and Nirit Yaron, 1994) and *Traição/Betrayal* (1999), all of which aspire to show an eclectic cross-section of social life in major metropolitan areas, where – as Joan M. Díez Clivillé writes – 'despite proximity, people can be total strangers' (2000).

The second episode features the same woman from the first episode, here joined by her mother, whom she meets at a food market. Together they walk to a public park and sit on an outdoor bench below the full moon. The older woman begins to read from a book of poetry, an object that serves as a reminder that *Carícies* is an adaptation of a pre-existing text, Belbel's play. The daughter reacts negatively to these pedantic, pretentious words, which actually reveal her mother's melancholic mindset. Although they apparently used to argue all the time, the old woman misses her daughter and feels that she is going mad. Her daughter, who later interrupts the woman just as she had been interrupted by her husband in the earlier episode, suggests that she go live in a retirement home, an idea that carries forth into the next episode, set in just such a space.

After another interstitial shot of the metropolis, this time comprised of images of Barcelona's Metro stations accompanied by melancholic piano music, the third episode begins. With this episode, the film's structural pattern becomes clear. Each autonomous section of the narrative chain hinges upon a disjointed conversation between two people. Each couple is made up of someone who had been introduced in the previous episode as well as someone who will carry over to the subsequent episode. The same mother presented to us minutes before is thus one of the main characters in this third segment of the film, only this time joined by another older woman: her dance partner at a retirement home. Actually, this newly introduced character is the woman's lover, a lesbian who prefers the tango to rock 'n' roll. Telling her companion that she had hated her baby as a young mother and that, when pregnant, she used to dance at the local bars, the woman reveals a very different side of her personality from the one shown earlier, going so far as to refer to her off-screen daughter as a 'stupid parasite that sucked my blood for seven months'. The episode concludes with the two older women escaping from the pains of their pasts by dancing together to two imaginary soundtracks, one to tango music and the other to rock 'n' roll.

Driving rock music and careening cars speed us through the streets of Barcelona in the next interstitial, which then segues to the film's fourth episode, a tête-à-tête between the lesbian lover and her unshaven brother, a homeless man digging through the city's trash for food. Noting the sad state of her sibling, the woman urges him to return with her to the retirement home before the doors close at ten o'clock. He refuses, stating that all he wants to do is stay cold, fart and defecate when and where he pleases. With these words the man throws an inedible, salty sardine at his sister and sends her away. Interestingly, the emphasis on time in this sequence, wherein the woman keeps checking her watch in the minutes leading up to ten o'clock, takes on deeper meaning once we realise that the ailing woman is expected to die soon, and that the wife of her brother (whom she hasn't seen in ten years) died at a young age. It is curious, though, that the time recorded by the woman (who notes that it is 9.45 p.m. on her watch before leaving) is set five minutes before the time shown on a bedside clock in the previous episode, suggesting that what appear to be linear progressions in the film's chain of events are in fact recursive moments that may indeed be transpiring on different nights and/or in non-chronological order. However, this too will be thrown for a loop by the time the penultimate episode arrives, recapitulating the first scene of the film.

Prior to that arrival are several other episodes plunging us deeper into the underbelly of the city. The homeless man, shown pushing his cart through the city at an accelerated speed during the interstitial, encounters a punk dressed in black, a 13-year-old boy who kicks the bum awake and demands money only to eventually sit down beside the man and offer him a cigarette. The kid then relates a story, accompanied by grainy video footage (the film's only flash-back), about how he bought some hash and stole the dealer's lighter. In one of the green-tinted flashback sequences, set in the same park depicted earlier, the two women from the second episode (the daughter and mother sitting on a bench) can be seen in the background, their momentary presence a reminder that episode films are frequently multi-perspectival, reiterating single events that are made plural in the process of a narrator system switching to a different point of view.

The unusual friendship struck by the homeless man and the glue-sniffing punk in the fifth episode – a kind of surrogate father–son relationship – is echoed in the sixth episode, which shifts to a domestic scene involving the same teenaged boy and his biological father, who joins his son in the bath. The incestuous tone of this scene, which culminates with the boy getting an erection in the presence of his father, then gives way to another interstitial, taking us to Barcelona-Sants, the train station where the same father meets and berates his girlfriend. This seventh episode marks a return to the theme of the first episode, with the woman – having taken so much abuse – turning the tables on him. Telling the man that, in her premonition-like dream, she has seen him saying these same things and that his train will crash, the woman takes control of the situation and gets the last laugh.

Leaving her married boyfriend to deal with his ill-fated future, the woman makes her way to her father's house, where the old man is seen making salad (yet another throwback to the first episode). And, as in earlier sequences, a painful argument ensues, with the daughter and father's first meeting in over a month being trivialised by her withering remarks. The 50-year-old man finds a more receptive listener in the ninth episode, set in the flat of a young homosexual. As one of the film's many conversations that cross a generation gap, this meeting between young and old differs insofar as it culminates with an orgasmic release of tensions, the outcome of a sex act between the two main characters in this episode. It is significant that the two share a physically intense moment in the presence of a large mirror, the old man's gift to his young companion which doubles their images. This doubling motif assumes rich connotations for attentive viewers, who notice that this same young man was seen in the opening seconds of the film, in the lead-up to the first episode when he passed by the abusive husband in the hallway of an apartment building.

For audiences who may have missed that connection, Pons soon makes it explicit by first showing the hands of the clock above the central Plaza de Catalunya spinning backwards, and then repeating the opening scene, albeit from a different angle. This leads to the tenth episode, with the same young man now returning to his mother's apartment, where, through the thin walls, the couple upstairs (from the first episode) can be heard arguing. Stopping by long enough to use the bathroom (during which time his mother steals some money from his wallet), the young man soon leaves. This brings about the final episode of the film, in which the woman is left momentarily to her loneliness, only to hear a knock on her door. Opening it, she sees the husband from upstairs, his face now bloody from the beating that his wife dispensed. He has come to the older woman looking for a small cup of olive oil, to be used on the salad that his wife is preparing. Letting the man in, the woman attends to his wounds and begins caressing his face. This titular touch on the cheek has been a long time coming, the emotional payoff for audiences who have weathered one devastating episode after another. Although episodically arranged, the stories comprising *Carícies* amount to a kind of serial psychoses, a mounting 'sense of estrangement and simmering rage' that, according to Gerard Dapena, makes this film representative of Pons's world-view (2001: 54). However, that final gesture of compassion breaks the chain of despair and suggests a way out of the cycle of miscommunication and violence, something similarly apparent in Pons's most challenging film from a stylistic as well as structural point of view, *Morir (o no)*, a series of 'what if' scenarios showing how the altering of a single person's destiny can have a kind of 'butterfly effect', changing the course of narrative events and guaranteeing the survival of several (initially ill-fated) individuals.

Conclusion: a trend in Catalan cultural productions?

Over the past twenty years, dozens of important works from Catalonia have begun attracting international attention, from Pere Portabella's *Pont de Varsòvia/Warsaw Bridge* (1989), with its multiple storylines, to Álvaro Fernández Armero's *El arte de morir/The Art of Dying* (2000), a flashback-filled thriller that is claimed to be the first Catalan-language film selected by Venevisión International 'to be distributed in the U.S. as part of a pilot project' (*Cineinforme*,

2001: 58). What is notable about this renaissance is the number of multi-story ensemble films being produced for a large and diverse demographic of viewers throughout Spain and the rest of Europe. Ramon Térmens' and Carles Torras's *Joves/Youth* (2004), for instance, interweaves three tales about the trials and tribulations faced by teenagers, while Cesc Gay's *A la ciutat/In the City* (2003) explores the day-to-day rituals of several thirtysomethings whose lives intersect on the streets of Barcelona. While older filmmakers and documentarians like Jaime Camino and José María Forn habitually turned to significant moments in the nation's history, Pons and his contemporaries continuously prod the viewer to examine present-day conditions and look ahead so as to imagine new possibilities of sociopolitical change.

If Spanish cinema has been marginalised compared to other Western European cinemas, Catalan filmmaking has been doubly marginalised. It is perhaps not too surprising, then, that one of the most marginalised genres (or meta-genres) of cinema – the episode film – has proven to be so effective in challenging the *grands récits* of the nation and providing alternate visions of contemporary life in a country that is culturally, ethnically and sexually diverse. Poised against earlier traditions and generic conventions, Pons's collections of anecdotal vignettes, which are rooted in regional issues and feature the local language, capture a heterogeneity of experience in keeping with Catalonia's multicultural climate. *El perquè de tot plegat*, *Carícies* and *Morir (o no)* are thus major contributions to a supposedly 'minor' type of film praxis, one fittingly predisposed to evoking the *magnitude* of minoritarian contributions to Catalan culture and society. As the recipient of numerous awards and as the subject of several career retrospectives, Pons has done much to shed light on Barcelona's thriving, cosmopolitan film culture. Perhaps the critical attention being paid to the three episode films comprising his Minimalist Trilogy will also lead to a re-evaluation of an overlooked narratological genre, one that has become increasingly relevant in these fragmented, uncertain times.

Notes

1 Terenci Moix has called *Ocaña* 'the first authentic portrait of post-Franco Spain'. See Anabel Campo Vidal's *Ventura Pons: la mirada lliure* (2000: 93).

2 This passage is quoted in Steven Marsh's excellent book *Popular Spanish Film under Franco: Comedy and the Weakening of the State* (2006), which attempts to 'politicise Bakhtin's insights' about carnivalism and heteroglossia.

3 Readers who are interested in *Morir (o no)* are invited to consult my essay 'Alternate Futures, Contradictory Pasts' (Diffrient, 2006), a portion of which interrogates the themes and structure of that particular film in the context of similar 'forking path' narratives produced throughout the world.

References

Anderson, Benedict (1991) *Imagined Communities: Reflections on the Origin and Spread of Nationalism*, London: Verso.

Bakhtin, Mikhail (1984) *Rabelais and His World*, Hélène Iswolsky (trans.), Bloomington: Indiana University Press.

Campo Vidal, Anabel (2000) *Ventura Pons: la mirada libre*, Huesca: Festival de Cine de Huesca.

Cineinforme (2001) 'El plan de Venevisión para la distribución de cine español en Estado Unidos, en marcha', 739, November, 58.

Dapena, Gerard (2001) 'Tainted Love', *Film Comment*, 37: 6, November–December, 53–5.

Díez Clivillé, Joan M. (2000) 'I'm a Catalan! An Internet Project on Catalonia and Her People', www.geocities.com/TheTropics/Lagoon/6202/catalan.htm.

Diffrient, David Scott (2006) 'Alternate Futures, Contradictory Pasts: Forking Paths and Cubist Narratives in Contemporary Film', *Screening the Past*, 20, www.latrobe.edu.au/screeningthepast/20/alternate-futures.html.

D'Lugo, Marvin (2002) 'Catalan Cinema: Historical Experience and Cinematic Practice', in Catherine Fowler (ed.), *The European Cinema Reader*, London: Routledge, 163–74.

Fernàndez, Josep-Anton (2004) 'The Authentic Queen and the Invisible Man: Catalan Camp and Its Conditions of Possibility in Ventura Pons's *Ocaña, retrat intermittent*', *Journal of Spanish Culture*, 5: 1, 69–82.

Klein, Andy (1999) 'The Lucky Bidder Beware', *New Times Los Angeles*, 10–16 June, 45.

Marsh, Steven (2006) *Popular Spanish Film under Franco: Comedy and the Weakening of the State*, Basingstoke: Palgrave.

Smith, Paul Julian (2003) *Contemporary Spanish Culture: TV, Fashion, Art, and Film*, Cambridge: Polity Press.

10

Horror of allegory: *The Others* and its contexts

Ernesto R. Acevedo-Muñoz

Alejandro Amenábar's first international co-production, *Los otros/ The Others* (Spain/US, 2001) poses the question of the translatability of generic formations and the elasticity of the concept of national cinema. Parting from his Spanish-language (and Spanish-style) psychological 'thrillers', *Tesis/Thesis* (1996) and *Abre los ojos/Open Your Eyes* (1997), Amenábar's *Los otros* built upon the director's prestige as a young, energetic and original director for marketing the Nicole Kidman vehicle. On the surface *Los otros* is dressed as a classically inclined horror movie of the haunted house variety with a strong stylistic debt to gothic novels and films (like Alfred Hitchcock's *Rebecca* (1940) and Robert Siodmak's *The Spiral Staircase* (1946)), eloquent plays of light and shadows, and a conventionally cued dramatic score.[1] However, as in his earlier contemporary-set films, the weight of Spanish political and cultural history allows for an allegorical reading of *Los otros* that extends the localised context of Madrid and the metaphors of monstrosity seen in *Tesis* and *Abre los ojos* into a more universal film language. Through the adaptation of classic conventions of genre, Amenábar is able to mould an essentially Spanish narrative into an elastic generic form whose national context is even underscored by the non-specificity of its setting. In this chapter I explore the ways in which contemporary Spanish directors, but Amenábar in particular, have evolved their nationalist concerns into generic hybrids or into revisionist generic arrangements that emphasise allegorically and metaphorically the Spanish contexts of cultural and political isolation, tradition, Catholicism, repression and motherhood.[2] Amenábar's *Los otros* reflexively reconfigures these Spanish themes into a horror format that obliquely refers to Spain's recent traumatic past and to the contemporary need to face and acknowledge the nation's evolution from 'horror' to 'deception' and eventually, to a compromise between past and present.

In his seminal essay 'The Mummy's Pool', Bruce Kawin analyses the logic of the horror genre in its recreation of dreams and nightmares, and the correlation between the systems of signification proper to films and dreams. Kawin writes:

> [O]ne goes to a horror film in order to have a nightmare – not simply a frightening dream, but a dream whose undercurrent of anxiety both presents and masks the desire to fulfil and be punished for conventionally or personally unacceptable impulses. This may be a matter of unconscious wish fulfilment . . . of confronting a hidden evil in the culture. (1999: 680)

The formal simplicity of the horror film and its reliance on visible and audible conventions that impose atmosphere and mood are usefully adapted to many contexts, as the history of the genre from 1920s German expressionism to Hollywood's 1930s Universal Studios classics, to the 1970s *slashers* and Italian exploitation horror of the 1980s clearly indicate. The basic formal and narrative conventions of horror, which Kawin eloquently lists, constantly refer us precisely to the genre's 'imitation' or recreation of dream states (of characters and spectators) in order to create a temporary sense of relief upon awakening from the fear and anxiety-causing nightmare (1999: 687). In other words, the pleasure of the classic horror film is the illusion of stability created by the temporary destruction (or freezing, or removal) of the threat, although it may return in sequels and remakes (as it so often happened from Karl Freund's *The Mummy* (1932) to Dracula's many incarnations; from *Frankenstein* (James Whale, 1931) to *Bride of Frankenstein* (James Whale, 1935) to *Son of Frankenstein* (Rowland V. Lee, 1939); from *Jaws* (Steven Spielberg, 1975) to *Jaws 2* (Jeannot Szwarc, 1978) to *Jaws 3-D* (Joe Alves, 1983); from Michael Myers to Jason and Mrs Voorhees). As the social function of all classical genres is to create and uphold the illusion of social stability, it is especially telling that the horror genre so often *fails* to create permanent stability, thus the monsters and threats are apparently welcome back so often.

The classic horror film is almost always a tale of repression in its latent content. Just like our dreams allow us some form of unconscious representation of our hidden, often unrecognised fears and desires – as Freud taught us in *The Interpretation of Dreams* – the horror film is commonly a revalidation of those fears in ways that exploit the 'terror of pleasure', as Tania Modleski has called it (1999). There is a consistent visible substance of repression in our dreams and nightmares, a logical manifest and latent content that allows us access to our own repression. As Luis Buñuel so perfectly showed us in *Un chien andalou* (1929) and *L'Age d'Or* (1930), and as Hitchcock so eloquently explored in *The Birds* (1963), there is temporary release of such fears and desires that is expressed in the cinematic form (Williams, 1990; Gordon, 2008). These canonical examples show the pendular motion between the rationality and irrationality of the horror scenario: in her nightmare the woman in *Un chien andalou* (Simone Mareuil) struggles against the man (Pierre Batchef) and his sexual assault until, in a final childish gesture, she sticks out her tongue and walks away from the enclosed (nightmarish) setting of the apartment into a sunny beach and the company of another young man she may actually desire. Melanie Daniels' victimisation in *The Birds* brings up the confusion between desire of a potential sexual partner and a maternal figure, as it is evident in the movie that Mrs Brenner (Jessica Tandy) is a bit young and wears her hair similarly to Melanie Daniels (Tippi Hedren). Both films offer faux happy endings in which the women protagonists are temporarily relieved of their respective threats. The sexual repression and forbidden desires (specifically for a lover or a maternal figure) explored in these films, however, very rarely address children's fears of abandonment, which may or may not be unconsciously sexual. In *L'Age d'Or*, for instance, both the man and woman repressed lovers express their frustration of 'the unbearable agony of desire' as Arthur Schnitzler called it (1990: 76), by sucking on a statue's big toe and falling asleep in the mother's bed, both childish gestures expressing the unconscious desire to return to the maternal 'dwelling'. Between sexuality and maternity, the horror film and dreams oscillate among the negotiation of fear and desire, and the fear of desire itself.

There is a long tradition in Spanish cinema of films about childhood that revisit and reappropriate the conventions of the classic horror film, with various generic intersections with melodrama and fairy tales. Coinciding significantly with the long end of Franco's regime in the early 1970s, *El espíritu de la colmena/Spirit of the Beehive* (Víctor Erice, 1973), *Furtivos* (José Luis Borau, 1975), *Cría cuervos/Cria!* (Carlos Saura, 1976) and a few other films adopt conventions of horror, introduce monsters and ghosts and various 'uncanny' figures and situations to their plots in ways that are potentially allegorical to the nation's cultural and political transitions of the period.[3] Following in the tradition of these films, Alejandro Amenábar's *Los otros* and Guillermo del Toro's *El espinazo del diablo/The Devil's Backbone* (2001) and *El laberinto del fauno/Pan's Labyrinth* (2006) all return to the context of the Spanish Civil War (1936–39) and its bigger sister, World War II (1939–45) to tell stories about children caught between reality, fantasy, horror and allegory.

In his essay on 'Historical Allegory', Ismail Xavier offers a history and analysis of the persistence of allegory in Western narrative since the classics as one of the logical forms of articulating national and regional foundational fictions. Allegory is necessary, writes Xavier, because it is a way for a cultural artefact to make sense in 'a specific frame of reference' (1999: 333). Specifically in the cinema, Xavier argues that allegorical strategies allow the filmmaker to 'thematize the position of his or her country in human history'. Furthermore, whereas 'intentional allegories' are by definition rather transparent, storytelling might also take the form of 'unconscious' allegory where the intervention of a 'competent reader' is necessary (1999: 335). Drawing from wide and varied examples from Hollywood as well as many other national cinemas including D. W. Griffith's *Intolerance* (1916), Fritz Lang's *Metropolis* (1926), Luis Buñuel's *Un chien andalou*, Jean Renoir's *La Marseillaise* (1936), Sergei Eisenstein's *Alexander Nevsky* (1938), Victor Fleming's *Gone with the Wind* (1939), John Ford's *The Searchers* (1956), Glauber Rocha's *Terra em transe/Land in Anguish* (1967), Rainer Werner Fassbinder's *Die Ehe der Maria Braun/The Marriage of Maria Braun* (1979), and even contemporary Hollywood films like Barry Levinson's *Wag the Dog* (1997), Xavier elaborates on the intention and interpretation of allegory in different contexts to mediate historical and social conflicts. And, while authorial intention or generic design may often dictate certain readings of allegory, the emergence of unconscious allegories and pragmatic allegories, those in which 'the underlined analogies between past and present are taken as . . . a form of raising a question about the present using the past' continue to determine, or at best mediate meaning (Xavier, 1999: 354). Significantly, genre categories and expectations also play a crucial role in our understanding of allegories and their meaning since popular genres by design present a type of shorthand for interpretation in each national context. As Rick Altman (1999) has argued, genres are not static categories but evolving forms. Contexts, whether they be cultural, historical, or of conditions of reception and consumption, inevitably shift the experience and interpretation of genre films. The concerns and social anxieties addressed in the horror genre are variable according to historical contexts so that the British and US classic horror film, for instance, concentrate on policing women's sexuality with recurring warning moral tales about vampirism and serial killers whose victims are almost always, inevitably, young white women in danger of sexual activity. The German horror films of the Weimar era (*The Cabinet of Dr Caligari* (Robert Wiene, 1919), *The Golem* (Carl Boese and Paul Wegener, 1920), *Nosferatu* (F. W. Murnau, 1922)), as Kracauer suggested, seemed to warn the Germans about the rise of false leaders and the dangers they presented to the population, driving somebody to an untimely and horrible physical or mental death. In the Spanish context, at least since the 1970s it seems as if the conjunction of maternity, horror and allegories of the Civil War is rather stable.

Xavier's approach can help us understand the intersection of horror and allegory in Spanish cinema after 1970. Allegory's potential to mediate the meaning of cultural and historical intersections comes to mind when acknowledging the insistent presence of the specific historical junctures of the Civil War and the *dictablanda* surrounding the narrative lives of children and young people in many Spanish films. And, while allegorical content or interpretation is not expressly present, it is however inferred from the narrative and/or character arc of these films. For instance, in Erice's *El espíritu de la colmena* the little girl Ana (Ana Torrent) is, quite literally, mesmerised in 1940 by the cinematic fantasy of James Whale's *Frankenstein*. Ana believes that she is caring for and befriending Frankenstein's monster. While little Ana is at first genuinely terrified by Dr Frankenstein's creature, she comes to appreciate and even to be seduced by the monster's presence in her life. Like dreams themselves, Ana becomes confused somewhere between 'reality' and 'fantasy' and that which lies between them, hallucinations. Ana is mystified by her parents' strained, silent relationship, lost in the medieval frost of a Castilian village that still resorts to a town crier for public announcements. Ana's 'monster' (who is actually a wounded *Maquís* still escaping from the wave of violence that followed the official end of the Civil War) comes to be, arguably, the only thing that makes sense in her life. At one point in the film the child seemingly attempts to commit suicide by ingesting mushrooms that her father had warned her were poisonous. But death is not something that this generation of Spanish children in films seems to fear.

In Saura's *Cría cuervos*, the main character, another little girl also named Ana (and, of course, played by Ana Torrent as well) attempts to and believes that she has in fact killed her father (Héctor Alterio, seen in military uniform). He is the patriarchal and abusive military head of a family ran as a Francoist barrack and trapped, quite literally, in the past. The little girl has very real visions of her dead mother's ghost (played by Geraldine Chaplin), whom she may have seen die. Ana interacts calmly and peacefully with her mother's ghost, who manifests herself only to Ana at various times in the movie. And rather kindly, in what comes across in the film as a loving gesture, little Ana offers to do the favour of killing her grandmother, paralysed and mute after an apparent stroke. Yet, little Ana is never frightened by the bizarre events that intersect her life, her imagination, hallucinations and dreams. As in *El espíritu de la colmena* this little Ana in *Cría cuervos* is very close to death: she finds her father's corpse, is haunted by memories of her mother dying, and is even attracted to decaying corpses (she is, we may recall, fascinated by the ever-present plate of chickens' feet in the refrigerator). This Ana, too, comes very close to committing suicide herself by ingesting what she believes are the same poisonous powders with which she attempted to kill her father. In a world that seems out of her control, with dead parents, a paralysed history (symbolised by the wheelchair-bound and mute grandmother), and contained by the presence of a sexually repressed aunt, Ana in *Cría cuervos* finds solace only in the dark intersections between life and death, and in the incongruously cheery tempo yet sad lyrics of the pop song '¿Por qué te vas?', which emerges as a sort of melancholy ode to abandonment.

Guillermo del Toro's *El espinazo del diablo* largely circumvents the allegorical approach by presenting a rather literal representation of horror in the world of children. Squarely set in 1939 towards the end of the Civil War and populated by desperately weak characters still loyal to the Republic, the film elaborates and extrapolates from the frame of reference set up by the earlier films by Erice and Saura in its creation of a world where children, 'monsters' and ghosts constantly interact. Significantly set in a remote orphanage, a place whose meaning is both literal and symbolic, the film's protagonist, a boy named Carlos (Fernando Tielve) and the other children, mostly orphans made by the Civil War, see themselves haunted by the ghost of a murdered boy (Junio Valverde), an unexploded bomb in the courtyard (depicted as a reminder of the horrors of Guernica), and a laboratory shelf with deformed foetuses conserved in glass jars full of brandy. The setting alone makes for the constant presence of death intersecting the past and present: the orphans' parents are dead, the foetuses are dead, Santi's ghost is dead, and the bomb promises more death soon to come. Part historical allegory about the Civil War and its immeasurable trail of death and destruction, and part a combination and literalisation of many death similes and metaphors, del Toro's *El espinazo del diablo* once again places children in a juncture where they will need to face and come in close contact with death in order to understand their lives and, yes, their history.[4] The fact that the child ghost Santi solves the mystery of his own murder serves to contextualise the film's position on the fatality and inescapability of history: as in Saura's *La caza/The Hunt* (1965) the guilty are inevitably brought to the surface. On the one hand, though, because the setting of *El espinazo del diablo* is so literal, its allegorical function is somewhat transparent: it is historical allegory in the Xavier sense of a story of the past helping make sense of the present, of the need to retain and preserve historic memory and prevent the return to the errors of the past. Literal and symbolic, *El espinazo del diablo* does not deny the potential power of allegory, particularly when dealing with events concerning the Civil War and its aftermath; its physical, psychological, emotional and even infrastructural devastation on Spain and its people and even the ineffectual efforts of Republican forces to turn around its outcome.

Del Toro's *El laberinto del fauno* also presents a child principal character, Ofelia (played by Ivana Baquero), who finds herself trapped in the netherworld between horror and fairy tales shortly after the end of the Civil War. In this netherworld children die, a princess has to fulfil three tasks, and there are numerous monsters and 'fauns' and fairies that are never as terrifying as the reality of military and fascist repression of the post-Civil War period. Not only is Ofelia's stepfather (Sergi López) the military authority of another sleepy, lost Spanish town, but his brutal government and the resistance fighters that surround the town are turned into a fantastic allegory of rebellion and survival in the girl's imagination. Ofelia's interactions with the incredible characters, the giant toad hidden in a cavern that is turned inside out to reveal a key, the faun or satyr with its human body, cold, expressionless eyes and phallic horns, and the eyeless gruesome child-eating pale man (both played by the wonderful Doug Jones), patterned, also allegorically, on Goya's *Saturno devorando a su hijo* (1820–23), never really make her as fearsome as Captain Vidal's brutality. An evil parental figure like so many others in Spanish cinema after 1970 (as in *Cría cuervos* and *Furtivos*), Captain Vidal's repressive, murderous hold on the town, its people and its resources, leads Ofelia to a personal sacrifice in the service of resistance. As in all fairy tales, the film's content is also peppered with references to sexuality, deaths and births, and with the traumatic transition from girlhood to womanhood. But it is the horror intersection, the one more precisely represented by the upperworld, where Ofelia's story, like that of Carlos and Santi in *El espinazo del diablo*, takes on its most eloquent allegorical value. Ofelia's death at the hands of Captain Vidal comes in as the sacrifice of 'the blood of the innocent' spilled, literally by fascism and repression under Franco. While Ofelia struggles to understand the Faun's tests, she also takes on the responsibility of protecting her newborn half-brother from the father's claims of patriarchal control. And so in the movie's conclusion Ofelia's two worlds collide when she refuses to spill the baby brother's blood and instead offers her own when shot in the stomach by Captain Vidal, paradoxically fulfilling the third task that proves her nobility. Ofelia's death at the conclusion of *El laberinto del fauno* arguably puts in evidence the oscillation between horror, allegory and fairy tale in this film; through her death, Ofelia fulfils the task proper of fairy tale, dies at the hands of the horrific monster and, in historical-allegorical fashion, refuses to spill innocent blood. Both of del Toro's films, *El laberinto del fauno* and *El espinazo del diablo*, serve to rewrite and revise Spanish history.

These and other Spanish films about childhood made after 1970 continuously make reference to the intersection of the horror genre, allegory and dreams, and repeatedly present children under grave threats, either real or imagined, who yet seem to be fearless. The weight of repression and tradition that Saura, Erice, Almodóvar,

Amenábar and other directors explore has been often associated to
the potential power and reliance of Spanish cinema on allegory in
order to speak about repression under repression (as in Saura's *La
caza*, for instance). The two contextual historical bookends of the
1970s and the period around the Civil War inform the entirety of
these films about childhood and the confusion of their protagonists
between reality, fantasy and history. In the post-Franco years since
the transition to democracy, horror has become once again popular
in some Spanish films that seem to re-address the anxieties of the
past from the perspective of those who didn't live them. Thus,
Amenábar's previous feature films – *Tesis* and *Abre los ojos* – present
metaphors of monstrosity as ways for his generation to arguably find
ways of addressing their own fears of violence, repression and the
weight of history itself. *Tesis* introduces us, provocatively, to the
grown-up Ana (indeed Ana Torrent, now iconic for her generation)
becoming self-reflexively involved in the production of a type of
'horror' film in which she herself becomes the victim. In *Tesis*
Amenábar also rehearses a horrifying parable of contemporary
Spain's damaging fixation with media and media intersections of
history, like in Almodóvar's *Kika* (1993) and *Matador* (1986). The
engrossing, pornographic attention to violence in Spanish media of
the last decade and a half is evidently intersecting Amenábar's gory
tale in which 'reality' and fiction are essentially fused, where there
are no boundaries left between violence and the representation of
violence. But unlike her childhood self in *El espíritu de la colmena*,
Cría cuervos, *Elisa, vida mía/Elisa, My Love* (Carlos Saura, 1977)
and even *El nido/The Nest* (Jaime de Armiñán, 1980) this Ana at
thirty years of age is susceptible to fear and cannot escape, except by
violence itself, from the horror of her own nightmare. And in *Abre
los ojos* César (Eduardo Noriega) not only lives within the eternal
confusion of dreams, reality and hallucinations but sees himself also
turned into a monster by the difficulty of understanding his own
past, not unlike 'Tony' Wilson, the character played by Rock
Hudson in John Frankenheimer's *Seconds* (1966). It is only through
the intercession of Sofía (Penélope Cruz) whose name, of course,
means 'knowledge', that César is able to understand anything, to
'open his eyes' and effect the exorcism of the 'traumas' of the past.
Arguably, César's narrative trajectory allegorically addresses the
'horrors' and 'scars' of the past, the dangers of not confronting and
understanding our own history, and the need to mediate and look

ahead. It's as if Amenábar's first two features were suggesting the evolution of the allegories of horror and metaphors of monstrosity into the denouement of reconcilement with the past. As Kawin argued in 'The Mummy's Pool', in the horror film 'there is no safety in ignoring the Id/Underworld/monster . . . but there is considerable strength in confronting the danger' (1999: 686).

Mothers and monsters abound in classic, recent and contemporary Spanish cinema, literature and culture; characters such as Martina (Lola Gaos) in *Furtivos* (José Luis Borau, 1975), and of course the title character of García Lorca's *La casa de Bernarda Alba* (1936/1945) herself is another mother figure turned into a 'monster' by the weight of her own repression: that imposed by Bernarda on her daughters, and by tradition on herself. In Amenábar's *Los otros*, Grace Stewart[5] (Nicole Kidman) and her children Anne and Nicholas (Alakina Mann and James Bentley) embody a new and yet paradoxically classical revisitation of the horror genre in its recent Spanish variation. In spite of the film's setting in the Isle of Jersey, a British island near the French coast of Brittany near the end of World War II, the film is insistently conscious of themes that are historically present in Spanish cinema that Amenábar's co-production strategy with the US-based Cruise/Wagner productions cannot conceal. There are especially the particularly (if certainly not exclusively) Spanish topics of Catholicism and repression. Grace's most powerful weapons in the control of her household (and she is, arguably, a type of 'Bernarda Alba' herself) are both isolation and religion. Not only is Grace Stewart's house self-contained and literally darkened by the lack of electricity and the eternally drawn drapes (ostensibly to protect her children from sunlight),[6] but Grace and her children live in a type of perennial mourning while awaiting the return of her husband from the war. The theme of darkness present throughout the movie literalises the metaphor of 'obscurantism' in Grace's education and upbringing of her children. In his autobiography, Luis Buñuel refers to turn of the twentieth-century Spain as being stuck in the 'middle-ages' and Amenábar seems to extend that metaphor into 1944, which is significantly the same year as the story-time of *El laberinto del fauno*. The isolation of Grace's household is dramatised by the fact that they live in a sort of 'limbo'; the Isle of Jersey, separated by water from both England and France, and arguably, as is Don Jaime's estate in Buñuel's *Viridiana* (1961) or even the real town of Hoyuelos in *El espíritu de la colmena*, living permanently in the nineteenth century.[7] The isolation motif is especially telling in comparison to Franco's isolationism during and after World War II that lead to protectionist deals with the US and the UN, while the wave of repression of the post-Civil War is also played up in the Stewarts' life.

Yet it is probably the insistence on religion as a tool of repression that better works to locate *Los otros* (the first non-Spanish-language film to win the Goya Award for Best Picture) within a critically Spanish context. In his work on the idea of national cinema, Andrew Higson describes some of the ways in which a country's cinema can be called 'national' or given some sort of official imprimatur through the exchanges that occur in national and international film festivals. Higson's study on British cinema suggests how the 'formation of intellectual film culture' helps to invent and cement ideas of national cinema by making distinctions from Hollywood. Thus the formation of the London Film Society in 1925 and later of the British Film Institute in 1933 helped articulate an idea of national cinema made official by distribution and exhibition practices (1995: 13–14).[8] Among the companies that were engaged in financing and production incentives of *Los otros* were TVE (Televisión Española) and the Spanish Ministry of Culture. The film was shot entirely in Spain with a mostly Spanish crew, although actors came from Britain, the US and, in Nicole Kidman's case, from Australia. Spoken in English, although released originally in Spain in a Spanish-dubbed version, the film was particularly embraced by Spanish critics and public (where it became the highest grossing film of the year at the box office) and the Spanish Goya Awards. Thus 'officially' nationalised, *Los otros* can be seen as earning the label of national cinema from the perspectives of economy and industry ('the infrastructure of production, distribution and exhibition'), consumption ('which films are audiences watching?'), national cinematic activity ('privileging particular film movements or directors', as in the National Goya Awards) and representation ('sharing of common themes, motifs and preoccupations') (Higson, 1995: 4–5).

Los otros has thus been named 'national' cinema very clearly in the economic, industrial and artistic categories; when it comes to 'motifs, themes, and preoccupations' we can see how, by drawing again on some of Xavier's readings of allegory, we can also solidly find it in the national map. For instance, in recent and contemporary Spanish cinema the relationship of the Catholic Church to the State and to repression has a long history of serving as a symbol for Franco's strategies of 'marrying', so to speak, the Church to his own Fascist, repressive regime. As we have seen, for instance, in Pedro Almodóvar's *Entre tinieblas/Dark Habits* (1983), *Matador, La ley del deseo/Law of Desire* (1987) and *La mala educación/Bad Education* (2004), the presence of the Church in the transition from dictatorship to democracy has been treated as symptomatic of Spain's isolation and backwardness, and its difficulty in emerging from 'the past'.[9] Grace Stewart's stubborn adherence to a strict Catholic upbringing for her children (which is somewhat in contrast to her British background) emerges as her most effective strategy to torture her children psychologically by threatening them with eternal damnation if they do not behave as she and God command. Very tellingly, Grace Stewart's repression of her children often results in rebellion, especially from the part of her daughter, Anne. Like her near-namesakes 'Ana' in *El espíritu de la colmena* and *Cría cuervos*, this little Anne is aggressively fearless, curious, even seduced by the strange and unexplained sounds, ghosts and unseen horrors that Grace's house bears, and that Anne insists are the doings of 'the others', the mysterious presence haunting their household and that initially Anne alone can see and feel. Anne challenges her mother about the reality of hell and limbo, a heretical system of beliefs that causes Grace great distress and provokes the imposition of various chastisements on the little girl. The more repressive Grace turns, the more fearless Anne becomes.

The intrusion of 'the others' into Grace's household, the insistence on literalising the metaphor of 'darkness' that Amenábar and his cinematographer Javier Aguirresarobe impose on the sets, even in the daytime scenes, and the eternal fog that surrounds the estate, while recognisable as conventions of classic horror and gothic films and literature, help to recreate a potentially allegorical understanding of *Los otros*, in the ways that *Abre los ojos* and *Tesis* arguably suggest Amenábar's own understanding of contemporary Spanish society's danger of becoming numb to the nation's violent history and its various media representations. While the two previous generations of Spanish filmmakers that include Luis Buñuel, Carlos Saura, Víctor Erice, Vicente Aranda, Pilar Miró and Pedro Almodóvar saw themselves 'negotiating' repression and the transition to democracy as something frantic and difficult, it seems as if Amenábar's generation, including Mateo Gil (Amenábar's screenwriting partner and

director of *Nadie conoce a nadie*/*Nobody Knows Anybody* (1999))
has gone through a process of revisionism that emphasises the dangerous weight of the past in their lives. Significantly, all of Grace
Stewart's repressive strategies on her children, her housekeeper
(Fionnula Flanagan), groundskeeper and maid fail to contain the
inevitable revelation of the horrific truth that neither Grace nor the
children themselves seem to recognise. That is, of course, the fact
that Grace has murdered her children and killed herself, and yet all
three fail to acknowledge, to understand or 'see' that they are dead.
As in *Tesis* and *Abre los ojos*, there is a terrible, violent, traumatic
truth to which Alejandro Amenábar's characters need in fact to
'open their eyes'.

   Los otros denies the apparent safety inspired by the destruction of
evil in the classic horror film. In its 'dreamlike' function, the classic
horror film's moral is that after going through the (admittedly titillating) journey of fear and death, there is generally confidence of
safety at the end of the tunnel; the knowledge that order will be
restored, that the monster will be killed and that then we will
awake from the nightmarish trance (Kawin, 1999: 687, 690). But
Amenábar's *Los otros*, like its closest narrative and generic relatives – Erice's *El espíritu de la colmena*, Saura's *Cría cuervos* and del
Toro's *El espinazo del diablo* and *El laberinto del fauno* – fails to
transition from nightmare to the awakening sense of 'safety' that
Kawin identifies in classic horror. Instead, death seems to almost
always win out and the children in these films, especially the girls
'Ana', 'Ana', 'Anne' and 'Ofelia', have to make the hardest of transitions from childhood to maturity, negotiating grown-up difficul-
ties, death, monsters, ghosts. For Grace, Anne and Nicholas Stewart,
isolation, repression, death, even hell, heaven and limbo have to be
recognised before their healing process can begin. Amenábar adds
the self-reflexive strategy of photographs of mostly unknown characters that are found in an abandoned attic. These are the types of
portraits of dead men, women, children and infants popular in the
late daguerreotype period and early photography in the 1880s and
1890s; they are also a morbid form of memory-keeping, of historical record. These death photographs include a group portrait of the
'family' of housekeepers that Grace has hired for help (and who are
there to tell Grace that she and her children are dead). The presence
of the photographs in the third act of the movie, after 'the others'
have been trying to make themselves manifest in many ways, offers

a conclusion that emphasises the self-reflexivity of a historical narrative. An attic is a place where people customarily store the useless remnants of the past, where things are left to be forgotten. Yet, in this film Grace finds in her attic room the key to understanding her family's present death, by discovering the historical past; a morbid reality preserved in the proto-cinematic form of the death photographs.

In Alejandro Amenábar's *Los otros* death itself is the last mediation of history. There is really no evil from without to destroy in the film; the only real threat, the monsters and ghosts that Grace and her children are stubbornly trying to escape might be history itself. As in many of its cinematic predecessors listed above, *Los otros* resorts to the confluence of historical context, conventions of the horror genre and children protagonists. There is also the certain degree of self-reflexivity added by the story-book drawings that run with the opening credit sequence (and which reminds us of *El espíritu de la colmena* and its model *To Kill a Mockingbird* (Robert Mulligan, 1962)), as well as the death photographs, both of which emphasise the generic hybridisation of horror, history and fairy tales or children's stories.[10] Film genres are historically determined; they answer to context and become malleable and hybridised in response to real or perceived social anxieties that are apparently resolved, even forced, in the destruction of a threat to the social setting of the story (as the 1950s hybridisation of horror and science fiction, beginning with the Japanese *Gojira* films and later followed in Hollywood, suggests).[11]

In these Spanish films that inform, contextualise, precede and follow *Los otros*, it seems that the most consistent convention is the insistence on forwarding historical context, as if history itself was the monster to escape from, vanquish, eliminate and eventually overcome. The emphasis on children serves perhaps to offer the promise, or simply suggest that history can still be remade and rewritten. And finally, the intersections of horror and children's narratives allow for the possible overlapping of themes such as innocence, death and violence. Through those intersections in *Los otros*, Anne, Nicholas and their mother Grace all ultimately become aware and awaken to the nightmare of history and in the process come to heal some of the wounds of the past. Genres evolve and adapt precisely because they serve mythical functions, because through them, as Rick Altman has argued, nations make and remake themselves. 'Given the extent to

which the process of genrification involves the creation or rein-
forcement of virtual communities', writes Altman, 'it is not surprising to find that our understanding of genres . . . furnishes insights
into broader cultural questions involving nations . . . and public
spheres' (1999: 87). Put differently: while the cultural and historic
trauma of the nation remains a topic of concern of the cultural establishment, films like these will find ways of retelling some episode or
episodes of the national history, until we understand its real meanings. These contemporary Spanish films are perhaps trying to remind
us that the weight of history cannot be ignored or trivialised, regardless of the sense of safety we might feel upon awakening from our
'nightmarish trance'.

Notes

I am thankful to the editors of this volume and to Carlos R. Acevedo-
Muñoz, Melinda Barlow and Larissa Rhodes for their helpful comments
about this chapter.

1 Alejandro Amenábar's authorial signature includes the composition of
   all of his own musical scores from his original 1992 short
   'Himenóptero' to his 2005 feature *Mar adentro/The Sea Inside*.
2 See my article 'The Body and Spain: Pedro Almodóvar's *All About My
   Mother*' (Acevedo-Muñoz, 2004).
3 For more on the 'cultural anxiety' of Spain's transition to democracy,
   see Yarza (1999: Chapter 1).
4 In his recent book *La guerra persistente. Memoria, violencia y utopía:
   representaciones contemporáneas de la Guerra Civil española* (2006),
   Antonio Gómez López-Quiñones traces and analyses the insistent presence of the War in Spanish fiction and films since the 1990s. He examines, among other topics, the uses of the Civil War as a referent to grasp
   contemporary anxieties about violence and historical memory in novels
   and films including del Toro's *El espinazo del diablo*.
5 Jay Beck has pointed out the Hitchcock reference in the character's
   name – a playful appropriation and rearrangement of Grace Kelly and
   James Stewart of *Rear Window*. In *Los otros*, though, the characters
   refuse to even look outside.
6 The children suffer from a rare genetic skin condition called *xeroderma
   pigmentosum*, a type of allergy to sunlight that causes skin cancer, pre-
   mature ageing and potentially death.
7 In the Criterion DVD release of *El espíritu de la colmena*, Paul Julian
   Smith points out that Erice chose the town precisely because it still had
   a town crier in 1972, and she of course plays herself in the film.

8 See especially 'British Film Culture and the Idea of National Cinema', in Andrew Higson (1995: 4–25).
9 See Acevedo-Muñoz (2007), as well as Yarza (1999) and Smith (2000).
10 Mulligan's film *The Other* (1972), as well as *To Kill a Mockingbird* (1962), are both referential markers for Amenábar's *Los otros*. In both films children are under threat and/or are the cause of harm and danger to people around them. Unavailable in the US for many years, Mulligan's *The Other* presents a pair of twin boys with telepathic and telekinetic powers and murderous intentions. The film also features a surprise finale in which the acknowledgement of death itself becomes the last signifying feature of the movie.
11 From *Them!* (Gordon Douglas, 1954) to *Tarantula* (Jack Arnold, 1955) to *The Blob* (Irvin Yeaworth Jr, 1958), the Hollywood hybrids of horror-science fiction naturally exploited the social anxieties of the Cold War, the nuclear race and the fear of Soviet invasions.

References

Acevedo-Muñoz, Ernesto R. (2004) 'The Body and Spain: Pedro Almodóvar's *All About My Mother*', *Quarterly Review of Film and Video*, 21: 1, 25–38.
—— (2007) *Pedro Almodóvar*, London: BFI.
Altman, Rick (1999) *Film/Genre*, London: BFI.
Gordon, Paul (2008) *Dial 'M' for Mother: A Freudian Hitchcock*, Madison, NJ: Fairleigh Dickinson University Press.
Higson, Andrew (1995) *Waving the Flag: Constructing a National Cinema in Britain*, Oxford: Clarendon Press.
Kawin, Bruce (1999) 'The Mummy's Pool', in Leo Braudy and Marshall Cohen (eds), *Film Theory and Criticism, Introductory Readings, Fifth Edition*, Oxford: Oxford University Press, 679–90.
López-Quiñones, Antonio Gómez (2006) *La guerra persistente. Memoria, violencia y utopia: representaciones contemporáneas de la Guerra Civil española*, Madrid: Editorial Iberoamericana.
Modleski, Tania (1999) 'The Terror of Pleasure: The Contemporary Horror Film and Postmodern Theory', in Leo Braudy and Marshall Cohen (eds), *Film Theory and Criticism, Introductory Readings, Fifth Edition*, Oxford: Oxford University Press, 691–700.
Schnitzler, Arthur (1990) *Dream Story*, Otto P. Schinnerer (trans.), Los Angeles: Sun and Moon Press.
Smith, Paul Julian (2000) *Desire Unlimited: The Cinema of Pedro Almodóvar*, 2nd edition, London: Verso.
Williams, Linda (1990) *Figures of Desire: A Theory and Analysis of Surrealist Film*, Berkeley: University of California Press.

Xavier, Ismail (1999) 'Historical Allegory', in Tobi Miller and Robert Stam (eds), *A Companion to Film Theory*, Oxford: Blackwell Publishers, 333–62.

Yarza, Alejandro (1999) *Un caníbal en Madrid: la sensibilidad* camp *y el reciclaje de la historia en el cine de Pedro Almodóvar*, Madrid: Ediciones Libertarias.

11

Love, loneliness and laundromats: affect and artifice in the melodramas of Isabel Coixet

Belén Vidal

The trajectory of director Isabel Coixet is both atypical and highly significant of the new routes and possibilities explored by Spanish cinema in the 1990s. Coming into fiction filmmaking after developing a successful career in advertising, her less than auspicious beginnings have given place to an increasingly assured profile in the Spanish film scene. The disastrous critical reception and commercial failure of her debut film *Demasiado viejo para morir joven/Too Old to Die Young* (1988), set in her native Barcelona, discouraged the tyro director to the extent that she would not embark in another film venture until six years later. Her second feature, *Cosas que nunca te dije/Things I Never Told You* (1996) was shot in a small town in Oregon, USA and made outside the production structures of the Spanish industry when the project failed to secure institutional funding.[1] In contrast, her fifth feature film, *La vida secreta de las palabras/The Secret Life of Words* (2005), has met with wide recognition in Spain, garnering two top prizes – Best Film and Best Director – at the annual Spanish Academy ('Goya') Awards in 2006. And yet, *The Secret Life of Words*, Coixet's third feature conceived and shot in English after the success of *Mi vida sin mí/My Life Without Me* (2001) consolidates a body of work that deliberately confounds national markers. Set in an oilrig off the west coast of Ireland, it features a multinational cast headed by North American actors Sarah Polley and Tim Robbins, whose participation reinforces the independent flavour of the production.

The string of small-scale hits achieved by the English-language films of Isabel Coixet raises intriguing questions regarding film authorship in Spain, and the relocation of the construct 'Spanish national cinema' as a transnational phenomenon. Carlos F. Heredero and Antonio Santamarina place Coixet in a group of Spanish filmmakers who, entering the Spanish industry in a moment of stable democracy and full-fledged participation in the global economy, favour a hybrid aesthetic informed by comic books, music videos and advertisement, as well as generic narratives naturalised by mainstream Hollywood cinema. These elements inform, nevertheless, projects carried out within what has traditionally been considered an auteur mode of production (Heredero and Santamarina, 2002: 62–4). This hybridisation is all the more noticeable in the case of filmmakers shooting in English and/or shooting abroad – a list that would include 1990s directors like Marta Balletbò-Coll (*Costa Brava: A Family Album*, 1995), Álex de la Iglesia (*Perdita Durango*, 1997), Julio Medem (*Los amantes del Círculo Polar/Lovers of the Arctic Circle*, 1998), María Ripoll (*Lluvia en los zapatos/If Only*, 1998) or Alejandro Amenábar (*Los otros/The Others*, 2001). Among these examples, Coixet's case is most significant in her consistent adoption of English and the imagined landscapes of American cinema not merely as a strategic career choice, but out of a self-conscious gesture of cinephilia – a love of cinema embedded in practices of intertextual allusion and appropriation.

In terms of industrial make-up, themes and style, the 'Spanishness' of Coixet's films remains, at best, elusive. The director has fashioned herself as the auteur-star at the centre of independently produced projects written in 'accented' global English. Hamid Naficy's term is useful in this context, not in the sense of an exilic or diasporic inflection of a dominant culture (Naficy, 2001: 22), but as the product of a negotiation between the local and the global (Triana Toribio, 2006) carried out at different levels: from production and casting decisions to choice of location and language. As Núria Triana Toribio notes, Coixet is part of a generation of Spanish filmmakers at ease with both mainstream Hollywood styles and the aesthetic of what has become known as American independent cinema. These referents function 'not as film styles/languages they "read in translation" but as film languages they "speak" at an almost native level' (2006: 58–9). In her films, the international casts, non-specific transatlantic settings and the focus on intimate, character-driven stories throw into question the very notions of 'home' and 'abroad'. Like their secretive protagonists, Coixet's films may be leading a double life: as idiosyncratic auteur cinema in Spain, and as genre cinema across borders.

This double passport of sorts raises intriguing questions about the ways in which Coixet's films may be perceived, decoded and consumed. Triana Toribio has highlighted the ambivalence implicit in Coixet's personal interventions and work towards a dominant mode of filmmaking identified as 'Spanish' mostly due to its commitment to represent contemporary social issues via stylistic markers associated with a conventional, script-driven realism.[2] Instead, the postmodern taste for offbeat humour, clichéd melancholic motifs and quirky dialogue in the familiar imaginary of her North American films, *Things I Never Told You* and *My Life Without Me*, ultimately contributes to what Valeria Camporesi (2007) calls the 'sincerity' and 'usefulness' of Coixet's cinema, that is, the desire to have an impact in the real world through affective storytelling. The iconography and narratives of 'indie' melodrama, which bring together a remarkably coherent body of work, also provide a generic mode of address that potentially facilitates the circulation of her films within and beyond the domestic market.[3] Against this background of complex relations with contested notions of Spanishness, I would like to focus instead on some of the textual motifs and strategies involved in the particular take on melodrama deployed by *Things I Never Told You* and *My Life Without Me*, the films that established Coixet's reputation as a recognised auteur in Spain. My reading of these films argues that Coixet's profile as both a nostalgic cinephile and a versatile multimedia auteur informs a style and themes that make her cinema readable to national and international audiences (albeit in diverse ways). This duality stems from one of the most distinctive traits of her cinema: the search for an affective mode of address through a self-conscious engagement with generic narratives and traditions.

Coixet's five films are at the centre of a network of texts that seeks to connect with the reader/viewer through cultural tastes and everyday experiences strongly located in a modern, urban identity. These texts include lavish spreads in weekend magazines to coincide with the releases of her films, as well as an official website where Coixet addresses her presumed audience under the host name of 'Miss Wasabi', also the name of her production company (Coixet, 2007). With spaces for chat, film information and leisure recommendations, the website (which is partially available in English) is notable by the ways in which cultural criticism freely mingles with brand endorsement (see Triana Toribio, 2006: 53). A class-coded narrative space drawn from *My Life Without Me* – the trailer – here functions as a two-dimensional, logo-like motif that encapsulates Coixet's 'universe', providing interactive access to the different sections of the website. The highlighting of lifestyle choices and products is, perhaps, not surprising coming from a former advertising executive whose films may be considered part and parcel of the circuits of specialist knowledge and discerning consumerism. In this respect, Coixet thrives as a savvy auteur in a mediascape where alternative consumer cultures and high-concept strategies combine towards marketable hipness and effective self-promotion.

The writing by and about Coixet (notably the interview format) has contributed to construe the director as a significant example of what Timothy Corrigan has called the postmodern 'auteur of commerce' (1991: 105–8). Following Corrigan, we could argue that Coixet's public persona deploys a 'commercial dramatization of self' that plays as a motivating agent of textuality towards the ways in which her films have been identified and consumed in the nation-state. Cinephilia plays a major role in this self-constructed image. In her volume of collected short essays *La vida es un guión* (*Life is a Script*) (2004), family memories of the Civil War and postwar periods passed down from parents and grandparents, as well as anecdotes, weaknesses and phobias (such as the melancholia of Sunday afternoons, or the compulsive checking of property listings), are registered as snapshots, alongside tributes to favourite film endings, actors (Katharine Hepburn and Marie Trintignant are the object of two short tributes) and auteurs – notably Wong Kar-Wai, a filmmaker invoked by Coixet as object of cinephilic devotion and as a kindred spirit (2004: 15–26, 42–4, 68–9, 75–8, 86–94). Coinciding with the general release in Spain of *The Secret Life of Words*, Coixet presented 'Las películas de mi vida' (2005) in the mainstream press – an annotated list of the 'ten films that changed my life', in which her (very canonical) selection (which includes titles by Billy Wilder, Jim Jarmusch, Ingmar Bergman, François Truffaut and John Cassavetes) is peppered with comments about her personal discovery of these films, and their inspirational role in her own filmmaking. Through such carefully staged interventions, the director inserts herself into a preferred lineage of cinephile filmmakers, bypassing other more contested categories such as a 'Spanish director' or even 'Spanish woman director'.[4]

In this respect, the one-off ninety-minute cultural talk show *Carta Blanca*, which Coixet was invited to host on the state television channel TVE2 (aired on 19 October 2006), gives a strong indication of how this self-construction as an auteur feeds on a cinephilia that opens spaces for dialogue, affinity and collaboration. For this show, Coixet selected four guests (actress and director Maria de Medeiros, writer Carlos Fuentes, architect Benedetta Tagliabue and critic and novelist John Berger, whose work is cited in *My Life Without Me* and *The Secret Life of Words*) and discussed with them specific film extracts (screened as part of the show). The eclectic selection included *Greed* (Erich von Stroheim, 1924), *The Apartment* (Billy Wilder, 1960), *La Femme d'à côté/The Woman Next Door* (François Truffaut, 1981), *Chungking Express* (Wong Kar-Wai, 1994), *Saraband* (Ingmar Bergman, 2003) or *Grizzly Man* (Werner Herzog, 2005), among others. As Christian Keathley has noted, 'cinephilia begins with the individual film lover and the idiosyncrasies of his and her relationship with the cinema. But cinephilia extends from there into a network of other like-minded people, and at its strongest moments, this sharing has grown into a cultural force as well' (2006: 39). Cinephilia proper belongs to the secondary moment of reflection, in which the love of cinema goes beyond the private obsession to become a cultural practice, informed by extratextual practices such as informal discussion as well as critical writing.

The director's active engagement with a new, yet nostalgic cinephilia (which could be extended to other knowledgeable cine-literate auteurs from Coixet's generation, such as Amenábar and de la Iglesia) strikes me as deeply symptomatic of a moment in contemporary film culture where style manifests in a self-reflexive overvaluation of the fragment and the detail, as well as in the multiplication of levels of reference. Such cinephilia poses a throwback to the practice of allusion as an expressive device for previous generational movements, such as the New Hollywood directors' taste for quotation and genre reworkings.[5] However, more than in any previous moments, the new cinephilia has become, in the words of Thierry Jousse, 'horizontal, digital and rhizomatic' (2003: 219). As films become available in a multitude of formats, the old genealogical models that seek historical patterns of influence do not work any more in the same fashion. Rather, both filmmakers and spectators are free to pick and choose, forging unexpected, 'customised' connections. Coixet's films could be said to ask for an spectator who is both attentive and involved, participating of the traditional pleasures of identification and absorption offered by classic genres, and

at the same time typically displaying the cinephile's 'panoramic perception' (Keathley, 2006: 44): the supplemental glance that isolates
the detail as complex focus of emotion. Her trendsetting interventions in the public sphere identify cinephilia as another form of alternative consumption, via a personalised mode of address that speaks
about individual connections through shared moments of feeling,
rather than seeking to elicit a blanket response from mass audiences.
This intimate mode of address, already encapsulated in titles such as
Things I Never Told You or *A los que aman*/*To Those Who Love*
(1998), also characterises *My Life Without Me*. The film opens with
a fade in white, followed by a series of close-ups of Ann's face
and body, raindrops rolling down her hair, face and neck. A soft
voiceover starts as the images fade in – 'This is you. Eyes closed, out
in the rain' – and proceeds to describe the minute feelings and sen-
sations going through Ann's body and mind. The utterance 'this is
you' (as opposed to the more conventional 'this is me') encloses the
spectator in Ann's fantasy. She pictures herself carrying out the kind
of spontaneous gestures (standing still in the rain) that she associates
with 'all the things they talk about in the books that you haven't
read'. Thus begins a film that seeks to involve the audience through
attention to fleeting moments, character and detail, as well as
through elaborate conversations about seemingly unimportant,
everyday experiences.

   My Life Without Me has an overtly melodramatic premise. Ann
(Sarah Polley) is 23 and lives in a cramped trailer stationed in her
mother's back garden, along with her husband and their two young
daughters. When she learns that she is dying from cancer, she decides
to keep her condition a secret and writes a list of things to do before
she dies, which includes both the trivial (things like 'Get false nails.
And do something with my hair') and the more serious business of
finding her also twenty-something husband 'a new wife who the girls
like', as well as making someone fall in love with her. The use of
hand-held camerawork keeps close for the most part to the bodies
and faces of the characters, registering minute gestures and events.
The film thus aligns with Ann's point of view, showing her tender
bond with her daughters and husband, as well as the somehow
fraught relations with her embittered mother (played by Blondie
singer Deborah Harry). Like *Things I Never Told You*, *My Life
Without Me* fetishises the quirks of an array of characters who Ann
meets in her last days, such as her diet-obsessed friend Laurie

(Amanda Plummer), as well as working-class women in beauty parlours and coffee shops, who flesh out a community of eccentric
characters. The emotional centre of the film, however, is the 'brief-
encounter' love story (reminiscent of *The Bridges of Madison
County* (Clint Eastwood, 1995)) between Ann and the sensitive but
love-shy Lee (Mark Ruffalo). The film unfolds as a low-key affair
marked by the proximity of Ann's death, which only the spectator is
privy to until the end.

In Spain, the release of *My Life Without Me* was accompanied by
features in the weekend editions of mainstream papers focusing on
the director and leading actress,[6] as well as a series of meetings with
the public to discuss the film in the forum provided by FNAC outlets
(a book, DVD and electronics chain store, which also hosts Coixet's
official webpage). The film circulated as another stepping-stone
towards her auteurist persona, consistent with her earlier film,
Things I Never Told You. Sporting low-budget production values
and featuring Lili Taylor as Ann, a young woman experiencing loneliness and depression, *Things I Never Told You* had all the trappings
of the contemporary American independent ('indie') film. For the
purposes of my argument, I use this category to refer to the narratives and iconography characteristic of a series of small-budget
American films released since the mid-1980s. The indie film distances itself from mainstream genre fare through distinctive styles
and concerns attached to authorial expressivity. Basic working definitions of the indie film in the 1990s have stressed the aesthetic and
rhetoric of social engagement and/or aesthetic experimentation,
episodic and character-driven narrative patterns, self-reflexive style
and offbeat subject matter, as well as the use of actors dissociated
from Hollywood stardom (Holmlund, 2005: 2–3; Tzioumakis,
2006: 1–2). An added dimension of special relevance in this discussion is the indie film's considerable presence in the art-house circuit
in European urban centres such as Madrid and Barcelona, and in
major European film festivals, which reinforces its circulation as
auteur or 'specialist' cinema.[7] This exposure constitutes the backdrop against which Coixet's first English-language film would be
read. Upon its release in 1996, *Things I Never Told You* successfully
found a niche audience in Spain, striking a chord with audiences and
reviewers already familiar with the drab yet stylised vision of urban
alienation and small-town eccentricity presented by the likes of Alan
Rudolph, Hal Hartley, Alexandre Rockwell or Jim Jarmusch,[8] all of

whom *Things I Never Told You* was evoking. *My Life Without Me* (which was supported by Agustín and Pedro Almodóvar's production company El Deseo, thus securing American distribution through Sony Classics) feels in many ways like an upgraded follow-up to *Things I Never Told You*, and a latter-day variation on the low-key aesthetic and unconventional narrative patterns pertaining to what could be grouped as a consolidated cycle of indie films, which would include *Stranger Than Paradise* (Jim Jarmusch, 1984), *Choose Me* (Alan Rudolph, 1984), *Trust* (Hal Hartley, 1990), *In the Soup* (Alexandre Rockwell, 1992) or *Smoke* (Wayne Wang, 1995).

In contrast, a cross-sample of the North American and UK reviews of *My Life Without Me* shows that non-Spanish critics tended to focus on the melodramatic elements of the film. The reviews reveal an underlying mistrust towards the populist subgenre of the 'terminal illness' movie (often associated with soap opera and low-quality drama in daytime television). Keywords such as 'indie weepie', 'tear-jerker' and 'cancer movie' dominate across the board, with a consistent focus on Sarah Polley's persona and performance as the familiar element that holds the film together (the reviewer in the *Village Voice* goes as far as to introduce the film as 'a Sarah Polley weepie').[9] Such approach has echoes of the low critical standing originally associated with classic melodrama (on the grounds of its manipulativeness and its association with femininity).[10] The low critical esteem afforded to contemporary women's genres (often conflated under the derogatory 'chick flick' in the US market)[11] stands in contrast to the masculine mystique of the auteur still prevalent in the male-dominated market for alternative films.[12] Further to this, the list of approximately a hundred comments posted by IMDb.com users based in countries where the film has had circulation either in theatrical and/or DVD release is perhaps more telling of the varied ways in which international audiences reacted to *My Life Without Me*.[13] Online users are sharply divided between enthusiastic responses to the film's story and a strong resistance to its perceived manipulativeness, along with criticism of the moral choices made by the protagonist.[14] Postings that describe the experience of being 'moved to tears', or even 'devastated' by the film alternate with sceptical and overtly mocking responses (including one 'crying with laugher') to the alleged implausibility of some situations and characters' reactions. Whether complying with or resisting the injunction to empathise with Ann's predicament, the emotional responses elicited by its 'excessive' melodramatic premise become the basis for the active engagement – or disengagement – of the viewers with the film.

As Steve Neale has noted, 'crying is fully compatible with – perhaps the fundamental mark of – the kind of paradoxical structure of fantasy, satisfaction and pleasure that melodrama fundamentally involves'. The sense of loss is part and parcel of such fantasy (1986: 20, 22). From *Love Story* (Arthur Hiller, 1970) and *Terms of Endearment* (James L. Brooks, 1983), to *Dying Young* (Joel Schumacher, 1991) or *Stepmom* (Chris Columbus, 1998), the 'terminal illness' motif appears as the main signifier of such loss, in films that update traditional Hollywood subgenres (such as the melodrama of maternal sacrifice) to the tastes and expectations of contemporary audiences. *My Life Without Me*, however, departs from the Hollywood reworking of the woman's film by refusing to spectacularise female suffering or to fall back on clichéd class images. Although numerous scenes highlight the intimacy between Ann and her daughters, the film sidesteps the emphasis on maternal sacrifice. Early in the narrative, we see Ann's mother indulging in a good cry while watching *Mildred Pierce* (Michael Curtiz, 1945) on television. But when Ann finds her later retelling the film's story to her granddaughters, whom she is babysitting, she angrily accuses her of filling the children's heads 'with stupid stories about mothers making dumb-ass sacrifices'. Ann's resolution to pursue her own desires flies in the face of this generic convention. The film holds an ambivalent relation with the pathos of classic melodrama, which is both evoked with affection and disavowed from the perspective of its resourceful protagonist.

The pleasures of melodrama have been reclaimed in the spectacular recuperation of the genre carried out by film theory since the 1980s, as well as through the revisionist possibilities opened up by modern pastiches by R. W. Fassbinder (*Alle Türken heißen Ali/Fear Eats the Soul*, 1974) or more recently, by Todd Haynes (*Far from Heaven*, 2002) and François Ozon (*8 Femmes/8 Women*, 2002). Beyond its origins in specific generic forms and film cycles (such as the 1940s Hollywood 'woman's film'), melodrama has been retrieved as a cultural mode focused on the drama of repression and revelation in scenarios where social conflict is expressed in terms of personal struggle.[15] This melodramatic mode is central to a modern sensibility that attempts to make the world morally legible (revealing, in the words of

Peter Brooks, the 'moral occult') through moments of gestural, visual
and musical excess (1976: 1–23). In the above films (as well as in contemporary melodramas by other influential figures such as Pedro
Almodóvar or Wong Kar-Wai), this aesthetic of excess is associated
with a mise-en-scène of vibrant and 'hot' colours which construe a
mood of both heightened emotion and distanced revision. In contrast,
Coixet's films constitute their own brand of 'cool' melodrama. They
show preference for muted, dark, and desaturated colour schemes. As
in the opening sequence from in *My Life Without Me*, bluish and rainy
settings often set the tone. Instead of the flamboyant clothing and
make-up of melodrama divas, Lili Taylor and Sarah Polley wear unre-
markable, everyday clothes. Their feelings are not amplified by
overblown orchestral soundtracks à la Elmer Bernstein or Frank
Skinner, but fleetingly captured by a mixture of low-key incidental
music and alternative pop bands. This tendency to visual understate-
ment makes Coixet's melodramas instantly 'modern' and accessible,
along the lines of many indie films. However, we should not mistake
this cool sensibility for absence of style or, worse, for realism. *My Life
Without Me* builds on a carefully orchestrated mise-en-scène that alternates humour, suppressed pathos, and emotion. For example, as Ann
awakes to the proximity of her death, her feelings of alienation and
her desire to escape into romantic fantasy surface in a sequence set in
a supermarket, where customers and staff suddenly break into a muted
dance to the ballad '*Senza Fine*' ('Without End'). This song, which
creates a connection with an earlier, romantic encounter with Lee, the
voiceover ('nobody thinks of death in a supermarket'), and the choreography transform the nondescript space of the supermarket into the
setting for an elaborate moment of emotional relief amidst the drab-
ness of Ann's surroundings.

This sequence points at one of the most salient strategies in Coixet's
films. Anonymous public spaces like supermarkets, beauty parlours,
coffee shops, car parks, train-crossings or coin-laundries become the
improvised stage for the drama of inarticulate feelings and the difficulty of personal relations. Rather than referring to specific social
realities, these spaces yield an intriguing geography of loneliness and
hidden inner lives charted by the films. Such spaces refer to what
Triana Toribio calls 'anyplace North America', in which:

> the setting that is looked for is a generic, imagined 'Indie' cinematic
> North American that can be that 'anyplace' that the narrative and

characters demand . . . It is also arguable that 'anywhere, anyplace North America' is a generic convention of the *indie* film itself. (2006: 61–2)

This argument suggests that, by the early 2000s, repetition has fossilised into convention, and the landscapes of 'anyplace North America' have become ripe for generic appropriation in a post-indie moment. Interestingly, the 'American' films of Isabel Coixet emerge at the precise moment in which the very existence of an independent cinema in USA has been thrown into question by the co-opting of the signifiers of alternative filmmaking by mainstream circuits of production and consumption. Whilst independent cinema has always been a relational term, meaningful only in relation to and in constant dialogue with the aesthetics and economics of mainstream Hollywood filmmaking (Kleinhans, 1998: 308), the notorious 'Hollywoodisation' of former reservoirs for independent practice (such as the Sundance Film Festival and the production/distribution company Miramax), have turned it into an extremely problematic category since the mid-1990s (Hillier, 2001: xv–xvi; Holmlund, 2005). Neither identifying with a Spanish imaginary nor belonging within the troubled economy of American independent cinema, the self-enclosed indie universe of Coixet's films may perhaps be best understood, retrospectively, as the mobilisation of cinephilic affect for an exhausted moment in recent cinema. This would entail, borrowing from Noël Carroll, a 'two-tiered system of communication', (1982: 56) or mode of address, where the non-ironic pleasures of melodrama and emotion are compounded with a knowing deployment of the markers of the American indie film, reinforced by strategic casting choices (Lili Taylor and Seymour Cassel in *Things I Never Told You*; Sarah Polley and Mark Ruffalo in *My Life Without Me*; and Sarah Polley and Tim Robbins in *The Secret Life of Words*), intertextual quotations and playful self-referencing (such as the repetition of character names throughout her films).

Rather than denoting a mode of production, *Things I Never Told You* and *My Life Without Me* come across as indie films mostly through connotation. They present naturalistic environments that provide purely stylistic as well as narrative motifs hinting to an already branded indie tradition. The coin-laundry or laundromat in particular (a setting that appears in both *Things I Never Told You, My Life Without Me*, and which was included in the first cut of *The*

Secret Life of Words)[16] fulfils to perfection the iconographic demands of the indie film. The preference for the American variants 'laundromat' and 'laundrymat' in the dialogue further places the characters in North American culture. Not only this, but these words are visually conveyed in establishing shots showing neon banners. The laundromat functions as a self-conscious caption that highlights the importance of the setting both as a realistic location for deracinated and working-class characters, and as a key emotional space. In *Things I Never Told You*, Don (Andrew McCarthy) and Ann's night conversation in the laundromat is framed through static two-shots which, while highlighting the economy of the low-budget film, deny the emotional 'suturing' of the shot/reverse shot structure for the first three minutes of the sequence. The long take, frontal framing and occasional cutaways to exterior shots of the laundromat (in which the camera looks in at the two solitary figures through the glass walls of the establishment) are a nod to the urban images of American painter Edward Hopper (whose *Nighthawks* (1942) somewhat hovers over the nocturnal atmosphere and precise framing of the sequence),[17] underscoring the privileged yet removed vantage point of the non-diegetic spectator. After Ann is gone, Don remains, looking in from outside the laundromat. In the reverse shot, we see him framed by the glass wall, entwined in a slow dance with Ann, in a brief interlude not dissimilar from the supermarket dance in *My Life Without Me*. Don's position as both passive onlooker and active participant in the scene, framed through the mirror-like glass window of the laundromat enacts melodrama's elaborate staging of fantasy in a self-conscious way. In both films, the everyday space of the laundromat nurtures the romantic fantasy of falling in love with a stranger – a fantasy that draws in the spectator through identification and displacement.

The repeated motif of the laundromat suggests that, by mobilising an American indie aesthetic as a ready-made idiom, Coixet's films are also able to borrow its ironic and detached stance as a deliberate artifice that, paradoxically, gives expression to a search for a visual vocabulary of intimacy and affect. Words lie at the centre of such visual vocabulary of small details. Words acquire weight; they become tangible objects and gestures at the centre of an elaborate mise-en-scène. A book hidden in a laundry bag as a tentative love gift (from Lee to Ann); the cassettes with birthday messages recorded by Ann for her daughters; or Ann's written lists, superimposed in the shot, feature in *My Life Without Me*. A mobile phone storing an illicit love message is secretly intercepted by Hannah (also played by Polley) in *The Secret Life of Words*; a declaration of love recorded in a videotape and sent to an absent lover lands in the hands of an unrequited admirer in *Things I Never Told You*. These motifs highlight the shifting and unreliable nature of words. Moreover, the films showcase sequences focusing on oral perform-ance – moments that embrace and yet disavow melodramatic excess, in which characters struggle to communicate their feelings in elabo-rate musings, off-the-wall dialogues, and small stories in which they reveal intimate secrets in indirect ways – an aspect that places Coixet's films nearer to the literariness of *Smoke* (scripted by Paul Auster) than to the terse writing of Hartley or Jarmusch. The prawn joke that Ann (Lili Taylor) records in one of the videos to her estranged boyfriend, nurse Ann's (Leonor Watling) story about the doomed conjoined twins, or Hannah's horrific account of her ordeal in the unexpected revelation at the end of *The Secret Life of Words*, are just some such moments in which characters try to come to grips with different kinds of loss. From romantic disappointment in *Things I Never Told You*, to the proximity of death in *My Life Without Me* and guilt and (historical) trauma in *The Secret Life of Words*, there is a continuous line in which the often contrived staging of words touches on hidden areas of experience, thus fulfill-ing one of the fundamental remits of the melodramatic mode as a modern sensibility: helping us make sense in a post-sacred universe by putting forth a moral truth that, paradoxically, and as the titles of the films suggest, cannot be fully spoken in words (Williams, 1998: 52–3).

Following up from this point and to conclude my argument, I would like to look briefly at the ways in which the letter (the ulti-mate token of language as artifice) acts as one of the central melo-dramatic gestures in Coixet's films. The letter represents a potent metaphor for the archetypal mechanisms of desire, time and loss embedded in the structures of melodrama (Vidal, 2006) where, as Neale has pointed out, timing and point of view are crucial to its effectiveness upon the spectator. Delay exploits our feelings of pow-erlessness: when characters finally achieve the same knowledge the spectator has had all along, it is always too late (Neale, 1986: 11). The ending of *My Life Without Me* uses the letter to achieve, never-theless, a different effect: it both pays tribute to the time-honoured fantasy of loss in classic melodrama and restores some power to the spectator by refusing to confine female subjectivity to the 'perpetual staging of suffering' of the classic woman's film (Doane, 1987: 293).

In the last scene in the trailer, Ann watches from her bed how nurse Ann, the friendly next-door neighbour whom she has invited for dinner, labours in the kitchen to get the food ready. As this other Ann commands the girls and Don (Scott Speedman) to wash their hands before sitting at the table, she assumes 'naturally' the maternal role that the dying Ann is too weak to perform. Like in the laundromat scene examined earlier, the main character's vantage point 'inserts' the non-diegetic spectator into a privileged yet removed spectatorial position in the text. As Ann looks on with satisfaction, the scene beautifully condenses the melodramatic and somewhat narcissistic scenario central to the film – 'my life (goes on) without me' – but also critically mobilises selected cinephilic pleasures. The idealised picture of Ann's family life, captured through the curtain made of coloured plastic beads that separates the bed from the kitchen area, provides a '*Stella Dallas* moment' in which, as Mary Ann Doane has pointed out, the scenario of 'watching the child from afar' emerges as a 'privileged tableau of the genre'.[18] But there is also the closeness of affective detail, captured through the montage of images and sounds that we know already belong to Ann's memories. The close-ups and medium shots of Don, the children and nurse Ann (who has already replaced the dying Ann in her and our imagination) are shot through a foreground of translucent beads. Out of focus, the beads reflect and decompose the light in myriad colours over their smiling faces, in a non-ironic take on the tears-of-melodrama motif of the diamond-shower opening credits in Douglas Sirk's *Imitation of Life* (1959).

Finally, there is a '*Letter from an Unknown Woman* moment' in which the famous line uttered by Lisa (Joan Fontaine) in voiceover ('by the time you read this letter I may be dead')[19] is rewritten in typically understated manner in Ann's final 'letter' to Lee: 'My darling Lee, I guess by the time you get this tape you'll know that I am dead – and, well, all that.' The serene and affectionate mood conveyed by this sequence is captioned by the second-person voiceover and the fade in white which effectively bookend the film. Avoiding the masochistic pathos of the dying woman's body, this letter magically 'sends' Ann's voice through time and space. As we hear her last letter to Lee, a montage of tracking shots cut together rhythmically to the first bars of the moody Alpha theme 'Sometime Later' brings together simultaneously mourning as loss (shifting images of a grieving Don, Lee and of the doctor in charge of delivering Ann's birthday-message tapes to her daughters are cut together) and as a way of overcoming loss. Ann's mother, looking happy and rejuvenated, chats with a date in a bar; Don and the new Ann take the children to the car for a day-trip to the beach. Even as she 'fades out', Ann's extended voiceover letter unambiguously claims loneliness, love and feminine desire as the motor of melodrama.

As this chapter has endeavoured to illustrate, the cinephilic recuperation and rebranding of 'cool' melodrama provides a possible avenue of entry into the visual and narrative pleasures granted by the cinema of Isabel Coixet, and its significance in contemporary filmmaking. If, as Linda Williams has remarked, 'in a post sacred world, melodrama represents one of the most significant, and deeply symptomatic, ways we negotiate moral feeling' (1998: 61), the attraction of these films may be partly due to the emotional response elicited by their stories and characters through their attention to detail. In *Things I Never Told You* and *My Life Without Me* the familiar motifs of unrequited love, death and desire are filtered through the distance created by the cinephilic allusion to a certain tradition of American independent cinema. Coixet's preference for 'foreign' yet familiar references gives her cinema the credentials of a cinephile auteur among national audiences, while paving the ground for exposure abroad thanks to the familiar generic markers of her style.

As Coixet continues to shoot outside Spain, the need for a visual vocabulary of affect that transcends linguistic barriers has become the ongoing motor in her fictions. One of her recent fiction features, a segment in the portmanteau film *Paris, je t'aime* (2006) distils in barely six minutes most of the familiar tropes of her cinema. Sergio (Sergio Castellitto) splits with his younger air-hostess girl-friend (Watling) to reunite with his estranged wife (Miranda Richardson) upon learning that she is dying from leukaemia. Humorous voiceover entirely replaces on-screen dialogue, a text message/goodbye letter provokes Watling to faint spectacularly, and references to other films are lovingly signposted (Richardson's character hums the song '*Le tourbillon*' from *Jules et Jim* (François Truffaut, 1962), which echoes the brisk pace of the film). The ironic, cine-literate tone of this melodrama-in-a-nutshell devised as affectionate homage to a Paris seen through Truffauldian in-jokes yields, nevertheless, a quiet moment of revelation at its very end. The husband's solicitous attention to his dying wife mutates into genuine emotion, which the French voiceover narration summarises in the following way: 'In his effort to behave like a man in love, he became again a man in love.' The film's non-ironic moral lesson could be that the trappings of emotion engender true emotion. The love for artifice thus creates the perfect scenario where affect may thrive.

Notes

I would like to thank Valeria Camporesi and Núria Triana Toribio for generous access to their work in progress. Thanks are also due to the editors of this volume for extremely valuable suggestions, and to Dona Kercher for a productive conversation about *My Life Without Me*. This chapter is dedicated to Dot, for her support and many shared moments of cinephilia and indie films.

1 See interview with Isabel Coixet in Camí-Vela (2005: 67–79).
2 For a development of this argument in depth, see Triana Toribio (2006: 64). For a critique of the aesthetics of realism in contemporary Spanish cinema, see Quintana (2005, 2006).
3 *Things I Never Told You* was the first of her films to be picked up for international (if very limited) theatrical distribution, whereas *My Life Without Me* has had the widest exposure so far, with both theatrical and DVD releases in North America, as well as in Europe, Latin America and Japan. At the time of writing, *The Secret Life of Words* has been given a selective rollout in the US, and it is still awaiting distribution in the UK.
4 Like many of her peers, Coixet shows a marked resistance to the concept of women's cinema, or even the existence of a 'feminine gaze' in cinema (Cami-Vela, 2005: 67–9). In her conversation with Maria de Medeiros in the course of the show *Carta Blanca*, Coixet suggestively uses the latter notion to discuss an extract from Wong Kar-Wai's *Chungking Express* (1994). The term has come under fire in the context of the Spanish film industry, not the least because of the perceived lack of a continuous tradition and role models for women filmmakers (who only from the 1990s on start joining the industry in significant numbers).
5 On the practice and politics of allusion, see Noël Carroll (1982: 52–56).
6 See the interview with well-known novelist and journalist Rosa Montero (2003) for the Sunday magazine *El País Semanal* entitled 'Isabel Coixet. La directora más original', and Ciro Krauthausen's (2003) profile of Sarah Polley and Coixet in the youth-oriented *El País de las Tentaciones*.

7 Some salient examples include the awarding of the Palme d'Or in the 1989 Cannes Film Festival to Steven Soderbergh's *Sex, Lies and Videotape*, of the Golden Lion in the 1993 Venice Film Festival to Robert Altman's *Short Cuts*, or the inclusion of no less than three American indie films in the Berlin Film Festival's main competitive section in 1995 – Abel Ferrara's *The Addiction*, Richard Linklater's *Before Sunrise* (recipient of a Silver Bear to Best Director) and Wayne Wang's *Smoke* (recipient of the Grand Jury Prize).

8 See, for example, Rafael Miret (1996: 18–19) and the entry 'Things I Never Told You/Cosas que nunca te dije' in Pérez Perucha (1997: 962).

9 See US reviews by Roger Ebert in the *Chicago Sun Times* (17 October 2003); A. O. Scott in the *New York Times* ('With Just a Few Months to Live, A Lifetime of Changes to Make', 26 September 2003); Michael Miller in *The Village Voice* ('Preparing for the Not So Sweet Hereafter in a Sarah Polley Weepie', 30 September 2003, 24); Edward Guthmann in the *San Francisco Chronicle* ('Polley's truthfulness shines through in 'My Life Without Me', 10 October 2003)' or UK critic Peter Bradshaw in the *Guardian* (7 November 2003). Daniel Etherington (from 16 March 2003) introduces the film as a 'Canadian-Spanish drama presented by the Almodóvar brothers' and a 'poignant, indie tear-jerker' with Sarah Polley as a young woman diagnosed with terminal cancer. BBC films reporter Jamie Russell gives perhaps the most positive review, noting that 'this intelligently pitched emotional melodrama avoids every pitfall of the few-weeks-to-live theme' (www.bbc.co.uk/films/2003/10/14/my_life_without_me_2003_review.shtml, dated 3 November 2003). A selection of these reviews can be accessed through IMDb at www.imdb.com/title/tt0314412/externalreviews and www.rottentomatoes.com/m/my_life_without_me accessed 1 March 2007.

10 See Gledhill (1987: 34), Williams (1998: 43) and Doane (1991: 304).

11 Although a discussion of the term 'chick flick' (films targeted at women and girls) falls beyond the scope of this chapter, it should be noted that this soubriquet is certainly one avenue through which mainstream audiences may encounter *My Life Without Me*. See the sympathetic entry of *My Life Without Me* (cited as 'surprisingly uplifting') in *Chick Flicks: Movies Women Love*, in the section 'Life's a Bitch: Romantic Dramas and Melodramas' (Berry and Errigo 2004: 107).

12 Christina Lane has noted that in the expanding of the market for independent films in the mid- to late 1990s, 'it became less likely that films would be advertised on the basis of a "woman director", meaning that women filmmakers and "female" genres became less marketable and less marketed, in a reciprocal spiral' (2005: 201).

13 www.imdb.com/title/tt0314412/usercomments, accessed 1 March 2007.
14 One thread develops a heated discussion (eighty-three comments) over Ann's decision to hide her illness and sleep with another man, with users arguing vigorously for and against her reasons, at www.imdb.com/ title/ tt0314412, accessed 1 March 2007.
15 See Gledhill (1987: 28–36) as well as the useful summary of the debates around melodrama in Mercer and Shingler (2004: 81–6).
16 Included in the deleted scenes of the DVD edition of *The Secret Life of Words* (Cameo, 2006).
17 Whether intentional or casual, this connection is suggested by Coixet's explicit interest in Hooper's work, noted by Triana Toribio (2006: 53), which in some ways blends naturally with her search for a certain American aesthetic in her films.
18 As noted by Doane, *Stella Dallas* (King Vidor, 1937) is the archetypal example of maternal melodrama (1991: 286).
19 From *Letter from an Unknown Woman* (Max Ophüls, 1948).

References

Berry, Jo and Angie Errigo (2004) *Chick Flicks: Movies Women Love*, London: Orion.

Brooks, Peter (1976) *The Melodramatic Imagination: Balzac, Henry James, Melodrama, and the Mode of Excess*, New Haven, CT: Yale University Press.

Camí-Vela, María (2005) *Mujeres detrás de la cámara. Entrevistas con cineastas españolas 1990–2004*, Madrid: Ocho y medio.

Camporesi, Valeria (2007) 'A ambos lados de todas las fronteras. Isabel Coixet y el cine español contemporáneo', in C. Peña Ardid and M. A. Millán Muñio (eds), *Las mujeres y los espacios fronterizos*, Zaragoza: Prensas Universitarias de Zaragoza, 55–69.

Carroll, Noël (1982) 'The Future of Allusion: Hollywood and the Seventies (and Beyond)', *October*, 20, 51–81.

Coixet, Isabel (2004) *La vida es un guión*, Barcelona: El Aleph.

—— (2005) 'Las películas de mi vida', *El País*, section EP3, 21 octubre, 20–1.

—— (2007) www.clubcultura.com/clubcine/clubcineastas/isabelcoixet/ index.htm.

Corrigan, Timothy (1991) *A Cinema without Walls: Movies and Culture after Vietnam*, New Brunswick, NJ: Rutgers University Press.

Doane, Mary Ann (1987) 'The "Woman's Film": Possession and Address', in Christine Gledhill (ed.), *Home is Where the Heart Is: Studies in Melodrama and the Woman's Film*, London: BFI, 283–98.

—— (1991) 'The Moving Image: Pathos and the Maternal', in Marcia

Landy (ed.), *Imitations of Life: A Reader on Film and Television Melodrama*, Detroit: Wayne State University Press, 283–306.

Gledhill, Christine (1987) 'The Melodramatic Field: An Investigation', in *Home is Where the Heart Is: Studies in Melodrama and the Woman's Film*, London: BFI, 5–39.

Heredero, Carlos F. and Antonio Santamarina (2002) *Semillas de futuro. Cine español 1990–2001*, Madrid: Sociedad Estatal España Nuevo Milenio.

Hillier, Jim (2001) 'Introduction', in Jim Hillier (ed.), *American Independent Cinema. A Sight and Sound Reader*, London: BFI, i–xvii.

Holmlund, Chris (2005) 'Introduction: From the Margins to the Mainstream', in Chris Holmlund and Justin Wyatt (eds), *Contemporary American Independent Film: From the Margins to the Mainstream*, London: Routledge, 1–19.

Jousse, Thierry (2003) *Pendant les travaux, le cinéma reste ouvert*, Paris: Cahiers du cinéma.

Keathley, Christian (2006) *Cinephilia and History, or The Wind in the Trees*, Bloomington: Indiana University Press.

Kleinhans, Chuck (1998) 'Independent Features: Hopes and Dreams', in Jon Lewis (ed.), *The New American Cinema*, Durham, NC: Duke University Press, 307–27.

Krauthausen, Ciro (2003)'Cara de seda, alma de hierro. Sarah Polley: activista política, actriz "indie". Y madre coraje en "Mi vida sin mí", el nuevo filme de Isabel Coixet', *El País*, section *El País de las Tentaciones*, 28 February, 10–12.

Lane, Christina (2005) 'Just Another Girl Outside the Neo-Indie', in Chris Holmlund and Justin Wyatt (eds), *Contemporary American Independent Film: From the Margins to the Mainstream*, London: Routledge, 193–209.

Mercer, John and Martin Shingler (2004) *Melodrama: Genre, Style and Sensibility*, London: Wallflower.

Miret, Rafael (1996) 'Cosas que nunca te dije. All you need is love', *Dirigido por . . .*, 246, 18–19.

Montero, Rosa (2003) 'Isabel Coixet. La directora más original', *El País Semanal*, February, 10–15.

Naficy, Hamid (2001) *An Accented Cinema: Exilic and Diasporic Filmmaking*, Princeton: Princeton University Press.

Neale, Steve (1986) 'Melodrama and Tears', *Screen*, 27: 5, 2–22.

Pérez Perucha, Julio (ed.) (1997) *Antología crítica del cine español, 1906–1995: flor en la sombra*, Madrid: Cátedra/Filmoteca Española.

Quintana, Ángel (2005) 'Modelos realistas en un tiempo de emergencia de lo político', *Archivos de la Filmoteca*, 49, 11–31.

—— (2006) 'Madrid *versus* Barcelona o el realismo tímido frente a las hibridaciones de la ficción', in Hilario J. Rodríguez (ed.), *Miradas para un nuevo milenio. Fragmentos para una historia futura del cine español,* Madrid: Festival de Cine de Alcalá de Henares, 279–84.

Triana Toribio, Núria (2006) 'Anyplace North America: On the Transnational Road with Isabel Coixet', *Studies in Hispanic Cinemas,* 3: 1, 49–66.

Tzioumakis, Yannis (2006) *American Independent Cinema. An Introduction,* Edinburgh: Edinburgh University Press.

Vidal, Belén (2006) 'Labyrinths of Loss: The Letter as Figure of Desire and Deferral in the Literary Film', *Journal of European Studies,* 36: 4, 418–36.

Williams, Linda (1998) 'Melodrama Revised', in Nick Browne (ed.), *Refiguring American Film Genres: Theory and History,* Berkeley: University of California Press, 42–88.

Part IV
Multilingual imaginaries, borderless Spain

12

Dancing with 'Spanishness': Hollywood codes and the site of memory in the contemporary film musical

Pietsie Feenstra

The film musical has a long-established tradition in Spain. Since the 1980s, the genre has undergone a revival that explicitly incorporated Spanish musical traditions from previous decades and, at the same time functioning within a process of historical inscription, attached them to a wider cinematic memory. Despite the fact that the Spanish musical incorporates other globally operative modes of address such as the Hollywood musical, it has not typically succeeded in travelling abroad. Two factors that may explain this fact are the use of the Spanish language and the particular relationship of music to Spain's own cultural memory. Even if a musical partakes of a set of transnational generic practices, it also functions by way of the songs and music that are closely related to its own country and its perception of history.

This chapter analyses the Spanish musical from the 1990s until today, focusing on how transnational quotations transform it and create sites of memory attached to the specificities of the Spanish cultural imaginary. Two categories will be studied. The first category is made up of those films that return to the period of the 1930s by dancing with the *españolada*: *¡Ay, Carmela!* (Carlos Saura, 1990) and *La niña de tus ojos/The Girl of Your Dreams* (Fernando Trueba, 1998). The second category represents several successful productions treating contemporary relationships by integrating pop songs from different countries and periods: *El otro lado de la cama/The Other Side of the Bed* (Emilio Martínez Lázaro, 2002), *20 centímetros/20 Centimetres* (Ramón Salazar, 2005) and *¿Por qué se* *frotan las patitas?* (Álvaro Begines, 2007).[1] How can we define the contemporary Spanish musical by analysing transnational influences on national questions and generic displacements? Can we speak of a Spanish genre that creates its own 'generic approach' in which 'Spanishness' has its own specific place related to cultural memory?

Spanish musicals

Over the last thirty years, the Spanish musical displays a tendency of honouring the nation's heritage. While it is therefore important to describe the history of the genre, considering the impressive number of films produced this always results in a reduction in order to categorise the different eras. I will therefore only comment on those musicals that have been 'honoured' or referred to from the 1990s until today. Barry Jordan and Rikki Morgan-Tamosunas introduce a convincing periodisation that relates the political context to the way in which the musical functions inside Spain (1998: 105–7). They mention several periods, starting with the so-called Golden Era of the 1930s and 1940s, and refer to films like *Carmen, la de Triana* (Florián Rey, 1938) or *Suspiros de España* (by Benito Perojo, 1938) as typical productions of the *españoladas*. They then consider the years following the Civil War as the next period, when Francoism used the genre for its own interests. For the 1950s and 1960s, they note the introduction of *tonadilleras* as 'light songs', citing stars such as Lola Flores and Rocío Jurado. The 1960s was also the period in which Marisol began her cinematographic career with *Un rayo de luz* (Luis Lucia, 1960): her character carried strong ideological implications, as several studies have already demonstrated.[2] The next stage, the 1970s, is described by Jordan and Morgan-Tamosunas as a period without remarkable musical production. They explain this fact by the changing political circumstances, as the transition period to democracy generated hope due to the newly acquired political freedom, and they subsequently explain the revival in the 1980s and 1990s as a period when new disillusions emerged towards politics, and relate this to the creation of retro or revivalist musicals (*La corte de Faraón* (José Luis García Sánchez, 1985), *Las cosas del querer/The Things of Love* (Jaime Chávarri, 1989) and *El día que nací yo* (Pedro Olea, 1991)).

The musical has always worked to create dreams and make people forget daily misery, even if ideological messages, and not always optimistic ones, were clearly included. This characteristic is important when we make a reading of the contemporary musical. In general, Spanish cinema in the 1990s pays particular attention to its own past – this tendency began in 1975 and the musical, as a genre, confirms this preoccupation. The musical can be characterised by some basic elements such as the function of music (dance, songs, etc.) that directly forms part of the story and is not simply utilised to create an atmosphere. For this chapter, I have chosen films that integrate in a specific way transnational codes (from Hollywood and Europe), while at the same time utilise other codes that are closely related to Spanish society.

Questioning the genre

Analysing musicals leads us automatically to Hollywood, which gave birth to the genre in the 1930s and 1940s (the so-called 'Golden Era'). The Hollywood musical created some prototypical models for narrative that have been analysed by Rick Altman in his book *The American Film Musical* (1987). Altman observes three subgenres of the musical: the fairy tale, the show and the folk musical. These subgenres determine most of the Hollywood productions and have introduced some specific codes that marked the musical. The three categories are each related to certain periods of US film history and have a specific way of integrating music and dance into the story. For example, in fairy-tale musicals, the music expresses the love between the two main characters. This is different from the show musical, where putting on a show is the central narrative focus that determines the structure of the film. In the folk musical, the community is most important and their identity is questioned with a focus on cultural memory and the music is often related to the past. In all three forms of storytelling, a man and a woman always fall in love, and the use of music is directly related to their romance.

The birth of the three subgenres can be related to some specific historical periods from the United States. However, as Altman explains, the distinction between the different subgenres changed after the Golden Era. The show and fairy-tale musicals increasingly integrated elements of the folk musical (Altman, 1987: 354): this means that cultural memory became a central issue for all three subgenres. Without intending to directly compare the Hollywood musical with Spanish ones, the generic model described by Altman provides some elements (what I describe as codes) that illustrate the way in which the genre functions in Spain. Many Spanish musicals are still based on classical narrative conventions, but their textual specificity represents a clear reflection on the past through the way in which music is introduced. It is in the so-called *lieux de mémoire* (Nora, 1984) that cinema can create this effect and in which music plays a decisive role. Because the Spanish musical had a long history (both during and after the Francoist years), its updating throughout the 1990s inscribed it into a wider *transnational musical memory*. Even if Altman's method was developed in an American context, some aspects are useful to illustrate how the genre can be read. For example, his definitions of the function of 'backstage' – the ways in which space is used and the music is included in the story – is revealing when one studies the sites of the Spanish past in the musical.

To give a short illustration of these codes, it should be noted that the films in the first section – *La niña de tus ojos* and ¡*Ay, Carmela!* – are show musicals, and their stories take us backstage to underline the creative process. In so doing, the creation of a show is revealed and we are given a new vision of the past. It is also evident that, though these films are set during the Civil War, they could not have been made in the same way during that period. The second section examines the updating of the fairy-tale musical via contemporary topics, inscribing it into a wider cinematic memory. Because Hollywood musicals and US and UK music videos were widely transmitted all over the world, we find references to songs inside these modern Spanish musicals. As a result, a memory site is constructed by the way in which the songs are integrated into the story – referencing both the original use of the songs and their new context.

Theatricalising memory

Before scrutinising the films, it is important to define the historical interrogation and engagement these musicals put forth. I propose the term 'cinematic theatricality', based on the way that the past is represented in the narrative, creating a theatrical view of it. In both of the following sections, the films refer to a turning point in Spanish history that requires a thorough analysis.

The philosophy of history, defined by Walter Benjamin, is revealing for an analysis of the filmic forms created for the musical. He explains that a traumatic experience for a culture creates a rupture in the way in which the past is perceived (2000b: 431). The Civil War is most evidently a sensitive point in Spanish history. This is all the more true as Francoism did not permit Republican visions in its cinema and the musical was often used to transmit the ideology of the dictatorship. Concerning the contemporary musical, the past also demonstrates a rupture, as the end of the 1970s in Spain witnessed a fundamental change in legislation concerning relationships. In my book *Les Nouvelles Figures mythiques du cinéma espagnol (1975–1995). A corps perdus* (2006), I studied the relationship between this new legislation on homosexuality and the place of women in society, considering how Spanish cinema created new images for these identities. In the contemporary musical, we observe that taking back songs from earlier periods is related to this important legal breaking point, making new forms of cultural identity and types of relationship possible. The so-called historical rupture creates a place for this part of our collective memory by quoting songs from other contexts.

The first two films under examination, however, treat a more complicated issue for Spanish society: the Civil War. The show musical is revealing for how the contested site of memory is situated inside the film, as the skits on stage contrast frequently with what we see backstage. Observing a play in a film creates an effect of theatricality: through the energy between an audience and the skits on stage (Amo-Sánchez *et al.*, 2005: 18). In the musical, however, this effect is intensified. Altman illustrates the importance of space in the show musical to create a double effect of theatricality: the film underlines that we are watching a play and the spectator can also observe 'real life' backstage. A spectator of a play is never able to see this part of the story behind the curtain. The backstage space creates a feeling that we are observing 'real life', while the show creates a 'fake' effect (Altman, 1987: 207–8). This contrast is particularly revealing for the way in which the past is integrated in Spanish show musicals.

Cinematic theatricality can therefore be defined, for the first set of films, as observing the process of creating a show, underlining the filmmaker's vision of the past, while the camera stimulates an impression of 'realness', of being 'authentic'. When Walter Benjamin wrote about the aura of art, he referred to the process of stimulating feelings of authenticity (2000a: 71–3). In the show musical, this process is underlined. The past is integrated in new stories, it is the Other. Thierry Maurice noted that Spanish history of the 1980s was disguising its memory through the characteristics of *la movida* (2000: 115–16). The musical is a good example of this 'disguising' of history, of the theatricalising of memory to chase away a painful past through song and dance, at the same time creating a feeling of authenticity in this contemporary vision. For the second set of films, cinematic theatricality represents the dialectical relationship between the original use of the songs and their contemporary use that creates revised vision of the topics treated in each film. This negotiation between transnational pop songs, national popular songs and a cinematic memory integrates the past into the present, imposing a new vision on it. I will illustrate this effect by focusing on the role of music during both periods.

Dancing with 'Spanishness'

The use of the Spanish language and cultural references in Spanish music forms a large part of its heritage and decisively determines the characteristics of its musicals. In this respect, Núria Triana-Toribio links the question of national cinema to the idea of Spanishness:

> The term 'Spanishness' cannot be avoided in discussion of Spanish national cinema: it has been in effect 'imposed' on me by its continuous appearance, in two different forms (as *españolada* (generally pejorative) and *españolidad* (usually complimentary)) in the discourse on Spanish cinema of all epochs throughout analyses of all kinds, from debate which took place in intellectual fora to popular film magazines. (2003: 7)

Her book illustrates how these two aspects have been updated in different periods and political contexts. The groundbreaking book by Valeria Camporesi, *Para grandes y chicos: un cine para los españoles 1940–1990* (1994), must also be mentioned. Camporesi analyses reactions towards the perception of national cinema, concentrating on both of these terms. As Triana-Toribio confirms, '"Spanishness" proves to be an astonishingly slippery signifier' (2003: 7). For the contemporary musical, the question is how the genre treats Spanishness and how their filmic forms create Spanish connotations, for example through music, or how the stories are related to the country's culture and history. The two sections in this chapter can be considered as two subgenres of the show musical, inspired by Triana-Toribio's distinction between *españolada* and *españolidad*. The first, 'Dancing with the *españolada*', is defined by the skits on stage functioning as a masquerade of Spain. The second, 'Pop music revisited', quotes music from different periods and countries in order to set up dialectical relationships between the past and the present, the national and the transnational.

Dancing with the *españolada*

To begin with this subgenre, the concept of the *españolada* should be defined, as a theatrical form in the show musical. In Spanish musicals, the *españolada* is often represented by typically clichéd characteristics: stereotypes of the exotic aspects of flamenco dance, gypsy culture and Andalusia. Among others, it is necessary to mention *Bienvenido Mister Marshall* (Luis García Berlanga, 1953), a film dealing with a small village being made over by *españoladas* to please the Americans and receive Marshall Plan dollars. This light-hearted comedy is not a show musical, but the disguising of the whole village in Andalusian style reveals how the stereotypes embodied in the *españolada* were transmitted to foreigners (Feenstra, 2006: 23–8). In Spanish cinema, the figure of the *españolada* has often been used as a masquerade to negotiate other interests (even when other readings were possible). Jordan and Morgan-Tamosunas describe it as a domestic genre used after the Civil War to represent the Francoist mythology: 'offering a seductive but false notion of Spanishness for both internal and external consumption' (1998: 106). But how should one read this filmic figure in the contemporary musical?

The *españolada* implies a contrast in itself. The term incarnates the so-called 'binary opposition' introduced by Claude Lévi-Strauss (1956: 235–65), which means that two topics cannot be united, but are closely related to each other, for example the past and the present, falseness and authenticity. The *españolada* is not an authentic representation of Spain, but, at the same time, it represents in a highly recognisable way some of the country's 'typical' characteristics. It is an act in itself, an act of performance where mise-en-scène masquerades as nation, allowing the audience to immediately recognise the cultural origins of the film. Actualising the genre, through show musical codes, integrates the *españolada* and creates a mise-en-scène of Spanishness.

Updating the Carmen myth
The first musical to be analysed, *La niña de tus ojos*, was inspired by Florian Rey's *Carmen, la de Triana*. The original film was a folk

musical, made when Nazism was emerging and during the period of the Spanish Civil War. Trueba interpolates this cinematic represen-tation of the Carmen myth and transforms it into a show musical by imposing a filmic gaze on the past, the production of the film and the particular historical circumstances under which it was made.

In *La niña de tus ojos*, music and dance take place only once in a very recognisable sequence, confirming a cinematic memory via the fictional reconstruction of filming a multilingual *Carmen, la de Triana* at Ufa studios in 1938. 'Carmen's' first and only singing act represents a typical scene of the *españolada* when she sings 'Los piconeros' – originally written by Juan Mostazo and Ramón Perelló, and performed by Imperio Argentina in Rey's film – yet here the song is heard in both Spanish and German versions. Eduardo Rodríguez Merchán illustrates that this way of filming can be compared with the musical productions of the 1930s. He analyses how the camera is used to create a recognisable image of the Carmen adaptation, inscribing it into the history of cinema (2007: 57–70). In fact, the whole film is enrolled in a wider cinematic memory by different cinephilic references. These are first related to the Carmen myth, borne of Mérimée's 1845 novel, that represented a French view of a Spanish woman in the nineteenth century, later adapted in Bizet's 1875 opera and subsequently returned to Spanish audiences in musi-cals like *Carmen, la de Triana*. The point of view of a foreigner is rooted in the origins of the Carmen myth, stimulating a stereotypi-cal interpretation of its image that is closely related to the charac-teristics of the *españolada*. In 1998, Penélope Cruz reinterprets Carmen through her character of Macarena Granada – two names that represent directly Andalusia – who inscribes this version into the long cinematic memory. Many cinephilic references exist in *La niña de tus ojos*: most tellingly, the NO-DO (*Noticiarios Documentales*) newsreels shown over the titles of the film, as well as the 1972 show musical *Cabaret* by Bob Fosse and starring Liza Minnelli. Without being exhaustive, Trueba's film is constantly quoting musical references – Spanish and non-Spanish – and inscrib-ing them into a wider memory by underlining one difference: we can now look behind the curtains at the 'backstage', as indicated by Altman (1987: 208), to observe 'real life' behind the *españolada*.

Cinematic theatricality is revealed when the producer shouts 'cut' during 'Los piconeros' and critiques Macarena for not respecting the rhythm of the song. The room is filled with extras who are actually prisoners taken from a concentration camp. Exhausted, they are asked to clap their hands as Macarena speaks about the rhythm of Spain, the rhythm of her heart, and tries to teach it to the Jewish-Russian prisoner who at first refuses. Entering into contact with him, Macarena becomes more aware of the historical situation surrounding the production of the film in which she is involved. The second time she performs the act, everything works well: the rhythm, her dance steps and her German interpretation of the song. This scene is a revealing example of the masquerades of the *españolada* and how it becomes a disguise for the horrors of Nazism, explicitly the link between Hitler's and Franco's use of cinema as propaganda. Dressed up as a typical *españolada* version of Carmen, Macarena discovers the truth about what really happens backstage and is shocked: after the skit the prisoners are locked up again and treated as mere 'material' to fill up the mise-en-scène of the film. We all know the performance is fake and that the producer wants to make money directing these films, but we are concerned for the now-enlightened Macarena.

The role of Carmen is known worldwide for being a femme fatale; yet in this film she becomes a femme fatale who intervenes in history. Having had an affair with the producer, himself a married man, their relationship is directly related to the show being produced. After Macarena falls in love with the Jewish-Russian prisoner, and escapes with him to Paris, we do not know if the show can go on. Returning to Hollywood musical codes, the film confirms Altman's assertion that the relationship between the couple is crucial for the success of the show (1987: 239). In *La niña de tus ojos*, history is transforming the Spanish musical: we do not know if the show will go on; it is open-ended, but with a new understanding of the past.

The second film in this section, *¡Ay, Carmela!* (1990), is also an example of the subgenre of 'dancing with the *españolada*'. However, whereas Trueba's film referred directly to the Carmen myth, its relationship to *¡Ay, Carmela!* is less obvious. The title refers to the main character, Carmela (Carmen Maura); however, the etymology of her name (on screen and off screen) is also related to Carmen as a figure of freedom – a revolutionary who prefers to die than to betray herself or her country. 'Ay, Carmela' is also the title of an anarchist song from the eighteenth century with its own historical connotations. This song was composed in 1808 during the battle against Napoleon and rewritten for the Civil War with reference to the battle of the Ebre: an impressive, 114-day long effort of resistance against Franco's army in 1938 that caused more than 100,000 deaths on both sides.[3] The International Brigades, who participated in the battle, play a central role in the film.

In relation to *¡Ay, Carmela!*, Altman's concept of 'backstage' space for the show musical is revealing (1987: 208). Set during the Civil War, the main characters – Gustavete, Paulino and Carmela – are all Republican actors who must perform in order to survive, because they are accidentally detained in a Nationalist camp. New choreography is invented for their numbers, the discourse of their poems is altered, and Carmela tries to dance and sing her *pasodobles* to honour Franco directly. Although the act of the *españolada* serves to disguise their political views, the song 'Ay, Carmela' is authentic and ultimately causes the death of the main character. Carmela, embarrassed by performing for prisoners from the International Brigades, meets the Polish Brigade in prison where she communicates with the soldiers by using gestures; pronouncing her name, they all start singing 'Ay, Carmela'. The second time the song is performed, Carmela is on stage with the Republican flag wrapped around her naked body in a blatant act of resistance. Understanding the gesture, the soldiers start to sing the song as an act of revolt: unable to contain her emotions, Carmela starts to sing with them only to be shot and killed for her actions. The narrative dynamics of the film create a memory site, as the backstage of the show musical becomes a historical backstage when Gustavete and Paulino visit Carmela's tomb. In the 1990s, both films danced with the *españolada* as a way of surviving, and their emphasis on cinematic theatricality shows that they had no choice. Behind their curtains we discover the site of memory.

Pop music revisited

This second subcategory of musicals I deal with stems from the combination of fairy-tale musical with folk elements. As Altman illustrated, the main marker of the folk musical is an emphasis on the seasons of life: birth, school, marriage and adulthood (1987: 354). This is expressed by the way in which the music is used: 'the rhythm of life already constitutes a dance' (Altman, 1987: 307). The narratives of films like *El otro lado de la cama, 20 centímetros* and *¿Por qué se frotan las patitas?* question contemporary interpersonal relationships and explore previously forbidden or underexamined topics in Spanish cinema such as infidelity, homosexuality and transsexuality. Folk elements are introduced in each of the films by the use of music from an earlier period in Spanish and international popular music history. Spanishness is represented through both songs and cinematic references, as these musicals foreground a dialectical relationship between modern images combined with songs from earlier periods.[4] This is what I define as 'theatricalising memory', as the songs are well-known from other periods – indeed, they become a place of memory and they carry prior associations that accompany these new takes of relationships. As mentioned above, at the end of the 1970s laws on sexuality and relationships were adapted. It is thus important to mention that divorce became legal in 1981, homosexual marriages were legalised in 2005 and since 2006 transsexuals have been able to change their name and gender on their passport. With this new understanding of relationships in both legal terms and within the Spanish social imaginary, quoting well-known songs from earlier periods and integrating them into contemporary stories historically reinscribes the meaning of these songs into a new political and social context, creating a comical juxtaposition by ideologically displacing well-established songs within the Spanish musical tradition.

El otro lado de la cama was so successful when it was released that a second version was made in 2005: *Los dos lados de la cama*. The film resembles a modern fairy tale; it is a light-hearted comedy that questions 'love' and 'relationships', and the title of Marina Díaz López's article on this film – '¡Viva la diferencia (sexual)!' – is revealing. She compares the relationships of the central characters with the Peter Pan complex of adults who refuse to grow up (Díaz López, 2008). Like eternal teenagers, they are looking for new experiences and testing their freedom, and at the end of the film all appears to be forgiven and forgotten: life goes on. The limits of sexual freedom are tested, with two couples being unfaithful and homosexual relationships explored. Throughout the film the male point of view dominates as the characters consider how to live their love life. Different songs drawn from the early 1980s period of *la movida* accompany and punctuate the different twists in the story. In turn, these pop songs are often staged to ballet and modern dance choreographies. The film opens with two couples, edited in parallel. Paula and Sonia are singing to their respective partners, Javier and Pedro: 'Tienes que levantarte' ('You need to wake up'). The two women are moving their bodies in the bed in a sensual manner, like a soft dance of waking up next to the person you love. Yet their love lives are about to change abruptly when Paula tells her boyfriend Pedro that she is in love with another man, and, though she does not mention it, she is having an affair with Javier, Sonia's partner.

As they probe and question their relationships, the songs express the feelings of the characters and are combined with dancers who do not fit within the diegetic space of the film. For example, when Paula is singing and dancing to seduce her lover, the mise-en-scène resembles the famous scene from *9½ Weeks* (Adrian Lyne, 1986). Kim Basinger's seductive dance impressed international audiences and the effect is now interpolated by Paula, who dances for Javier while singing the song 'Dime que me quieres' ('Tell Me That You Want Me'), originally by Tequila.[5] Her body dominates the scene with her energy, while Javier sits in a corner and observes her, overwhelmed by her sensual movements. It is here where we observe the effect of 'cinematic theatricality': her body is accompanied by three other female dancers, who also have long hair and are dressed in the same way. Multiplying Paula's movements with the dancers' anonymous bodies visually reinforces the emotions that Paula expresses. She is sensually overwhelming Javier, and his desire is translated in the visual representation of the dance.

Another sequence translating male desire features Rafa, a typical macho who sings 'Las chicas son guerreras' ('Girls Are Warriors'), also originally by Tequila. Rafa believes that he controls his girlfriend, his sex life and all the world's women. Convinced at the beginning of the film, his views are completely different at the end. However, he explains to his friends how to engage in sex with women at any moment, at which point the song 'Las chicas son guerreras' is sung by all of them. As the song unfolds, Rafa finds himself in the middle of a group of different dancers, who move towards him and jump upon him. They express the intensity of Rafa's male fantasy as well as his nervous fear of women being so demanding when they see him, and, once again, the dancers appear without a clear identity to multiply his emotions and desire.

This effect of multiplying bodies translates the individual experience into a feeling concerning the whole community. As Altman wrote, the couple in the folk musical represents not only their own relationship, but also the desires of the whole community (1987:

309). This feeling is also illustrated by the way in which the characters react to each other. For example, when Javier discovers that Pedro was having an affair with Sonia, he tells him that at least he forms part of the family, and that life should go on. Yet throughout most of the film, the music and the dance sequence theatricalise the characters' feelings of community. The words of the songs underline their emotions, and the choreography forces us to have a look at their intensity. The human body expresses these contradictory feelings through dance: throwing itself from one place to the other, approaching or retreating in space and in emotion, towards the other. The music questions the relationship and the dance translates the individual emotions into a general feeling of desire that engages the whole community.

Swinging transsexuals

Another original musical, *20 centímetros* drew massive Spanish audiences to cinemas. This film treats the topic of transsexuality through its knowing use of songs. It examines the plight of Marieta (whose real name is Adolfo) who would like to become a woman by getting rid of 'twenty centimetres'. Watching the film, we are immediately able to connect it to a national and transnational cinematic memory. The list is too long, but transsexuality has been a central issue in Spanish culture and cinema with titles such as *Mi querida señorita* (Jaime de Armiñán, 1973), which was nominated for an Academy Award – a curious choice for representing Spain in Hollywood at the end of Francoism – and *Cambio de sexo* (Vicente Aranda, 1977), which introduced Bibí Andersen to Spanish cinema as the character who undergoes a sex-change operation. In the 1980s, Almodóvar's *La ley del deseo/Law of Desire* (1987) shows gender confusion by contrasting Carmen Maura, who plays a post-op transsexual, who adopts the daughter of Bibí Andersen's character, acting as if she is the child's biological mother. In fact, this confusion of gender identity is systematic in Almodóvar's cinema and symptomatic of major changes in Spanish culture and society.

In *20 centímetros*, we feel firmly within Almodóvar's microcosm as Marieta, played by Mónica Cervera, physically resembles co-star Rossy de Palma with her cubist face. But the narrative and the songs also inscribe the film into a larger cinematic memory. The film opens with Marieta dumped out of an anonymous van in the desert. A narcoleptic, Marieta can fall asleep during the day, whereupon she enters into a fantasy world constructed around her own interpretations of popular songs. Still asleep, her first dream replays the title song from *Tómbola* (Luis Lucia, 1962) featuring Marisol. A colourful sequence illustrates the song as Marieta dances through the streets of Madrid surrounded by many people. Initially a brunette, Marieta enters a revolving door and emerges blonde and brave, re-entering the city as a modern reinterpretation of Marisol. After waking up, we observe Marieta's real life as a prostitute, and the lurid quality of the images reminds us of Agrado and her fellow prostitutes in Almodóvar's *Todo sobre mi madre/All About My Mother* (1999). But Marieta would love to work somewhere else; yet when she is dressed up as a woman, presenting herself for a job, her identity card still bears the name Adolfo. Because the film was released in 2005 before new legislation made it possible for transsexuals to change their name, it is requested that she dress as a man when cleaning Atocha station at night.

Without a doubt, Marieta dreams of becoming a woman, and she falls in love with a muscular man whom she met at a market. Extremely impressed by his physical beauty, she immediately falls asleep and dreams while singing Madonna's 'True Blue', accompanied by dancers who resemble characters from *Grease* or *The Rocky Horror Picture Show*. When she wakes up, her muscular man is standing next to her, having declared that he is now her husband. Their love affair continues, but he wants her to keep the 'twenty centimetres', while Marieta has a different ending in mind. One of the last musical sequences shows her in hospital, like the end of *Cambio de sexo*, and instead of sleeping Marieta is completely awake for the last song: her version of Queen's 'I Want to Break Free'. Dressed up in blue, she is ready for surgery and all the doctors and nurses – Rossy de Palma among them – are dancing together. This song, originally sung by the openly gay Freddie Mercury, was well-known for its video clip with the singer dressed up as a woman in a short black leather skirt, cleaning house and longing to change his life. Marieta also wants to break free, and when she leaves the hospital the film finishes with a smiling blonde Marieta reborn as a latter-day Marisol. Walking in the city, she looks happy, having finally rid herself of her twenty centimetres: her dream came true.

If the Hollywood musical often transmitted, and transmuted, dreams through music and dance, this postmodern production updates the genre by referring to some recognisable musical traditions, domestic and international. Marieta's dreams are inscribed into a long-existing tradition where musical quotations are related to specific time periods and become sites of popular memory. This story is theatricalised by imposing a new gaze on the life of this transsexual, filled with dreams. Richard Dyer underlined the importance of Judy Garland for gay communities (1986: 141–94), and in *20 centímetros* both Marisol and Madonna form the inspiration for the entirely Spanish Marieta. As life changes, the musical continues to tell stories about new issues by adapting traditional codes to create modern love stories.

The film *¿Por qué se frotan las patitas?* confirms this tendency by revisiting pop music. The question in the title – 'Why do they rub their legs?' – is posed by a punk when he sees a fly doing so. At the end of the film, he comes back to it, talking to his dog and explaining that it prevents anything getting stuck. In the film, this is a metaphor for relationships, as three women – a mother, a wife and a daughter – abandon their respective lives. The men they abandon try to get them back, going so far as to hire a private detective. The songs illustrate their visions of life and distress, rearticulating famous pop songs by adding a flamenco touch. The way in which the songs are integrated into the film and the narration remind us of *On connaît la chanson/Same Old Song* (1997) by Alain Resnais, in how it showed daily life and distress in Paris. *¿Por qué se frotan las patitas?* foregrounds its Spanishness through its interpretation of the songs and its own forms of communicating, such as the tele-reality of 'Encuentros con Carla' or singing to each other via a mobile phone. The songs are often accompanied by flamenco gestures, but in a comical way, that gives the film a recognisably Spanish touch in parodying the *españolada*. The women choose their own destinies and, as the songs express them, the male characters feel completely lost (like in *El otro lado de la cama*). Even if the film does not directly represent its society or legislation, the grandmother Niña María refers frequently to the legal possibility of divorce, regretting her own marriage and the fact that she gave up her career as a singer for her husband. Though played by the venerated Spanish actress Lola Herrera, when Niña Maria sings the voice we hear is that of flamenco singer Carmen Linares. The three generations of women create a memory site in this contemporary musical, connecting their current issues to a history of personal rights in Spain by theatricalising them with their own appropriation of well-known Spanish musical traditions. Their voices symbolise the female point of view as they too wished to change their lives.

Conclusion

The aesthetic originality of the Spanish musical is impressive. However, while the Hollywood musical had a strong economic structure behind it, European cinemas have never been able to create the same kind of globally effective mode of production and circulation. One limitation is language; even if songs could be translated, this would not have the same impact that English-language pop music has experienced historically worldwide. In addition, the Hollywood musical was so successful internationally because it succeeded in creating dream and fantasy worlds in a cinematic language that is widely understood, passing the test of cultural translatability all around the world. In addition, the Spanish musical generally did not travel transnationally due to its cultural and historical characteristics, which are not so easily comprehended by foreign audiences. Even if a few Hollywood musicals have treated racial or political issues, we should not forget that many people continue to wish to see them in order to dream. By contrast, contemporary Spanish musicals treat issues that are closely related to the country's own culture and past, and should therefore be compared with other national cinemas for how they reflect their own national identities. For example, several contemporary French musicals – such as *On connaît la chanson*, *Jeanne et le garçon formidable* (Olivier Ducastel and Jacques Martineau, 1998), *8 Femmes/8 Women* (François Ozon, 2002) – reprise the country's popular musical history, so deeply rooted in their French culture, and therefore the films do not have the same effect on international audiences as they do on French audiences. Songs are like the veins of cultural memory, each leading their own life over decades. This effect, so intrinsically related to a culture, cannot be translated by words alone: the songs often already have their own life. The Spanishness of the musical can therefore be defined by the specificity of the music and importance of its cultural and political context. Memory sites are a permanent issue and songs revisit the past, transforming it into something new. The two studied subgenres of the musical – 'Dancing with the *españolada*' and 'Pop music revisited' – integrate different concepts of the past and confirm how Otherness requires its own place in Spanish cinema. Cinematic theatricality creates a vision of this Otherness by summoning the past, disguising it and integrating it into a genre meant to let people dream a bit more.

Notes

1 These films are all well-known in Spain, a fact confirmed by the box office and the number of Goya Awards they have received.
2 I refer in particular to the analysis of Núria Triana-Toribio in her book *Spanish National Cinema* (2003: 84–92), and Peter Evans's article 'Marisol: the Spanish Cinderella', in *Spanish Popular Cinema* (2004), 129–41.
3 Wikipedia, about the song 'Ay Carmela' and 'El paso del Ebro'.
4 In Spanish cinema, other filmmakers use this strategy, for example Pedro Almodóvar. In her article '¿Qué he hecho yo para merecer esto? (Almodóvar, 1984)', Núria Triana-Toribio (1999) analyses this process for the film *¿Qué he hecho yo para merecer esto?*, contrasting songs from different periods. Even if it is not a musical, Almodóvar is very clever in mixing up genres.
5 'Dime que me quieres', written by Alejo Stivel and Ariel Rot, was a number one hit for Tequila in the Spanish music charts for two weeks in August of 1980.

References

Altman, Rick (1987) *The American Film Musical*, Bloomington: Indiana University Press.

Amo-Sánchez, Antonia, Monique Martinez Thomas, Carole Egger and Agnès Surbezy (2005) *Le Théâtre contemporain espagnol. Approche méthodologique et analyses de textes*, Rennes: Presses Universitaires de Rennes.

Benjamin, Walter (2000a) 'L'Œuvre d'art à l'ère de sa reproductibilité technique (première version 1935)', in *Œuvres III*, Paris: Editions Gallimard, 67–113.

—— (2000b) 'Sur le concept d'histoire', in *Œuvres III*, Paris: Editions Gallimard, 427–43.

Camporesi, Valeria (1994) *Para grandes y chicos: un cine para los españoles 1940–1990*, Madrid: Ediciones Turfán.

Díaz López, Marina (2008) '¡Viva la diferencia (sexual)! o *El otro lado de la cama* (Emilio Martínez-Lázaro, 2002)', in Pietsie Feenstra and Hub Hermans (eds), *Miradas sobre pasado y presente en el cine español (1990–2005)*, Rodopi: Amsterdam.

Dyer, Richard (1986) *Heavenly Bodies. Film Stars and Society*, New York: St Martin Press.

Evans, Peter William (2004) 'Marisol: the Spanish Cinderella', in Antonio Lázaro Reboll and Andrew Willis (eds), *Spanish Popular Cinema*, Manchester: Manchester University Press, 129–41.

Feenstra, Pietsie (2006) *Les Nouvelles Figures mythiques du cinéma espagnol (1975–1995). A corps perdus*, Préface de Michèle Lagny, Paris: Harmattan.

Jordan, Barry and Rikki Morgan Tamosunas (1998) *Contemporary Spanish Cinema*, Manchester: Manchester University Press.

Lévi-Strauss, Claude (1956) *Anthropologie structurale*, Paris: Editions Plon.

Maurice, Thierry (2000) 'La *movida* ou l'impossible mémoire du franquisme', in *Les Historiens et le travail de mémoire*, Esprit, 266–7, August/September 2000; 103–18.

Nora, Pierre (1984) *Les Lieux de mémoire*, Paris: Gallimard.

Rodríguez Merchán, Eduardo (2007) 'De *Carmen, la de Triana* a *La niña de tus ojos*: la búsqueda de una armonía estilística de un modelo cinematográfico populista en el transcurso del tiempo', in Jaivier Marzal Felici and Francisco Javier Gómez Tarín (eds), *Metodologías de análisis del film*, Madrid: Edipo, S.A., 57–73.

Triana-Toribio, Núria (1999) '¿Qué he hecho yo para merecer esto? (Almodóvar, 1984)', in Peter William Evans (ed.), *Spanish Cinema: The Auteurist Tradition*, Oxford: Oxford University Press, 226–41.

—— (2003) *Spanish National Cinema*, London: Routledge.

13

Immigration films: communicating conventions of (in)visibility in contemporary Spain

Maria Van Liew

'Why haven't I ever seen you people before?'
'Because we are the people you do not see. We are the ones who drive your cars, clean your rooms, and suck your cocks.'
Dirty Pretty Things (2002)

'Siento sus ojos clavados aquí. No nos quieren aquí.'
Las cartas de Alou (1990)

In Stephen Frears' *Dirty Pretty Things* (2002), we encounter an ethnically diverse group of immigrants specific to the political, geographic and cultural time and place of twenty-first-century England – including a 'corrupt Spaniard' played to horrific excellence by Catalan actor Sergi López. This 'dramatic thriller' does not discriminate along lines of race, gender or national affiliation in doling out the suffering. Even 'Mr Sneaky' (Sergi López) gets his in the end! For many, the film in its treatment of 'peripheral collectivities' contributes to a field of academic research and criticism known as 'European' or 'international cinema'.[1] But, as Tim Bergfelder rightly points out, 'research into European cinema still equals research into discrete national cinema' (2005: 315). A plethora of co-productions and shifting audience formations have led to discussions of the possibility of a 'supranational' cinema that seemingly fails to account for the persistence of the regionally specific social realist foci of many accounts of the immigrant experience, newly familiar when merged with recognisable modes of storytelling such as the case of Spanish immigration films.

In response to the racial and ethnic differences posed by a rapid growth in immigration to Spain and public attention to its increasing visibility in the streets by the mid-1980s due to press coverage of the famous *ley de Extranjería*,² Spanish film directors begin to explore the 'illegal' immigrant's difficult integration into the fabric of Spanish social and economic developments. Fertile ground for explorations of recent shifts in national identification, integration and exclusion, Spanish immigration films help to distinguish the European Union as a hotbed of transnational cultural and political activity, while exhibiting distinctive national and regional social and aesthetic parameters.³ In this heterogeneous cluster of films, the social and political landscape becomes the aesthetic borderland where insider and outsider meet, shrouded in the unifying guise of a melodramatic mode of storytelling. The term 'transnational' connotes a certain transcendence of traditional national borders, while the modern national model of community identification persists in guiding and determining the lived reality and cultural practices of the transnational subject. Likewise, aesthetic interpretations of these experiences are woven into traditional modes of storytelling, allowing for a critical look at mythical notions of 'authentic' national identity and perceived threats to the same.

Fictional representations of the search for 'a better life' involve predictable conflicts and the intellectual and spiritual development of heroic protagonists. Several films of varying degrees of distribution and commercial success have set a tone of great humanity and attitudinal diversity on both sides of the migratory divide: *Las cartas de Alou/Letters from Alou* (Montxo Armendáriz, 1990), *Bwana* (Imanol Uribe, 1996), *En la puta calle/Hitting Bottom* (Enrique Gabriel, 1996), *Cosas que dejé en La Habana/Things I Left in Havana* (Manuel Gutiérrez Aragón, 1997), *Saïd* (Llorenç Soler, 1998), *Flores de otro mundo/Flowers from Another World* (Iciar Bollaín, 1999), *Poniente* (Chus Gutiérrez, 2002), *Extranjeras* (Helena Taberna, 2003), *El tren de la memoria* (Marta Arribas and Ana Pérez, 2005) *Princesas* (Fernando León de Aranoa, 2005). They also exhibit flashes of racism, ethnocentrism and the need for clearer national immigration policies alongside varying degrees of Spanish cinematic 'traditions' that either favour or disfavour certain ethnic groups such as Hispanic Americans and Africans.⁴ What these films have in common is the ability to exhibit new cultural formations and alliances that are at a crossroads with Spanish/European immigration policy. Central to these texts are constructions of spaces for transnational subjectivity as a reciprocal experience that fuels conflicts, forges alliances and forces individuals to confront their assumed 'normalcy' as contingent upon a global array of differentiation that transcends the dichotomous notion that difference is located outside the 'authentic' national self. The tendency of Spanish immigration films is to represent variance on both sides of the immigrant/host divide, demonstrating that immigrant characters are equally capable of 'Othering' those with whom interaction produces a space of reciprocity, thereby offering 'new' aesthetic possibilities.

Acknowledging a Continental mode of competitive industrial practices, Bergfelder describes European cinema as more than the sum total of its divergent national film styles, preferring 'a cinema of Diaspora' that is 'defined by the simultaneous agencies of dispersal and recentring [sic], which perpetually challenge easy solutions to the questions of identity and "home"' (2005: 319). This description speaks to the tendency to combine social realism and allegorical fantasy in presenting newly classical situations of migration, which in fact contribute to the transgeneric quality of contemporary immigration films. As Bergfelder proposes, an alternative history of European cinema needs to avoid narratives and discourses of containment in favour of 'charting the fluidity of identities' that through greater inclusiveness are more representative of 'the European idea on a larger scale' (2005: 329).

Engaging this fluid mode of address, films about recent migrations exhibit hybrid qualities that merge the dramatic techniques of social realism, romance, thriller, road trip/odyssey, bittersweet comedy with 'new' social developments.[5] These 'real' social references, as Christopher Williams points out, 'do necessarily tangle with conventional ways of seeing the truths and emotions of social and cultural life. But this involvement does not mean the adoption of fixed positions for the subject, the audience, or the medium' (2000: 211). Rather, these films articulate the space for transnational subjectivity to develop and expand along with an encompassing melodramatic mode.

In this 'large-scale' environment, Spanish directors address waves of human migrations from Latin America, Africa and Asia with stories as varied as the peninsula's already diverse cultural, political and physical landscape. Likewise, the generic conventions engaged in telling these stories are equally fluid and diverse. 'Genres are fictional worlds, but they do not stay within fictional boundaries: their conventions cross into cultural and critical discourse, where we – as audiences, scholars, students, and critics – make and remake them' (Gledhill, 2000: 241). These generic border crossings set human endeavour, liberal sympathies and bigotry in melodramatic dialogue, allowing for the eruption of moral and emotional consequences:

> Melodrama, as an organizing modality of the genre system, works at western culture's most sensitive cultural and aesthetic boundaries, embodying class, gender, and ethnicity in a process of imaginary identification, differentiation, contact, and opposition. But, as we have seen, bodies belong not only to generic worlds. They circulate as representations of ourselves within cultural verisimilitude and are subject to challenge. (2000: 238)

Implying that melodrama facilitates international exchange and debate, Gledhill recognises the persistence of a 'public space of social imaginings within a culturally conditioned aesthetic framework', (2000: 232) such as Spain's political, social and geographic conditions that contribute to composing and framing the daily experience of immigration. Linda Williams concurs that melodrama drives the production of a great variety of familiar film genres, and even today compensates 'the ongoing loss of moral certainty . . . by increasingly sensational, commodified productions of pathos and action' (2001: 23). By establishing the historical development of a melodramatic mode that encompasses myriad genres, Gledhill insists that questions of 'how to live, who is justified, who are the innocent, where is villainy at work now, and what drives it are embodied, personified, and enacted in different social and gendered arenas and historical periods' (2000: 234). Melodrama thus drives Spanish immigration cinema toward a transgeneric borderland where cultural and aesthetic encounters occur.

Las cartas de Alou (1990)

Cultural encounters, cohabitation, rejection, acceptance, prohibited romance, deportation and the determination to return represent a (re)cycle that follows the pattern of many 'new' genres in literature, theatre, video and so forth. The male protagonism of the earliest immigration films, spearheaded by Montxo Armendáriz's *Las cartas de Alou* (1990),[6] coincides with Spain's acceptance into the Common European Market, increasing press coverage of immigration issues, and changing laws to accommodate what for Spain is a newer phenomenon than for many northern European countries.

This shift begins in *Las cartas de Alou* with a nauseating traversal of the Straits of Gibraltar, which disorients the spectator attempting to discern in the darkness a small *patera* carrying an ethnically diverse group of African men to Spanish shores. Alou explains in voiceover Senagalese the contents of a letter destined for his friend Mulai, who has already established himself as a 'businessman' in Catalonia. This technique offers a challenge to the 'Spanishness' of Spanish cinema, much like Steven Spielberg implements with his enslaved characters, Cinqué and Kai Nyagua a.k.a James Covey ('the translator'), in *Amistad* (1997). Nyagua tells his story in his native language and we, as spectators, are initially locked out of his commentary due to the intentional lack of subtitles, thereby offering a glimpse into the experience of 'arrival' accompanied by linguistic and cultural exclusion and confusion. What both films achieve is a certain alienation of the spectator who, perhaps, expects to understand what is happening within the frame – that is, to see her or himself in the protagonist. While explaining his hopes and intentions for having left his homeland – 'We cannot survive on what I earn here' – spectatorial disorientation is increased by an unruly ocean and the defiance of Western 'normalcy' in this dangerously illegal method of arrival. Alou's precarious journey is underscored by the apparent drowning of a seasick Moroccan occupant of the *patera* who falls overboard. Despite Alou's protestations, they are forced to abandon the victim and, once on shore, must run into the grey twilight that renders them but dark silhouettes melding with a new landscape. Interestingly, this 'victim', Moucef, resurfaces later in the film in the province of Lérida (Catalonia), where he teaches Alou the game of '*blanco come negro*' ('white eats black') in *damas*, an important motif that leads Alou to his eventual love interest, Carmen, and a difficult situation for her father, who views Alou as a worthy 'opponent' but unacceptable as a romantic partner.

By framing numerous interactions such as this in Almería, Madrid and Barcelona from Alou's point of view, powerful sentiments are evoked that transcend the sentimental 'excess' often attributed to melodrama. Linda Williams insists that 'melodrama is neither archaic nor excessive but a perpetually modernizing form that can neither be clearly opposed to the norms of the "classical" nor to the norms of realism' (2001: 12), but rather entails images that move people through depictions of 'virtuous victims' and 'leering villains'. Alou's odyssey is told in a mode crucial to the establishment of his 'moral goodness' (despite being a practising Muslim!) by echoing the 'unspeakable truth' of current migratory trends and ensuing resentments that, ultimately, make no sense though upheld by the law. Thus, Alou's encounters with other immigrants, some of whom exploit him in this capitalist milieu and others who are crucial to his success (in learning the language, learning the 'games' people play) are just as damning as his encounters with Spanish nationals of equally exploitative or helpful capacity. Ultimately, the 'villain' is the political landscape that undercuts any attempt by a 'virtuous victim' to attain legal status while contributing to the Spanish economy.

Firmly established as an 'upstanding' non-citizen – 'I don't steal, I don't drink, and I don't sell drugs. What more do they want?'– Alou's greatest transgression is this relationship with a 'white' woman, whose father, generally accepting of the migratory diversity of his small town, cannot accept. Over a game of *damas*, Carmen's father, upon making his move, advises Alou to stay away. Framed in symmetry with the bi-coloured *tablero de damas*, he asks if this 'intruder' understands. Alou makes his move on the board (white eats black) and responds 'yes'.[7] The civility of this tightly framed scene remains underscored by the continuation of 'the game' despite growing resentment and fear on both sides of the board. But, as Paz Villar-Hernández points out, 'no image allows Alou to be tarnished as an inferior being, as we can see during his apprenticeship as a checkers player. His dexterity and skill is such that he wins notable sums of money by competing with town locals in the province of Lérida' (2001–2: 4).[8] He and Carmen pursue their relationship, despite her father's fear of potential consequences. Tolerant of the game of 'winning' or 'losing' until it crosses the threshold of family relationships, he exhibits what filmmaker Helena Taberna calls 'the little Hitler we all carry inside' (2003). Not only worried about 'losing' his daughter, he seems conscious, by daily interaction with migrant workers in his bar, that their life is a difficult and marginalised existence. Armendáriz comments: 'We're not racist until the problem affects us directly. When the problem crosses the threshold into our home, we change our attitude . . . such that open violence or monstrous persons are not necessary for racism to exist and manifest itself' (*Las Cartas de Alou*, 2002: 4).[9] Carmen's father is 'afraid', much like Spencer Tracy's otherwise liberal father role in *Guess Who's Coming to Dinner* (Stanley Kramer, 1967), fearing for his daughter's future of dealing with social pressures working against her potential happiness if involved in an intercultural/racial union (with Sidney Poitier's character, whose class standing as a medical doctor would otherwise be perfectly acceptable to the wealthy family). Quite often, close encounters with new migrants challenge liberal sentiments and a 'cosmopolitan' sense of privilege that pervades more positive theoretical views of globalisation. An intercultural dialogue persists along these lines of an equally interconnected discourse on the impact of globalisation, European Union immigration policy, and frustrations with individual national policy such as Spain's 'more lax' rules and treatment of recent arrivals.[10] Carmen's father is also terrified of his own abandonment, which is another 'real' reference point developed more extensively in Iciar Bollaín's *Flores de otro mundo*, which examines the depopulation of the Spanish rural countryside and the reality/fantasy of importing Latin American women for the project of repopulation.

Alou's arrivals are often accompanied by 'expulsions' (the first thing a Spaniard says to him in Almería is: 'Hey, you [tú], outta here, you can't be here!'). Thus, Carmen's father's resistance is only one in a series of 'legal' obstacles leading up to Alou's official deportation (profiled in the train station), to which he responds by explaining to his father (in voiceover while we watch him undertake the journey across the strait once more): 'I don't belong here [Senegal] any more. I've learned to live with white people', thus ending the film with his return, confirming the undeniable insertion of this 'other' within 'authentic' Spain. And Alou is not unique as the film's 'hero'. Thought victim of the treacherous crossing of the Straits of Gibraltar, Moucef's reappearance, optimistic attitude and photos of his family in Algeria suggest that his life and home are both here and there, and that nothing can stop the process of perpetual return.

With his expulsion due to lack of *papeles*, the film ends with the cycle of determination that drives Alou and others to return to their liminal status within Spain/Europe, rather than stay at 'home'. As the camera follows this migratory subject through rural and urban environments, Alou's established membership in an illegal 'we' that exists within Spain challenges the notion that he is on the outside of a presumed national 'authenticity' by inserting his sense of morality – 'I've learned to live with white people' – into the social and economic landscape comprised, as the film insists, of diversity, racism, resistance, fear, mutual need and determination.

Spain's relationship with its own recent history of emigration to northern Europe in the 1960s makes its 'allure' to current immigration all the more powerful in the Spanish national imagination by contributing to its liberal democratic image as one of the 'big players' in the European Union. While the 'transnational subject' is a fixture in most European films about immigration, the aesthetic result often remains intimately linked to the social and political structures of the host region/city/town – a landscape which, in turn, exhibits traces of its Eurocentric national 'past'.[11] In *Flores de otro mundo*, a rural landscape plays hostile host to 'loved' migratory subjects, whose ability to defy their liminal status within Spain pivots on their ability to compromise romantically for the sake of legitimacy.[12]

Miscegenation by invitation

Bollaín's contemporary tale of imported love offers insight into a global system that allows a wealthy European country to invite women from a geopolitical locus, whose postcolonial history coincides with its own. The transnational subjectivity exhibited is constructed out of an effort to merge Spain's contemporary social and economic reality of uneven urban/rural development with the fantasy of the transformative powers of migration. The inclusion of female characters as desirable subjects helps depict the changing coordinates of the Spanish contemporary milieu in which romance plays a pivotal role. As explained above, once Alou develops the ability to communicate in Spanish, his relationships with Spaniards develops into 'love'. Distinctive in the inclusion of Hispanic characters is that their 'authentic difference' is an accent, while the language with which they arrive is 'the same'. This linguistic quality of mutual understanding promotes complex misunderstandings that fulfil the melodramatic mode, the failure to communicate thus leading to the failed romantic plot.

From the disparate yearnings for greener pastures, to the romantic desires of Spanish nationals, emerges a set of 'love stories' between urban centres (Havana, Santo Domingo, Madrid and Bilbao) and the Castilian village of Santa Eulalia. Three tenuous relationships take shape in different ways. A wealthy middle-aged builder, Carmelo imports Milady, a 20-year-old Cuban who promptly asks upon her arrival: 'Is everything so ugly around here?' while the more mature, independent Patricia of the Dominican Republic must contend with two small children, her 'ex'-husband, and a meddlesome mother-in-law through marriage to shy villager Damián. A third relationship forms between two older Spanish nationals, Alfonso and Marirrosi, divorced and living in Bilbao as a nurse and single mother, serving as an important point of contrast to the Caribbean women's situations. This Basque resident has no intention of sacrificing her autonomy by moving to Santa Eulalia. Her voiceover letters to her *novio* Alfonso, who refuses to visit or move to Bilbao, offers an interesting parallel with Alou's letters, representing the fluidity of belonging through longing for a 'home' and companionship. Marirrosi's letters also serve as a contrastive voice to the intransigent male villagers, determined to import 'someone' rather than export themselves, emphasising the significant role these exotic 'flowers' play in the repopulation of rural Spain, a metaphor for the national need for human importation due, in part, to the sexual liberation of many Spanish women and their subsequent abandonment of traditional gender roles.[13]

Many cinematic representations include the 'threat' of non-Hispanic immigration in the form of linguistic, racial, and religious challenges to the status quo, as well as feeding national anxieties regarding difference (Flesler, 2004; Molina Gavilán and Di Salvo, 2006). Daniela Flesler's study insists that Spanish cultural productions on the topic of current immigration reveal less about the real lives of the newcomers and more about Spain's anxiety regarding its own liminal location in Europe, insinuating further in her study that: 'Even though a number of these films strive to show positive images of immigrants, they also reveal, through failed romance plots, a profound anxiety about racial/cultural contagion and miscegenation' (2004: 104).[14] While 'failures' are a necessity for the melodramatic mode to function, certain questions of morality need to be posed carefully. Flesler points out that positive images of immigrants (as morally sound) do not exonerate them from the role of carriers of potential contamination in the national imaginary, a resistance we see played out in *Las cartas de Alou*. While a disturbing xenophobic reality confronted by non-'white' immigrants, the function of this 'profound anxiety' does not taint all failed romance plots in the same way. In Manuel Gutiérrez Aragón's *Cosas que dejé en La Habana* (1997), two undocumented 'white' Cubans fall in love in Madrid, but cannot be together. This failure is premised on a distinct notion of 'contagion' in that they cannot help each other attain legal status. 'When I see a Cuban woman like you, I run,' states Igor, the film's Cuban male love interest. Similarly, in *Dirty Pretty Things*, 'black' Okwe and 'white' Senay cannot be together though in love, since the romance would compromise their ultimate goal of escape attained by changing their identities into members of the 'First World', thus sending them in different directions. While all three relationships implode in Bollaín's film, one interethnic romance recovers due to the development of intercultural communication skills that allow the 'truth' to emerge.

Potential conflict arrives with a busload of women hopefuls who gawk and giggle at the town and its inhabitants. Their first impressions allow the spectator to see the locals as 'the other' (Santaolalla, 2005: 194).[15] Their traversal through the human passageways and town streets is more pleasant than Alou's (he certainly does not have a group of women holding roses waiting for him!), but similar in that this hopeful arrival will culminate in disillusion and 'a return to crude and tedious reality' (2005: 195). An initially warm welcome by locals turns into critical hostility regarding the situation of cohabitation, posing obstacles and expectations that must be overcome in order to stay. The urgency to secure legal status in *Flores de otro mundo* is key to understanding the desire for interethnic relationships that can resolve problems for lonely Spanish nationals and desperate immigrants (in need of *papeles*). What *Flores de otro mundo* achieves is the expansion of the economic issues of the male centred immigration story towards a greater emphasis on national identity as impetus.

The 'permanence' of these migrations is represented through the marriage contract between Patricia and Damián, who installs his new bride and her two children in his mother's house. A series of conflicts ensue between mother (Gregoria) and daughter-in-law, demonstrating that crossing borders and thresholds is not always liberating for the immigrant, but equally invasive and challenging. Shots of Gregoria always accompany moments of intimacy between Patricia and Damián, implying that interracial intimacy is not private, but of 'public' concern. In this manner, Gregoria is framed as the rigid, frustrated 'other' in the family dynamics of this now multiethnic household, implying that the cinematic representation of 'others' requires reflection about one's own membership in any group that is neither stable nor fixed.

In the introduction of her excellent study, *Los 'Otros': etnicidad y 'raza' en el cine español contemporáneo*, Isabel Santaolalla poses a question that aligns itself with Gledhill's (2000) proposition for the melodramatic mode: 'Which identities tend to be presented as the normative ones, and which as the marginal?' Santaolalla asserts that possible answers work in conjunction with a long established us/them dichotomy premised on historically specific and, thereby, shifting traditions of national mythmaking practices. While her study reveals moments of overt Eurocentric racism towards the 'other', it also demonstrates that the questions circulating in recent Spanish cinema such as 'who are "we"' and 'who are "they"' render the dividing line between 'our' normalcy and 'their' marginality ever finer, much like the paper-thin wall that barely separates Gregoria from her son's intercultural romance. Immigrant subjects, both strange and familiar, 'make evident the fine line existing between the "I" and the "not-I", between what could have been, is and will be, and what will not' (2005: 13).[16] Along these thin lines of differentiation, many of the Spanish films produced between 1990 and 2006 offer social criticism while celebrating Spain's developing racial and ethnic diversity through overt sympathy with 'irregular others'. What is fascinating about many of these stories is that 'the other' is recognisably within: within Spain, within Europe, and within the individual, demonstrating that myths of 'otherness' continue to pervade contemporary storytelling premised on 'new' developments in national identity formation.

Without attempting to speak for the Caribbean 'other', Bollaín creates a portrait of transnational subjectivity as a shifting relationship of *mutual* need, desire and disdain, which calls for romance to express the melodramatic mode of interaction and misunderstanding. For the Caribbean protagonists, their linguistic skills contribute to constant negotiation with local attitudes and reactions toward their presence in town. Gregoria's control of the non-intimate spaces of the household, especially the kitchen, finally escalates into the threat of abandonment by her son. Damián concurs that his mother is in control of 'her' house, and that if she continues harassing his wife, they will leave. Burying their differences in the cemetery while attending to Damián Sr's gravesite, symbolic of their ability to now communicate as women, Gregoria learns to 'see' Patricia as an ally and not as a threat, and ultimately becomes the matriarchal force that keeps the marriage from breaking apart.

Attempting to speak her collaboration honestly, Patricia explains that she would not have married Damián had it not been for her need for *papeles*, and that she did not legally end her former marriage. Outraged at 'the truth', he expels her from the house until Gregoria intervenes. The final family portrait, taken during a Catholic ritual of 'arrival' for their daughter, Milai at her first Communion, is utopic in its ethnic inclusiveness. Yet, not all is resolved, as the cycle recurs in the arrival (similar to Alou's return) of a second round of 'love bus' members, echoing the melodramatic continuum through its expansion towards representations of the arrival of yet greater racial and cultural difference.

As a self-proclaimed 'European conscript', Stuart Hall offers the perspective of being 'in but not of Europe', a vantage point that disputes Europe's claim to be somehow autochthonous and capable of producing itself from within. Evoking what Ernesto Laclau and Judith Butler would call its 'constitutive outside', Hall explains that European identity, though premised on an imagined 'sameness', is constructed through difference, thereby affirming the importance of what is, in fact, outside: 'So nations – and supranational communities – if they are to hang together, and construct a sense of belongingness amongst their members – cannot simply be political, economic or geographical entities; they also depend on how they are represented and imagined: they exist within, not outside, representation, the imaginary' (2002–3: 61).

The shifting boundaries due to current rezoning of European borders are becoming the recognisable norm that marks a generic fabric as equally mutative in its fickle inclusiveness. This is of course a very unstable process of marking lines of difference from 'them': the lowering of barriers within Europe, the coming together around the 'lingua franca' of a common market in goods, capital and ideas, the incorporation of a 'wider Europe' which the modern 'myth' of the Euro is supposed to symbolise, each continues to display its reverse side. *What is 'open' within is increasingly barred without'* (Hall, 2002: 67, my emphasis). Upon arrival, 'they' – Patricia and her children – shake things up from the inside, and force Spain to reimagine or re-present itself differently in order to justify the transition as 'native' and 'natural', thereby including the liminal qualities of immigration 'drama'.

Milady's arrival offers comedic spectacle, occurring somewhat differently than Patricia's and Marrirosi's. Driven by her 'host' to the centre of town, she emerges clad in red, white and blue 'Italian lycra', stars and stripes emphasising the spectacle of her height and sleek, black, 20-year-old body deployed cinematically as an instrument of disruption, arriving with the message, 'I am not like you at all.' A chorus of old men, reminiscent of Spike Lee's hilarious Greek chorus of neighbourhood denizens in *Do the Right Thing* (1989), express their racial confusion and sexist reactions:

Old man 1: Wow, she's beautiful! Which one is she?
Old man 2: The Cuban.
Old man 3: Wasn't she Dominican?
Old man 2: No! The Dominican is Damián's! Don't you get it!
Old man 1: Hey, I think this one is better than the other.
Old man 2: Yes, much better.
Old man 3: What teeth! What lips!
Old man 2: What kisses she must plant on him! If only. . .
Old man 1: Ah, to be thirty again!

This receiving party, seemingly innocuous due to their advanced ages, serves as precursor to the racism and sexist violence that Milady, the darkest and youngest of the romantic trio of transnational protagonists, will endure. Yet, she mirrors their attitudes and judgements back at them throughout the film. When Patricia declines an offer to go out, Milady accuses her of becoming like 'them', insinuating that her Caribbean-ness is being compromised by contact with the Santa Eulalians. In boredom, she 'escapes' to Valencia for a night of dancing and fun, posing as a 'tourist just visiting friends', employing the social and economic position of Spanish sex tourist she encountered in Cuba.

Upon her return to a now extremely hostile environment, Carmelo brutally attacks Milady. Her subsequent docility and housebound status quell her colourful wardrobe, which turns toward the tones of the host landscape – shades of brown and grey. What this change implies is that Milady's arrival offers 'the finality of representational and representative *hubris*', something R. Radhakrishnan warns against, since the 'diasporic hybrid conjuncture' proposed by Carmelo's importation of her becomes the site of a paradox where (self) representation and political truth collide violently (2000: n.p.). Without resources, Milady abandons Santa Eulalia with another local, whom she quickly abandons, too – thus the final shot of her trekking autonomously and most likely toward the coast and urban Spain. Her vulnerability to the real effects of racism and sexism inflicted on her body in this rural locus forces her away from participating in 'diasporic hybridity' (forming a family with fifty-plus Carmelo), thereby remaining liminal to the transnational subjectivity explored as a shared possibility in the film. The town's inability to absorb the three 'foreign' imports unfolds in a manner that resists celebration of Spain's status as a European Community member, and 'focuses on the hybrid temporalities that crowd the margins of this inclusion' (Martín-Cabrera 2002: 48). As Luis Martín-Cabrera suggests here, the hierarchies of difference established in a modern European notion of time are 'irrevocably entangled' in the insistent though flawed heterogeneity of Bollaín's film (2002: 49). Consistent with its sympathetic connection to the development of transnational subjectivity as premised on a shared responsibility, *Flores de otro mundo* releases Milady from her position of abused but desirable subject/object to face other possible arrangements lingering beyond the frame – deportation, another unequal loveless relationship, financial autonomy – continuing her migration in search of a location within Europe and 'First World' capitalism.

Villar-Hernández suggests that in studying Spanish films we can observe a tendency to treat immigration from the viewpoint of conflict rather than contribution. She states that this is particularly acute in the representation of sub-Saharan and Moroccan immigrants, 'which can contribute to the creation of a more negative social imaginary than in existence already. To the contrary, with respect to Latin-American immigration, the image is more "alegre" and usually is accompanied by the feminine figure, who in general is rebellious and transgressive' (2001–2: 6).[17] The contemporary inclusion of 'the Latin American friend' seems to consistently represent cause for celebration due to the 'alegría' he or she brings to the party, while Africans bring 'problems'; their stories usually a series of conflicts to overcome.

While the circularity of Alou's odyssey is closed in a cycle of departure/return, Milady and Marrirosi present the possibility of the female melodramatic mode as more prone to an open-ended transience. Numerous Spanish films offer transient female characters less likely to cooperate in closure, resolution or containment. These characters do not die, nor marry for security or safety. Marrirosi returns to the security of her national autonomy in Bilbao, while

Milady disappears into an unknown outcome, beyond the boundaries of an established, though less rigid, national imaginary.

Nostalgia in the new millennium

While theories of 'the Other' include notions of the other within, as
Helena Taberna notes: 'We all harbour a racist inside, a little Hitler
that must be domesticated' (2003).[18] Taberna and other filmmakers
have been developing strategies that defy 'traditional notions of
inflexible hierarchy and normative type-casting' that would only
propagate the inhospitable 'European gaze' (Rodríguez, 2003: n.p.).
María Pilar Rodríguez has studied the traditional cinematographic
documentary mode, demonstrating on the one hand 'a constant
social, political and cultural concern for its content', while on the
other suffering 'an almost endemic hierarchical relationship' to the
same. She attributes this 'disequilibrium' to a manifest sense of supe-
riority on the part of the director with respect to the selected other
as subject of analysis, thereby creating 'patterns of hierarchy' (2003:
n.p.), such as Martín-Cabrera suggests are irrevocable entanglements within a European notion of time (2002: 49). Rodríguez
asserts that Taberna defies these hierarchical representational patterns in her documentary *Extranjeras* (2003) of integrated women
immigrants to the neighbourhood of Lavapíes in Madrid:

> By means of a series of visual strategies that break from traditional
> notions of inflexible hierarchy and normative type-casting, Taberna
> brings us irreversibly closer to the subjects of her film, *making us
> accomplices and responsible*, obligating us to a radical questioning of
> our [own] prejudices and stereotypes. (2003: n.p.)[19]

The visual strategies employed by Taberna that signal storytelling as
revelatory of a new autochthonous 'Other'. Taberna controls the
context and framing of her immigrant subjects, but remains silent
and allows their voices and experiences (both successful and tragic)
to flow in collaborative control of a heterogeneous discourse that
merges voices and images into a melodious cacophony of final
celebration of their multicultural, multiethnic contributions to an
adoptive and adopted home. By investigating these 'new' strategies,
Taberna, Rodríguez and others highlight transnational 'disruptions'
as moments shared by immigrants ('we are the people you do
not see') and Europeans who believe their 'normalcy' (Western

citizenship in wealthy, technologically advanced countries) renders them equally invisible. This interaction between two 'seeing' and 'unseen' entities underscores the significance of recent Spanish immigration cinema without circumscribing this space of confrontation and collaboration.

What should happen in the near future is the expansion of this transgeneric mode of storytelling in the hands of non-native Spanish direction that will tell yet 'Other' stories that continue to question established notions of Spanish national identity, and that will perhaps move on from the expected conflicts arising from the rapid and recent influx of people from other cultures in search of 'a better life'. Taberna (2003) affirms that 'the difference between the first generation [of women] who arrive to Spain and second generation daughters is great and becomes curious to listen to them speak with a *madrileño* accent and foreign features'.[20] In the meantime, existing stories of immigration in Spain exhibit an introspective melodramatic mode that allows 'the "Other" within' to emerge – creating the shared responsibility of transnational subjectivity that encompasses the space, time and place of these cultural encounters.

Notes

1 Gonzalo Navajas considers *Dirty Pretty Things* one of 'the new narratives', in which 'peripheral collectivities' are represented as borderless but vulnerable in their 'nation-less' state. His hope is that their presence in contemporary artistic production can produce 'an inclusive and antinormative paragon of individual and collective identity'. While he does not confine the 'new' borderless and post-national self to immigration, the point is well taken that, 'although international law has had increasing visibility and functions in the world, it is a fact that the law of the nation still is the ultimate agent and arbiter in legal affairs' (2006: 5).

2 Enrique Santamaría distinguishes between press coverage and fictional renditions of Spain's encounter with 'new' immigration: 'La configuración social de la "inmigración" que la prensa ejecuta es indisoluble, es el reverso, de la producción social de una figura de la identidad: el "nuevo" autóctono, el ciudadano europeo' (1993: 71).

3 This tendency is visible in the predominance of concern with such issues in the selection of films for international competition, such as for the Palme d'Or for Best Film at the 2006 Cannes International Film Festival: Only four of the twenty selected were not concerned to any extent with

issues of immigration; see http://movies.monstersandcritics.com/features/article_1167775.php/Themes_of_immigration_injustice_mark_C annes_film_festival.

4 Isabel Santaolalla's chapter 'Antecedentes: Breve historia de la representación de la "otredad" étnica en el cine del siglo XX' (in Santaolalla, 2005) offers a thorough explanation of the historical bases for the particular cinematic treatment of different ethnic groups in an effort to allay the notion that all outsiders are 'othered' in the same way in contemporary Spanish cinema.

5 Pedro Almodóvar's artistry in the 1980s is a good prior example of how Spanish, European and Hollywood genres can merge with new social and political developments particular to the social landscape in Spain and, thereby, influence the same.

6 José Luis Borau is often recognised for his contribution with *Río abajo/ On the Line* (1984), an English-language film about the border situation of Mexican immigrants in the United States. But Armendáriz's film is recognised for engaging with a specifically 'Spanish' situation.

7 Mónica Cantero-Exojo elaborates this aspect of the film: 'Los jugadores de esta partida representan las dos partes antagonistas: los nacionales y los ilegales, con la ironía que el final, son estos inmigrantes (un marroquí y un africano) los que casi siempre ganan la partida de damas. Esta situación de enfrentamiento con el otro refleja el malestar de la multiculturalidad y de tan decisiva transformación en la que se vive, que produce toda una serie de sentimientos encontrados en el seno de la sociedad' (2007: n.p.).

8 'Ninguna imagen nos permite tachar a Alou de ser inferior, como podemos ver durante su aprendizaje del juego de las damas. Su maña es tal que consigue una cantidad notable de dinero compitiendo con los locales de ese pueblo de la provincial de Lérida.'

9 'No somos racistas mientras el problema no nos afecta. Cuando tenemos el problema dentro de casa cambiamos de actitud . . ., de manera que no es necesario que haya violencia directa o personas monstruosas para que el racismo exista y se manifieste.'

10 Christopher Caldwell's in-depth exploration of Spain's 'uniquely lax' immigration controls offers comparison with other European countries' 'stricter' legislation: 'Spain is the unlocked side-door of the European Union's house' (2006: 2). Nevertheless, Spain is quickly catching up with its 'Western' neighbours: 'More than 11 % of the country's 44 million residents are now foreign-born, one of the highest proportions in Europe. With hundreds of thousands more arriving each year, Spain could soon reach the U.S. rate of 12.9 %' (2006: 5). The fact that Spain's extremely high 'building bubble' has 'burst' (it is not at 18 per cent of economic production), perhaps promoting a less tolerant environment

if unemployment rates, lowered to 8.6 per cent from the over 20 per cent average of the 1990s, begin to rise again.

11 Such is the focus of the emergence of a nostalgic turn in the immigration genre. Preceded by the documentary *El tren de la memoria*, *Un franco, 14 pesetas* (Carlos Iglesias, 2006) is a fictionalised biographic film about the economic exodus of Spanish émigrés to northern industrial jobs in countries like Switzerland in the 1960s. The thematic offers a point of comparison (the immigrant experience of the Spanish national of yesteryear) with the experience of playing national host to immigration today. The idea that the immigrant has the obligation to eventually 'go home', despite an inferior quality of life awaiting him or her, is promoted in the tone and ending of the film, which gives cultural expression to a sense of national anxiety regarding Spain's current situation of economic magnet to poorer communities and a sense of guilt regarding national behavior towards the same.

12 By the latter 1990s, directors begin exploring the relationship between Spain and women immigrants, predominantly from Latin America, whose numbers rose dramatically coincident with the appearance of these narratives. From a sociological viewpoint, Angeles Escrivá published a report in 2000 stating that 'while migrant men – especially of African origin – were visible within the Spanish landscape, women have remained invisible to the public and in the eyes of some social scientists dealing with migration issues' (2000: 199). The appearance of women migratory subjects abound in cinematic representations of twenty-first-century Spain, though whether these films are widely seen is disputable.

13 I develop this study more extensively in 'Importing Love: Transnational Subjectivity in Iciar Bollaín's *Flores de otro mundo* (1999) (Van Liew, 2007).

14 She offers examples from the following films: *Las cartas de Alou*, *Bwana*, *Saïd*, *Poniente*, and especially *Tomándote* (Isabel Gardela, 2000) and *Susanna* (Antonio Chavarrías, 1996).

15 'Mientras los del pueblo y las forasteras se examinan nerviosamente a través de los cristales del autobus, la negociación entre estos dos mundos (el "femenino" frente al "masculino", el de "aquí dentro" y el de "allí fuera") se transmite visualmente de forma escueta pero muy efectiva.'

16 'Pondrá[n] en evidencia la fina línea que existe entre el yo y el no-yo, entre lo que pudo, puede o podrá ser y lo que no.'

17 'Lo que puede contribuir a crear un imaginario social más negativo del que ya existe sobre ellos. Por el contrario, respecto a la inmigración latinoamericana, la imagen es más alegre y suele ir acompañada de la figura femenina, que en general es una figura rebelde y transgresora.'

18 'Todos llevamos un racista dentro, un pequeño Hitler que hay que ir domesticando.'
19 'Por medio de una serie de estrategias visuales que rompen con las nociones tradicionales de inamovible jerarquía y normativa tipificación, Taberna se/nos acerca irreversiblemente a los sujetos que muestra su cámara, *nos hace cómplices y responsables* y nos obliga a un cuestionamiento radical de prejuicios y estereotipos.'
20 'La diferencia entre la primera generación que llega a España y la siguiente que ya es hija de los inmigrantes es muy grande y resulta curioso escuchar a gente con un acento madrileño pero rasgos extranjeros.'

References

Bergfelder, Tim (2005) 'National, Transnational or Supranational Cinema: Rethinking European Film Studies', *Media, Culture and Society*, 27: 3, 315–31.

Caldwell, Christopher (2006) 'Europe's Future: The Senegalese – and the Malians, Mauritanians, Gambians, *et al.* – are coming to Spain – and staying', *Weekly Standard*, 12 April, V 12, I 12, 1–9.

Cantero-Exojo, Mónica (2007) 'El discurso de la inmigración en el cine hispano: tragedias personales y realidades sociales', presented at Cine-Lit VI, Portland State University, Portland, Oregon, 21–24 February.

Las Cartas de Alou (2002) Guía didáctica, 1–6, www.edualter.org/material/intcine/cartase.htm.

Escrivá, Ángeles (2000) 'The Position and Status of Migrant Women in Spain', in Floya Anthias and Gabriella Lazaridis (eds), *Gender and Migration in Southern Europe: Women on the Move*, Oxford: Berg, 199–225.

Flesler, Daniela (2004) 'New Racism, Intercultural Romance, and the Immigration Question in Contemporary Spanish Cinema', *Studies in Hispanic Cinemas*, 1: 2, 103–18.

Fuchs, Dale (2003) 'The Love Bus: In Spain's Lonely Countryside, a Cupid Crusade', *Christian Science Monitor*, 10: 1, 14.

Gledhill, Christine (2000) 'Rethinking Genre', in Christine Gledhill and Linda Williams (eds), *Reinventing Film Studies*, London and New York: Arnold and Oxford University Press, 221–43.

Hall, Stuart (2002–3) 'In But Not of Europe: Europe at its Myths', *Soundings: A Journal of Politics and Culture*, 22, Winter, 57–69.

Martín-Cabrera, Luis (2002) 'Postcolonial Memories and Racial Violence in *Flores de otro mundo*', *Journal of Spanish Cultural Studies* 3: 1, 43–55.

Molina Gavilán, Yolanda and Thomas Di Salvo (2001) 'Policing Spanish/European Borders: Xenophobia and Racism in Contemporary Spanish Cinema', *Ciberletras*, 5, www.lehman.cuny.edu/ciberletras/v05/molina.html.

Navajas, Gonzalo (2006) 'Transnational Aesthetics: Literature and Film Between Borders', *Ciberletras*, 14, www.lehman.cuny.edu/ciberletras/v14/navajas.htm.

Radhakrishnan, R. (2000) 'Adjudicating Hybridity, Co-ordinating Betweenness', *Jouvert: An Online Journal of Postcolonial Studies*, 5: 1, Autumn, http://social.chass.ncsu.edu/jouvert/v5i1/con51.htm.

Rodríguez, María Pilar (2003) *Extranjeras*, presented at Cine-Lit I, Portland State University, Portland, Oregon, March, www.lamiaproducciones.com/extranjeras/textompilar.htm.

Santamaría, Enrique (1993) '(Re)presentación de una presencia. La "inmigración" en y a través de la prensa diaria', *Archipiélago*, 12, 65–72.

Santaolalla, Isabel (2005) *Los 'Otros': etnicidad y 'raza' en el cine español contemporáneo*, Madrid: Ocho y medio, Zaragoza University Press.

Taberna, Helena (2003) 'Taberna: "Todos llevamos un pequeño Hitler dentro que hay que domesticar" ' (2003) *Diario de Noticias* (Valladolid), 27 October, 1–2, www.lamiaproducciones.com/extranjeras/notadn.htm.

Van Liew, Maria (2007) 'Importing Love: Transnational Subjectivity in Iciar Bollaín's *Flores de otro mundo* (1999)', *Letras Femeninas*, 23: 1, 153–73.

Villar-Hernandez, Paz (2001–2002) 'El Otro: conflictos de identidad en el cine español contemporáneo', *University of Pennsylvania Working Papers in Romance Languages and Literatures*, 6, http://ccat.sas.upenn.edu/romance/gra/WPs2002/paz_1.htm.

Williams, Christopher (2000) 'After the Classic, the Classical and Ideology: The Differences of Realism' Christine Gledhill and Linda Williams (eds), in *Reinventing Film Studies*, London and New York: Arnold and Oxford University Press, 206–20.

Williams, Linda (2001) *Playing the Race Card: Melodramas of Black and White from Uncle Tom to O. J. Simpson*, Princeton: Princeton University Press.

14

Spanish-Cuban co-productions: tourism, transnational romance and anxieties of authenticity

Mariana Johnson

It's by now accepted that a delimited scope on the nation as the organising principle in film and media studies is inadequate to account for the constantly shifting landscapes in which film and media are made, distributed and consumed. In the current period of globalisation and mobile capital, deterritorialisation and resettlement, and migrations imagined and real, a shift has taken place from the myopics of national culture to the relationality of transnational flows. This has involved, to name just a few important frameworks of analysis, studying diasporic and exilic films for their distinct subjectivity and style (Hamid Naficy, Laura Marks); looking at media uptake across borders, attentive to the ways in which it can be used to build communities, maintain local cultures, and promote or retard progressive action (Marie Gillespie, Louisa Schein); analysing the impact of international financing on questions of cultural representation and reception (Nestor García Canclini); using critical political economy to expose the inequities of the new international division of cultural labour (Toby Miller); and reorienting Eurocentric tendencies in cultural studies to interrogate their nationalist premises (Robert Stam and Ella Shohat).

In their volume *Multiculturalism, Postcoloniality and Transnational Media*, Shohat and Stam argue that 'communities, societies, nations, and even entire continents exist not autonomously but in a densely woven web of connectedness, within a complex and multivalent relationality' (2003: 1). This reality demands an attentiveness not only to the interrelationship between dynamic geographies but also to the usefulness of diverse theoretical grids, 'of deploying multiple historical and cultural knowledges, [and] of envisioning the media in relation to mutually co-implicated communities' (2003: 17). This chapter aims to bring this kind of relational, transnational lens to one facet of contemporary Spanish cinema. It moves away from national cinema and auteur models to analyse the relationship between tourism and representation in Spanish-Cuban co-productions. It expands the purview of what typically falls under the heading of Spanish cinema by looking at recent Spanish films set in Cuba, or that represent Cuban immigrants in Spain, as well as films by Cuban directors that are supported by Spanish funding. Such a contrapuntal approach is useful in understanding the workings of genre figuration and reformulation in the age of mobile capital, as new generic categories emerge and contract across borders in accordance with both industrial and sociocultural practice. While genre studies are attentive to the ways in which genre categories evolve *within* cultures and industries, there is a need to reorient our gaze to examine the ways in which genres evolve *across* them. This is not meant merely as a means to celebrate some form of cultural or formal hybridity or enumerate genre-bending tendencies or innovations, but rather to interrogate the repetitions and differences of generic development as the representations of new transnational spaces reveal familiar and, in some cases, reactive cultural anxieties.

In Spanish-Cuban co-productions what is most apparent is the ascendancy of films projecting heterosexual romance between Spaniards and Cubans. Although generic diversity exists among the films themselves – from the low-budget Spanish-directed sexcapade movies of the early 1990s to more ambitious, politically nuanced works by such well-respected directors as Manuel Gutiérrez Aragón in Spain and Fernando Pérez in Cuba – Spanish co-productions with Cuba are dominated by transnational romance, usually in variations of the romantic comedy. Whether projecting relationships between Cuban nationals and European tourists in Havana (e.g. *Cuarteto de La Habana/Havana Quartet* (Fernando Colomo, 1999), *La vida es silbar/Life is to Whistle* (Fernando Pérez, 1998), *Hacerse el sueco* (Daniel Díaz Torres, 2001), *Habana Blues* (Benito Zambrano, 2005)), or Spanish citizens and Cuban immigrants in Spain (*Cosas que dejé en La Habana/Things I Left in Havana* (1997), *Flores de otro mundo/Flowers from Another World* (1999)), various configurations of transnational coupling have been projected in Spanish and Cuban cinema since 1990, after Fidel Castro declared 'the Special Period in Times of Peace', a period of sustained economic decline following the collapse of the island's socialist trading partners. The

Special Period initiates a more conciliatory reconfiguration of the transnational/national relationship, one that is both more transparent and more subtly and strategically deployed – more transparent in that cultural interdependence and mutual recognition are more likely to be explored rather than foreclosed upon; more subtly and strategically deployed in that, while foreigners are increasingly being reincorporated into Cuban productions, this process has evolved during a historical period when non-Cubans and especially Europeans have become a more indispensable part of the Cuban economy than ever before. Tourism has replaced sugar as the dominant source of hard currency earnings in Cuba, and the filmic representations of romance between Cubans and Spaniards should be understood within this historical and economic context.

Cuban cinema may depend on Spanish financing for its very existence, but what have these transnational collaborations meant for both cinemas? To what extent are Spanish representations of Cuba engaged in constructing a transnational imaginary with imperial nostalgic undertones? How is Cuba negotiating its entry into the global film marketplace, and what is at stake? To some extent transnational romance in Spanish-Cuban co-productions is constructing a kind of Latino-Iberian 'foundational fiction' for the globalised economy, one in which mutual economic interests are opening up new spaces for cultural and sexual exchange and simultaneous national expansion. Yet, insofar as foundational fictions posit cultural and physical *mestizaje* as an ideal based on the already existing reality of racial amalgamation, these co-productions project familiar anxieties about cultural purity and nationhood. Even the most culturally nuanced and politically sensitive of these films, such as the recent and critically acclaimed *Habana Blues*, reveal a lingering romanticisation of cultural purity in an age of instant commodification. This essay provides an overview of these trends, analysing Spanish-Cuban co-productions made on both sides of the Atlantic, specifically drawing attention to the ways in which mobile capital is mediating representations of transnational romance.

Spain has long invested in filmmaking in Latin America, but the last ten years have witnessed a burgeoning of Spanish/Latin American co-productions in the region. Spain's assertive economic policies, which expanded their holdings in Latin American telecommunications, finance and energy in the 1990s, also helped encourage co-production initiatives at the Institute for Cinema and Audiovisual

Arts, Television Española and the Agency for Cooperation and International Development. These changes increased Spanish investment in Latin American films, with the aim of developing a powerful Spanish-speaking cinema market. One result of these policies was the establishment of Ibermedia, the multiplatform consortium specifically designed to promote co-productions among Spanish and Portuguese-speaking countries (Hoefert de Turégano, 2004). Of the films made in Mexico, Brazil and Argentina, 50 per cent are international co-productions, but during the ongoing Special Period in Cuba nearly all film projects rely on international funding. The Cuban film industry, in fact, cannot exist in its present state without securing funding from the outside, and Spain is the leading financial contributor to the island's productions.

There are plenty of reasons why Cuban national film finds itself in a state of crisis. From 1989 to 1992, the country's gross national product declined by thirty percent, and the Cuban government passed a series of measures mandating sacrifice and bracing for further shortages. At the 1991 meeting of the Fourth Congress of the Communist Party, Castro pressed for self-financing in the culture industries. The state-subsidised film industry Instituto Cubano de Arte e Industria Cinematográficos (ICAIC), established immediately after the Revolution in 1959 by the first official cultural decree of the new government, has during the last fifteen years opened itself up to the logic of the international market. It has now become impossible to make a feature film in Cuba without external financing, a reality that has in turn provoked serious debate over how to represent national culture while working with transnational capital. Much as with Néstor García Canclini's questions regarding what happens to the production of national cultural identity in Latin America during an age of transnational corporations (1997), Cuban filmmakers have attempted to reformulate the meanings of revolutionary cinema as they simultaneously negotiate Cuba's economic restructuring and the forces of globalisation. My argument likewise places the transnational and national side by side, attentive to their interplay rather than privileging or segregating one from the other. By moving from an examination of films made in Cuba with transnational, predominantly Spanish, funding to films made by Spanish directors and financed by Spain that are either set in Cuba or that use Cuban actors, I wish to demonstrate that these issues play out along a continuum of interconnected cultural flows.

Studies of transnational co-productions have tended to raise questions about the erasure of national cultures, bringing attention to the uneven playing field in which most of these collaborations take place. R. Ruby Rich warned that, 'with Spanish television recently poised to expand into a large-scale agenda of co-productions', Latin American cinema should be wary about the pressures of self-exoticisation, and feared that 'contemporary fictional themes would no longer arise out of the specificity of an identifiable set of national circumstances' (1997: 294). Although histories of imperialist oppression and economic powerlessness in the Third World practically demand the construction of national authenticity and cultural heritage as strategies for self-determination, there persists in third-worldist discourse a tendency to fetishise cultural authenticity along nationalist lines. This tendency has resulted in a quasi-moralistic discourse, in which migrancy in the Latin American mediascape is read always in terms of loss, assuming that collaboration with First World partners must involve a collusion with hegemonic perspectives and a dilution of national cultures (Stock, 1995).

The onus for preserving national culture continues to fall heaviest on the least privileged party, with Latin American countries expected to be more protective and assertive of their national cultural identities, whereas First World cultures are already accepted as too fragmented, complicated and modern for naive notions of purity. In the case of Cuba, a blockaded island and the last vestige of a socialist utopia, this tendency to romanticise authenticity is magnified. Indeed one of the most potent conceptions of Cuba proliferating outside the island, particularly in North America and Europe, is that it is sealed off from the rest of the world, dwelling in a kind of permanent time warp. That it is an insular place defined by its own decay. Without attending to the historical specificity of US foreign policy, the myth of Cuban isolation as a form of cultural purity is one of the most frequently recycled clichés in international discourse about the nation and influences most representations of the island in the non-Cuban media. While the devastating impact the embargo has on ordinary Cubans cannot be overstated, this typically one-way view of history, which assumes that US trade restrictions have managed to keep Cuba culturally separate from the rest of the world, is patronising and false. It is, nonetheless, an extremely powerful perspective that structures popular (and to some extent academic) ideas about the island.

The popular currency of this idea is nowhere more evident than in the discourse surrounding the *Buena Vista Social Club*, first a Grammy-winning album in 1997, then a popular documentary directed by Wim Wenders in 1999, and now a veritable brand used to promote all things Cuban, including the tourist industry. In an interview that aired on the American Broadcasting Company television news programme *Nightline* in April 2000, Wenders discussed his Cuban subjects as follows:

> Some of the little things, well, can give bigger pleasures than all these gigantic and bombastic pleasures we're living with. These people are really very clear about who they are and where they belong so it's a sense of identity that is really pretty difficult to find anywhere else in the world.

The Cubans' identities are discussed as an absolute, or, to borrow Stuart Hall's phrase, as 'an already accomplished fact' (2003: 234). They are simple, organic and grateful; we are complicated, fragmented and decadent. The depiction (however false) of a bounded space and culture that have been 'sealed off from the fall out of a hyper-organised and noisy world', as Ry Cooder described it in the booklet accompanying the *Buena Vista* compact disc, suggests the nostalgia for cultural authenticity pervading discursive representational practices that fetishise Cuban insularity. In some ways, the increase in the flow of globalisation and transnational capital, rather than hastening the deconstruction of this mythology, has worked to intensify it. Those invested in maintaining an illusion of Cuba as the great 'unspoiled', the last holdout in a world of multinational conglomerates, may have difficulty reconciling their romantic image of the 'sealed-off' nation with its transnational reality (of which, ironically, *Buena Vista* is itself an index).

At the same time, the myths of island insularity and authentic culture are not solely confined to outsider perspectives. Revolutionary anti-imperialism has consistently utilised island geography as a trope in articulating oppositional politics and culture. The idea of a 'harshly besieged and blockaded country', to quote from a recent article by Cuban artist Tonel (Antonio Eligio Fernández) (2002: 80), has figured prominently in the David and Goliath-like narrative of Cuban anti-imperialist struggle. And national destiny and cultural authenticity have been ongoing, pervasive forces in the discourse of the Revolution. These discourses have also, again ironically, been used as a marketing strategy for the tourist sector. Cuba's Ministry of Tourism has appropriated those iconic images of 1950s Chevys and peeling paint. Meanwhile metaphors involving time travel and virginal pristineness abound on the Ministry's website. They appeal to external gazers as potential tourists on a global level, appropriating the transnational imaginary in a strategic orientalising of culture that is not atypical in the marketing of tourism from within the Caribbean. Their tagline 'Viva Cuba' itself invokes the continued existence of the island as a selling point, affirming national identity at the same time as it evinces a kind of pre-elegiac quality. This sense that something pure still exists in Cuba, but that it's always on the brink of disappearing, has become an operative representational mode in various forms of contemporary cultural production inside the island and out.

I spend a few pages summarising these issues of island insularity and authentic culture because they are essential to my reading of contemporary Spanish-Cuban co-productions and the emergent generic category of the transnational romance. Time and time again these films reveal tensions between transnational cosmopolitanism and national cultural purity, and these tensions assert themselves most forcefully through representations of, and narratives focused on, heterosexual romance. Films like *La vida es silbar* and *Cosas que dejé en La Habana* are concerned with the evolving social realities of intensified travel, migration and mobile capital in both Cuba and Spain. At the same time they suggest a longing for stability of place and identity, a palpable nostalgia for an island nation perceived as coherent and pure.

Throughout the 1990s tourism and migration made indelible marks on the mise-en-scène of Cuban cinema. The inclusion of tourist characters, either as part of the backdrop, making up the social fabric of the city, or as major players who actively shape narrative development, has become commonplace. Topics once considered taboo, such as emigration and reconciliation with the exile community, are increasingly addressed in some of the most popular and internationally successful films the island has produced (e.g. *Miel para Oshún/Honey for Oshun* (Humberto Solás, 2001), *Suite Habana* (Fernando Pérez, 2003), *Viva Cuba* (Juan Carlos Cremata Malberti and Iraida Malberti Cabrera, 2005)). Indices of life in the Special Period – dollars, prostitutes, unemployment, hotels, passports, and an urban landscape marked by transnational travelers of all kinds – receive considerable attention in contemporary visual culture. In addition to the high visibility of the José Martí International Airport and Spanish tourists, the representation of new social spaces such as hotel lobbies and stores accepting US dollars embodies the tensions between the national and international, as filmmakers explore Cubans' liminal experience – dwelling between, on one hand, segregated areas of capitalism jointly controlled by foreign companies and the Cuban state, and state-enforced socialism on the other.

Within this milieu several Cuban-directed co-productions with Spain have represented romantic entanglements across the Atlantic. In *La vida es silbar*, directed by Fernando Pérez and co-produced by ICAIC and Spain's Wanda Films, the search for Cuban national identity and cultural authenticity is transparently allegorised through the main character Elpidio's search for his mother, named Cuba, who abandoned him when he was a child. His search, however, is interrupted and challenged when he falls in love with a European tourist, Chrissy, and must decide whether or not to leave the country. This film, like many others, links the Cuban's romantic involvement with a tourist to economics. Not only does Elpidio steal Chrissy's wallet before he meets and has a passionate affair with her, but his street hustling and his involvement with her together provoke a crisis for his identity and integrity. The conflation of romance and economics is most directly evident in a scene in which a taxi driver, a foil for Elpidio, weeps as he relates a story of finding $50,000 that a tourist left in the back of his cab and then returning it and refusing the reward. Shot in a long take close-up the driver weeps as he says, 'It is the happiest day of [my] life.' The driver's story serves as counterpoint to Elpidio's *jineterismo* (a term that covers all manner of hustling, which marks the social and economic landscape of the Special Period). The subsequent slow track into Elpidio's reaction as he stares directly into the camera works too to underscore the allegorical nature of it all. The tourist, the outsider, is a symbol of compromise; the driver's decision, to whatever extent it comments on his personal integrity or sense of independence, is at the same time a gesture of renunciation. His tale casts the choice before Elpidio, who otherwise is content to move through intersecting grey areas, in the starkest of terms.

This is not to say that Chrissy, or even that tourists in general, are represented unsympathetically in Cuban films of the Special Period. (The tourist in this instance is played by the popular, fair-skinned

Cuban Isabel Santos, who, significantly for the purposes of this chapter, has performed both Spanish and Cuban characters in films produced in both countries.) In another of the film's vaguely cloaked symbols, Pérez's camera lovingly shapes Chrissy as a kind of saintly mother figure. Almost every erotic scene between the couple either begins or ends with a close-up on Elpidio's totemic tattoo, 'there is nothing like a mother's love'. That Elpidio's primary crisis is about whether or not to forsake his search for his true mother or leave with the tourist – a mother substitute – makes the national allegorical weight of the relationship clear. The film offers up unification with a European as one possible solution to revolutionary crisis, but at the film's climax, in which Afro-Cuban music pounds as he searches the city for signs of his mother, his departure is pre-empted and his fate remains ambiguous.

Juan Carlos Tabío's Spanish-financed films *Lista de espera/ Waiting List* (2000) and *Aunque estés lejos/So Far Away* (2003) also represent transnational couplings of Cubans and Spaniards. The female lead in *Lista de espera* is poised to leave the country with her Spanish fiancé when she falls in love with a young Cuban engineer, played by Vladimir Cruz. In this romantic comedy, she finds herself stranded with a group of passengers awaiting bus repairs. Eventually they overcome their petty differences and rehabilitate the weathered bus terminal as a (national) community. As in *La vida es silbar*, the Cuban woman's choice is presented as a litmus test of national loyalty and cultural authenticity, and when her fiancé comes to rescue her, vehicles – ever-charged icons in Cuban visual culture – become important markers of her dilemma: does she go off with the Spaniard in his Land Rover, or get on the decrepit bus, whose engine is finally running? Again, the film concludes obliquely, with the audience wondering in the last scene whether or not the entire thing has been a dream.

Aunque estés lejos, on the other hand, is a more self-reflexive film that centres precisely on issues involved in the making of Spanish-Cuban co-productions. This film takes a critical stance toward contemporary Cuban cinema's international collaborations, as it explores cultural difference in transnational filmmaking as well as transnational romance.

Given the ascendancy of tourism, and particularly sex tourism, in the Special Period, it is perhaps not surprising that Cuban films would grapple with questions of self-exoticisation and collusion with outsiders' perspectives. Although there is relatively scant scholarship on this question, Cuban filmmakers themselves are vocal about feeling restricted as to what they can or cannot represent on the screen. Self-censorship, as some have described it, is commonplace in contemporary Cuban filmmaking, but not for the reasons critics typically assume – the curtailing of freedom of expression by the government – but because, some filmmakers say, the demands of securing external financing for their productions require that they present a superficial, touristic image of the country. 'Foreign investors in co-productions want to impose their conception of our reality', Humberto Solás says in an interview with *Film Quarterly*. 'With a few notable exceptions it is very difficult to find a producer who wants to invest in a film about the Cuban reality and not tell the director what to do or what point of view to take' (Martin and Paddington, 2001: 10). In an interview with eight contemporary Cuban directors published in *El Kinetoscopio*, the issue of self-censorship (as the curtailing of national expression to meet the demands of an international market) and the 'danger' of co-productions come up several times. Enrique Álvarez, director of *La Ola* (1995) and *Miradas* (2001), asserts that 'economic censorship is in fact more powerful than ideological censorship because ideological entails the confrontation of ideas, which can be discussed and debated . . . But with economic censorship, there can be no discussion. You cannot argue with money' (Ricciarelli, 2001: 44).

Given the importance in Cuba of gaining access to hard currency, property and income-earning arenas, émigrés, transnationals and tourists have become an increasingly vital part of the Cuban economy, which in turn has contributed to their influence and representation on the island. The move to self-financing in the 1990s, which opened the film industry to the logic of the international market for the first time, has required that filmmakers develop new ways of presenting a national identity that would be more in tune with international expectations. None of which is to deny the existence of recent Spanish-Cuban films that, while playing to themes, tropes and representational practices seen as reliably 'attractive' to international audiences, and while directly or indirectly promoting tourism, manage to do so in a manner that is critically engaged, or even double-voiced. Daniel Díaz Torres's co-production *Hacerse el sueco*, for instance, is about a self-described Swedish literature professor, Bjorn, who arrives in Cuba and ends up renting a room from a family headed by a retired policeman nostalgic for the old days of the Revolution (Enrique Molina). His hosts soon become his surrogate family, and the Swede falls in love with the policeman's daughter. It is quickly revealed, however, that the 'Swedish professor' is actually a criminal on the run who repeatedly holds up the city's inhabitants and steals their dollars; worse yet, he is planning a major jewel heist. Light-hearted in tone and briskly paced, the film was reviewed internationally as a 'broad' and 'straightforward comedy', and indeed, in many respects, it functions as one (De Alberi, 2001). But at the same time, by making the blond-haired, blue-eyed tourist the serial criminal that has Havana on edge, Torres subverts and interrogates many of the popularly circulated narratives about tourism and crosscultural encounter that posit the 'native' as dangerous other of whom the First World 'visitor' must be wary. As one Cuban character, a petty black market hustler, complains, 'there's a real problem when you can't trust the tourists enough to sell to them'.

Hacerse el sueco also contains a scene foregrounding Afro-Cuban music and dance, but Torres's depiction of it is far from being an uncritical replication of an orientalising gaze. In this particular sequence, the 'professor', who wants to get out of town, says he must go to the country because he needs more 'local colour' for his research. Not wanting to lose her tenant and love interest, the daughter orchestrates a raucous scene in the apartment courtyard, in which her neighbours put on a mock-spontaneous show of 'local colour' for the unwitting Swede, complete with an ecstatically dancing Santera, Afro-Cuban percussionists, and chickens. Here the film's title, 'hacerse el sueco', which is an idiomatic expression meaning 'to play dumb', takes on a subtle irony, with Torres emphasising the multiple layers of performance that characterise all manner of inter- and crosscultural encounters.

These subtleties notwithstanding, *Hacerse el sueco* does ultimately endorse a new Cuban cosmopolitanism that reflects the interests of the tourist sector. Torres's film ends happily with the union of a Cuban and a European, in this case, 'el sueco'. In fact, of all the Cuban directed co-productions representing transnational romance, this film is most suggestive as a 'foundational fiction' narrative, since in the end the tourist is redeemed and incorporated into the now-extended (inter)national family. At the most basic level, the emphasis on the coupling of a Cuban and a European broadens the potential audience and allows for points of identification that cross national borders. But, to the extent that the film endorses transnational union as a metaphor for a socialist nation entering the world market, it is a foundational fiction on Cuba's terms, one that remains fully wedded to the Cuban characters' perspectives and deeply parodic about the structural paradoxes of contemporary life on the island.

Cuban co-productions, while incorporating émigrés and tourists on to their screens and making strategic compromises about the representation of culture in a global economy, betray a deep-seated ambivalence toward transnational coupling. It would be impossible not to consider the role sex tourism plays in these anxieties. Any consideration of transnational romance in Spanish-Cuban co-productions cannot escape the island's long history of being fetishised by outsiders, with the touristic gaze focused on the 'beautiful Cuban señorita' (to borrow a phrase from Tomás Gutiérrez Alea's *Memorias del subdesarrollo/Memories of Underdevelopment* (1968)), reproduced globally in visual culture as a metaphor for unspoiled resources as well as a promise of sexual fulfilment. This promise has become significantly pronounced during the Special Period, given the rampant (actual and discursive) rise of Cuban sex tourism.

In May 2007, Spain's national airline Iberia ran an animated advertisement promoting tourism to Cuba in which a white baby is transported to Cuba through the airline's website. Once on the island, dancing mulattas in bikinis feed and massage the little tourist as he sings 'feed me mulattas – come on little mamas, take me to my cot'. After complaints that the airline was promoting sex tourism, Iberia discontinued the advertisement, and a spokesperson for the company dismissed the ad as being 'completely trivial'. This is but one example of the degree to which simultaneously racist and sexist images have come to be iconically associated with Cuba, especially where it is represented to outsiders. This is a process that takes place on and off the island and involves the interplay of mutual self-interests. At any rate, it comes as little surprise that popular Spanish cinema's representations of sexual conquest and romantic involvement on the island trade on exoticism and fetishisation. During the 1990s, several low-budget Spanish films used the island for this purpose, with films like *Calor . . . y celos* (Javier Rebollo, 1996), *Sabor latino* (Pedro Carvajal, 1996) and *Demasiado caliente para ti* (Javier Elorrieta, 1996) suggesting the emergence of a virtual Cuban exploitation genre.

Fernando Colomo's comedy *Cuarteto de La Habana* (1999), which was funded entirely in Spain but shot on location in Cuba with Cuban actresses, is self-consciously comedic about sex tourism on the island, lightly criticising it even as it lingers visually on sexy mulattas and trades on the familiar hooker-with-a-heart-of-gold cliché. The film's narrative spends much time focused on the Spanish men's search for exotic sex partners, poking fun at the incompetent tourists in the process. While certainly the sexual and racist objectification of Cuban bodies is worth interrogating in this film, as is the way in which the film attempts to criticise the very thing that it exploits (sex tourism), it is the film's projection of Cuba as a place where the fully modern Westerner goes to reconstitute his or her identity – presented here through the main character Walter's search for his long-lost mother – that is perhaps most worth noting.

As in *La vida es silbar*, the search for the maternal is constructed alongside the pursuit of transnational romance. Walter, a jazz musician in Madrid, undertakes the transatlantic trip after learning that his long-lost mother is, in fact, a Cuban woman (played by Mirta Ibarra). Once there he falls in love with a beautiful young Cuban who turns out to be his half-sister; as with several of the other films under discussion here, the transnational romance ends in failure. The charter plane that carries Walter and his oversexed friend to Havana is named '*la lechera*', a quiet symbol almost prescient of the sexist Iberia ad linking Cuba at once to sex and nurturing. That Cuba is represented as the place where one searches for his mother – a theme engaged from within Cuba in *La vida es silbar*, from a Spanish perspective in *Cuarteto de La Habana* and from a Miami exile perspective in *Miel para Oshún* – suggests how powerfully the myth of Cuban insularity as cultural purity has become. In all of these films, Cuba is the place where one might recover an identity fragmented by the disconnections between place and culture that characterise late capitalism and the 'post-national'.

The nostalgia for a lost past and the idealisation of the *campo* that have been identified in several studies on Spanish cinema are in some ways analogous to representations of Cuba – or, if not Cuba itself, then the idea of it – as another backdrop for the reformulation of national identity in Spanish cinema (D'Lugo, 1997). The connection between this backward-looking tendency and the representation of Cuba as a blank slate is most apparent in Spanish films that use Cuba as historical backdrop, such as *Havanera 1820* (Antoni Verdaguer,

1992), *Mambí* (Santiago and Teodoro Ríos, 1998) and the Basque-produced *Maite* (Eneko Olasagasti and Carlos Zabala, 1994). Yet even Spanish films about Cuba that are firmly rooted in the contemporary context, and that deal with immigration and transnational travel in politically nuanced ways, place a heavy burden on Cuban characters to maintain their cultural integrity and sense of self. It is not this fact alone that warrants attention, of course, but the fact that the representation of Cuban cultural authenticity almost always expresses itself in relation to two problematic issues: sex or capital (and often both).

Manuel Gutiérrez Aragón's *Cosas que dejé en La Habana* (1997), though a densely layered film about Cuban immigrants in Madrid, also expresses European neuroses about purity and places a heavy burden on its characters to stay true to their Cubanness, even though they have left the country. This is expressed through the portrayal of romance. In this film the male protagonist Igor, played by Jorge Perugorría (another Cuban star who has successfully crossed over into the Spanish market), is a kind lothario who seduces 'well-fed' Spanish women to get '*plata y cama*'. Then at a nightclub he meets and falls deeply in love with Nena (Violeta Rodríguez), an aspiring actress who has only just arrived from Havana with her two sisters. Their immediate mutual attraction is presented as the union of like with like: 'Cuban women's saliva tastes better than Spanish women's saliva', Igor says; and later Nena, dancing closely, tells him, 'you smell of Cuba'. The purity of their relationship is contrasted against the opportunistic Spanish-Cuban couplings in the film (Igor's continued charade of a relationship with an older Spanish woman, and the 'arranged' marriage of one of the Cuban sisters to a wealthy gay Spaniard in need of a beard).

Although assertively anti-racist and highly critical of the exploitation of immigrants in Spain, *Cosas que dejé en La Habana* duplicates fears about *mestizaje* that characterise much Spanish immigration cinema (Santaolalla, 2002). The tension between Spain's understanding of its truly heterogeneous cultural history and its simultaneous investment in myths of ethnic homogeneity expresses itself in these representations of Cuban romance. *Cosas que dejé en La Habana* strives to be frank and open about cultural mixing and economic negotiation even as it laments these things. Igor's exploitation of Spanish women, furthermore, is a reversal of the infinitely more frequent power dynamic shaping Spanish-Cuban transnational romance – that of European men seeking sex tourism – in its focus on the Cuban as economic/sexual predator. In *Cosas que dejé en La Habana* money becomes a corrosive force that strips Cubans of their authenticity: the evil assimilated Cuban aunt with her successful fur store; Igor's transplanted *jineterismo* and his work securing illegal papers that forces him to 'fuck other Cubans over'; the Cuban playwright who has sold out the integrity of his work to produce a play that caricatures his culture for the tastes of a non-Cuban audience. In this the film reveals what is arguably the most powerful dimension in the representation of Cuban transnational romance inside the island and out; namely, a preoccupation with cultural purity as economic purity, or a romanticisation of Cuba's virginity within the global market.

These collaboratively created and financed films are a product of Cuban culture industries' opening themselves up to the international market, yet this is precisely the situation that many of the individual film texts lament. Spanish filmmakers are willing to take advantage of the economic disparity in the international distribution of cultural labour, and Cuban filmmakers, while doubtless possessing little real choice whether to cooperate with foreign investors, at the same time show signs of self-exoticisation and collusion with the tourist market. Yet the transnational imaginary being constructed by these films is riddled with anxieties concerning cultural purity and authenticity. The condition of compromise, understood as systemic to co-productions in a general sense, but particularly fraught in the case of Cuba – the last holdout in an era of multinationals – is projected as a kind of mourning. It's because of this that Cuban characters and the island itself are inescapably allegorical in Spanish co-productions. The onus of cultural authenticity weighs heavily on these films, a phenomenon nowhere more evident than in a recent Spanish film, *Habana Blues*, directed by Benito Zambrano.

Like *Cosas que dejé en La Habana*, *Habana Blues* is complicated in its representational politics. The film follows the destinies of two Cuban popular musicians, Ruy and Tito, struggling to make it in present-day Havana, as well as Ruy's wife, Caridad, and their children. Zambrano, a young Spanish director who studied at Cuba's International Film School, encourages multiple points of identification in the film, adopting shifting points of view that share a sympathy toward the challenges facing different characters who, at times, pursue divergent agendas. The film hovers over the problem of 'selling out' to an international market, of maintaining one's integrity in a world of complex cultural haggling and economic oppression. And again, these issues are played out in tandem with a story of transnational romance between a Cuban and a Spaniard that is, eventually, presented as a corrosive force.

To give a brief synopsis of the plot, best friends Ruy and Tito opportunely meet a pair of Spanish music producers, one a hard-edged, attractive woman with whom Ruy has an affair. The musicians are given the opportunity to make a record in Spain but discover later that in order to do so they will have to compromise their music by making it less local and assuming a critical posture toward the Cuban regime. Not only, it is implied, does this mean that they'll be distorting their political perspectives – they will also, as a result, not be allowed to reenter the country. Tito, for his part, is willing to concede to whatever demands the label makes, but at the final contract meeting Ruy refuses, breaking up their alliance and rejecting (both here and later sexually) the Spanish producer with whom he's been having an affair. Meanwhile, Ruy's wife Caridad has grown tired of her husband's lack of support and makes arrangements to travel with her children in a *balsa* to Miami to reunite with her mother.

The tagline of the film '*vivir es elegir*' refers to the central questions facing the three main characters, and Zambrano refrains from making overly moralistic or simplistic judgements, attending to the complexities of the individual choices involved. While textually speaking there is much one could analyse in this well-made film, including the degree to which it ironically indulges some of the exoticising demands of tourism and the international film market, it is the lingering romanticisation of cultural purity in an age of instant commodification filtered through yet another tale of Spanish Cuban coupling that stands out most immediately. There is little question that, although the film is respectful toward both Tito's decision to stick with the label and go to Spain and Caridad's decision to leave for Miami, at the end the true heroic, tragic and sublime figure is Ruy, the one who stays. Like the taxi driver in *La vida es silbar*, he may not have chosen pragmatically, but he has chosen the best. The concluding scene of the film depicts a much-awaited Havana concert that brings the estranged Tito and Ruy back together before Tito's departure for Spain. After an ecstatically unifying performance of a song that celebrates post-nationalism and the unity of Cubans wherever they are, the final number focuses on Ruy, intercutting footage of his now teary-eyed performance with a flash-forward, which shows him bidding his wife and children farewell as they leave in a boat, with the music continuing to play over the image. Cutting from that scene back to the performance, Ruy is cloaked in a blue-black light. Everyone else has left the stage – it's as if he is performing to no one. His final line alludes to being left in 'the sands of solitude'. The final shot before the credit sequence reveals the moon shining through a large hole in the ceiling of the auditorium.

The Cuban artist Tonel has written about the currency of 'insular consciousness' in Cuban plastic art, of how the image of the island map conjures:

> an isolation deeper than that created by relative geographic solitude: an insularity seen as distance from everything and everyone, as an extreme precariousness of communications. Opportunely this interpretation stands as one of the pillars of contemporary Cuban political ideology: the idea of a harshly besieged and blockaded country, of the walled fort, subject to an inescapable tragic destiny. (2002: 80–1)

The tragic romanticism of Ruy at the conclusion of *Habana Blues* likewise conjures this sense that the island's inescapable destiny is constitutive of the Cuban imaginary. Zambrano summons a curious aesthetic pleasure from Ruy's lonely fate, a kind of doomed-but-lovely quality that bespeaks a long-standing Spanish preoccupation with myths of purity and cultural identity. Sympathetic, complex portrayals like this one nonetheless depict a kind of Cuban purity that is vulnerable to the taint of capitalism. At the same time, the existence of the films themselves is an index of increasing cultural negotiation and transnational capital flow. This, I would argue, is the underlying tension that appears and reappears throughout the body of Spanish-Cuban co-productions.

I have attempted to read Cuban cinema's engagements with Spain, and Spanish cinema's engagements with Cuba, against the critical discourse of loss to examine the ways in which an emergent transnational imaginary is being constructed in and through cinematic representation. For me, such a perspective does not constitute a 'post-national praxis', since such a designation downplays the power of nation-states to regulate all manner of transnational encounter, a fact brutally evident in the case of Cuba. Nonetheless, in the interstices between socialist ideals and capitalist practice, familiar anxieties about purity, heterosexual romance and cultural identity are emerging, suggesting that transnational realities are generating reactive expressions as well as new markets that trade on national nostalgia.

References

De Alberi, Attilio L. (2001) 'Cuba Now', *LA Weekly*, 28 February, www.laweekly.com/film+tv/film/cuba-now/5012/.

D'Lugo, Marvin (1997) *Guide to the Cinema of Spain*, Westport, CT: Greenwood Press.

García Canclini, Néstor (1997) 'Will There Be Latin American Cinema in the Year 2000? Visual Culture in a Postnational Era', in Ann Marie Stock (ed.), *Framing Latin American Cinema: Contemporary Critical Perspectives*, Minneapolis: University of Minnesota Press, 246–58.

Hall, Stuart (2003) 'Cultural Identity and Diaspora', in Jana Evans Braziel and Anita Mannur (eds), *Theorizing Diaspora*, Malden, MA: Blackwell Publishing, 233–46.

Hoefert de Turégano, Teresa (2004) 'The International Politics of Cinematic Coproduction: Spanish Policy in Latin America', *Film and History: An Interdisciplinary Journal of Film and Television Studies*, 34: 2, 15–24.

Martin, Michael T. and Bruce Paddington (2001) 'Restoration or Innovation? An Interview with Humberto Solás: Post-Revolutionary Cuban Cinema', *Film Quarterly*, 54: 3, 2–13.

Ricciarelli, Cecilia (2001) 'Conversaciones con los Realizadores Cubanos', *El Kinetoscopio*, 12: 58, 44.

Rich, R. Ruby (1997) 'An/Other View of New Latin American Cinema', in Michael T. Martin (ed.), *New Latin American Cinema*, vol. I, Detroit: Wayne State University Press, 273–97.

Santaolalla, Isabel (2002) 'Ethnic and Racial Configurations in Contemporary Spanish Culture', in Jo Labanyi (ed.), *Constructing Identity in Contemporary Spain: Theoretical Debates and Cultural Practice*, Oxford: Oxford University Press, 55–71.

Shohat, Ella and Robert Stam (eds) (2003) *Multiculturalism, Postcoloniality and Transnational Media*, New Brunswick, NJ: Rutgers University Press.

Stock, Ann Marie (1995) 'Migrancy and the Latin American Cinemascape: Towards a Post-National Critical Praxis', *Revista Canadiense de Estudios Hispánicos*, 20: 1, 19–30.

Tonel (Antonio Eligio Fernández) (2002) 'The Island, the Map, the Travelers: Notes on Recent Developments in Cuban Art', Kenya Dworkin (trans.), *boundary 2*, 29: 3, 77–89 (see http://boundary2.dukejournals.org/cgi/content/citation/29/3/77).

Index

CPSIA information can be obtained at www.ICGtesting.com
Printed in the USA
BVOW071547190513

321052BV00001B/4/P